This book provides a clear and elegant account of the development of Spanish over the last 2000 years. Although it is principally oriented towards 'internal' history, 'external' history is considered in outline in the Introduction and is referred to throughout. The four principal chapters deal in detail with phonological development, and with morpho-syntactical, lexical and semantic change. Professor Penny's treatment of the sound-system is in terms both of broad patterns of change and specific phonemic developments and is described in two main phases: spoken Latin to medieval Spanish, and medieval to modern Spanish. In the chapter on morpho-syntax, grammatical morphology and lexical morphology are treated separately, with particular attention paid to word formation. The sources of Spanish vocabulary, inherited and borrowed, are discussed in chapter 4, and chapter 5 is concerned with the causes, typology and effects of semantic change.

Though *A History of the Spanish Language* is written as a textbook, the comprehensive coverage of the major varieties of Spanish given here will be welcomed by scholars and students alike.

A History of the Spanish Language

A History of the Spanish Language

Ralph Penny
Department of Hispanic Studies
Queen Mary and Westfield College
University of London

CAMBRIDGE
UNIVERSITY PRESS

Published by the Press Syndicate of the University of Cambridge
The Pitt Building, Trumpington Street, Cambridge CB2 1RP
40 West 20th Street, New York, NY 10011-4211, USA
10 Stamford Road, Oakleigh, Melbourne 3166, Australia

© Cambridge University Press 1991

First published 1991
Reprinted 1992, 1993

Printed in Great Britain at the Athenaeum Press Ltd.
Newcastle upon Tyne

British Library cataloguing in publication data
Penny, Ralph
   A History of the Spanish Language.
   1. Spanish language, to 1985
   1 Title
   460.09

Library of Congress cataloguing in publication data
Penny, Ralph J. (Ralph John), 1940–
   A History of the spanish Language/Ralph Penny.
      p.   cm.
   Includes index.
   ISBN 0-521-39481-2, – ISBN 0-521-39784-7 (pbk.)
   1. Spanish language – History. 1. Title.
PC4075. P46 1991
460'. 9 – dc20 90-1869 CIP

ISBN 0 521 39481 3 hardback
ISBN 0 521 39784 7 paperback

VN

Contents

Preface   *page* xiii
List of abbreviations and symbols   *xiv*

1 Introduction   1

  1.1 Latin   1
  1.2 The Latin of Spain   5
    1.2.1 Archaism   7
    1.2.2 Conservatism   8
    1.2.3 Dialectalism   9
    1.2.4 Innovation   10
  1.3 Conquest and Reconquest   11
    1.3.1 The Visigoths   11
    1.3.2 Moors and Christians   13
  1.4 Standard Spanish   15
  1.5 Spanish overseas   17
    1.5.1 The Canaries   17
    1.5.2 America   18
    1.5.3 The Mediterranean and the Balkans   21
    1.5.4 The Philippines   24
  1.6 'Castilian' and 'Spanish'   25

2 Phonology   27

  2.1 Phonological change   27
    2.1.1 Conditioned change   27
      2.1.1.1 Assimilation   27
      2.1.1.2 Dissimilation   28
      2.1.1.3 Epenthesis   28
      2.1.1.4 Metathesis   29
    2.1.2 Isolative change   29
    2.1.3 Changes affecting the phonemic system   29
      2.1.3.1 Split   30
      2.1.3.2 Merger   30
    2.1.4 Change of incidence of phonemes   31
  2.2 Transmission   32
    2.2.1 Popular words   32
    2.2.2 Learned words   32
    2.2.3 Semi-learned words   32
    2.2.4 Doublets   33

2.3   Suprasegmental features   33
  2.3.1 Position of the accent   33
  2.3.2 Nature of the accent   34
  2.3.3 The syllable   35
2.4   Development of the vowel-system   36
  2.4.1 The Latin vowel-system   36
  2.4.2 Tonic vowels   39
    2.4.2.1 Metaphony   39
    2.4.2.2 Diphthongization   43
    2.4.2.3 The Latin diphthongs   44
    2.4.2.4 New diphthongs   45
    2.4.2.5 Medieval developments   45
    2.4.2.6 Summary of tonic vowel development   46
  2.4.3 Atonic vowel development   47
    2.4.3.1 Initial vowels   47
    2.4.3.2 Final vowels   49
    2.4.3.3 Intertonic vowels   50
    2.4.3.4 Hiatus   51
2.5   Development of the consonant-system   52
  2.5.1 The Latin consonant-system   52
  2.5.2 Developments from Latin to Old Spanish: (1) the creation
    of the palatal order   53
    2.5.2.1 Consonantization of /i/   53
    2.5.2.2 Palatal developments of consonant + [j]   53
    2.5.2.3 Palatalization of syllable-initial velars 56
    2.5.2.4 Palatalization of syllable-final velars   60
    2.5.2.5 Palatalization of -LL- and -NN-   62
    2.5.2.6 Palatalization of PL-, CL-, FL-   62
    2.5.2.7 Summary of palatal developments from Latin to Old
    Spanish   63
  2.5.3 Developments from Latin to Old Spanish: (2) the creation
    of the voiced fricative series   64
    2.5.3.1 The appearance of /ĵ/ and /β/   64
    2.5.3.2 Lenition   65
    2.5.3.3 Further effects of lenition: consonant + R or L   73
    2.5.3.4 The Old Spanish voiced fricative series   73
  2.5.4 Final consonants   74
  2.5.5 Secondary consonant groups   75
  2.5.6 The development of Latin F   79
  2.5.7 Other initial consonants   82
  2.5.8 The Old Spanish consonant system   84
2.6   Phonological change since the Middle Ages   84
  2.6.1 The merger of Old Spanish /b/ and /β/   84
  2.6.2 The Old Spanish sibilants   86
  2.6.3 The sibilants in Andalusian and American Spanish   89
  2.6.4 The phonologization of /f/ and /h/   90
  2.6.5 Learned consonant groups   91
  2.6.6 *Yeísmo*   93
  2.6.7 Weakening of syllable-final /s/ and /θ/   93
2.7   Chronology of phonological change   95

3 Morpho-syntax   98

3.1 General concepts   98
     3.1.1 Morphological change   99
3.2 The noun   101
     3.2.1 Case and number   101
     3.2.2 Gender   106
           3.2.2.1 Neuter nouns   106
           3.2.2.2 Gender-marking of the noun   110
     3.2.3 Noun-classes   112
3.3 The adjective   114
     3.3.1 The adjective endings   114
     3.3.2 Comparison of adjectives   115
3.4 The adverb   117
3.5 The pronoun   119
     3.5.1 Personal pronouns   119
           3.5.1.1 Forms of address   123
     3.5.2 The possessive   125
     3.5.3 Demonstratives and articles   128
           3.5.3.1 The demonstratives   128
           3.5.3.2 The articles   130
     3.5.4 Relatives and interrogatives   132
     3.5.5 Indefinites   133
3.6 The numeral   133
     3.6.1 Cardinals   133
     3.6.2 Ordinals   136
     3.6.3 Multiples and fractions   136
3.7 The verb   137
     3.7.1 Voice   137
     3.7.2 Person/number   137
     3.7.3 Aspect   140
     3.7.4 Tense   145
     3.7.5 Mood   146
     3.7.6 Verb-classes   147
     3.7.7 Verb paradigms   150
           3.7.7.1 Present indicative and subjunctive   150
                   3.7.7.1.1 The palatal glide [j]   150
                   3.7.7.1.2 The present tense endings   151
                   3.7.7.1.3 Consonantal alternation   153
                   3.7.7.1.4 Vocalic alternation   156
                   3.7.7.1.5 Irregular present tense forms   161
           3.7.7.2 Imperative   166
           3.7.7.3 Imperfect indicative and subjunctive   167
                   3.7.7.3.1 Imperfect indicative   167
                   3.7.7.3.2 Imperfect subjunctive   169
           3.7.7.4 Future and conditional   173
                   3.7.7.4.1 Future indicative   173
                   3.7.7.4.2 Conditional   177
                   3.7.7.4.3 Future subjunctive   178

3.7.7.5 Preterite   179
     3.7.7.5.1 Weak preterite   180
     3.7.7.5.2 Strong preterite   183
3.7.8 Non-finite verbal forms   189
  3.7.8.1 Infinitive   189
  3.7.8.2 Gerund   191
  3.7.8.3 Participle   192
3.8 Other word-classes   194
  3.8.1 Preposition   194
  3.8.2 Conjunction   198
3.9 Conditional sentences   201
  3.9.1 Open conditional sentences   202
  3.9.2 Improbable and impossible conditional sentences   203

4 Lexis   208
4.1 Vocabulary inherited from Latin   208
4.2 Words of pre-Roman origin   208
4.3 Latinisms   210
4.4 Hellenisms   211
4.5 Germanic borrowings   215
4.6 Arabisms   217
4.7 Mozarabisms   223
4.8 Gallicisms and occitanisms   224
4.9 Amerindianisms   228
4.10 Anglicisms   230
4.11 Catalanisms   231
4.12 Lusisms   233
4.13 Italianisms   234
4.14 Word-formation (including affective suffixes)   237
  4.14.1 Prefixation   237
  4.14.2 Derivation   241
     4.14.2.1 Lexical derivation   242
     4.14.2.2 Affective derivation   246
  4.14.3 Composition   251

5 Semantics   254
5.1 Causes of semantic change   254
  5.1.1 Linguistic causes   255
  5.1.2 Historical causes   255
  5.1.3 Social causes   256
  5.1.4 Psychological causes   257
     5.1.4.1 Fear taboo   258
     5.1.4.2 Delicacy taboo   259
     5.1.4.3 Decency taboo   259
  5.1.5 Foreign influences which cause semantic change   260
  5.1.6 The need to name a new concept   262
5.2 Types of semantic change   262
  5.2.1 Metaphor   263
  5.2.2 Metonymy   264

5.2.3 Popular etymology 265
5.2.4 Ellipsis 265
5.3 Consequences of semantic change 266
5.3.1 Change of semantic range 266
5.3.2 Change of affectivity 268

References 270
Index of Latin words 277
Index of Spanish words cited
Subject index 314

Preface

The aim of this *History of the Spanish Language* is to provide the reader with as complete a picture as possible of the development of Spanish over the last two thousand years. The book is concerned essentially with the internal history of Spanish (with what used to be called, rather forbiddingly, 'historical grammar'), although the external history of Spanish (the account of the circumstances in which Spanish has been spoken and written over time) is discussed at some length in the Introduction. In writing this book, I had in mind the needs of undergraduate and postgraduate students of Spanish and other Romance languages, but more advanced scholars will, I trust, find it a useful source of reference.

My indebtedness to other scholars will be evident on almost every page, but I have not sought to acknowledge this debt in detail at each moment; such acknowledgement is to be found in the list of references on pp. 270–6. Where I make reference in the text to the work of a particular scholar, it is with the specific aim of directing the reader to a source in which a more complete discussion may be found of the issue in question than is possible within the confines of a textbook.

Help in the writing of this book has come from many sources, from many cohorts of students who have participated over the years in my seminars on the history of Spanish, from colleagues with whom I have discussed many of the issues concerned, and from those who have read drafts of the text. I am indebted to the readers to whom the proposed book was referred by Cambridge University Press, and particularly to Professor Thomas J. Walsh, of Georgetown University, whose constructive and detailed comments brought about a host of improvements to the original version. All shortcomings, it need hardly be said, are entirely my own.

Abbreviations and symbols

*	Reconstructed form (see 1.1, end)
x > y	x becomes y in the course of time
x < y	x is the descendant of y
x → y	y is created on the basis of x (e.g. through word-formation)
Sp.	Spanish
OSp.	Old Spanish
MSp.	Modern Spanish
JSp.	Judaeo-Spanish
Gal.	Galician
Ptg.	Portuguese
OPtg.	Old Portuguese
Leon.	Leonese
Arag.	Aragonese
Fr.	French
OFr.	Old French
Occ.	Occitan
Cat.	Catalan
It.	Italian
N. It.	North Italian
C. It.	Central Italian (including Tuscan)
S. It.	South Italian
Sic.	Sicilian
Sard.	Sardinian
Rum.	Rumanian
Gmc.	Germanic
Germ.	German
Eng.	English
Ar.	Arabic
GA	Golden Age
Lat.	Latin
CL	Classical Latin
VL	Vulgar Latin
[xxxx]	phonetic transcription
/xxxx/	phonemic transcription
Ø	null segment (e.g. [h] > [Ø] = '[h] ceases to be pronounced')
'	stress accent
:	length

In the case of Latin words (for which small capitals are used), long vowels are indicated by a macron, thus Ā, Ē, Ī, Ō, Ū. Any vowel not so marked should be understood to be a short vowel.

The phonetic and phonemic symbols used are those of the International Phonetic Association, but with the following modifications:

[ĵ] is used for the mid-palatal fricative (as in *mayo*) to distinguish it from the (frictionless) glide [j] (as in *tierra*).

[s̺] and [z̺] are used for all dental fricatives (whether predorsal, coronal, etc.), as used in Andalusia, America, etc., to distinguish them from the apico-alveolar [s] and [z], typical of central and northern Spain.

[l̺] and [n̺] are used for the interdental lateral and nasal, respectively, and [l̪] and [n̪] for the dental lateral and nasal.

[r̄] indicates the vibrative (as in *perro*), while [r] symbolizes the flap (as in *pero*).

In the following chart on p. xvi, a symbol at the left of its box represents a voiceless sound, one on the right indicates a voiced sound. In the case of glides with double place of articulation, the symbol within parentheses indicates the secondary locus.

Consonants	Bilabial	Labiodental	Interdental	Dental	Alveolar	Prepalatal	Midpalatal	Velar	Laryngeal
Plosive	p b			t d				k g	
Fricative	φ β	f v	θ ð	ş ẓ	s z	ʃ ʒ		x ɣ	h ɦ
Affricate				ts dz		tʃ dʒ	ǰ		
Lateral			ḷ	ḻ	l		λ		
Vibrative					r̄				
Flap					r				
Nasal	m	ɱ	ṇ	ṇ	n		ɲ	ŋ	
Glides									
opening	ʍ w						j	(ʍ) (w)	
closing	u̯						i̯	(u̯)	

Vowels	Front	Central	Back
high	i		u
high-mid	e		o
low-mid	ɛ		ɔ
low	æ	a	ɑ

I
Introduction

This history of Spanish is conceived as an account of the 'internal' development of the language, a discussion of the way in which its phonology, its morpho-syntax, its vocabulary and the meanings of its words have evolved, and of the reasons for these developments (insofar as they can be established). It is therefore what used to be called a 'historical grammar' of the Spanish language. However, although it follows that the book is not essentially concerned with the social contexts in which Spanish is and has been used, it is appropriate to give a brief account of these contexts, by way of introduction to the main matter which follows. More detailed accounts of the 'external' history of Spanish (notably Lapesa 1980) are available to the reader, and what is discussed here consists of an outline of the circumstances under which Spanish and its antecedents have been spoken over the centuries, an outline which is sufficient to explain the chronological and social terms used in later chapters.

1.1 Latin

Latin is the ancestor of Spanish (and, by definition, of all other Romance languages) in the sense that there is an unbroken chain of speakers, each learning his or her language from parents and contemporaries, stretching from the people of the Western Roman Empire two thousand years ago to the present population of the Spanish-speaking world. An alternative way of expressing the relationship between Latin and Spanish is to say that Spanish *is* Latin, as Latin continues to be spoken in parts of Europe, Africa and America. Similar claims are of course justified in the case of Portuguese, Catalan, French, Italian, Rumanian, etc., and the main reason the term 'Latin' is not used for these various kinds of speech and writing is one of convenience: some forms of contemporary Latin (i.e. some Romance languages) have become mutually unintelligible and it is inconvenient to use a single label for mutually unintelligible forms of language. Another reason for the use of distinctive labels such as 'Spanish', 'French', etc., is that the rise of the nation-state in Europe has demanded a separate linguistic identity for each state, as an expression of its cultural and political identity.

It is self-evident that contemporary 'Latin' speech (in the sense used here to embrace what are otherwise referred to as 'the Romance languages') is not uniform, but it is equally important to recognize that Latin speech can never have been uniform. All language displays variation (and Latin speech can have been no exception) in three main ways: it varies diatopically (i.e. in space), diachronically (i.e. over time), and sociologically (i.e. in the same place and at the same time it varies in accordance with factors such as the age, sex, education, occupation, etc. of the speaker). In addition, variation is inherent not only in speech-communities, but in individuals, in the sense that individuals normally vary their speech according to the circumstances in which they are speaking. The fact that we are deprived of the opportunity (for the most part) of observing such variation in the case of Latin should not blind us to the fact of its existence in the Latin-speaking world of two thousand years ago.

Evidence of diatopic variation in Latin is scarce, owing to the fact that those who wrote were trained to do so in a variety of Latin (an educated, literary variety, traditionally called 'Classical Latin') which by its nature rejected merely local characteristics. However, some evidence is available and, insofar as it refers to the Latin of Spain, it will be discussed in the following section (1.2). Evidence of diachronic variation is more plentiful, and comes from comparison of the language used by writers at different periods, and from comments made by Latin grammarians on the antiquated or obsolete status of certain features of the language.

It is the evidence of sociological variation which has received most attention from students of the Romance languages, although this aspect of variation is not traditionally described as 'sociological'. Since at least the nineteenth century, it has been known that the Romance languages do not descend from Classical (i.e. literary) Latin, but from a non-literary type, most usually referred to as 'Vulgar Latin'. To take a simple and well-known lexical example, the word meaning 'horse' in literary Latin is EQUUS, a form which is clearly not the ancestor of the Romance words for this concept (Sp. *caballo*, Ptg. *cavalo*, *Fr. cheval*, It. *cavallo*, Rum. *cal*, etc.). The latter forms descend from CABALLUS, which, where it appears in literary Latin, means 'nag; workhorse', but which in non-literary language was evidently used in the generic sense 'horse'.

Definitions of 'Vulgar Latin' have abounded, and many have rested on historical models that can now be seen to be mistaken. Thus, Romance linguists have long since rejected the notion that Vulgar Latin is a later form of Latin than the Classical variety, despite the fact that much of the evidence for Vulgar Latin comes from the later centuries of the Empire and despite the fact that many of the features of Vulgar Latin are revealed as more 'advanced' than the corresponding features of Classical Latin.

Harder to die is the notion that Vulgar Latin and Classical Latin are sharply different codes, and that the two terms represent mutually exclusive concepts. This view cannot be sustained since all varieties of Latin of which we have knowledge share most of their vocabulary, most of their morphology and most of their syntactical rules. The model adopted here is that 'Latin', like any language observable today, represents a gamut or spectrum of linguistic registers, ranging from the codified, literary register at one end to the raciest slang at the other, with a smooth gradation of intermediate registers. On this model, 'Classical Latin' occupies one extreme of the spectrum, representing essentially written registers (un-spoken except in 'performance' or 'reading aloud' mode), while Vulgar Latin represents almost the whole of the remainder of the spectrum, perhaps with the exception of the spoken language of the educated classes (for which a separate term is required) and with the exception of the language of marginal social groups at the other extreme, since the slang of such groups is known to be unstable and therefore unlikely to have affected the speech of the great mass of the population in any consistent way.

This view of Vulgar Latin, although expressed differently, is in broad agreement with one of the more satisfactory earlier definitions of the term, that adopted by Herman (1967: 16) and some predecessors: 'the spoken language of those classes who were uninfluenced or scarcely influenced by the teaching of the schools or by literary models'. However, it is important to make clear certain corollaries which flow from the definition of Vulgar Latin adopted here.

First, Vulgar Latin has no implicit chronological limits. It is contempor-ary with Classical Latin and as soon as it is meaningful to refer to Classical Latin (i.e. from the first century BC) it is also meaningful to use the term 'Vulgar Latin', despite the fact that most evidence of the nature of Vulgar Latin comes from later centuries. At the other extreme, the term 'Vulgar Latin' ceases to be useful once locally divergent forms of language begin to be recorded in writing (the ninth century AD in Northern France), and the term 'Romance' is then used for any or all vernacular descendants of Latin, written or spoken. However, some scholars also use the term 'Romance' to refer to the spoken language of earlier centuries, while other scholars use the term 'Proto-Romance' to indicate those forms of spoken language which constitute the ancestor of the Romance languages, and which by definition belong to a period prior to the appearance of texts written in Romance.

Second, there can be no such thing as a 'Vulgar Latin text'. Texts of all kinds are composed, by definition, by the educated and therefore in the codified or 'standard' variety of Latin in which such writers have inevitably been trained. This is not to say that textual evidence of spoken registers of

Latin is unavailable (it will be outlined below); what we do find is that certain types of text contain a greater or lesser proportion of forms (spellings, words, constructions, etc.) which differ from the standard and which reveal particular features of spoken Latin. Such information is inevitably incomplete and cannot amount to a 'full' picture of Vulgar Latin.

Third, like 'Latin' considered in its entirety, Vulgar Latin is inherently variable. The term includes reference to all the chronological, local, and social varieties of Latin as spoken by the majority of the relevant populations. It cannot therefore be described in the 'grammar-book' way that is appropriate to codified or standard varieties.

What then are the sources of information about the features of Vulgar Latin? Full discussion is inappropriate here (and can be found in works on Vulgar Latin such as Väänänen 1968: 39–49), but may be summarized as:

> literary writing purporting to reflect popular speech (dramatists such as Plautus, Ennius, Terence; satirists such as Petronius);

> Christian writings, which generally rejected the exclusivist standard language in favour of a style more suited to a proselytizing religion, especially those written for an unsophisticated audience (such as the fourth-century AD account by a Spanish nun of her pilgrimage to the Holy Land, the *Peregrinatio ad loca sancta*);

> technical writing, which because of its practical intent and the modest education of its intended readership was usually unpretentious in style and allowed the use of vocabulary and expressions belonging to speech; such writing includes works on cookery, farming, building, medicine, veterinary science, etc.;

> writing for various purposes, literary and non-literary, from the late Roman period (third–fifth centuries AD) and from the following centuries, when standards of education and culture among the literate were lower than they had earlier been and when writers consequently may lapse into non-Classical modes of expression;

> informal inscriptions, including gravestones but especially including painted graffiti (such as those of Pompeii and Herculaneum, which include advertisements, announcements, slogans, obscenities, etc.) and *defixionum tabellae* (metal plaques on which magical spells are scratched);

> writings of grammarians, especially insofar as they condemn forms as incorrect, since this assures us of their existence in speech; particularly noteworthy is the so-called *Appendix Probi*, a sixth- or seventh-century (see Robson 1963) list of 227 forms to be avoided in writing, in which each recommended expression is placed alongside its condemned equivalent (e.g. BACULUS NON VACLUS, AURIS NON ORICLA, GRUS NON GRUIS, TRISTIS NON TRISTUS); of almost similar importance, especially for Spain, are the linguistic observations of St Isidore, bishop of Seville (*c.* 570–636), in his *Origines sive etymologiae*;

glosses of various dates from the first century AD on, where some reader has inserted into a text interlinear or marginal equivalents for words or expressions which were obsolete and therefore posed difficulty for readers, the replacements sometimes being drawn from spoken registers;

borrowings made by Latin from other languages, and vice versa, in which the manner of adaptation of the borrowed word to the borrowing language may reveal features of pronunciation (e.g. German *Kaiser* reveals that when Germanic borrowed the Latin word CAESAR its initial consonant was articulated [k]).

Alongside this testimony drawn largely from ancient texts is to be placed the evidence deducible from the Romance languages themselves. We have already seen that by comparing certain Romance forms it is possible to deduce that in VL the word CABALLUS had the generic sense 'horse', and it is possible to apply this procedure to any linguistic feature, on the hypothesis that if the same feature is observed in a broad range of Romance languages then that feature belonged to spoken Latin. Thus, by comparing Romance words for 'green' (e.g. Sp., Ptg., It., Rum. *verde*, Fr., Cat. *vert*), it is possible to make the minimal deduction that their spoken Latin ancestor had no more than two syllables, despite the fact that the Latin word for 'green' that we find in writing has three: VIRIDIS. On this occasion, our deduction is confirmed by the author of the *Appendix Probi*, who prescribes VIRIDIS NON VIRDIS. However, in a large number of cases, such confirmation from written sources is not forthcoming, and many forms have been deduced (on the basis of the comparison of Romance forms) as belonging to spoken Latin without their existence being confirmed by any written source. Thus, a comparison of the Romance verbs meaning 'to be' (e.g. Sp., Ptg. *ser*, Cat. *ésser/ser*, Fr. *être*, It. *essere*) reveals that their spoken Latin ancestor is likely to have had three syllables and that the last syllable was -RE, by contrast with the CL form ESSE 'to be'. On the basis of known facts about the development of each Romance language, it is possible to refine the deduced VL form to *ESSERE. It will be noted that in such cases an asterisk indicates the lack of confirmation from written sources, and therefore the hypothetical (but not necessarily doubtful) status of the word concerned.

1.2 The Latin of Spain

Latin came to be used in Spain as a result of the gradual incorporation of the Peninsula into the Roman Empire and of the consequent romanization of its diverse cultures. Romanization began in 218 BC, at the beginning of the Second Punic War, when Roman troops were disembarked in northeastern Spain to forestall any Carthaginian advance across the Pyrenees and the Alps in the manner of Hannibal's earlier famous march. After the defeat of the Carthaginians and the capture of their Peninsular capital, Cádiz, in 206 BC, military enterprise became a process of colonization and settlement. This process was relatively slow, progressing in a westerly and northwesterly direction over the next two centuries and culminating in the conquest of the northern coastal area (now Galicia, Asturias, Santander and part of the Basque Country) in 19 BC.

In the wake of conquest and settlement came latinization. The use of Latin was not enforced (and scarcely could have been), but was learned by the local populations, as a matter of convenience and prestige, from Roman settlers, administrators, soldiers, traders, etc. This process was rapid in some areas (the east and south), slower in others (the centre, west and north), and is still incomplete in one area (the Basque Country). Any such language-change implies bilingualism over at least several genera-tions, and since bilingualism persists today in the Western Pyrenees it is likely that it persisted in other areas remote from the major Roman cities (that is, in parts of the north and west) at least until the end of the Roman period, in the fifth century, and in the remotest areas probably later. Such bilingualism, between Basque and Latin and between Celtic and Latin, has often been cited as the cause of certain changes which are evident in the Peninsular descendants of Latin (see 2.5.3.2, 2.5.6, etc., for discussion), and it is certain that it allowed the borrowing of words by Latin from the languages with which it coexisted (see 4.2). Latinization was evidently much more rapid in the east and south, where Iberian and Greek (in what is now Catalonia and Valencia) and Tartessian (in Andalusia and Southern Portugal) appear to have been displaced entirely by Latin by the first century AD at latest.

Pace of latinization is probably correlated with distance from the 'educated standard' of the 'average' Latin spoken at any given date. The factors which encouraged rapid latinization (close contact with central Italy, the growth of large cities, good road communications, the conse-quent fostering of trade, etc.) are the same factors which encouraged the use of forms of Latin which were closer to the prestigious end of the sociolinguistic spectrum (see 1.1). It is therefore likely that the 'average' Latin spoken by people in the remoter, less developed, parts of the Peninsula was considerably further from the prestige norm (that of upper-class Rome) than was the speech of the eastern and southern cities. This factor is particularly relevant to the history of Spanish, since Spanish has its geographical roots in what is now the northern part of the province of Burgos, an area of the northern meseta which was remote from the centres of economic activity and cultural prestige in Roman Spain, which was latinized fairly late, and where the Latin spoken must consequently have been particularly remote from the prestige norm (that is, particularly 'incorrect') at the time of the Roman collapse. With the end of the Roman state came the effective removal of the linguistic model towards which, however distantly and ineffectually, speakers strove to adhere, so that any 'incorrect' features of local speech were likely to be perpetuated (unless challenged by some other prestige model, which was not to be the case in the Burgos area). Spanish has often been described as a rather idiosyncratic form of Peninsular Romance (even of Romance *tout court*), a view associated with Menéndez Pidal (1964a: 472–88) and which can be defended at least with regard to the consonantal phonology of Spanish. Such linguistic idiosyncrasy can plausibly be accounted for by the conditions under which the northern meseta was latinized.

It is also appropriate to consider here the ways in which the Latin spoken in Spain differed from that spoken in other provinces. Such a consideration must not assume that the Latin of Spain was in any sense uniform; we have just seen that it was probably far from uniform. But it is at least arguable that there are some characteristics shared by all or most of the surviving varieties of Peninsular Romance (and which therefore belonged to the Latin spoken in most if not all of the Peninsula), which may be contrasted with the corresponding features of Gallo-Romance, Italo-Romance, etc. The characteristics which have been assigned to the Latin of Spain, at different times by different scholars, are its archaism, its conservatism, and its Osco-Umbrian dialectalism. Paradoxically, there are a number of features which allow the Latin of Spain to be described as innovatory. Each of these characteristics will be considered in turn.

1.2.1   Archaism

The early date at which the latinization of Spain began (the end of the third century BC) implies that the Latin carried to Spain represents an earlier phase in the development of Latin than that represented by the language carried to other areas. For example, the latinization of northern Italy and southern Gaul begins in the second century BC, at a time when all but the northwest of Spain was under Roman rule, while the latinization of the rest of Gaul does not begin until the first century BC, and that of Dacia (approximately modern Rumania) does not begin until the second century AD. On the hypothesis that colonized areas often retain features of speech which are abandoned in the parent-state (a hypothesis which finds some support in the history of English and Spanish in America, as elsewhere), it is predictable that Hispano-Romance will retain some features of third- and second-century BC Latin which were then abandoned in the Latin of Rome and other, more recently latinized, provinces. Such an argument may apply to the widespread appearance in Peninsular speech of bilabial [φ] (corresponding to the spelling F; see 2.5.6) rather than its successor, the labiodental [f], which is used in most of the rest of the Romance-speaking world. However, it is in the field of vocabulary that such archaism has been most closely studied. The following expressions are ones whose antecedents appear in pre-Classical writers (Plautus, Ennius, Terence, etc.) but not in the works of those writing from the first century BC onwards, facts which suggest that the words concerned had fallen out of use in Rome (while continuing in use in the Latin of Spain):

Sp., Ptg. *cansar* 'to tire' < CAMPSĀRE 'to bend, to round (a headland)', an early borrowing from Greek not found in literature after the second century BC.

Sp. *cueva*, Ptg. *cova* 'cave' < the pre-Classical adjective COVA 'hollow', by contrast with CL CAVA 'id.', whence Fr. *cave* 'cellar', etc.

Sp. *cuyo, -a*, Ptg. *cujo, -a* 'whose' < CŪIUS, -A, -UM 'id.', a form already obsolescent in the first century BC.

Sp. *(a)demás*, Ptg. *demais* 'besides' < DĒMAGIS, not found in writing after the second century BC.

Sp. *hablar*, Ptg. *falar* 'to speak' < pre-Classical FABULĀRĪ 'to converse'.

Sp., Ptg. *querer* 'to wish' probably reflects the pre-Classical sense of QUAERERE 'to wish', found in Terence (early second century BC), but whose sense later became 'to seek'.

1.2.2   Conservatism

Conservatism cannot be sharply distinguished from archaism, since both terms refer to the retention of forms which elsewhere disappear. What is meant by the conservatism of the Latin of Spain is the retention of forms which appear in Classical Latin (and which were presumably once current in the spoken Latin of many areas besides Spain) by contrast with their eventual rejection in those areas which formed the cultural centre of the late Roman Empire (central and northern Italy and Gaul). Thus, the Latin numerals QUADRĀGINTĀ ... NŌNĀGINTĀ 'forty ... ninety', retain the stress on the penultimate vowel I (later > /e/) in their Spanish and Portuguese descendants: *cuarenta ~ quarenta ... noventa* (see 3.6.1), whereas in other Romance areas a stress-shift to the preceding syllable produced forms with tonic /a/: Fr. *quarante*, It. *cinquanta*, etc. But it is again in vocabulary that most evidence of conservatism is forthcoming; in the following cases, Spanish (together usually with Portuguese) retains a form which is normal in Classical Latin but which, if it appears outside the Peninsula, appears only in similarly 'remote' areas (e.g. the Alpine area, southern Italy, Sicily, Sardinia, Rumania):

Sp. *arena*, Ptg. *areia*, Rum. *arină* 'sand' < CL ARĒNA 'id.' (cf. Fr. *sable*, It. *sabbia*).

Sp. *ciego*, Ptg. *cego*, Cat. *cec*, C. It. *cieco* 'blind' < CL CAECU 'id.' (cf. Fr. *aveugle*, N. It. *orbo*).

OSp., Sard. *cras*, S. It. *crai* 'tomorrow' < CRĀS 'id' (cf. Fr. *demain*, It. *domani*, Rum. *mîine*).

Sp. *hervir*, Ptg. *ferver*, Rum. *fierbe* 'to boil' < CL FERVERE 'id.' (cf. Fr. *bouillir*, It. *bollire*, Cat. *bullir*).

Sp. *hombro*, Ptg. *ombro*, Rum. *umăr* 'shoulder' < CL UMERU 'id.' (cf. Fr. *épaule*, It. *spalla*, Cat. *espatlla*).

Sp., Ptg. *ir*, OSp., OPtg. *imos*, S. It., Sic. *immu*, OSp., MPtg. *ides*, Sp., Ptg. *ido* forms of the verb 'to go' which descend from corresponding forms of CL ĪRE 'id.' (cf. Fr. *aller*, *allons*, It. *andare*, *andiamo*, Cat. *anar*, *anem*, etc.).

Sp., Ptg. *mesa*, Rum. *masă* 'table < CL MĒNSA 'id.' (cf. Fr. *table*, It. *tàvola*, Cat. *taula*).

Sp. *queso*, Ptg. *queijo*, C. It. *cacio*, S. It. *caso*, Rum. *caş* 'cheese' < CL CĀSEU 'id.' (cf. Fr. *fromage*, It. *formaggio*, Cat. *formatge*).

Sp., Ptg. *rogar*, Rum. *ruga* 'to beg' < CL ROGĀRE 'id.' (cf. Fr. *prier*, It. *pregare*, Cat. *pregar*).

Sp., Ptg. *sanar*, S. It., Sard. *sanare* 'to cure' < CL SĀNĀRE 'id.' (cf. Fr. *guérir*, It. *guarire*, Cat. *gorir*).

Sp. *yegua*, Ptg. *égua*, Cat. *egua*, Rum. *iapă* 'mare' < CL EQUA 'id.' (cf. Fr. *jument*, It. *cavalla*).

It can be seen from these examples that there is a strong correlation between those varieties of Romance which preserve older forms and those which are located in peripheral parts of the Romance-speaking area, i.e. those that were remotest from the trend-setting centres of the late Roman period. However, this correlation is not solely evident in the preservation and distribution of forms which also appear in Classical Latin. It is also evident in the distribution of Vulgar Latin innovations, where earlier innovations are typically found in peripheral regions and later innovations are observable in the central territories of Romance-speaking Europe. This distribution can be seen in the Vulgar Latin replacements of the synthetic forms of the comparative adjective (see 3.3.2), where the earlier innovation MAGIS (+ adj.) is preserved in Sp. *más*, Ptg. *mais*, Cat. *mes*, Rum. *mai*, by contrast with the later type PLŪS (+ adj.) seen in Fr. *plus*, It. *più*. In vocabulary, this pattern is frequently repeated; e.g.:

Sp. *hallar*, Ptg. *achar*, S. It. *acchiare*, Rum. *afla* 'to find' < AFFLĀRE 'to breathe out' (see 5.3.1) (cf. Fr. *trouver*, It. *trovare*, Cat. *trobar* < *TROPĀRE).

Sp. *hermoso*, Ptg. *formoso*, Rum. *frumos* 'beautiful' < FŌRMŌSU 'shapely' (cf. Fr. *beau*, *bel*, It. *bello* < BELLU).

Sp. *pájaro*, Ptg. *pássaro*, Rum. *pasere* 'bird' < VL PASSAR (CL PASSER) 'sparrow' (cf. Fr. *oiseau*, It. *ucello*, Cat. *aucell* < AVICELLU).

For further details, see Rohlfs 1960.

1.2.3 Dialectalism

At the time that the latinization of Spain began, at the end of the third century BC, Latin was far from having ousted its Italic competitors (Oscan, Umbrian, etc.) from Central and Southern Italy; there is evidence of the use of Oscan until at least the first century AD. And since it seems likely that many

Roman soldiers and settlers who came to Spain were drawn from areas of Italy where Latin was spoken bilingually with Oscan or Umbrian, it has been claimed that the Latin of such speakers was likely to have contained non-standard features resulting from this bilingual contact. A detailed case of this kind can be seen in Menéndez Pidal 1960, where phonological changes such as MB > /m/ (see 2.5.3.2) and -LL-, -NN-, -RR- > /ʎ/, /ɲ/, /r̄/ (see 2.5.3.2[9]) are assigned to this origin. Similarly, the tonic vowels of the ancestors of *nudo* 'knot', *octubre* 'October' and *cierzo* 'north wind' have sometimes been explained on the basis of interference between Latin NŌDU, OCTŌBER and CIRCIU and cognate Oscan or Umbrian forms with tonic ū and ĕ (namely hybrid *NŪDU, *OCTŪBER, *CĔRCIU), an interference which did not arise outside southern Italy and Spain (cf. NŌDU > Fr. *noeud*). The distribution of forms cognate with Sp. *dejar* 'to leave' (Ptg., Cat. *deixar*, Gasc. *dechà*, Sic. *dassari*, S. It. *dassare*, OSard. *dassare*), by contrast with descendants of LAXĀRE (OSp. *lexar*, Fr. *laisser*, It. *lasciare*) has sometimes been explained on the basis of a dialectal Latin form *DAXĀRE, whose D- would be due to interference from Oscan. A similar distribution of the meaning 'to arrive' associated with descendants of PLICĀRE (CL 'to fold'), such as Sp. *llegar*, by contrast with those Romance forms which retain the Latin sense (e.g. Fr. *plier*, It. *plegare*, as also Sp. semi-learnęd *plegar*), is also cited as a case of the dialectal nature of the Latin of Spain. However, it cannot be said that there is general agreement on the origin of any of the instances of putative Osco-Umbrian influence so far adduced.

1.2.4 Innovation

Despite the general characterization of Hispanic Latin as archaic and conservative, there are a number of features displayed by its descendants which reveal innovatory changes which were evidently limited to the Peninsula. Among these innovations can be counted the total merger of the Latin 2nd and 3rd verbal conjugations (see 3.7.6), so that infinitives like DĒBĒRE and VENDĔRE, originally distinct, became identical in type (Sp. *deber*, *vender*, Ptg. *dever*, *vender*), rather than remaining separate as they do in other varieties of Romance (e.g. Fr. *devoir*, *vendre*).

Some Hispanic innovations consist of new cases of word-formation, as in:

> CIBU 'food' → CIBĀRIA > *cibera* '(animal) feed, etc.', now only in rural use.
> CIBU 'food' → CIBĀTA > *cebada* OSp. 'feed', later 'barley'.
> AMĀRU 'bitter' → AMĀRELLU 'yellowish' > *amarillo* 'yellow'.
> ARGENTU 'silver' → ARGENTEU 'of silver' > OSp. *arienço* 'a (specific) coin, unit of weight'.
> CATĒNA 'chain' → CATĒNĀTU 'chained' > *candado* 'padlock'.

CENTĒNI 'hundredfold'→CENTĒNU 'rye' > *centeno* 'id.'.
COLUMNA 'column'→COLUMELLU 'canine (tooth)' > *colmillo* 'id.'.
FŌRMA 'shape, mould'→FŌRMĀCEU 'mud-brick wall' > *hormazo* 'id.', now antiquated.
PĀCĀRE 'to pacify'→*ADPĀCĀRE 'to extinguish' > *apagar* 'id.'.

On other occasions the innovation consists of a change of meaning which is peculiar to the Latin of Spain and its descendants:

CAPTĀRE 'to seize' > *catar* 'to look'.
FRĀTRE GERMĀNU 'true brother (i.e. one who shares both parents)' > GERMĀNU 'brother' > *hermano* 'id'; thus also GERMĀNA > *hermana* 'sister'.

Other innovations of course include the borrowing of words from the pre-Roman languages of the Peninsula (see 4.2).

1.3   Conquest and Reconquest

1.3.1   The Visigoths

From the fifth to the early eighth century, Spain was controlled by a Visigothic monarchy and aristocracy. The Visigoths had forced an entry into the Roman Empire in the late fourth century and following their sack of Rome in 410 established (as *foederati*), a semi-autonomous kingdom in southwestern Gaul, with their capital at Toulouse. While remaining subjects of the Roman state, they expanded their territory to include much of the Peninsula, which, together with their lands north of the Pyrenees, became an independent kingdom on the collapse of Roman administration in the West. Expulsion from Gaul by the Franks (early sixth century) was followed by the successful absorption (completed in AD 585) of the Swabian kingdom of the northwest (in modern terms, Galicia, northern Portugal, and the provinces of Asturias and León), and by the eventual expulsion (in the early seventh century) of the Byzantine forces who dominated parts of eastern and southern Spain on behalf of the Eastern Roman Emperor.

The Visigoths were partly romanized before their entry into the Peninsula and it is likely that from the first they spoke Latin, bilingually with their East Germanic vernacular. The latter never achieved the status of written language in Spain and Latin continued to be the language of culture and administration throughout the Visigothic period. The influence exercised by Visigothic upon the Latin of Spain was therefore small. Apart from a number of lexical loans (see 4.5), such influence is limited to a few morphological features:

The introduction of a new noun-declension type in Nominative -Ā, Oblique -ĀNE (plur. -ĀNES), alongside the three types already existing in late spoken Latin (see 3.2.3). This pattern was mostly restricted to personal names of

Germanic origin (e.g., OSp. *Froilán* < FROILANE, beside *Fruela* < FROILA, both names applied to the same Visigothic monarch), but was occasionally applied to common nouns (usually personal, usually borrowed from Germanic). In one instance, Spanish shows descendants of both the Nominative and Oblique forms of this paradigm: *guardia* 'guard, policeman' < WARDJA 'guard(sman)', *guardián* 'guardian' < *WARDJANE 'id.'.

The introduction of the suffix *-engo* (< Gmc. -ING), for deriving adjectives from nouns. This suffix has always been of low productivity and is found in: *abadengo* 'belonging to an abbey', *realengo* 'belonging to the Crown', and, now substantivized, *abolengo* 'ancestry' (originally 'pertaining to one's ancestors').

The possible introduction of the suffix *-ez, -oz*, etc., found in names which were once patronymic and are now surnames (e.g. *Rodríguez, Fernández, Muñoz*). The genitive of the latinized form of certain Germanic names in -IKS, e.g. RODERĪCĪ '(son) of Roderick', may explain certain patronymics (e.g. RODERĪCĪ > *Rodriz* > *Ruiz*). By comparison with the short form of the corresponding given name (e.g. *Ruy*), it was possible to extract an element *-z* with patronymic value, which could then be applied to other given names, including their 'full' forms: *Rodrigo* → *Rodríguez, Fernando* → *Fernández*, etc.

The ruling Visigothic group constituted a small fraction of the total population of the Peninsula, and despite their political supremacy, they sooner or later abandoned bilingualism and their speech became entirely assimilated to that of their subjects, who were not only numerically superior but, even in these 'Dark Ages', enjoyed a culture which was more prestigious than that of their rulers. Throughout this period, the large majority continued to speak Latin, no doubt with considerable and increasing variation between one locality and another.

It was probably this divorce between political power and cultural prestige which allowed centrifugal, linguistically diversifying, forces to gain the upper hand over centralizing and linguistically unifying forces. Despite the fact that the Visigoths eventually ruled the whole Peninsula, they presided over a period in which diatopic variation of speech was increased rather than diminished. However, there is one political event of this period which was to have great linguistic significance at a later date: the establishment of Toledo as the centre of government. For the first time in Peninsular history, the seat of political power was situated in the central meseta and, after the collapse of Visigothic Spain and the Moorish conquest of the early eighth century, Toledo therefore assumed great symbolic importance to the northern Christians, who to some extent saw their mission as the reestablishment of Christian Visigothic Spain. The fact that Toledo fell (in 1085) to Castilian reconquerors endowed Castilian speech with a prestige it might otherwise not have enjoyed, and can therefore be seen as an important factor in the rise of Castilian to national status (see 1.4).

1.3.2   Moors and Christians

The Islamic invasion of 711 had enormous linguistic consequences. It was not merely that it brought Hispanic Latin and its successors into contact with the language of a culture which was soon to be more developed and prestigious than that of Christian Europe, thereby creating the conditions for substantial lexical and semantic borrowing from Arabic (see 4.6, 5.1.5), for the modification of the syntax and phraseology of Hispano-Romance (see Galmés 1956; also Lapesa 1980: 156–7 for the Arabic origin of phrases like *que Dios guarde/que Dios mantenga, si Dios quiere, Dios le ampare, bendita sea la madre que te parió*, etc.), and for occasional morphological borrowing (e.g. the suffix *-i*; see 4.14.2.1). The linguistic effects of the Moorish conquest were even more profound, since the dialectal map of Spain was entirely changed, and importance was given to varieties of Romance which, in the absence of this political upheaval, would have remained insignificant and peripheral. The reason is, of course, that the Moorish armies failed to conquer the entire Peninsula. Between 711 and 718 they established control over approximately three quarters of its territory, but allowed the survival of Christian nuclei in the extreme north and northwest. These were precisely the areas which had been remotest from standardizing influences during the Roman period and from such linguistic levelling processes as obtained during the period of Visigothic rule. It can therefore be argued that they were the areas of the Peninsula where speech was most distant from the 'norm' of eighth-century Hispano-Romance speech. This was no doubt particularly so in the case of Cantabria (modern Santander, northern Burgos and adjacent areas), the southern part of which is the area where Castilian has its origins and which was especially resistant to Roman and Visigothic rule and whose language in the eighth century is likely to have been particularly 'abnormal'. (It is recognized that there can have been no single accepted prestige-norm for speakers of eighth-century Hispano-Romance, and the term 'norm' here is a means of referring to those linguistic features which were common to most varieties of Hispano-Romance speech.)

The linguistic effects of the Christian Reconquest of the Peninsula are similarly great. Varieties of Hispano-Romance speech which were hitherto peripheral (in both geographical and linguistic terms) are extended southwards at the expense of those varieties which one can presume were previously the most prestigious and the most in keeping with the Romance spoken outside the Peninsula. And among these peripheral varieties of Hispano-Romance, it was one of the most 'abnormal', namely Castilian, which was to have the greatest territorial and cultural success. At first typical only of the speech of the Burgos area of southern Cantabria, Castilian linguistic characteristics were carried south, southeast and southwest, in part by movement of population, as Castilians settled in reconquered territories, and in part by the adoption of Castilian features by those whose speech was originally different. The creation of the kingdom of Castile in 1035 no doubt sharpened awareness of the separate identity of Castilian speech and the capture of Toledo in 1085 has already been noted as having considerable linguistic significance, by reason of the prestige that this success afforded to Castile and to Castilian speech. After what proved to be temporary setbacks at the hands of Almoravid and Almohad reformers of Islamic Spain in the late eleventh and twelfth centuries, the Castilian advance continued with the capture of the major cities of northern and western Andalusia (Córdoba 1236, Jaén 1246, Seville 1248, Cádiz 1250) and with control over the kingdom of Murcia (1244). By the mid-thirteenth century, then, Castile had expanded to comprise something over half of the Peninsular territory and Castilian speech was on the way to displacing its competitors, Arabic and Mozarabic, the latter term indicating those varieties of Hispano-Romance which had continued to be widely spoken in Islamic and ex-Islamic Spain. The contact between Castilian and Mozarabic produced some effects upon Castilian, largely restricted to borrowing of Mozarabic vocabulary (see 4.7), but perhaps including the development of the sibilant consonants in Andalusian (and, later, American) varieties of Castilian (see 2.6.3). However, it is likely that Mozarabic speech was assimilated to Castilian patterns (or was abandoned in favour of Castilian speech) during the thirteenth and fourteenth centuries.

Between the mid-thirteenth century and the end of the fifteenth, Islamic Spain consisted only of the mountainous southeastern parts of Andalusia, namely the kingdom of Granada. When this area was captured in 1492 by the Catholic Monarchs, Ferdinand and Isabella, it was largely resettled by speakers of Andalusian varieties of Castilian, so that in the course of six centuries Castilian had come to occupy a territory stretching from the Cantabrian coast to the Atlantic and the Mediterranean.

However, it should be made clear that Castilian speech-characteristics were spread not simply to those central and southern Peninsular territories into which the kingdom of Castile expanded. At the same time as this southward development was taking place, people in neighbouring kingdoms were adopting Castilian manners of speech. In the case of León, the westward spread of Castilian is firmly attested, in literary and non-literary writing, well before the final union of Castile and León in 1230. Unattested, but presumably no less real, was the northeasterly advance of Castilian at the expense of Basque. Similar encroachment of Castilian features upon Aragonese territory is observable in texts written in Saragossa in the fourteenth and fifteenth centuries, that is, before the union of the crowns of Castile and Aragon in 1479. At this stage, only Galicia and the Catalan-speaking areas (Catalonia, Valencia and the Balearics) remained, for the most part, outside the Castilian sphere of linguistic influence.

The reasons for this lateral spread and imitation of Castilian features lie in the political prestige of Castile, stemming from its increasingly predominant role in the Reconquest, and in the development of its literature (see 1.4), which had no comparable counterpart in the kingdoms of León and Aragon. The castilianization of these kingdoms was of course not rapid (although it was undoubtedly more swift among the educated than among the majority) and it is still incomplete today, in rural areas of Asturias, western León, northern Huesca, etc.

1.4 Standard Spanish

The creation of standard Spanish is arguably the result of the work of one man, Alfonso X the Learned, king of Castile and León (1252–84). Writing by means of a spelling-system which was able to specify vernacular pronunciation, by contrast with writing in Latin, goes back to the period following the reforms of the Council of Burgos in 1080 (see Wright 1982), and vernacular writing in the kingdom of Castile, both literary and non-literary, becomes ever more frequent in the twelfth and early thirteenth centuries. However, until the period of Alfonso X, all writing can be seen to be dialectal, in the sense that the language used shows some features characteristic of the writer's region, rather than representing any supra-regional variety. Thus, the twelfth-century *Auto de los reyes magos* reveals features of the speech of Toledo (perhaps due to contact with Mozarabic) not shared with the rest of the kingdom, while the *Poema de mio Cid* displays a number of characteristics which locate its language in the northeast of Castile. Non-literary writing is no different in this respect; the *Fuero de Madrid*, which reached its final form in 1202, is recognizably from New Castile.

Such regional characteristics disappear, for the most part, in the later thirteenth century, as a result of the scholarly activities of the king and his collaborators. On the one hand, the use of Castilian as the vehicle of an enormous output of scientific, historiographical, legal, literary, and other work, was bound to lend great prestige to the chosen medium, Castilian, by contrast with other varieties of Hispano-Romance, such as Leonese or Aragonese, which enjoyed little literary cultivation. On the other hand, the king's express concern over the 'correctness' of the language of his scholarly output is a witness to the creation of a standard form of Castilian. Certainly, as just stated, by the end of Alfonso's reign it is no longer possible to identify a specific regional flavour in the writing of Castilians, and it is reasonable to assume that the new supra-regional literary standard was based upon the speech of the upper classes of Toledo, a form of speech which, we have seen, originated in the Burgos area and had been extended to Toledo at the time of the Reconquest of New Castile.

A further important aspect of Alfonso's activities was the consistent use of Castilian as the language of administration. Latin had been partly abandoned in the previous reign, but was now definitively superseded, by Castilian, which had the culturally unifying advantage of being religiously neutral, by contrast with Latin (or Arabic, or Hebrew). In Alfonso's reign, the entire business of the state was carried out in an increasingly standard form of Castilian and documents issuing from the royal chancery could stand as models of correctness in writing wherever they were read, copied or imitated.

The use of the Castilian vernacular as a medium of scientific, legal, administrative and other writing required the expansion of its expressive resources. The syntax of Castilian becomes considerably more complex and subtle during the Alfonsine period, and the vocabulary is enormously expanded, in part by borrowing from Latin and Arabic (see 4.3, 4.6), in part by word-formation (see Penny 1987).

It should not be assumed, however, that the speech of Toledo, which we have seen forming the basis of the written standard, immediately provided the only spoken standard. Other cities were cultural rivals to Toledo, and the speech of their educated classes no doubt continued to pose a challenge to that of the central city. In particular Seville. At the time of its reconquest and for centuries thereafter, Seville was the largest and economically the most flourishing city of the kingdom. The speech of its educated classes must consequently have enjoyed great prestige in its region. This factor, together with the geographical remoteness of Seville from the central cities, was responsible for the establishment of a spoken norm which to some extent rivalled that of Toledo. This norm was characterized by a number of phonological features which sooner or later (but almost certainly by the sixteenth century) included *seseo* (see 2.6.3). Other features which contributed to the Sevillian 'norm' were *yeísmo* (see 2.6.6), preservation of the phoneme /h/ descended from Latin F- (which was eliminated from central Spanish in the sixteenth century under northern influences; see 2.5.6 and 2.6.4), weakening of syllable-final /s/ (see 2.6.7), and the weakening and merger of syllable-final /r/ and /l/. At the morphosyntactical level, Sevillian Spanish was characterized by, among other features, etymological distinction of the pronouns *lo* and *le*, in contrast with central Spanish, which was *leísta* (see 3.5.1). Between these two varieties there were no doubt also considerable lexical differences, which are now difficult to reconstruct.

Therefore, at the time of the overseas expansion of Spanish, there were two main norms, that of Toledo (superseded in the 1560s by Madrid) rivalled by that of Seville. It cannot be claimed that they were of equal status, and in Spain the Madrid norm was to establish a firm priority during the Golden Age of Spanish literature. However, in areas outside the Peninsula to which Spanish was extended, the two norms continued in much more equal contention, as will be seen in the following section.

It is also during the Golden Age that Castilian becomes the main language of literature and of the educated in Galicia and the Catalan-speaking areas, giving rise to bilingualism in those parts of the Peninsula, a bilingualism which was intensified in the following centuries through the almost exclusive use of Castilian as the medium of education. From the late nineteenth century onwards, however, and despite their suppression during the Franco era, Catalan (and to a lesser extent Galician) have regained the status of languages of literature and culture. From the sixteenth century, Basque has also acquired some literary and other written use, and now coexists bilingually with Castilian in Guipúzcoa, eastern Vizcaya, northern Navarre and the northern fringe of Álava.

1.5   Spanish overseas

In the fifteenth and sixteenth centuries, Spanish was carried outside the Peninsula to a number of other parts of the world, by soldiers, settlers, priests, colonial administrators, etc. The main areas to which Spanish was extended were the Canaries, America, the Mediterranean and the Balkans, and the Philippines.

1.5.1   The Canaries

The conquest of the Canary Islands and their incorporation in the crown of Castile was a fifteenth-century undertaking not completed until the reign of the Catholic Monarchs. The enterprise was launched and sustained from Andalusian ports and the participants were in all probability drawn from Andalusia; the clear evidence is that they were speakers of southern (i.e. Andalusian) Spanish and that the prestige norm by which they were influenced was that of Seville. Thus Canaries Spanish is in all cases *seseante* (see 2.6.3), it retains the aspirate /h/ descended from F- (see 2.5.6, 2.6.4); at least in part of the relevant vocabulary and among many speakers, it suffers weakening of syllable-final /s/ (usually to [h]; see 2.6.7), and merger (among some speakers) of syllable-final /r/ and /l/, all features found to a greater or lesser extent in Andalusian and American Spanish.

The Canaries were an indispensable stepping-stone and staging-post on the route to and from America, in closer contact with the American colonies than was most of the Peninsula, and therefore sharing with American Spanish certain features which are absent, or largely absent, from Spain. Such features are often lexical (like the use of *guagua* 'bus'), but include other characteristics, such as the absence of contrast between second-person plural informal and formal address (*ustedes* + third-plural verb is almost universal in Canarian Spanish, and is identical to the universal American usage and to that of parts of western Andalusia; see 3.5.1.1).

1.5.2   America

Columbus's route of discovery took him from southern Spain to the Canaries and thence across the Atlantic to the West Indies. Colombus's landings, on each of his four voyages to America, were in the Caribbean: the island of La Española (now the Dominican Republic and Haiti), Cuba, etc. He established small settlements in these islands and they became thereafter an essential staging-post for the conquest and settlement of the northern and southern continents. The conquest of Mexico by Cortés was launched from La Española, and eventually led to the acquisition by Spain of large parts of North America (now New Mexico, Texas, Arizona, California, as well as Mexico proper).

Following the discovery of the Pacific in 1513, the conquest of the Inca empire was carried out by Pizarro, who thereby extended the chain of communication from the Caribbean down the Pacific side of the Andes to Lima in Peru.

These routes of discovery and conquest then became the normal lines of communication between Spain and America and within America:

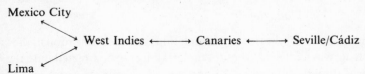

Mexico City and Lima became the main administrative and cultural centres of Spanish America. They were the seats of the king's representatives (the viceroys), the headquarters of the Church, and the places where the first universities in America were founded (already in the sixteenth century). From these centres, subsidiary lines of communication eventually came to feed the rest of Spanish America. But it should be noted that, except in the case of parts of the Caribbean, communication with Spain was for centuries effected only via Mexico and Lima. As a result, some areas (like Argentina/Paraguay/Uruguay, Central America, New Mexico) remained much more remote (geographically and culturally) than the territories connected by the main lines of communication. For example, until the nineteenth century, Buenos Aires was accessible only by an enormous overland journey down and across the southern continent.

This pattern of conquest, settlement and communication, in addition to explaining the sources of most of the words which are borrowed by Spanish from Amerindian languages (that is, explaining why they are borrowed from the languages of the Caribbean, the Mexican plateau and the central Andes; see 4.9) also helps to account for the relative influence of the Seville norm and the Toledo/Madrid norm in the speech of different parts of America. Thus, the speech of highland Mexico and of Peru/Bolivia has remained closer to the central Peninsular standard, while in areas remoter from the main cultural centres of colonial America southern Peninsular features have been more successful in establishing themselves. Such southern features have more easily spread through society in those areas, such as Argentina and Central America, which were geographically remote, in terms of sixteenth- and seventeenth-century communications, from the American centres which were responsible for radiating the central Peninsular norm (namely, Mexico City and Lima).

These similarities and dissimilarities from central Peninsular Spanish have sometimes been explained by reference to physical geography and choice of location by early settlers; it has been claimed that settlers from the Castilian meseta preferred the highland areas of America (the Mexican plateau, the Andean area), while lowland and coastal areas of America were preferred by Spanish settlers from lowland and coastal areas of Spain, principally including Andalusia. Since there is absolutely no evidence of the exercise of such preferences by settlers of the New World, it is preferable to explain the broad differences between varieties of American Spanish in the way here expounded, in terms of proximity or distance from the main centres of colonial government and the cultural influence (including linguistic influence) they exercised. In these centres, speakers from the centre of Spain would be sufficiently numerous and prestigious to set the linguistic tone for such cities and for the areas in easiest communication with them. It is in this context that one can explain the distribution of certain key features in American Spanish (for details of the distribution of phonetic features, see Canfield 1981). For example:

Retention of syllable-final /s/ is typical of those areas of America which were under the greatest central Peninsular influence, namely Mexico (except the far south), Peru, Bolivia and Andean Ecuador. Most other areas show weakening and/or loss of the phoneme under these conditions, as in southern Peninsular and Canarian Spanish (see 2.6.7).
Use of the pronoun *tú* as the singular informal mode of address, as in Spain is found in a somewhat broader but essentially similar distribution: in Mexico and the southwestern United States, in most of Bolivia and Peru, but on this

occasion including the Caribbean islands and the major part of Venezuela. Such *tuteo* contrasts with the use of *vos* (see 3.5.1.1), which occurs in those regions which were remote from the main lines of communication, either in competition with *tuteo* (as in Chile, Ecuador, Colombia, etc.), or as the dominant form of address (as in Argentina, Uruguay, Paraguay and most of Central America up to southern Mexico).

On the other hand, there are many features of American Spanish which demonstrate that southern Peninsular tendencies have successfully gained the upper hand in all or most of Spanish America. Such features include *seseo* (see 2.6.3), *yeismo* (see 2.6.6), use of /h/ where standard Peninsular Spanish has /x/ (see 2.6.3–4), and *loismo* (see 3.5.1). The result is the predominantly 'Andalusian' character of most transatlantic Spanish, a character which was traditionally 'explained' by the assumption that the majority of American settlers came from Andalusia. However, this notion was rejected by Henríquez Ureña (1932), on the basis that many colonists came from the north of Spain (they were Galicians, Basques, etc.) and that a majority were non-Andalusian. He therefore came to the conclusion that the similarities between American and Andalusian Spanish were due to separate but parallel developments on each side of the Atlantic, favouring a now discredited climatological explanation.

However, more recent and more detailed examination of the regional origins of American settlers, by Boyd-Bowman (1956, 1964), has led to broad acceptance of an amended version of the earlier theory. Boyd-Bowman concludes that the similarity between Andalusian and American Spanish is due to inheritance of Andalusian (and specifically Sevillian) speech characteristics and adduces the following facts in support of his contention: There was a large majority of Andalusians among the early settlers of the West Indies, 78 per cent in the first two decades of settlement, when colonies were limited to the Caribbean. Subsequent waves of settlers usually spent at least some time in the West Indies before passing on to new areas of settlement. And significantly, most of the Andalusians were from Seville, with a very high proportion of Andalusian women, who were likely to pass on their Andalusian speech-patterns to the following generation.

Another factor which is relevant here is the fact that groups of colonists from all over Spain gathered in Seville before their departure and were often kept there for months waiting for a ship. It is understandable that such emigrants, with their diverse linguistic backgrounds, should have gravitated towards a common linguistic denominator, most conveniently furnished by the popular speech of Seville. This process of dialectal adjustment is now well understood and it can now be said that such processes are normal, even inevitable (see Trudgill 1986). Even before setting out, then, prospective settlers from the centre and north of Spain had probably already acquired at least some of the characteristic features of southern speech. Similarly important is the fact that the sailors on the ships that made the Atlantic crossings were almost exclusively Andalusians. Owing to their prestige as experienced men who had travelled back and forth to America, their speech may well have influenced that of the emigrants who travelled with them.

Nor should it be forgotten that almost all contact between Spain and its American colonies was channelled through Seville (or its dependent port of Cádiz), which for centuries enjoyed a powerful trade monopoly with Spain's American empire. This dominant position of Seville in all dealings with America no doubt favoured the continuing spread of Andalusian linguistic features to America, while the material wealth that this monopoly brought would have served to enhance further the prestige of the city and its speech. Only in the viceregal centres of Mexico and Lima were there sufficient concentrations of speakers of central and northern varieties of Spanish to challenge this prestige.

1.5.3 The Mediterranean and the Balkans

At the same time as the beginning of the settlement of America, and the completion of the Reconquest of the Peninsula upon the fall of Granada, came the expulsion of the Jews of Spain, in 1492. Faced with conversion to Catholicism or expatriation, many thousands chose to leave Spain. Some settled at first in Portugal, until their later expulsion from the neighbouring country, some in the cities of north Africa (Fez, Algiers, Cairo, etc.), some in Italy, but the majority in the cities of the Ottoman Empire, which by the early sixteenth century included not only Syria and Asia Minor but what are now the Balkan states of Greece, Albania, Yugoslavia, Bulgaria and much of Rumania. In Constantinople, Salonika, Sofia, Bucharest, Monastir, etc., the Spanish or Sephardic Jews established flourishing communities, which were later joined by Jews expelled from Portugal and those who found their way to the east via Italy. Within these communities, regional origins within the Peninsula (and probably also the associated dialectal differences) were at first distinguished; there were separate synagogues for those originally from Aragon, Castile, Portugal, Barcelona, Lisbon, Córdoba, etc. Merger of regional origins was no doubt accompanied by dialectal mixing, with the result that although the resulting Judaeo-Spanish speech (also called 'Ladino', or 'Judezmo', or simply 'Espaniol') is predominantly of Castilian tradition, it shows a considerable admixture of features from other regions of the Peninsula, especially western or specifically Portuguese features, while among its Castilian features we find a number which are specifically southern or Andalusian, as well as features preserved with little change from general fifteenth-century Castilian.

Among the non-Castilian features of Judaeo-Spanish can be cited the frequent absence of diphthong corresponding to Latin Ĕ and Ŏ (*quero* [= Sp. *quiero* 'I wish'], *preto* [= Sp. *prieto* 'black'], *rogo* [= Sp. *ruego* 'I beg']), in keeping with the non-diphthongization of Galician-Portuguese, although in other instances the diphthongs /ie/, /ue/ are found, and may even be analogically extended to unstressed syllables (e.g. *puedo→pueder*, standard *poder* 'to be able'; see 3.7.7.1.4 for parallel cases in the standard). In the Judaeo-Spanish of the Balkans, the system of final vowels is /i/ – /a/ – /u/, similar to that of Portuguese and like many varieties of Leonese, and unlike Castilian /e/ – /a/ – /o/ (e.g. *vedri* [= Sp. *verde* 'green'], *fijus* [= Sp. *hijos* 'sons']). Again like Galician-Portuguese and most of Leonese (but also like Aragonese and Catalan), Balkan Judaeo-Spanish often preserves latin F- as /f/ (e.g. *fazer* 'to do', *furmiga* 'ant', *fambri* 'hunger' [= Sp. *hacer*, *hormiga*, *hambre*]), although eastern varieties of Judaeo-Spanish (e.g. in Istanbul) most frequently show /h/ or no consonant (e.g. *hetcho ~ etcho* [= Sp. *hecho* 'done']). Again as in Galician-Portuguese and Leonese, Latin -MB- is widely retained as /mb/ (e.g. *palombika* [= Sp. *paloma* 'pigeon, dove']). Like Portuguese, syllable-final /s/ is palatalized (> /ʃ/), although in Judaeo-Spanish the change only occurs before /k/ (e.g. /móʃka/ 'fly', /eʃkóla/ 'school' [= Sp. *mosca, escuela*]).

All the data so far considered argue for a substantial western Hispanic (and specifically Portuguese) input into the dialectal mixture which in the sixteenth century produced Judaeo-Spanish. The Portuguese flavour of Judaeo-Spanish is further emphasized by the outcome in these varieties of the medieval sibilants (see 2.6.2–3). The medieval Portuguese sibilant system was identical to that of Castilian, but changed less, producing a system which is identical to that of Judaeo-Spanish, while the fundamental shifts of the Castilian system produce an outcome quite foreign to Judaeo-Spanish. The Portuguese and Judaeo-Spanish development can be summarized in the following way, showing merger of apico-alveolar fricatives and dento-alveolar affricates into dento-alveolar fricatives (i.e. *seseo*), but preserving the contrast between voiceless and voiced phonemes:

	medieval			*modern*		
prepalatal	/ʃ/	/ʒ/	>	/ʃ/	/ʒ/	prepalatal
apico-alveolar	/s/	/z/	>	/ş/	/ẓ/	dento-alveolar
dento-alveolar	/ts/	/dz/				

Examples of these developments in Judaeo-Spanish, in the order of the medieval phonemes as listed, include: OSp. *dixo, ojo, passo, casa, cinco, dezir* > JSp. /díʃo/ 'he said', /óʒo/ 'eye', /páşo/ 'step', /káẓa/ 'house', /şínko/

'five', /deʒír/ 'to say'. However, it should be noted that the incidence of the phonemes concerned in Judaeo-Spanish is generally the same as in Castilian (e.g. OCŬLU > JSp. /óʒo/ 'eye', by contrast with Ptg. *olho* 'id.').

A further case of agreement with Portuguese is the contrast made in some varieties of Judaeo-Spanish between *b* and *v*, sometimes in the form /b/:/β/ as in north-central Portugal, sometimes in the form /b/:/v/ as in the standard. However, the argument for Portuguese phonological input into Judaeo-Spanish is less strong in these cases, since sixteenth-century southern Castilian still showed the contrast /b/:/β/ (see 2.6.1), as do southern and Balearic varieties of Catalan.

In some respects, the phonology of Judaeo-Spanish concurs with southern varieties of Castilian. The main instance of this agreement is the merger of /ʎ/ and /ĵ/ (see 2.6.6). Such *yeísmo* is typical of most Andalusian and Canaries speech and of much American and southern Peninsular speech, and is universal in Judaeo-Spanish (e.g. *sevoya* 'onion', *fayar* 'to find' [= *cebolla*, *hallar*]). The resulting phoneme /ĵ/ is most frequently lost when adjacent to a front vowel: *ea* 'she', *amarío* 'yellow', *gaina* 'hen', *aí* 'there' [= *ella*, *amarillo*, *gallina*, *allí*]).

In many of its features, however, Judaeo-Spanish can be regarded as archaic, preserving characteristics of fifteenth-century Spanish which have elsewhere disappeared. Because Judaeo-Spanish was entirely cut off from contact with the Peninsula after the early sixteenth century, changes which have since then affected other varieties of Spanish have been unable to penetrate the language of the Sephardic Jews. This archaic character is clearly visible in vocabulary (see Zamora Vicente 1967: 361–77, Sala 1979), where Judaeo-Spanish maintains in use words which were current in Spain in the Middle Ages, but which have since then become obsolete or restricted to regional use. All new vocabulary (except that originating in word-formation) is due to borrowing from a variety of other sources, Italian, French, Turkish, Greek, etc. However, archaism is not restricted to vocabulary but can also be seen, for instance, in the morpho-syntax of Judaeo-Spanish. The second person plural verb-forms show the variation found in fifteenth-century Spanish (see 3.7.2), but with palatalization of the final /s/ in the shorter forms: /kantáʃ/ ~ /kantáis/, /keréʃ/ ~ /keréis/. With the exception of this palatal development, the shorter forms are therefore identical to those used in most American areas of *voseo* (see 3.5.1.1). However, unlike all other forms of Spanish, the innovation *vuestra merced* (whence modern *usted*) is unknown in Judaeo-Spanish, which contrasts informal *tú* (sing.), *vos* (plur.) with formal *el*, *e(y)a*, *e(y)os*, *-as* (see Malinowski 1983).

Despite its five hundred years' survival, Judaeo-Spanish does not have a rosy future. The rise of nationalism in the Balkan states from the nineteenth century (together with the concomitant pressure towards language uniformity), followed by decimation of many Sephardic communities during the Second World War, has brought about a dramatic decline in the use of Judaeo-Spanish. It continues to be used to some extent in the Balkan and Turkish cities where it has been spoken for centuries, but perhaps now survives best in Israel, as a result of further migration. There, however, it belongs essentially to the older generation, as is also the case in New York, the other principal destination of Sephardic Jews emigrating from erstwhile Turkish areas.

1.5.4   The Philippines

Discovered by Europeans in 1521 and incorporated in the Spanish Empire later in the century, the Philippine islands were administered via Mexico until Mexican independence in the early nineteenth century, and remained a Spanish possession until the war with the United States in 1898. By contrast with the Canaries and America, the Philippines were only superficially hispanized; Spanish became the language only of the ruling class, of civil and judicial administration, and of culture. By the time Spanish rule came to an end, Spanish was the language of approximately 10 per cent of the population, and although it has become an official language of the country (together with English and Tagalog), its use has probably declined in the twentieth century (see Whinnom 1954).

Long contact between Spanish and local languages has given rise to a series of pidgins and creoles, the latter of which are the language of a substantial proportion of the Philippine population (see Quilis 1980, Whinnom 1956).

It is unsurprising, given the fact that communication between Spain and the Philippines was for centuries mediated by Mexico, that Philippine Spanish is similar in its broad lines to American Spanish (see 1.5.2), not only in vocabulary but in pronunciation and grammar. Although some speakers distinguish /s/ and /θ/ (as in central and northern Spain), and /λ/ and /j/ (as some speakers do in the northern half of the Peninsula), Philippines Spanish is more generally characterized by *seseo* (see 2.6.3) and *yeismo* (see 2.6.6). It also reveals retention of /h/ (from Latin F-), uses the same phoneme to correspond to standard Peninsular /x/ (see 2.5.6, 2.6.2–4), and shows some evidence of merger of syllable-final /r/ and /l/. The atonic pronoun system is also similar to American Spanish (and to Canarian and Andalusian Spanish) in its preservation of *loísmo* (see 3.5.1). A local phonological development, under the influence of Tagalog, which lacks /f/, is the replacement of Spanish /f/ by /p/ (e.g. *Pilipinas* 'Philippines', *supri* 'to suffer').

1.6 'Castilian' and 'Spanish'

The terms *castellano* and *español* are now synonymous when they refer to the national language of modern Spain and of nineteen American republics. In this sense, their English equivalents, *Castilian* and *Spanish*, will be used interchangeably in this book. However, in other contexts the two terms are not synonymous, and some discussion of their meaning is called for. Much has been previously written on this topic (e.g. Alonso 1943, Alvar 1978) and remarks will therefore be kept to a minimum.

The language whose history is traced in this book is referred to in the Middle Ages as *castellano* or *romance castellano*, a term which at the written level can be contrasted with Latin, and at the written and spoken level with other varieties of Hispano-Romance (Portuguese, Aragonese, etc.), or, increasingly, with extra-Peninsular Romance (principally French and Italian). At this stage the term *español* (earlier *españón*) is rarely used of language; it is of course related to España, which in the early centuries of the Reconquest refers to Muslim Spain, then to the Peninsula as a whole (under the influence of Lat. HISPANIA?), and finally, after the union of the crowns of Aragon/Catalonia and Castile/León/Galicia, to the new nation-state.

It is in the sixteenth century that the term *español* is applied to the language of culture of Spain, and therefore becomes equivalent in this sense to *castellano*. The two terms have been used almost interchangeably since then, although political considerations have often led to preference for the older term (as in the current Spanish constitution and as in the usage of many American countries), in order to avoid the implication (sometimes seen as present in the term *español*) that the language concerned is the only language of the Spanish state or that the Spanish state has cultural hegemony over those, living in other states, who speak the same language.

There is, however, a further use of the term *castellano* (and of Eng. *Castilian*), which may give rise to misunderstanding. This is the use of the term to mean 'the speech (or dialect[s]) of Castile', a sense in which *castellano* is opposed to *leonés, gallego, aragonés, catalán*, etc., but which naturally refers to a different portion of the Peninsula at different times in history. In the earliest period (the ninth century) at which the name *Castile* occurs (as *Castella*, then *Castiella*) it refers to a very small area at the eastern extremity of the kingdom of Oviedo, which then comes to include Burgos (884). Only in the tenth century does Castile expand as far as the Duero (912) and the Guadarrama mountains (*c.* 950). Even this territory is less extensive than what is now called *Old Castile* (*Castilla la Vieja*), since areas such as that which now comprises the province of Palencia fell outside Castile until the eleventh century. After the conquest of the kingdom of

Toledo from the Moors in the late eleventh century, it becomes necessary to distinguish the newly acquired territory south of the Guadarrama (*New Castile*) from that to the north (*Old Castile*), and the maximum extent of *Castile* is achieved at the end of the twelfth century, when the Reconquest reaches the Sierra Morena. Beyond that, the term *Castile* did not apply; the territory to the south was, and is, *Andalusia*. In its more limited sense, then, *Castilian* can nevertheless refer, after 1200, to a considerable portion of the Peninsula.

2
Phonology

This chapter presupposes some knowledge of phonological theory, in particular of the concepts of the phoneme, the allophone, complementary distribution, and neutralization. Useful discussion of these matters can be found in Lyons (1968: ch. 3), and, with reference to Spanish, Alarcos 1965, Dalbor 1980, Macpherson 1975, Quilis & Fernández 1969.

2.1 Phonological change

Phonological change is motivated in a number of ways, although scholars are not in agreement on the number or relative importance of the factors which provoke such change. Among the main types of phonological change are the following:

2.1.1

Change caused (initially, usually at the allophonic level) by a neighbouring phoneme or phonemes in the spoken chain. Such change is in most cases motivated by the unconscious need to save articulatory energy and may take a number of forms:

2.1.1.1

Assimilation is said to occur when a phoneme is modified in one or more of its features in such a way that the phoneme becomes more similar to a neighbouring phoneme. The most frequent case is that of **anticipatory** (or 'regressive') assimilation, in which the modified phoneme precedes the modifying unit, as in the case of Latin /k/ (see also 2.5.2.2). Lat. /k/, until about the first century AD, appears to have had only velar articulation ([k]), but thereafter, in the spoken Latin of most areas, the allophones of /k/ used before front (i.e. palatal) vowels themselves became attracted into the palatal area (becoming at first [tʃ], later further fronted to [ts], etc., in some areas). Thus,

CĪNQUE (CL QUĪNQUE)	[kíŋkwe]	>	[tsíŋkwe]
CISTA	[késta]	>	[tsésta]
CERVUS	[kérβos]	>	[tsérβos]

(ultimately appearing in Sp. as *cinco*, *cesta*, *ciervo*), while, in cases where Lat. /k/ was followed by a non-front vowel, it remained unmodified and appears in Sp. as /k/:

CAPANNA	>	*cabaña*
CORONA	>	*corona*
CURRERE	>	*correr*

Assimilation less frequently results in modification of allophones under the influence of a preceding phoneme (this is termed **progressive** assimilation or assimilation 'by lag'). Thus, in cases where Latin presents the sequence /mb/, the second consonant is modified, in some areas, from non-nasal to nasal, producing /mm/ (later simplified to /m/, see 2.5.3.2[3]):

VL PALUMBA	>	Sp. *paloma*
LUMBU	>	*lomo*

Thirdly, assimilation may be **mutual**; two adjacent phonemes each change, in one or more of their features, and merge in a pronunciation which is physiologically intermediate between the two original phonemes. Thus, the Latin diphthong /au/, in which the low vowel /a/ is followed by the (high) labiovelar glide, is resolved in many Romance languages (including Sp.) as /o/, a single phoneme whose aperture lies between that of the two original phonemes, e.g.

CAUSA	>	*cosa*
AUDĪRE	>	*oír*
TAURUS	>	*toro*

2.1.1.2

Dissimilation springs from the difficulty of coordinating the articulatory movements required in the repetition, within a word or phrase, of a given phoneme. It arises especially when other phonemes intervene between the occurrences of the phoneme in question and leads (in one of the occurrences) either to **replacement** by a related phoneme or to **elimination**. Cases of vowel dissimilation can be seen in

> ROTUNDU > *ROTONDO > *redondo* (replacement of back vowel by front vowel)
> AUGUSTU > *agosto* (elimination of first occurrence)

and of consonant dissimilation in

> *RŌBORE > *roble* (replacement)
> ARĀTRU > *arado* (elimination of second occurrence)

2.1.1.3

Epenthesis, the addition of a phoneme to a word, normally occurs in order to aid the transition from a preceding to a following phoneme. Thus the appearance of /b/ or /d/ in the following examples (where syncope first eliminates an intertonic vowel; see 2.4.3.3) is due to a need to facilitate the articulatory movement between the preceding nasal and the following /r/:

| HUMERU | > | *hombro* |
| INGENERĀRE | > | *engendrar* |

2.1.1.4

Metathesis is less obviously energy-saving. It consists in the re-ordering of phonemes in the utterance; in some cases, at least, such re-ordering may be energy-saving. Cases of metathesis may involve the movement of a single phoneme:

| PR̥AESĒPE | > | *pesebre* |
| CR̥EPĀRE | > | *quebrar* |

or the interchange of two phonemes:

early OSp. *parabla* > *palabra*
early OSp. *periglo* > *peligro*
GENERU > *yerno*

2.1.2   Isolative change

Isolative change is the term used to refer to cases in which a phoneme is modified, without apparent influence of environmental factors, in all or most of its occurrences. For example, Lat. /w/ (spelt v) is regularly modified in such a way that it appears in OSp. as /β/ (still spelt *v*):

| VĪTA | > | *vida* |
| Early L. COVA | > | *cueva* |

The origins of isolative change are probably many: generalization of conditioned variants to all environments, influence from another language or dialect, etc.

It will be noted that individual changes of the types so far discussed do not, by themselves, create additional phonemes or otherwise alter the phonological structure of the language concerned. For structural changes, see the following section.

2.1.3   Changes affecting the phonemic system

Phonemes may be added to the system of a given language through the process of **split**, while the number of phonemes may be reduced through **merger**.

2.1.3.1

Split requires two changes for its accomplishment. It is not common in the history of Spanish, but may arguably be seen in the following case. OSp. /h/ (spelt *f*) probably came to have, for reasons of assimilation, the following allophonic variation (see 2.5.6):

> the glottal aspirate [h] was used before full vowels ([haβlár], [hóndo], *fablar*, *fondo*)
> the voiceless labiovelar fricative [ʍ] was used before the glide [w] ([ʍwérte], [ʍwénte], *fuerte*, *fuente*)

(There may well have been a third allophone [φ], used before consonants, which I shall ignore here.)

In some varieties of Spanish, [ʍ] > [f], perhaps spontaneously, perhaps under foreign (French?) influence, but so long as the conditioning factor (the following sound) remained stable, the unity of the phoneme /h/ was unaffected.

However, at a certain stage in later Old Spanish, the introduction of borrowings from neighbouring languages and from Latin created the possibility in Spanish of the sequence [f] + full vowel:

> Lat. FŌRMA was borrowed as [fórma]
> Prov. *faisan* was borrowed as [faisán]

From this point on, both [f] and [h] could occur in the same environment (i.e. before full vowels) and could therefore serve to distinguish the meanings of separate words, whereupon the phonemic split was complete:

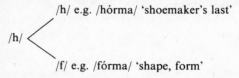

/h/ e.g. /hórma/ 'shoemaker's last'

/h/

/f/ e.g. /fórma/ 'shape, form'

The ultimate loss of /h/ in most varieties of Spanish (including the standard) does not affect the substance of the split examined here.

2.1.3.2

Merger is more common in the history of Spanish and consists of increasing neutralization of originally distinct phonemes (for which see Alarcos 1965: 97–8, 180–5), until there are no phonetic environments in which the two units remain distinct. At this stage, the two have fully merged and are henceforth a single phoneme. Thus, in the case of OSp. /b/ (spelt *b*) and /β/ (spelt *v*), spelling evidence suggests that the two phonemes were neutralized when they occurred in consonant clusters; the spellings *alba* and *alva* (< ALBA) alternate, as do *enviar* and *embiar* (< INVIARE), with apparent freedom. Similarly, in word-initial position after a nasal or pause, neutralization of /b/ and /β/ is also likely in OSp.; thus, in cases like the following,

lo han b̠axado	*b̠áxalo*
lo han y̠endido	*y̠éndelo*

it was probably true that realization of the phonemes /b/ and /β/ was uniformly [b]. Increasingly frequent neutralization in word-initial position was followed, in the fifteenth and sixteenth centuries, by neutralization of the two phonemes in intervocalic position; this is revealed in Golden Age verse, which increasingly allowed, say, *grave* to rhyme with, say, *sabe*. At this stage, the two original phonemes are no longer distinguished in any environment and the merger is therefore complete (see 2.6.1):

Further discussion of the reasons for phonetic and phonological change can be found in Bynon 1977 and Samuels 1972.

2.1.4 Change of incidence of phonemes

The particular phonemes which occur in a given word may be replaced, at any historical moment, by other phonemes. One motive for such change is popular etymology (see 5.2.3), but the main reason for this kind of phonemic replacement is **analogy**. A broad definition of analogy is 'the process by which related words become more alike in form', where 'related' can refer to relatedness either of meaning or of function. Analogical change of form motivated by relatedness of function will be of particular concern when morphological change is considered (see 3.1.1), and here we shall exemplify analogy motivated by similarity of meaning. The meaning relationships involved are many and include 'complementarity' and 'antonymy'. A well-known case of analogical change inspired by complementarity of meaning is that of Lat. SOCRUS 'mother-in-law' and NURUS 'daughter-in-law'; leaving aside the change of ending (for which see 3.2.2.2[1]), these two words might be expected to give *suegra* and **nora* (for tonic /o/ < ŭ see 2.4.2.6); however, the outcome of the second word was *nuera*, where tonic /ue/ is due to analogy with the corresponding segment of *suegra*. Opposite meaning may also induce change of form; thus DEXTRU 'right' (whence OSp. *diestro* 'id.') has influenced SINISTRU 'left' to produce an Old Spanish form with /ie/ (*siniestro* 'id.'), when, in the absence of analogy, a form with /e/ is predicted (see 2.4.2.6).

2.2 Transmission

It is convenient at this point to introduce discussion of the difference between **popular**, **learned** and **semi-learned** words.

2.2.1

Popular words are those which, in a given language, have a continuous oral history. In the case of Spanish, the term means that the word concerned has been transmitted from spoken Latin, generation by generation, by word of mouth, to modern Spanish (or until the word dropped out of use), undergoing in the process all the phonological and morphological changes which are characteristic of the development of Spanish. This book is largely concerned with the history of such popular words, but special reference will be made from time to time to words which have been transmitted to Spanish in other ways. The following are examples of popular transmission:

> FABULĀRĪ > *hablar* 'to speak' (Note treatment of F- [2.5.6] and loss of pretonic vowel [2.4.3.3])
> REGULA > *reja* 'ploughshare' (Note loss of post-tonic vowel [2.4.3.3] and /gl/ > /x/ [2.5.2.4])

2.2.2

Learned words are ones which have been borrowed by Spanish from Latin (Classical or Medieval), through the medium of writing. Such borrowings were already frequent in the Middle Ages and have taken place at all times since then. The words concerned do not undergo the changes typical of popular words, but merely suffer minor modification of their endings in order to fit them to the morphological patterns of Spanish. Thus, *fábula* 'fable' (a borrowing of Lat. FABULA) reveals its learned nature by the retention of post-tonic /u/ (see [2.4.3.3]) and by the appearance of /f/ (see [2.5.6]). Likewise *regular* (Lat. RĒGULĀRIS) 'regular, poor, etc.' is best described as learned, because of its retention of pretonic ŭ as /u/ and the consequent failure of /gl/ to evolve to /x/ (see 2.5.2.4).

2.2.3

Much dispute has taken place over the precise definition to be given to the term **semi-learned** (see, in particular, Wright 1976). The definition adopted here is that of words which, although (like popular words) orally inherited from VL, have been remodelled, usually during the medieval period, under the influence of Latin, as read aloud in the church, the law-courts, etc. Because of their oral transmission, they undergo some (but, by definition, not all) of the changes typical of popular words; however, in other features, semi-learned words are unevolved. Thus *regla* 'rule, ruler' shows loss of the post-tonic vowel (see 2.4.3.3) as in popular words, but owes its /gl/ group to influence from Med. Lat. REGULA. Similarly, despite showing the popular treatment of $C^{e,i}$ (see 2.5.2.3), *cruz* (< CRUCE) reveals its semi-learned status in its tonic /u/; in fully popular words, Lat. ŭ appears in Sp. as /o/ (see 2.4.2).

2.2.4

It will be evident from the examples given in the preceding sections that a given Latin word may be transmitted to Spanish by more than one means. Cases of double transmission are referred to as **doublets** and usually also show semantic differentiation, the popular form being associated with changed meaning, while the learned or semi-learned counterpart typically retains the Latin sense. Compare popular *reja* and semi-learned *regla* above, or learned *fábula*, above, with popular *habla* 'speech'.

2.3 Suprasegmental features

The main feature of concern here is the accent, and, in particular, its position and nature in Latin and Spanish. The accent serves as one of the devices which aids word-recognition, and in Spanish (but not in Latin) it also has a semantic role.

2.3.1

Throughout the development from Latin to Spanish, the position of the accent is highly stable; the accent of a Spanish word falls on the same syllable it occupied in the Latin ancestor of that word. In Latin words of two syllables, the accent fell on the first, while in words of three or more syllables the position of the accent was determined by the length of the penultimate syllable; if the penultimate syllable was long, the accent fell upon it; if the penultimate syllable was short, the accent fell on the antepenultimate. Since a Latin syllable was long **either** because it contained a long vowel or a diphthong **or** because its vowel, although short, was followed by at least two consonants (the first of which combines with the short vowel to provide a 'long' syllable), Latin polysyllabic words can be said to fall into three accentual categories:

1 The penultimate vowel (and therefore the penultimate syllable) is long (the accent falls on ít): DĒBĒRE (> deber), MOLĪNU (> molino), CONSUTŪRA (> costura);

2 the penultimate vowel is short, but is followed by two or more consonants (the accent falls on the penultimate); SAGITTA (> saeta), QUADRĀGINTĀ (> cuarenta); for one exception to this rule, affecting cons. + /r/ and cons. + /l/, see 3.2.3;

3 the penultimate vowel is short and is followed by a single consonant or by no consonant (the accent falls on the preceding syllable): VETULUS (> viejo), VIRIDIS (> verde), FĪLIUS (> hijo), CORRIGIA(> correa).

It follows from the above that the position of the Latin accent was determined by the phonological structure of the word concerned and never by its meaning. In Spanish, accent-position has acquired phonemic value, as can be seen in cases like *continuo* 'continual', *continúo* 'I continue', *continuó* 'he continued'.

As stated above, there are few cases of accent-shift in the history of Spanish; these fall into two main categories. On the one hand, words whose short penultimate vowel was followed by a consonant group whose second member was R were at first accented on the antepenultimate, because in such consonant-groups the first element was syllable-initial (unlike the case of the majority of consonant-clusters, in which the first phoneme was syllable-final) and could not therefore form a long syllable with the preceding (penultimate) vowel. Thus, TÉNEBRAE, ÍNTEGRUM (see rule 3, above). However, in spoken Latin, it seems that these consonant groups came to be articulated like other groups, with the consequences that a preceding short penultimate was now in a long syllable and therefore **could** bear the accent (rule 2): TENÉBRAE, INTÉGRUM (whence Sp. *tiniéblas*, *entéro*).

The other main category of words in which accent-shift took place consists of those in which a stressed antepenultimate was in hiatus (see 2.3.2) with the penultimate (e.g. MULIERE, FĪLIOLUS, PUTEOLUS, TĀLEOLA). The instability of hiatus in VL (see 2.3.2, end) led to transfer of accent to the more open of the two vowels concerned (and reduction of the first to a glide): /muljére/, /filjólo/, /potjólo/, /taljóla/ (> *mujer*, *hijuelo*, *pozuelo*, *tajuela*).

2.3.2

The nature of the accent, in various languages, is complex. Three main elements are involved, pitch, energy, and duration, with different prominence given to each in different languages.

1 Pitch refers to the 'height' of the musical note adopted in articulating a vowel. The vowel which bears the accent will tend to have higher pitch than other vowels in the word.

2 Energy refers to the muscular force with which air is expelled during articulation (this force is sometimes called **stress**) and therefore governs the loudness of vowels. The vowel which bears the accent will tend to be louder than others.

3 Duration is, of course, a matter of relative length. The accented vowel may be longer than other vowels.

It is thought that early Latin had a type of accent in which pitch was the predominant element. In the case of this type of accent (so-called **pitch-accent**), relative heights of musical notes reveal where the accent lies, while energy is more uniformly deployed, so that all vowels have similar loudness. (The third element can never have been important in Latin, since length was a distinctive feature of the vowel-system [see 2.4.1] and it is unlikely that length was associated with two separate values.) However, for reasons which remain obscure, spoken Latin underwent a change of accent-type and came to have an accent in which energy-deployment dominated. This type of accent (**stress-accent**) is the one which continues to characterize the majority of Romance languages (including Spanish) and is also the type used by English. The consequences of this change of accent-type can be seen elsewhere in the development of the Romance languages. The increasingly uneven deployment of energy over the word (more to the tonic, less to the atonics) accounts in large part for the different historical treatment of the Latin vowels in different positions. Concentration of energy on the tonic (and the greater audibility this brings) allows tonic vowels to be quite well differentiated and preserved, while lesser degrees of energy devoted, in decreasing order, to initial, final and intertonic vowels imply greater degrees of merger and loss (see 2.4.3). A second effect of the change to a stress-accent is the wholesale destruction of hiatus. Cases of hiatus (vowels which are adjacent but in separate syllables) were frequent in early Latin, but none (I would argue) survives in Spanish words of popular descent; for hiatus to survive, the vowels which constitute it must have similar degrees of energy/audibility, a condition which was precisely not fulfilled in later spoken Latin. Since adjacent vowels increasingly had different degrees of energy, cases of hiatus were reduced to monosyllabic pronunciation, either by loss of one of the vowels or by reducing the first of the two to a (non-syllabic) glide (see 2.4.3.4).

2.3.3

The other suprasegmental feature with which we need to be concerned is the syllable. The nature of the syllable will not be discussed here (see Abercrombie 1967: 34–41 for a good description), but only the matter of syllable-boundaries. Generally speaking, it seems that in the case of such boundaries Latin differed little from Spanish: a single consonant between vowels is syllable-initial (TE-PI-DUS), while in the case of groups of two consonants the boundary falls between the two (POR-CUS, DEN-TES, CUP-PA), except in the case of cons. + R and cons. + L, where the first consonant is syllable-initial (LA-CRY-MA, PE-TRA, CA-PRA). In groups of three consonants, the boundary falls after the first (AM-PLU) or after the second (CŌNS-TARE).

In discussing accent-position, which follows closely from syllable-structure, we have seen two types of syllable-boundary change, exemplified by IN-TE-GRUM > IN-TEG-RUM (some groups consisting of cons. + R, originally syllable-initial, come to straddle the boundary) and MU-LI-E-RE > MU-LIE-RE (where the boundary fell between vowels it was abolished, reducing two syllables to one, at the same time as converting the first vowel to a glide; see 2.4.3.4).

A further instance of syllable-boundary change (this time also affecting the word-boundary) occurs in the case of words which in Latin began with s + cons. Because the second consonant (typically P, T, C, QU or M) required maximum closure, speakers of Latin came to hear it as syllable-initial, preceded by an anomalous 'semi-syllable' consisting of /s/. This difficulty would be particularly noticeable where the preceding word, if any, ended in a consonant (e.g. AD SCHOLAM) and was resolved by turning 'semi-syllabic' /s/ into a full syllable, by means of the addition of a vowel (at first I, later evolving to /e/). Thus,

> SPERĀRE > *esperar*
> STĀRE   > *estar*
> SCHOLA > *escuela*

This remains a productive rule of Spanish, so that, when words are borrowed from languages which permit initial /s/ + cons., /e/ is added in the adaptation process:

> Eng. *snob* > Sp. *esnob*
> Eng. *smoking(-jacket)* > Sp. *esmoquin*

although this addition is not always noted in the spelling of neologisms (e.g. *snob, smoking*).

2.4   Development of the vowel-system

2.4.1   *The Latin vowel-system*

The early Latin vocalic system, perpetuated by the literary language, consisted of ten phonemes, which were contrasted on the basis of three distinctive features, aperture, locus and length. There were three distinctive degrees of aperture: high (/i/ /i:/ /u/ /u:/), mid (/e/ /e:/ /o/ /o:/) and low (/a/ /a:/). Front vowels (/i/ /i:/ /e/ /e:/) were distinguished from back vowels (/u/ /u:/ /o/ /o:/), with two vowels (/a/ /a:/) which were neither front nor back. Each point in this system was occupied by two vowels, distinguished on the basis of length (i.e. duration, indicated here by presence and absence of ':'); /i:, e:, a;, o:, u:/ were long, and /i, e, a, o, u/ were short. The system can therefore be represented in the following way:

	Front		Back
High	/i:/ /i/		/u:/ /u/
Mid	/e:/ /e/		/o:/ /o/
Low		/a:/ /a/	

The Latin system of spelling generally ignored differences of length and used only five letters, each indicating both a long and a short phoneme. (Grammarians later devised a graphical distinction, using the macron (¯) over a long vowel and a micron (˘) over a short vowel; here the micron is omitted.) Despite the general lack of written distinction between long and short vowels, the contrast of length was (by definition) meaningful, as can be seen by the following minimal pairs:

HĪC	'here'	HIC	'this' (masc. sing. Nom.)
LĪBER	'free'	LIBER	'book'
LĒVIS	'smooth'	LEVIS	'light in weight'
VĒNIT	'he came'	VENIT	'he comes'
MĀLUM	'apple'	MALUM	'evil, misfortune'
ŌS	'mouth'	OS	'bone'
PŌPULUS	'white poplar'	POPULUS	'people'

In addition to these ten simple vowels, literary Latin used three diphthongs (combinations of two vocalic elements belonging to a single syllable): AE [ai̯], OE [oi̯], and AU [au̯].

At the level of articulatory phonetics, it is likely that, within each pair of phonemes which shared the 'same' point of articulation, the long vowel was a little higher than the short vowel. Such relative raising of long vowels is observable in many modern languages. Taking into account this (small) difference of aperture (which does not affect the lowest pair of vowels), the ten simple vowels of literary Latin can be seen to have the following phonetic realizations (ignoring any allophonic variation stemming from environment):

Ī = /i:/: [i:]   Ū = /u:/: [u:]
I = /i/: [ɪ]   U = /u/: [ʊ]
Ē = /e:/: [e:]   Ō = /o:/: [o:]
E = /e/: [ɛ]   O = /o/: [ɔ]
Ā = /a:/: [a:]
A = /a/: [a]

Although the system just described appears to have persisted in educated speech, the vowel-system of popular spoken Latin gradually underwent a number of fundamental changes. The earliest of these (no later than the first century AD) was the loss of the distinctive feature of length, the functional load carried by this feature being transferred to that of aperture. There is no consensus over the motivation for this change; a phonological account can be seen in Alarcos 1965 (210–18) and a substratum explanation is sketched in Lausberg 1965 (208–9). What is clear is that as length ceased to be meaningful, the pre-existing (and hitherto non-significant) differences of aperture between pairs of vowels such as ī and I came to be the sole basis of distinction between the two vowels (and between the other pairs of vowels, except Ā and Ă, which simply merged). At this stage, then, after the transfer of distinctiveness from length to aperture and the merger of Ā and Ă, the vowel-system of spoken Latin can best be expressed in terms of the following nine units:

$$/i/ \qquad\qquad\qquad /u/$$
$$/\imath/ \qquad\qquad\qquad /\upsilon/$$
$$/e/ \qquad\qquad /o/$$
$$/\varepsilon/ \qquad /\mathupomega/$$
$$/a/$$

The effect of this change can be exemplified through a minimal pair such as HĪC/HIC (see above). While length continued to be distinctive, the contrast between these words can be represented as /hi: k/ vs /hik/; after the change, the contrast between the words can be shown as /hik/ vs /hɪk/.

The second major transformation of the Latin vowel-system is due to the change in the nature of the accent in spoken Latin (see 2.3.1). As a result of the differing degree of energy devoted to the different syllables of each word, the vowels of these syllables evolve differently. From this point on, we shall need therefore to discuss separately the treatment of vowels in **tonic** position (i.e. in syllables which receive the major word-stress), where there is a maximum of differentiation between phonemes, from their treatment in **atonic** positions (i.e. in syllables which do not receive the major stress), where mergers of phonemes are more frequent. Furthermore, we shall need to distinguish between various classes of atonic vowels, since merger is more extensive in some than in others. Among atonic vowels, those in **initial** syllables (the first syllable of the word, unless the main stress falls there, in which case the word has no initial syllable) preserve more distinctions than those in **final** syllables (the last syllable of the word, which in Latin may not bear the stress). Similarly, such final vowels preserve more distinctions than those in **intertonic** position (internal vowels, which may be further classified as **pretonic** (between initial and tonic) or **post-tonic** (between tonic and final). Vowels in intertonic position, because of the severely lessened amount of energy devoted to them in spoken Latin, suffer the greatest degree of merger and may be weakened to the point of effacement.

2.4.2 Tonic vowels

The nine-vowel system which emerged after the loss of the length contrast (see 2.4.1) was inherently unstable. Any system which depends upon the distinction of five tongue-heights (= five **degrees of aperture**) is likely to be modified, since the acoustic difference between the vowels concerned is probably too small for the accurate conveying of information. There is convincing evidence that, no later than the first century AD, there was a merger between tongue-heights three and four, and a consequent reduction from nine phonemes to seven in tonic position:

5	/i/			/u/		4	/i/			/u/
4		/ɪ/			/ʊ/	3		/e/		/o/
3			/e/	/o/		2		/ɛ/	/ɔ/	
2			/ɛ/	/ɔ/		1			/a/	
1				/a/						

The seven-vowel system which emerged from this merger is often referred to as the 'Vulgar Latin vowel-system', since it was evidently in use in much of the Latin-speaking world, including Spain. Notice that, in terms of spelling, the change just considered implies that, on the one hand, the phonemes written Ĭ and Ē have merged in /e/, and, on the other hand, the phonemes written Ŭ and ō have merged in /o/. Like all mergers, these changes led to uncertainty of spelling among the less well educated. Among the graffiti of Pompeii, we find the misspellings VECES and MENUS (for VICES and MINUS) while the *Appendix Probi* (see 1.1) recommends the spellings TURMA, COLUMNA and FORMOSUS and condemns TORMA, COLOMNA and FORMUNSUS.

2.4.2.1

Metaphony The vowels of the tonic system were subject, during the Vulgar Latin phase, to **metaphony** (assimilatory raising of vowels, in anticipation of a following, higher phoneme, typically a high vowel or a glide). Thus, in many areas, including the area where Castilian developed, the tonic vowels of Vulgar Latin were frequently raised, by one degree of aperture, through metaphony exercised by a following palatal glide [j] or [i̯] (see 2.4.3.2 and 2.5.2.4 for glide-formation) which occurred in the same syllable or in the following one, or by an /i/ in the final syllable. Naturally, the highest tonic vowels, /i/ and /u/, were exempt from this process. It is also true that the glide concerned sometimes combined early in spoken Latin with an adjacent consonant, thereby losing its identity and consequently failing to affect the preceding vowel; this is the case of the glide [j] preceded by Latin /t/ or /k/: in LENTEU > *lienzo* 'fabric', FORTIA > *fuerza* 'strength', etc., VL /ɛ/ and /ɔ/ are unaffected by metaphony and remain half-open vowels, subsequently receiving the normal treatment ·of such vowels, namely diphthongization to [jé], [wé] respectively (see 2.4.2.2).

However, in the majority of cases, the glide survived longer (as is always the case with a final high vowel) and produced **in principle** the following raising effects on tonic vowels:

> VL /e/ is raised to /i/: VINDĒMIA > *vendimia* 'grape harvest', FĒCĪ > *hice* 'I did' (cf. non-metaphonized PLĒNA > *llena* 'full')
> VL /ɛ/ is raised to /e/: MĀTERIA > *madera* 'wood', VENĪ > *ven* 'come!' (cf. PETRA > *piedra* 'stone')
> VL /ɔ/ is raised to /o/: FOLIA > *hoja* 'leaf' (cf. FOCU > *fuego* 'fire')
> VL /o/ is raised to /u/: *CUNEA > *cuña* 'wedge' (cf. CUPPA > *copa* 'wine glass')
> VL /a/ is raised to /e/: ĀREA > *era* 'threshing-floor' (cf. ANNU > *año* 'year')

We look in turn at the metaphonic effects of a glide and of final /i/.

The detailed effects of metaphony by the glide yod are complex (and are best studied in Craddock 1980), in that certain VL vowels sometimes escape raising, depending on the precise sequence of vowel, consonant and glide (or vowel, glide and consonant) which appears in a given word. In order to clarify the details of the way in which the VL vowels have been affected by metaphony, it is necessary to distinguish between five environments observable at the stage of spoken Latin:

1 The vowel is followed immediately by [i̯], by definition in the same syllable as the vowel. The glide may have arisen through one of a number of processes: reduction of /i/ in hiatus with the vowel concerned [see 2.4.3.2]; loss of a consonant between the vowel and an atonic /e/ or /i/, which thereupon is reduced to [i̯] by the preceding process; metathesis of a glide from the following syllable [see 2.5.2.2(6)]; palatalization of a syllable-final velar [see 2.5.2.4]. Ultimately, the glide is absorbed by the preceding vowel and/or by the following consonant.

2 The onset of the syllable following the vowel concerned contains (as it still does) a glide [j] (from earlier atonic /e/ or /i/ in hiatus [see 2.4.3.2]), the intervening consonant(s) being /b/, /m/ or a group such as /br/, /tr/, /mp/.

3 The vowel in question is followed by [j] (from earlier [gj], [dj]; see 2.5.2.2[4]). Ultimately, the consonant either survives intact or is absorbed by a preceding front vowel.

4 The vowel in question is followed by VL [ʎ] (from earlier [lj] [2.5.2.2(2)] or [kl], [gl] [2.5.2.4]). Ultimately [ʎ] becomes [ʒ] in Old Spanish and [x] in the modern language.

5 The vowel concerned is followed by [ɲ] (from earlier [nj] [2.5.2.2(3)] or [gn] [2.5.2.4]), which remains unchanged from spoken Latin to the present.

These five environments are listed in accordance with the proportion of VL
vowels which undergo metaphony in each. Thus, in environment (1), four
of the five susceptible VL vowels (/a/, /ɛ/, /ɔ/, /e/ and /o/) are affected, while
in environment (5) only one vowel is clearly affected. Considering each
relevant vowel in turn, the effects of metaphony can be seen to occur (√) or
not (×) in each environment:

/a/ 1 √ LAICU > *lego* 'layman'; CANTĀVĪ > VL [kantái̯] > *canté* 'I sang';
ĀREA > [ái̯ral] > *era* 'threshing-floor', BĀSIU > [bái̯so] > *beso* 'kiss',
SAPIAM > [sái̯pa] > *sepa* '(that) I know'; LACTE (CL LAC) >
[lái̯te] > *leche* 'milk', MATAXA > [matái̯sa] > OSp. *madexa* > MSp.
madeja 'skein'.

2 × LABIU > *labio* 'lip', RABIA > *rabia* 'rage'; FLACCIDU > [fláttsjo] >
OSp. *llacio* > *lacio* 'limp, lank'.

3 × RADIU > *rayo* 'ray, spoke', (ARBOR) FĀGEA > *haya* 'beech tree'.

4 × ALIU > *ajo* 'garlic', PALEA > *paja* 'straw'; NOVĀCULA > *navaja* 'knife,
razor'; COĀGULU > *cuajo* 'rennet'.

5 × ARĀNEA > *araña* 'spider', EXTRĀNEU > *extraño* 'strange'; TAM
MAGNU > *tamaño* 'size'.

/ɛ/ 1 √ GREGE > [grée] > [gréi̯] > grey '(bishop's) flock'; MĀTERIA >
[matéi̯ra] > *madera* 'wood', VL CERESIA (CL
CERASIA) > [keréi̯sa] > OSp. *ceresa* > *cereza* 'cherry';
DIRECTU > [deréi̯to] > *derecho* 'law; straight'; LECTU > [léi̯to] > *lecho*
'bed', VL INTÉGRU (CL ÍNTEGRU) > [entéiro] > *entero* 'whole'.

2 √ SUPERBIA > *soberbia* 'pride, vainglory', NERVIU > *nervio* 'nerve;
strength', PRAEMIU > [prémjo] > *premio* 'prize'. In TEPIDU, creation
of the glide (through loss of /d/) presumably came too late to
prevent /ɛ́/ receiving its normal treatment, diphthongization, so
that TEPIDU > [tjéβeðo] > *[tjéβjo], whence *tibio*, under the double
influence of preceding and following yod.

3 √ SEDEAT > [sɛi̯a] > *sea* (pres. subj. of *ser*).

4 √ SPECULU > [espéλo] > *espejo* 'mirror' (but VL VECLU [CL
VETULU] > [βéλo] > *viejo* 'old').

5 (no example)

/ɔ/ 1 √ OCTO > [ói̯to] > *ocho* 'eight', NOCTE > [nói̯te] > *noche* 'night',
COXU > [kɔi̯so] > OSp. *coxo* > *cojo* 'lame'.

2 √ OSTREA > OSp. *ostria* 'oyster' (> *ostra*), NOVIU > *novio* 'fiancé'.

3 √ PODIU > *poyo* 'stone bench', HODIE > [ói̯e] > *hoy* 'today'.

4 √ FOLIA > [fɔ́λa] > *hoja* 'leaf', COLLIGIS > [kóllees] > [kólljes] >
[kóλes] > *coges* 'you grasp', OCULU > [óλo] > *ojo* 'eye'.

5 (no example)

/e/ 1 × STRICTU > [estréi̯to] > *estrecho* 'narrow', TĒCTU > [téi̯to] > *techo*
'roof', CERVĒSIA > OSp. *cervesa* > *cerveza* 'beer', PIGNORA > [péi̯nra] >
prenda 'garment' (see 2.5.2.4 [end]).

2 √ VINDĒMIA < [βendémja] < *vendimia* 'wine harvest', LIMPIDU <
[lémpeo] > *limpio* 'clean', SĒPIA > *jibia* 'cuttlefish', VITREU >
[βétrjo] > *vidrio* 'glass'.

3 × CORRIGIA > [koréja] > *correa* 'leather belt, strap', VIDEAT >
[βéja] > *vea* (pres. subj. of *ver*).

4 × CILIA > *ceja*, CŌNSILIU > *consejo* 'advice', APICULA > [apéλa] > *abeja* 'bee', TĒGULA > [téλa] > *teja* '(roof)tile'.

5 × LIGNA > *leña* 'firewood', SIGNA > *seña* 'sign'.

/o/ 1 √ LUCTA > [lói̯ta] > *lucha* 'struggle', TRUCTA > [trói̯ta] > *trucha* 'trout', MULTU > [móu̯to] > [mói̯to] > *mucho* 'much', AUSCULTAT > [askóu̯tat] > [askói̯tat] > *escucha* 'he listens', VULTURE > [βóu̯tore] > [βói̯tore] > [βói̯tre] > *buitre* 'vulture' (see 2.5.2.4 [end]), IMPULSAT > [empóu̯sat] > [empói̯sat] > *empuja* 'he pushes'.

2 √ RUBEU > [r̄óβjo] > *rubio* 'fair-haired', PLUVIA > [pλóβja] > *lluvia* 'rain', TURBIDU > [tórβjo] > *turbio* 'cloudy'.

3   (no example; the frequently-cited case FUGIO > *huyo* 'I flee' is inconclusive, since tonic /o/ is excluded from the stem of *-ir* verbs [see 3.7.1.4])

4 × CUSCULIU > *coscojo* 'kermes-oak gall', VL GURGULIONE (CL CURCULIONE) > *gorgojo* 'weevil' (a back-formation from **gorgojón*), GENUCULU > OSp. *enojo* ~ *(h)inojo* ~ *finojo* 'knee'.

5 √ CUNEU > *cuño* 'die-stamp' (whence *cuña* 'wedge'), PUGNU > *puño* 'fist'.

Even this complex state of affairs leaves out of account certain recalcitrant data. In the following cases, /ɔ́/ or /ó/ (in environments 1 and 5) have combined with a following glide to produce [wé]:

CORIU > *cuero* 'leather'
SOMNIU > *sueño* 'dream'
AUGURIU > *agüero* 'omen'
CICŌNIA > *cigüeña* 'stork' (cf. *cuño*, *puño*, above)
SALE MURIA > *salmuera* 'brine'
VERĒCUNDIA > OSp. *vergüeña* 'shame'

Early textual evidence (*coiro*, *agoiro*, *salmoyra*, *cigoña*, *vergoña*, the latter forms perhaps representing [tsiɣóiɲa], [βerɣóiɲa]) suggests the following sequence: (1) /ɔ́/ is raised to /ó/ ([kɔ́i̯ro] > [kói̯ro]); (2) /ói/ evolves to /ué/ in accordance with the Castilian avoidance of off-gliding diphthongs (see Malkiel 1976), thus forestalling any metaphonic effect of [i̯] on preceding /o/.

A possible (partial) explanation of the differential effect of yod on preceding tonic vowels is one based on the length of survival of the glide in different phonemic environments. Where [j] was absorbed early through assimilation to preceding /t/ or /k/, it has no metaphonic effect, but where it has survived to this day (environment 2), it affects all vowels except /a/. A similar deep effect is seen in environment 1 (four out of five vowels affected) and it is probably the case that the glide survived for centuries where it arose through palatalization of /k/ before /t/ and /s/, through metathesis, or through loss of an intervocalic consonant; French *nuit*, etc., and Portuguese *noite*, *leigo*, *madeira*, *beijo* etc., provide evidence of its long survival in other territories.

Environments 3 and 4 represent chronologically intermediate positions; two vowels are affected (if *espejo*, rather than *viejo*, can be taken to represent the development of /ɛ́/), perhaps betraying a fairly rapid (but not immediate) absorption of the glide into the adjacent /d/, /g/ or /l/. Finally, environment 5 (in which only /o/ is affected) perhaps indicates that a glide adjacent to /n/ survived the shortest period (except for the glide following /t/ or /k/). There is also a case for separating instances like LIMPIDU (> *limpio*) and TURBIDU (> *turbio*) from environment 2, on the grounds that the glide of such forms can only be late in appearing (after the loss of -D-). And it has to be said that such a chronological account, although it receives some support from other Romance languages, is far from complete, since it fails to explain why particular vowels (and not others) are affected in a given environment.

Metaphony by final /i/ is less frequent than that caused by a yod, since the conditioning factor (/-i/) is relatively infrequent in Hispano-Romance. The main examples are:

/ɛ/ > /e/:	VENĪ > *¡ven!* 'come!' (but HERĪ > *(a)yer* 'yesterday')
/e/ > /i/:	VĒNĪ > *vine* 'I came', FĒCĪ > *hice* 'I made', MIHĪ, TIBĪ, SIBĪ > *mí, ti, sí* (see 3.5.1)

Metaphony can also be seen to operate in atonic syllables. The most usual case is raising of an initial vowel (see 2.4.3.1).

2.4.2.2 Diphthongization

In the late Roman period, the tonic vowel system underwent further modification in many areas, including the area where Castilian (and its immediate neighbours) originated. In this period, it seems there was a lengthening of tonic vowels in many regional varieties of spoken Latin; by contrast, the atonic vowels remain unlengthened. The reasons for this development are disputed (some see here the influence of Germanic speech on Latin, at a period when large numbers of Germanic speakers were allowed or forced their way into the Empire and were learning to speak Latin), but its effect on the tonic vowels was extensive. There have been many accounts of the way in which this effect was exercised, and no single account has gained general acceptance. What follows is one of a number of possible sequences of events.

The immediate effect of the lengthening of tonic vowels was to raise most such vowels, since the added muscular tension required for lengthening will cause added tensing of the jaw muscles, with consequent raising of the jaw and of the tongue-position of the vowel being articulated. However, /i/ and /u/, because of their already high position, were not susceptible to further raising. Since raising of all vowels but the highest implies that the physiological and acoustic difference between neighbouring vowels is lessened, this process gave rise to potential confusion. Thus, e.g.

> /ósso/ 'bear' (< ŬRSUS)
> /ɔ́sso/ 'bone' (< VL ŏSSUM)

must have become confusingly similar.

Any language so affected may seek some therapeutic device to preserve comprehension, and the device employed by some varieties of Romance, including Spanish, was a compensatory downward movement of the newly lengthened low-mid vowels, /ɛ/ and /ɔ/, leading to their fracture and the creation of incipient diphthongs:

> /i/   /u/
> /e/   /o/
> /ɛ/ > [eɛ]   [oɔ] < /ɔ/
>   /a/

Further differentiation between the on-glide and the off-glide of these complex sounds led to the true diphthongs already observable in the earliest Spanish and no doubt by then interpreted as sequences of two vowel phonemes:

> [eɛ] > [iɛ] > [je] (= /ie/)
> [oɔ] > [uɔ] > [wo] > [we] (= /ue/)

> e.g. BENĔ = /béne/ > *bien* 'well'
> PETRA = /pétra/ > *piedra* 'stone'
> BONUS = /bɔ́no/ > *bueno* 'good'
> OSSUM = /ɔ́sso/ > *hueso* 'bone' (thereby avoiding collision with *oso* 'bear')

Since the glide [j] may not in Spanish occupy syllable-initial position, the result of diphthongization of word-initial Ĕ (or HĔ) was a sequence of fricative consonant + /e/:

> EQUA > *yegua* 'mare'
> HERBA > *yerba* (later spelt *hierba*) 'grass'

The phonological effect of diphthongization is that, since two of the seven VL tonic vowels came to be interpreted as sequences, in each case, of two other vowels (or of consonant plus vowel), the number of tonic vowel phonemes in Spanish is reduced to five.

2.4.2.3 *The Latin diphthongs*

The three Latin diphthongs, AE, OE, and AU, were reduced to simple vowels, although at different rates. AE > /ɛ/ and OE > /e/ in VL, that is to say, early enough for the product of AE to be involved in the diphthongization process discussed in 2.4.2.2. Thus,

CAELUM = VL /kélo/ > *cielo* 'sky'
QUAERIT = VL /kwéret/ > *quiere* 'he wishes'
POENA = VL /péna/ > *pena* 'grief'
FOEDUS = VL /fédo/ > *feo* 'ugly'

However, although there were a few cases of reduction in VL of AU > /o/ (e.g. *Appendix Probi*: AURIS NON ORICLA), it was not until later that reduction of AU became regular in Spanish (as in most, but not all, Romance languages):

PAUCU > *poco* 'little'
TAURU > *toro* 'bull'
CAUSA > *cosa* 'thing'.

2.4.2.4 New diphthongs

As a result of the transfer of a glide into a preceding syllable (see 2.5.2.2[6]), certain new diphthongs came into existence in late VL or in Hispano-Romance. Where the new diphthong consisted of a front vowel or /a/ + palatal glide, there was a reduction of the sequence, through assimilation, to /e/:

MĀTERIA > /matéira/ > *madera* 'wood'
CĀSEUS > /káiso/ > *queso* 'cheese'
SAPIAT > /sáipa/ > *sepa* (3rd sing, pres. subj. of *saber*)

Where the new diphthong consisted of a back vowel + palatal glide, it was dramatically modified to /ue/, in part, no doubt, because by this time the diphthong /ue/ (< tonic ŏ) was extremely frequent and because diphthongs stressed on the first element were rare:

CORIU > /kóiro/ > *cuero* 'leather'
DŌRIU > /dóiro/ > *Duero* (river name)
SEGŪSIU > /sagúiso/ > *sabueso* 'bloodhound'

It is possible, too, for a labiovelar glide to be transferred to a preceding syllable, combining with tonic /a/ to produce /o/, as in the case of primary AU (see 2.4.2.3). The only examples are certain irregular preterites (see 3.7.7.5.2[1]):

HABUI > /áuβi/ > OSp. *ove* (MSp. *hube*)
SAPUI > /sáupi/ > OSp. *sope* (MSp. *supe*)

2.4.2.5 Medieval developments

After diphthongization and the emergence of the system of five tonic vowels, there were no further modifications to this system either in the medieval or the modern periods. However, there were some modifications of individual vowels, of which the most frequent cases are the occasional reduction of /ie/ to /i/ and of /ue/ to /e/.

/ie/ was reduced to /i/ in Old Spanish principally when followed by /λ/ (for the chronology of this change, see Menéndez Pidal 1958: 55–7 and Menéndez Pidal 1964a: 152–8):

> CASTELLU > OSp. *castiello* > MSp. *castillo* 'castle'
> CULTELLU > OSp. *cuchiello* > MSp. *cuchillo* 'knife'
> SELLA > OSp. *siella* > MSp. *silla* 'seat'

but may also occur before syllable-final /s/:

> VESPERA > OSp. *viéspera* > MSp. *víspera* 'eve'
> VESPA > OSp. *aviespa* > MSp. *avispa* 'wasp'

although this is not the case in *fiesta* (< FESTA), *siesta* (< SEXTA) or *hiniesta* (< VL GENESTA). There is also an ill-defined group of other words in which this reduction takes place, e.g.

> MERULA > OSp. *mierla* > MSp. *mirla* 'blackbird'
> SAECULU > OSp. *sieglo* (semi-learned) > MSp. *siglo* 'century'

Reduction of /ue/ to /e/ occurs in Old Spanish, probably for reasons of assimilation, after /r/ or /l/:

> FLOCCU > OSp. *flueco* > MSp. *fleco* 'fringe, tassel'
> FRONTE > OSp. *fruente* > MSp. *frente* 'forehead'
> VL COLOBRA > OSp. *culuebra* > MSp. *culebra* 'snake'

2.4.2.6   Summary of tonic vowel development

The developments studied in this section can be summarized in the following way:

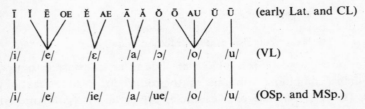

Examples of these developments, omitting the VL stage:

> Ī > /i/:   FĪLIU > *hijo* 'son'
>   FĪCU > *higo* 'fig'
>   VĪTA > *vida* 'life'
> Ĭ > /e/:   CISTA > *cesta* 'basket'
>   PILU > *pelo* 'hair'
>   SIGNAS > *señas* 'address'
> Ē > /e/:   PLĒNU > *lleno* 'full'
>   ALIĒNU > *ajeno* 'alien'
> OE > /e/:   POENA > *pena* 'grief'
>   FOEDU > *feo* 'ugly'

Ĕ > /ie/: PETRA > *piedra* 'stone'
           METU > *miedo* 'fear'
           SERRA > *sierra* 'saw, mountain range'
AE > /ie/: CAECU > *ciego* 'blind'
           CAELU > *cielo* 'sky'
Ā > /a/:   CĀRU > *caro* 'dear'
           PRĀTU > *prado* 'meadow'
Ă > /a/:   MANU > *mano* 'hand'
           PATRE > *padre* 'father'
Ŏ > /ue/: ROTA > *rueda* 'wheel'
           NOVE > *nueve* 'nine'
           NOVU > *nuevo* 'new'
Ō > /o/:   TŌTU > *todo* 'all'
           FLŌRE > *flor* 'flower'
           FŌRMŌSU > *hermoso* 'beautiful'
AU > /o/: MAURU > *moro* 'Moorish'
           CAULE > *col* 'cabbage'
Ŭ > /o/:   CUBITU > *codo* 'elbow'
           CUPPA > *copa* 'wine glass'
Ū > /u/:   FŪMU > *humo* 'smoke'
           CŪPA > *cuba* 'vat'
           ACŪTU > *agudo* 'sharp'

2.4.3 Atonic vowel development

As anticipated in 2.4.1, the different classes of atonic vowels receive different treatment, owing to the different degrees of energy with which they were articulated in VL. (See 2.4.1 for definitions of the various types of atonic vowels.) They will be considered here in order of decreasing energy.

2.4.3.1 Initial vowels

Vowels in this category, less energetically articulated than tonic vowels, are the most energetic of the atonics. They therefore show a greater degree of merger than the tonics but less than other atonics. The ten vowels of early Latin (preserved in literary Latin) were reduced to five in initial position in spoken Latin, and these five VL vowels have been directly inherited by OSp. and MSp.:

Although they probably began earlier, these mergers are not clearly attested until the third century AD. They are then revealed by misspelling of the kind FRECARE (for FRICARE) and by statements in the *Appendix Probi* (SIRENA NON SERENA, SENATUS NON SINATUS).

These developments may be exemplified by the following items:

ī > /i/:	RĪPĀRIA > *ribera* 'riverbank'
Ĭ > /e/:	PLICĀRE > *llegar* 'to arrive'
Ē > /e/:	SĒCŪRU > *seguro* 'sure'
Ĕ > /ɛ/:	SENIŌRE > *señor* 'sir'
.AE > /e/:	PRAECŌNE > *pregón* 'announcement'
Ā > /a/:	PĀNĀRIA > *panera* 'basket'
Ă > /a/:	CAPISTRU > *cabestro* 'halter'
Ŏ > /o/:	CORTICEA > *corteza* 'skin, rind'
Ō > /o/:	NŌMINĀRE > *nombrar* 'to name'
AU > /o/:	PAUSARE > *posar* 'to put down'
Ŭ > /o/:	SUSPECTA > *sospecha* 'suspicion'
Ū > /u/:	CŪRĀRE > *curar* 'to cure'

The main difference between tonic and initial development is that in initial syllables, Ĕ and Ŏ merge early with their long counterparts, so that the conditions for diphthongization (the need to keep the low-mid vowels, /ɛ/ and /ɔ/, separate from the high mid vowels, /e/ and /o/) do not arise, and diphthongization cannot therefore take place.

Metaphony, which has been studied in connection with tonic vowels (2.4.2.1), also occurs in the case of initial vowels. A following palatal glide (yod) may cause the raising of initial /e/ and /o/ to /i/ and /u/ respectively, from late VL onwards (i.e. after the mergers discussed earlier in this section), e.g.

RENIŌNE = VL [renjóne] > *riñón* 'kidney'
GENESTA > *hiniesta* 'broom'
CAEMENTUM > *cimiento* 'foundation'
TENEBRAS > *tinieblas* 'darkness'
COCHLEĀRE = VL [kokljáre] > *cuchara* 'spoon'
COGNĀTU = VL [koináto] > *cuñado* 'brother-in-law'
MULIERE = VL [moljére] > *mujer* 'woman'
CŌGITĀRE > [koidáre] > *cuidar* 'to take care of'

Although in most cases the system of initial vowels has proved stable (the five vowels of late VL persisting unchanged, and with the same incidence, through Old Spanish to the modern language), there is some sporadic evidence of a drift towards a three-vowel system. There are few cases of minimal pairs in which initial /u/ and /o/ or /i/ and /e/ are the differentiating elements and historically there has been some unconditioned drift from /o/ to /u/. In the following cases, initial /o/ was normal in Old Spanish, usually until the fourteenth century, but was gradually replaced by /u/:

jogar > *jugar* 'to play'
logar > *lugar* 'place'
polgar > *pulgar* 'thumb'
roido > *ruido* 'noise'

2.4.3.2   *Final vowels*

Change in the nature of the Latin accent (2.3.2) brought severe decrease of
energy to final syllables, with consequent intense merger and some loss.
Where Latin final vowels survived into Spanish, they had the following
outcomes:

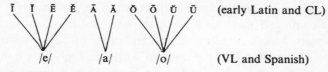

These developments may be exemplified by the following items:

Ī > /e/:	VĒNĪ > *vine* 'I came'
Ĭ > /e/:	IOVIS > *jueves* 'Thursday'
Ē > /e/:	PATRĒS > *padres* 'fathers'
Ĕ > /e/:	DE UNDE > *donde* 'where'
Ā > /a/:	CANTĀS > *cantas* 'you sing'
Ă > /a/:	CANTANT > *cantan* 'they sing'
Ŏ > /o/:	CITO > OSp. *cedo* 'soon'
Ō > /o/:	CANTŌ > *canto* 'I sing'
Ŭ > /o/:	VINU > *vino* 'wine'
Ū > /o/:	MANŪS > *manos* 'hands'

However, of the three final vowels which survive into early Old Spanish,
only /a/ and /o/ are almost entirely stable. /a/ is raised to /e/ (and
occasionally lost) in Old Spanish when in hiatus with a high tonic vowel:
mía > míe > mi 'my', *duas >* OSp. *dues* 'two (fem.)', *-ía > -íe* (imperf. endings
of *-er/-ir* verbs). Final /o/ was lost in a few words which habitually preceded
a noun or adjective: *primero > primer* 'first', *tercero > tercer* 'third',
santo > san 'Saint', DOMINU > *don* (honorific), *segundo > según* 'according
to', MULTU > **muito > muy* 'very'.

By contrast, final /e/ is highly unstable and suffered elimination in two
periods of the history of Old Spanish. In pre-literary texts of the tenth and
eleventh centuries (see Menéndez Pidal 1964a: 186–90), one can observe the
loss of /e/ where it followed a dental or alveolar consonant which at that
stage was ungrouped (i.e. preceded by a vowel):

PARIETE > *pared* 'wall'
MERCĒDE > *merced* 'mercy'
PĀNE > *pan* 'bread'
MARE > *mar* 'sea'
FIDĒLE > *fiel* 'faithful'
MĒNSE = VL /mése/ > *mes* 'month'
PĀCE = VL /pátse/ > *paz* 'peace'

Later, especially in the thirteenth century, certain varieties of Castilian
(urban, educated varieties, which are those reflected in writing) suffered

sporadic loss of /e/ in other phonological environments. In this period, perhaps under the influence of French (see Allen 1976, Lapesa 1951, 1975, 1982), /e/ could be absent after almost any consonant or consonant group:

> *nuef (nueve), nief (nieve), lech (leche), noch (noche), princep (príncipe), mont (monte), cuend (conde), part (parte), estonz (entonces),* etc.

The forms with /e/ never disappeared from the written record and it is likely that they continued to characterize popular styles of Castilian speech, which reasserted themselves towards the end of the thirteenth century and have been perpetuated into the modern language. Only in a handful of cases was this later loss of /e/ made permanent; where a consonant group preceding /e/ was simplified in later Old Spanish to /ts/ = ç (through vocalization and assimilation of /-l/ or through assimilation of /-s/ to following /ts/), forms without final /e/ were preferred:

> CALCE > *coçe* > *coz* 'kick'
> FALCE > *foçe* > *foz* > *hoz* 'sickle'
> FASCE > *façe* > *faz* > *haz* 'bundle'
> PISCE > *peçe* > *pez* 'fish'

This solution no doubt occurred because, after loss of /e/, these words ended with the same (now ungrouped) phoneme as many other previously existing words (*paz, cruz,* etc.).

2.4.3.3 Intertonic vowels

Unstressed internal vowels are those which suffer most from the development of a stress-accent in VL (see 2.3.2). With the exception of the vowel /a/, whose inherent audibility ensured its survival, Latin intertonic vowels have been entirely eliminated. In certain environments (contact with /r/ or /l/, sometimes with /n/ or /s/), intertonics were frequently lost in VL. This conditioned loss, which is evident in all Romance languages, is attested in (amongst other sources) the *Appendix Probi*:

> ANGULUS NON ANGLUS
> CALIDA NON CALDA
> SPECULUM NON SPECLUM
> STABULUM NON STABLUM
> VETULUS NON VECLUS
> VIRIDIS NON VIRDIS, etc.

Later, in pre-literary Spanish (and before the loss of final /e/, see 2.4.3.2), almost all surviving intertonics other than /a/ were eliminated. Examples of pretonic loss:

> CATĒNĀTU > *candado* 'padlock'
> LĪMITĀRE > *lindar* 'to border upon'
> SEPTIMĀNA > *semana* 'week'
> TEMPORĀNU > *temprano* 'early'

and of post-tonic loss:

> MANĬCA > *manga* 'sleeve, hose'
> RETĬNA > *rienda* 'reins'
> SANGUĬNE > *sangre* 'blood'

Examples of survival of /a/ are:

> CALAMELLU > *caramillo* 'type of flute'
> CANTHARU > *cántaro* 'pitcher'
> RAPHANU > *rábano* 'radish'

Latin words with two pretonic vowels other than /a/ lose the vowel closest to the tonic:

> INGENERĀRE > *engendrar* 'to engender'
> RECUPERĀRE > *recobrar* 'to recover'

It will be seen that the consonants brought into contact by the loss of intertonic vowels frequently undergo modification. This will be discussed in 2.5.5.

2.4.3.4 Hiatus

In 2.3.2 it was noted that hiatus could not survive the change in the nature of the Latin accent. Once the accent had become predominantly a stress-accent, neighbouring vowels received markedly different degrees of energy, conditions which militated against hiatus, which requires that its constituent syllables should be of similar intensity. The result is, on the one hand, loss of the weaker vowel (see 2.3.2 for the concept of 'weaker'), a result which is almost regular where the two vowels were identical, or became identical in VL, through regular change (see 2.4.1–2.4.3.3):

> PARIETE > VL PARĒTE > *pared* 'wall'
> QUIĒTUS > VL QUĒTUS > *quedo* 'still'
> DUODECIM > *doce* 'twelve'
> MORTUU > *muerto* 'dead'

But note MULIERE > /muljére/ > *mujer* 'woman'.

On the other hand, hiatus was more frequently destroyed by converting the weaker vowel into a glide, thereby changing a sequence of two vowels (each belonging to a separate syllable) to a sequence of glide + vowel (both belonging to the same syllable). The weaker vowel normally happens to be the first and if it is a front vowel it is converted into the front (i.e. palatal) glide [j], while if it is a back vowel the result is the back (i.e. labiovelar) glide [w]. That is,

> $\bar{I}/\bar{I}/\bar{E}/\bar{E} + V > [j] + V$
> $\bar{U}/\bar{U}/\bar{O}/\bar{O} + V > [w] + V$

(where V indicates any vowel). This change is evidently a case of neutralization; all front vowels came to be realized in the same way when one of them was originally the weaker member of a sequence of vowels in hiatus, and similarly all back vowels were neutralized under the same circumstances. Such a neutralization produced the usual uncertainty of spelling among the less well educated, and alternation between the spellings E and I, and between O and U, under these conditions, was common in non-literary Latin. In an attempt to redress this uncertainty, the *Appendix Probi* comments

> ALIUM NON ALEUM
> LANCEA NON LANCIA
> VINEA NON VINIA
> CLOACA NON CLUACA
> PUELLA NON POELLA, etc.,

indirectly demonstrating the total confusion between the phonemes concerned under conditions of hiatus.

The effect upon vowels of the palatal glide created in this way has been anticipated in the discussion of metaphony (see 2.4.2.1 and 2.4.3.1), as has the appearance of new diphthongs created when a glide was transferred to a preceding syllable (2.4.2.4). The effect of the glide upon consonants will be seen in 2.5.2.2.

2.5   Development of the consonant-system

2.5.1   The Latin consonant-system

The consonants in use in spoken Latin until the first century BC, and in literary Latin for longer, were organized in the following system of three orders and six series:

	labial	dental ~ alveolar	velar
voiceless plosives	/p/	/t/	/k/
voiced plosives	/b/	/d/	/g/
voiceless fricatives	/f/	/s/	/h/
nasal	/m/	/n/	
lateral		/l/	
trill		/r/	

To these thirteen phonemes, some would add two labiovelar phonemes /kʷ/ and /gʷ/, although the sounds spelt QU and GU in Latin can be regarded as sequences of the phonemes /k/ and /g/ followed by a non-syllabic (or glide) realization of the phoneme /u/. The productivity of the system was increased by the fact that most of these phonemes could appear, within the word, in **geminate** form (i.e. doubled), with the exception of /h/, which could not be geminated, and /f/, /b/, /d/, /g/, which rarely were in the native vocabulary.

The spelling of Latin at this stage seems to have been broadly phonemic, with one letter for each phoneme, although, as we have just seen, both Q and C could be said to represent the same consonant.

2.5.2 Developments from Latin to Old Spanish: (1) the creation of the palatal order

Of these thirteen consonants, /h/ (which was strictly glottal rather than velar) was lost by the first century BC, as can be seen from Latin versification, misspellings, and frequent direct comments by grammarians and others. The twelve remaining phonemes have all survived into Old Spanish (and modern Spanish), but have been joined by a number of others created along the way. The broad pattern of development of the system has been one of complication: the system grows in size and complexity until the late medieval period (after which a number of mergers reduces the range of phonemes). The kind of increased complexity which arises is twofold; on the one hand, a new (palatal) order of consonants comes into existence between the dental∼alveolar and the velar orders (see 2.5.2.1–6), and, on the other hand, a series of voiced fricatives was created (see 2.5.3), to match the pre-existing series of voiceless fricatives. In each case, a number of individual changes contributes to the restructuring, and we shall consider these changes in chronological order, beginning with those which contributed to the creation of the palatal order.

2.5.2.1 Consonantization of /i/

Word-initial /i/ before another vowel was non-syllabic from early times in Latin, no doubt articulated as the glide [j]. IĀNUĀRIUS was probably pronounced [ja:nua:rius], and the same is likely to have been true in other morpheme-initial positions such as the case represented by CONIUGES. In spoken Latin, the frictionless glide [j] became a consonant, presumably the fricative [ĵ] or even the affricate [dĵ] (in some areas [ʒ] or [dʒ]). The consonantal quality of I- under these circumstances is reflected in clumsy misspellings of the kind ZANUARIO (for IANUARIO), ZERAX (for HIERAX), SUSTUS (for IUSTUS), spellings which do no more than indicate the fricative or affricate nature of the initial phoneme. Word-initial I- may be regarded as a separate (voiced palatal fricative or affricate) phoneme in VL, and its appearance can therefore be considered the first step in the creation of a palatal order of consonants (and of the voiced fricative series; see 2.5.3). Further development of /ĵ/ will be considered together with that of /g/ (2.5.2.3), some of whose allophones merged with I-.

2.5.2.2 Palatal developments of consonant + [j]

The palatal glide [j] (emerging from atonic E and I in hiatus; see 2.4.3.4) was frequent in VL. Through the process of assimilation (2.1.1.1), this glide often modified the preceding consonant, changing its place of articulation by drawing it towards that of [j], and sometimes, in the process, changing its manner of articulation from plosive to affricate or fricative. Such an assimilatory process is referred to as **palatalization** and may or may not lead to the simplification of the two phonemes to only one. In general, the palatalizing influence of [j] is felt most readily on those consonants articulated closest to the palate (the dento-alveolars and the velars) but may be exercised at even greater distance (on the labials). We shall consider all the possible combinations of c + [j] (remembering that /h/ had been lost and observing that /f/, because it was rare in word-internal position, does not enter into combination with [j]) in the order in which, it seems, they were affected by palatalization.

1   /t/ + [j] and /k/ + [j]. The first stage of palatalization of these combinations (*c.* first century AD) produced

/t/ + [j] > [ts] (PUTEU > [pótso], MARTIU > [mártso])
/k/ + [j] > [tʃ] (ĒRĪCIU > [erítʃo], CALCEA > [kálʧa]),

pronunciations which are hinted at by such misspellings as VINCENTZUS (for VINCENTIUS) and TERSIO (for TERTIO). However, although most Romance languages maintained the contrast between these two results, the Latin of Cantabria (the area where Castilian developed) allowed them to merge in [ts]. This pronunciation survives into OSp. (spelt *c* or *ç*) where it was preceded by a consonant:

MARTIU > *março* 'March'
CALCEA > *calça* 'stockings', later 'breeches'

However, where it was preceded by a vowel (and was therefore intervocalic) it was subject to lenition (2.5.3.2) and produced OSp. /dz/ (spelt *z*):

PUTEU > *pozo* 'well'
ĒRĪCIU > *erizo* 'hedgehog'

There is some evidence (see Malkiel 1971, Wilkinson 1976) that [tj] and [kj], when following a vowel, were at first treated differently in Old Spanish, [tj] producing OSp. /dz/, but [kj] giving /ts/. The forms containing /ts/ < [kj] were then modified to /dz/, perhaps for reasons of analogy, since many of the relevant cases of /ts/ occurred in suffixes (e.g. -ACEU > -*aço*), which were open to influence from similar inherited derivational elements which in a majority of cases displayed voiced consonants (see 4.14.2.1).

Geminate /tt/ and /kk/ were also palatalized by following [j], producing in VL the geminate [tts], at which stage there was a merger, in Cantabria, between the product of /tt/ and /kk/ + [j] and the product of /pt/ + [j], /kt/ + [j] and /sk/ + [j], all these groups giving [tts], later simplified (through lenition, like other geminates, 2.5.3.2) to OSp. /ts/ (spelt *ç* or *c*):

MATTIANA > *maçana*, later *mançana* 'apple'
BRACCHIU > *braço* 'arm'

CAPTIĀRE > caçar 'to hunt'
DIRECTIĀRE > adereçar 'to prepare'
ASCIOLA > *açuela* 'adze'

2 /l/ + [j] widely became [λ] in VL, which persisted in most areas. However, in the late VL of Cantabria or in pre-literary Castilian, this [λ] was modified to /ʒ/ (voiced pre-palatal fricative, comparable with *s* in Eng. *leisure, measure*). This development from lateral to central articulation may have resulted from a need to maintain contrast between words originally containing /l/ + [j] and those containing /ll/, since the latter was being transformed into [λ] in the Castilian area (e.g. GALLUS > *gallo* 'cock'; see 2.5.3.2[9]). However, this argument cannot be regarded as conclusive since Eastern Hispano-Romance (Arag. and most of Cat.) allows the merger of /l/ + [j] and /ll/. Examples of the development of Lat. /l/ + [j] > Cast /ʒ/ (spelt *j, i, g*):

ALIU > *ajo* 'garlic'
FOLIA > *foja, foia* (later *hoja*) 'leaf'
VL MOLLIĀRE > *mojar* 'to soak'
MULIERE > *mugier* (later *mujer*) 'woman, wife'
MELIŌRE > *mejor, meior* 'better'

3 /n/ + [j] underwent mutual assimilation in VL, producing [ɲ], which survives as OSp. /ɲ/ (spelt *nn*, or its contraction *ñ*):

ARĀNEA > *araña* 'spider'
HISPANIA > *España* 'Spain'
SENIŌRE > *señor* 'sir'
VĪNEA > *viña* 'vineyard'

4 /d/ + [j] and /g/ + [j] were everywhere palatalized in VL and merged, probably as the geminate [ĵĵ], thereby entering into a further merger with intervocalic -I-. The sound represented by I in words like MAIUS, PEIUS, etc., was evidently a geminate (no doubt [ĵĵ]) in VL; this conclusion is based on direct comment by Roman grammarians and on the spelling of such words in inscriptions with a double-height I (*I longa*). Whatever its source, VL [ĵĵ] was subject to reduction, in Western Romance, through lenition (2.5.3.2) and normally appears in OSp. as /ĵ/ (spelt 'y', also 'i' in late OSp. and early MSp.):

PODIU > *poyo* 'hill, bench'
RADIĀRE > *rayar* 'to scratch, score'
EXAGIU > *ensayo* 'attempt'
FĀGEA > *faya* (later *haya*) 'beech tree'
MĀIU > *mayo* 'May'
MAIŌRE > *mayor* 'greater'

Where /ĵ/ was preceded in early OSp. by a front vowel, the consonant was lost through assimilation to the vowel:

SEDEAM > *sea* (pres. subj. of *ser*)
VIDEO > *veo* 'I see'
CORRIGIA > *correa* 'leather strap'
PĒIŌRE > *peor* 'worse'

Where Lat. /d/ + [j] was preceded by a consonant, the result of the palatalization process was OSp. voiceless /ts/:

HORDEOLU > *orçuelo* 'style'
VIRDIA > *berça* 'cabbage'
VERĒCUNDIA > *vergüença* (beside *vergüeña*) 'shame'

5 The labials /b/ and /m/ + [j] are largely unaffected by palatalization. Apart from the verbal case HABEAM > *haya* (pres. subj. *haber*), the consonants survive unchanged (apart from fricatization of /b/; see 2.5.3.2) into OSp. (and MSp.). The VL merger of -B- and -V- (2.5.3.1) must also be borne in mind, e.g.

RUBEU > *ruvio* (later *rubio*) 'blond'
NOVIU > *novio* 'fiancé', etc.
PLUVIA > *lluvia* 'rain'
PRAEMIU > *premio* 'prize'
VINDĒMIA > *vendimia* 'grape harvest'

6 Lat. /p/, /s/, /r/ + [j] are subject only to metathesis (see 2.1.1.4), without palatalization of the consonant. For the treatment of the glide, once transposed, see 2.4.2.4. E.g.

CAPIAM > *quepa* (pres. subj. *caber*)
BĀSIU > *beso* 'kiss'
MANSIŌNE > *mesón* 'inn' (for NS > /s/, see 2.5.3.2)
AUGURIU > *agüero* 'omen'
FERRĀRIU > *ferrero* (later *herrero*) 'blacksmith'

2.5.2.3 *Palatalization of syllable-initial velars*

The Lat. phonemes /k/ and /g/, when followed by a front vowel, were palatalized in later VL and contributed to the creation of the OSp. phonemes /ts/, /dz/, and /ǰ/, a process initiated by the assimilations discussed in 2.5.2.2.

As exemplified in 2.1.1.1, Lat. /k/ probably always had a fronted allophone ([k̑]) used when the following vowel belonged to the front series (/i/, /e/, or /ɛ/). In spoken Latin, this assimilatory fronting process was continued and exaggerated, so that the allophone of /k/ used before front vowels came to be palatal ([tʃ]), and was further fronted in some areas (including Spain) to [ts]. This phonetic adjustment, made possible by the absence of palatal phonemes from the Latin system, is reflected in occasional barbaric spellings like INTCITAMENTO (for INCITAMENTO) and NISEAM (for NICEAM). But the change is not merely phonetic, but has consequences for the phonemic system of Latin. In the first place, it implies neutralization, before front vowels, of /k/ on the one hand, and /t/ + [j] and /k/ + [j], on the other. Thus PĀCE [pátse], and FACIE [fátse] shared the same internal consonant.

In the second place, the sound [ts] could now occur before any of the VL vowels, and was therefore well on the way to phonemicization. For example, PRETIARE [pretsáre] 'to prize' was in minimal opposition to PRECARE [prekáre] 'to beg', and the sound [ts] can be seen before a range of vowels in ERĪCIU [erítso], MARTIU [mártso], CALCEA [káltsa], ACŪTIARE [akutsáre], FACIT [fátset], AMĪCĪ [amítsi], etc. Full phonemicization of /ts/ probably had to await the development of QUI-, QUE- > [ki], [ke] (see 2.5.7), at which stage /ts/ contrasts with /k/ in all environments.

The treatment of Lat. /k/ is therefore a case of incipient split, /k/ remaining velar before back vowels and /a/ and contributing towards the creation of the phoneme /ts/ when it occurred before front vowels:

> CIRCA > *cerca* (OSp. /ts/) 'near'
> CAELU > *cielo* (OSp. /ts/) 'sky'
>
> ---
>
> CAPANNA > *cabaña* (OSp. /k/) 'hut'
> CORŌNA > *corona* (OSp. /k/) 'crown'
> CŪPA > *cuba* (OSp. /k/) 'vat'

When VL /ts/ (< /k/ or any other source) occurred between vowels, it was subject, in Spanish (as in other W. Romance varieties) to lenition (see 2.5.3.2), and therefore appears in Old Spanish as the voiced phoneme /dz/ (spelt *z*):

> DĪCIT > *dize* 'he says'
> FACERE > *fazer* (later *hacer*) 'to do'
> VL RACĒMU > *razimo* 'bunch of grapes'
> VĪCĪNU > *vezino* 'neighbour'

Since Latin intervocalic /k/ before non-front vowels became voiced /g/ in OSp. (see 2.5.3.2[8]), it can be seen that Lat. /k/ in this position split into two OSp. phonemes, /dz/ and /g/:

> FACIT > *faze* (later *hace*) 'he does'
> IACĒRE > *yazer* (later *yacer*) 'to lie'
>
> ---
>
> LOCĀLE > *logar* (later *lugar*) 'place'
> IOCU > *juego* 'game'

The sequence QU, whether word-initial (see 2.5.7) or internal, retained its glide [w] following /k/ for a sufficiently long period to ensure that this /k/ is always treated like /k/ preceding a non-front vowel and never like /k/ preceding a front vowel: QUĪNDECIM > *quince* 'fifteen', SEQUERE (CL SEQUĪ) > *seguir* 'to follow'.

/kk̑/ and /sk̑/. Note that although few words with geminate /kk/ before front vowel have survived into Spanish, the Latin group /sk/ was frequent before such vowels. Both groups gave rise to a geminate /tts/ in the spoken Latin of Cantabria, thereby merging with the product of /kk/ + [j], /tt/ + [j], etc. (see 2.5.2.2[1]) and producing OSp. /ts/ (spelt *(s)ç* or *(s)c*), through the usual Western Romance simplification of geminates (2.5.3.2):

FLACCIDU > *llacio* (later *lacio*) 'lank'
FASCĒS > *faces* (later *haces*) 'bundles (of corn, wood, etc.)'
PĀSCERE > OSp. *pascer ~ pacer*, later only *pacer* 'to graze'
PISCĒS > *peces* 'fish'

The voiced velar /g/, like voiceless /k/, no doubt had always had fronted allophones when followed by any front vowel. As in the case of /k/, such fronted allophones were further fronted in later spoken Latin, a development made possible by the absence of palatal phonemes in Latin, and became the voiced palatal fricative [j̃]. In word-initial position, therefore, the product of /g/ (before front vowels) merged with the product of non-syllabic I- (see 2.5.2.1), so that henceforth words like GENESTA and words like IĀNUĀRIUS had the same initial sound. This neutralization of phonemes is reflected in the usual confusion of spellings among less well-educated writers of Latin; we find GEIUNA (for IEIŪNA) and GENARIUS (for IENUĀRIUS or, more correctly, IĀNUĀRIUS).

Palatal /j̃/ from these sources was sometimes preserved, in word-initial position, in Old Spanish, spelt *y*. E.g.

GEMMA > *yema* 'yolk', etc.
GYPSU > *yesso* (later *yeso*) 'plaster'
IACET > *yaze* (later *yace*) 'he lies'

However, loss or modification of /j̃/ was frequent in early Old Spanish, for a series of reasons. Sometimes, through analogy, word-initial /je/ in an atonic syllable was replaced by /e/, since /je/ was phonetically identical to the tonic syllable of words like *yegua* 'mare' < EQUA and *yerva* 'grass' < HERBA. But in *yegua*, *yerva*, etc. /je/ owed its existence to the diphthongization process (see 2.4.2.2) and was therefore limited to tonic syllables and corresponded to /e/ in atonic syllables (e.g. *ervage* 'fodder'). For this reason the **atonic** /je/ of words like **yermano* 'brother' (< GERMĀNU) or **yenero* 'January' (< IĀNUĀRIU) would have appeared anomalous and was brought in line with the prevailing morpho-phonological pattern by replacing /je/ by /e/:

*yermano > *ermano* (later *hermano*)
*yenero > *enero*

Similarly, IACTĀRE > *echar* 'to throw', GENUCULU > OSp. *(h)inojo* 'knee', VL IINIPERU > *enebro* 'juniper', GELĀRE > *(h)elar* 'to freeze', GINGĪVAS > *enzias* (later *encías*) 'gums'.

Early OSp. /j̃/ was also occasionally lost for reasons of dissimilation before another palatal phoneme, e.g.

*yayuno (< VL IĀIŪNU) > *ayuno* 'fasting'

Finally, /j̃/ was sometimes modified to /ʒ/ (spelt *j, i*), probably under the influence of medieval Latin, as read aloud in the church and the law-courts:

> IŪSTU > *yusto* > *justo* 'just'
> IŪDICĒS > *yuezes* > *juezes* 'judges'

For a full account of the various medieval treatments of /j̃/, see Penny 1988.

Intervocalic /g/ before front vowels was also palatalized, but in this position did not merge with non-syllabic -I-. The latter, it will be recalled (2.5.2.2[4]), corresponded to geminate /j̃j̃/, while the immediate VL product of intervocalic /g/ before front vowels appears to have been simple /j̃/, which was rapidly eliminated, by total assimilation to the following vowel, or through the lenition process (2.5.3.2). It is probably this total loss which is indicated by occasional misspellings like TRIENTA (for TRĪGINTA) and by the *Appendix Probi*'s recommendation CALCOSTEGIS NON CALCOSTEIS. Certainly, this loss is characteristic of all Romance languages, including Spanish:

> DIGITU > *dedo* 'finger'
> FRĪGIDU > *frío* 'cold'
> MAGISTRU > *maestro* 'master'
> SAGITTA > *saeta* 'arrow'

To summarize, Lat. /g/ underwent phonemic split. In initial position, it gave palatal results (which merged with I- and then suffered further changes, including loss) before front vowels, but remained velar before other vowels:

> GYPSU > OSp. *yesso* 'plaster'
> GENERU > *yerno* 'son-in-law'
>
> ---
>
> GALLĪNA > *gallina* 'hen'
> GAUDIU > *gozo* 'enjoyment'
> GUTTA > *gota* 'drop'

In intervocalic position, /g/ was palatalized and lost before front vowels, but before non-front vowels survived in some words as a velar (but a velar fricative, see 2.5.3.2), although elimination of this velar was frequent, so that the effects of the phonemic split are partially obscured:

> RUGĪTU > *roido* (later *ruido*) 'noise'
> DIGITU > *dedo* 'finger'
>
> ---
>
> NEGARE > *negar* 'to deny' (but LIGARE > *liar* 'to tie')
> AUGUSTU > *agosto* 'August' (but REGALE > *real* 'royal, real')

Where /k/ and /g/ occur as the second element of an internal group in Latin, they evolve in principle, as is generally the case for consonants under these conditions, in the same way as in word-initial position (see above). Thus, in the case of cons. + /k/ (in which case the consonant may be s [see /sk/ above], L, R, or N), we observe the same phonemic split as in the case of initial /k/: /k/ before non-front vowels, OSp. /ts/, MSp. /θ/ before front vowels:

SULCU > *surco* 'furrow'   *DULCE > *dulce* 'sweet'
PORCU > *puerco* 'pig'   *TORCERE (CL TORQUERE) > *torcer* 'to twist'
IUNCU > *junco* 'reed'   *VINCICULU > *vencejo* 'bond (for tying corn)'

However, in the case of cons. + /g/ the development of the velar is notoriously thorny, especially since many of the examples are verbs, where analogical interference in phonological development is likely to be involved (see Malkiel 1982 for a detailed account). Of the consonants that may be grouped internally with /g/ (L, R and N), only R and N occur with any frequency. For /rg/ the outcome is /rg/ before non-front vowels and (usually) OSp. /rdz/, MSp. /rθ/ before front vowels:

SPARGO > OSp. *espargo* 'I strew' (remodelled as MSp. *esparzo*; see 3.7.7.1.3[b])
ARGILLA > OSp. *arzilla* > MSp. *arcilla* 'clay'

For /ng/ we predictably find no change when a non-front vowel follows:

TANGO > OSp. *tango* 'I touch' (remodelled as MSp. *taño* 'I play [an instrument]'; see 3.7.7.1.3[b])

But, before a front vowel, /ng/ gives no fewer than three results:

OSp. /ndz/, MSp. /nθ/: GINGĪVA > OSp. *enzia* > MSp. *encia* 'gum'
OSp. and MSp. /ɲ/: RINGERE (CL RINGĪ) > *reñir* 'to scold'
OSp. and MSp. /n/ (i.e. with loss of /g/ as when intervocalic before a front vowel [see above]): QUĪNGENTŌS > *quinientos* 'five hundred'

2.5.2.4 Palatalization of syllable-final velars

A further source of OSp. palatal phonemes is provided by /k/ and /g/ when grouped, within the word, with a following consonant. In W. Romance (and therefore in Spanish) such syllable-final velars were first fricatized (to /x/) and then modified to [i̯]. This offglide has two effects which are observable in Spanish; on the one hand, through metaphony (see 2.4.2.1), it causes raising of the preceding vowel, often combining with it thereafter, and, on the other, it has an assimilatory effect on the following (syllable-initial) consonant, a process which gives rise to new palatal phonemes. The VL internal groups whose first member is a velar are the following: -X-(= /ks/), -CT-, -CL- (occurring chiefly in words where the group was formed by loss of an intertonic vowel, e.g. SPECLUM for SPECULUM, see 2.4.3.3), -GL-(likewise formed through loss of an intertonic; cf. *TEGLA for TEGULA, etc.), and -GN-. In the first two cases, the processes outlined above produced entirely new (palatal) consonants

-x- > /ʃ/:

    DĪXĪ > *dixe* (later *dije*) 'I said'

    MATAXA > *madexa* (later *madeja*) 'skein'

    TAXU > *texo* (later *tejo*) 'yew'

-CT- > /tʃ/:

    FACTU > *fecho* (later *hecho*) pp. *hacer*

    NOCTE > *noche* 'night'

    STRICTU > *estrecho* 'narrow'

The group LT, when preceded by U, has the same outcome as CT. Syllable-final /l/ was frequently velar in VL (as in MEng; cf. *wool, wall, old*), and this characteristic was no doubt exaggerated after a back (velar) vowel. This velar allophone of /l/ was then treated like other syllable-final velars (see above):

(U)LT- > /tʃ/:

    MULTU > *mucho* 'much'

    CULTELLU > *cuchiello* (later *cuchillo*) 'knife'

Note that where the vowel preceding -CT- was VL /i/, the glide (< -C) was quickly absorbed by the (homorganic) vowel and leaves the T- unaffected:

    FRĪCTU > *frito* 'fried'

    FĪCTU > *fito* (later *hito*) 'boundary-marker, target'

In the case of -CL- and -GL-, the result of palatalization of the second consonant was at first /λ/, an outcome which implies merger with the product of /l/ + [j] (see 2.5.2.2[2]) and the same Old Spanish outcome as that group:

-CL- > /ʒ/:

    LENTIC(U)LA > *lenteja* 'lentil'

    NOVĀC(U)LA > *navaja* 'razor'

    OC(U)LU > *ojo* 'eye'

    VERMIC(U)LU > *bermejo* 'red'

-GL- > /ʒ/:

    REG(U)LA > *reja* 'ploughshare'

    TEG(U)LA > *teja* 'tile'

Note that in the sequence -T(V)L- (where (V) indicates an intertonic vowel lost in VL), the first consonant was replaced by /k/ (*Appendix Probi*: VETULUS NON VECLUS, VITULUS NON VICLUS) and the group therefore shares the development of -CL-:

-T(V)L- > /ʒ/:

    *ROTULARE > *arrojar* 'to throw'

    VETULU > *viejo* 'old'

The outcome of -GN- again shows merger, this time with the product of /n/ + [j] (see 2.5.2.2[3]):

-GN- > /ɲ/:

    LIGNA > *leña* 'firewood'

    PUGNU > *puño* 'fist'

    STAGNU > *estaño* 'tin'

The groups concerned here have the full evolution described above only if the second consonant remains syllable-initial. The final stage (palatalization) does not take place if the group is (or becomes) word-final, or if, through loss of an intertonic vowel (see 2.4.3.3), one of the consonant groups under consideration here comes into contact with a following, third, consonant (for such secondary groupings, see 2.5.5). Under all these circumstances, the second consonant of the primary group necessarily ceases to be syllable-initial and becomes syllable-final. Since, throughout the history of Spanish, it has been impermissible for palatal consonants to occupy syllable-final position, a palatal result is precluded in this case. The glide which emerged from their velar consonant (see above) affects the preceding vowel but not the following consonant. Contrast the following cases with those quoted above (DĪXĪ > *dixe*, STRICTU > *estrecho*, MULTU > *mucho*, LIGNA > *leña*, etc.):

-x(C) > /(i̯)s/:	FRAXINU > (pre-lit.) *freisno* > *fresno* 'ash tree'
	SEX > *seis* 'six'
-CT(C) > /(i̯)n/:	PECTINĀRE > *peinar* 'to comb'
	LECTORĪLE > *letril* (later *atril*) 'lectern'
(U)LT(C) > /t̯/:	VULTURE > *buitre* 'vulture'
	MULT(U) > *muyt* (later *muy*) 'very'
-GN(C) > /(i̯)n/:	PIGNORA > *peyndra*, *pendra*, *prenda* 'pledge, garment'

2.5.2.5   *Palatalization of* -LL- *and* -NN-

One of the outcomes in Spanish of the lenition process was the palatalization of the Latin geminates /ll/ and /nn/. The motives for this change will be seen in 2.5.3.2, but we note here its contribution to the creation of the OSp. palatal order of consonants. While -LL- produces a new phoneme (we have seen [2.5.2.2, section 2, and 2.5.2.4] that late VL /ʎ/ (< /l/ + [j] and -CL-, -GL-) was modified in early Sp. to /ʒ/, perhaps owing to the change now under consideration), -NN- merges with the product of Lat. /n/ + [j] (2.5.2.2[3]) and -GN- (2.5.2.4):

-LL- > /ʎ/:	CABALLU < *cavallo* (later *caballo*) 'horse'
	GALLU < *gallo* 'cock'
	VALLES > *valles* 'valleys'
-NN- > /ɲ/:	ANNU > *año* 'year'
	CANNA > *caña* 'cane'
	GRUNNĪRE > *gruñir* 'to growl, groan'

2.5.2.6   *Palatalization of* PL-, CL-, FL-

It seems likely that the /l/ of these groups had a palatalized pronunciation already in the VL of some areas (see Lausberg 1965: 332–5). In pre-literary Spanish, the initial consonant was in most cases assimilated to the following [ʎ] and was absorbed by it, although there are some popular words (e.g. PLATEA > *plaça*, later *plaza* '(town) square', CLAVĪCULA > *clavija* 'peg', FLOCCU > *flueco*, later *fleco* 'tassel'; for detailed discussion see Malkiel

1963–4) which show retention of the group. Examples of the more usual (palatal) treatment are:

PL- > /λ/:	PLAGA > *llaga* 'wound'
	PLANU > *llano* 'flat'
	PLICĀRE > *llegar* 'to arrive'
CL- > /λ/:	CLĀMĀRE > *llamar* 'to call'
	CLAUSA > *llosa* 'enclosed field'
	CLĀVE > *llave* 'key'
FL- > /λ/:	FLAMMA > *llama* 'flame'
	FLACCIDU > *llacio* (later *lacio*) 'lank'

Where these groups occur internally following another consonant, the regular result is /tʃ/. In this case, it appears that the voiceless /p/, /k/ or /f/ has devoiced the following /λ/ before being absorbed:

(cons.)PL- > /tʃ/:	AMPLU > *ancho* 'broad'
	IMPLĒRE > *henchir* 'to cram'
(cons.)CL- > /tʃ/:	*MANCLA (CL MACŬLA) > *mancha* 'stain'
(cons.)FL- > /tʃ/:	INFLĀRE > *hinchar* 'to inflate, swell'

The same treatment is accorded, in a few words, to initial PL-, a development which no doubt originated under circumstances where the word was preceded by another ending in a consonant and where the post-consonantal treatment was eventually extended (for unknown reasons) to all uses of the word:

PL- > /tʃ/:	*PLATTU > *chato* 'snub-nosed'
	*PLŎPPU (CL PŎPULU) > *chopo* 'black poplar'
	PLUTEU > *chozo*, whence *choza* 'hut'

2.5.2.7 *Summary of palatal developments from Latin to Old Spanish*

As a result of the various processes considered in the preceding sections (2.5.2.1–6), Old Spanish came to have a palatal order of consonants, which had been lacking at first in Latin. In some cases (*viz.* the emergence of /ts/ and /dz/), although there had been an earlier palatal stage of development, the outcome was a new dental(-alveolar) phoneme. The Old Spanish phonemes created in these ways are now listed, together with the various sources of each phoneme and a single example of each development. Cross-reference is given to the earlier discussion of each change. (C) and (V) indicate that a Consonant or a Vowel is a necessary conditioning factor but does not participate directly in the outcome.

OSp. phoneme	Latin sources	Example	See
/ts/	(C)/t/ + [j]	MARTIU > *março*	2.5.2.2(1)
	(C)/k/ + [j]	CALCEA > *calça*	2.5.2.2(1)
	/tt/ + [j]	MATTIANA > *ma(n)çana*	2.5.2.2(1)
	/kk/ + [j]	BRACCHIU > *braço*	2.5.2.2(1)

OSp. phoneme	Latin sources	Example	See
/ts/ (cont.)	/pt/+[j]	*CAPTIĀRE > caçar	2.5.2.2(1)
	/kt/+[j]	*DIRECTIĀRE > adereçar	2.5.2.2(1)
	initial /k/(E/I)	CISTA > cesta	2.5.2.3
	/sk/(E/I)	PISCES > peçes	2.5.2.3
	/kk/(E/I)	FLACCIDU > lacio	2.5.2.3
/dz/	(V)/t/+[j]	PUTEU > pozo	2.5.2.2(1)
	(V)/k/+[j]	ĒRĪCIU > erizo	2.5.2.2(1)
	(V)/k/(E/I)	VĪCĪNU > vezino	2.5.2.3
/tʃ/	/kt/	FACTU > fecho	2.5.2.4
	(U)/lt/	MULTU > mucho	2.5.2.4
	(C)/pl~kl~fl/	AMPLU > ancho	2.5.2.6
/ʒ/	/l/+[j]	FĪLIU > fijo	2.5.2.2(2)
	(V)/kl/	OC(U)LU > ojo	2.5.2.4
	(V)/gl/	TEG(U)LA > teja	2.5.2.4
/ʃ/	/ks/(V)	MAXILLA > mexilla	2.5.2.4
/ǰ/	initial /i/(V)	IACET > yaze	2.5.2.1
	(V)/i/(V)	MĀIU > mayo	2.5.2.2(4)
	initial /g/(E/I)	GYPSU > yesso	2.5.2.3
	/g/+[j]	FĀGEA > faya	2.5.2.2(4)
	/d/+[j]	RADIĀRE > rayar	2.5.2.2(4)
	initial /ɛ́/	EQUA > yegua	2.5.2.3
·/ɲ/	/n/+[j]	VĪNEA > viña	2.5.2.2(3)
	/gn/	PUGNU > puño	2.5.2.4
	/nn/	ANNU > año	2.5.2.5
/λ/	/ll/	CABALLU > cavallo	2.5.2.5
	initial /pl/	PLŌRĀRE > llorar	2.5.2.6
	initial /kl/	CLĀMĀRE > llamar	2.5.2.6
	initial /fl/	FLAMMA > llama	2.5.2.6

2.5.3   Developments from Latin to Old Spanish: (2) The creation of the voiced fricative series

We come now to the second of the two major realignments which affected the VL consonantal system. As anticipated in 2.5.2, a series of voiced fricative consonants (a series of phonemes lacking in VL) was created as the result of a number of separate processes, the main one of which is lenition (2.5.3.2). Some of these processes have already been considered, since they contribute to both the major readjustments, providing not just new **palatal** consonants but **voiced** palatal **fricatives**.

2.5.3.1   The appearance of /ǰ/ and /β/

We have already seen how the voiced fricative /ǰ/ emerged, from initial non-syllabic I- (2.5.2.1) and intervocalic -I- (see 2.5.2.2[4]), and merged with /d/+[j], /g/+[j]. Just as non-syllabic I was consonantized in VL, so too was non-syllabic V, in words like VITA, AVIS, where the earlier Latin pronunciation was the glide [w] ([wi:ta], [a:wis]). And just as /ǰ/ (<I) entered into

mergers with other phonemes, so too did the product of v, the voiced bilabial fricative /β/ (see Väänänen 1968: 92–3). In intervocalic position, v seems to have been identical to в in VL, as witnessed by the extraordinary frequency of interchange of the spellings в and v in this position: SIVI (for SIBĪ), VIBA (for VĪVA), PLEBES NON PLEVIS (*Appendix Probi*), etc. The likely pronunciation was the voiced fricative /β/ for both, a pronunciation inherited by Old Spanish and spelt *v* or *u*:

> CABALLU > *cavallo* (later *caballo*) 'horse'
> BIBERE > *bever* (later *beber*) 'to drink'
> NOVU > *nuevo* 'new'
> VĪVERE > *bevir, bivir* (later *vivir*) 'to live'.

With regard to initial в- and v-, ancient misspellings suggest that there was some neutralization in VL of the two phonemes concerned (after a word-final nasal, it would be difficult to distinguish a bilabial plosive (в-) from a bilabial fricative (v-)). Spellings like BIXIT (for VĪXIT), BALIAT (for VALEAT), and the recommendations of the *Appendix Probi* (BACULUS NON VACLUS, VAPULO NON BAPLO) are evidence of this incipient (but unaccomplished) merger. However, it seems that in initial position the Latin phonemes represented by в- and v- maintained their contrast into the Old Spanish period, since Old Spanish spelling practice for the most part continues to distribute initial *b* and *v* according to whether the etymon had в- or v-:

> BUCCA > *boca* 'mouth'
> BENE > *bien* 'well'
> VĪTA > *vida* 'life'
> VACCA > *vaca* 'cow'

Only in a minority of instances does Old Spanish spelling show confusion of initial *b-* and *v-*, sometimes due to dissimilation of initial /β/ from a following /β/ (as in VĪVERE > *bevir* (see above), VĪVU > *bivo* 'alive', VERVĀCTU > *barvecho* (later *barbecho*) 'fallow', VOLVERE > *bolver* (later *volver*) 'to return' and sometimes no doubt through increasing neutralization of the two phonemes (e.g. *boz* for *voz* 'voice', *vando* for *bando* 'clan'). Full merger was not accomplished until the late medieval and early modern periods (see 2.6.1 and Penny 1976).

2.5.3.2 Lenition

Beginning in the last centuries of the Empire and continuing through the Dark Ages, W. Romance (therefore including Spanish) was affected by an interrelated series of consonantal changes, sometimes described as 'weakenings' and referred to by the name **lenition**. Almost all intervocalic consonants and all geminates were involved in these changes, one of whose major outcomes was the provision (in Old Spanish, etc.) of further voiced fricative phonemes.

The reason for the lenition changes is much disputed. Some have seen in them the influence upon spoken Latin of Celtic speech, since similar weakenings of intervocalic consonants are evident in the well-documented history of the Celtic languages, and since there is considerable (but not complete) correspondence between the areas of originally Celtic population and the areas of Romance speech where lenition is evident (Gaul, the Alps, N. Italy, W. Spain); see Baldinger 1972: ch. 8, Martinet 1974: 365–420. Others (e.g. Alarcos 1965: 241–7) have sought purely Latin explanations: an increase in VL of the incidence of geminates (see below) led to an unbalanced consonantal system, an imbalance which was redressed by the simplification of the geminates, a process which had the consequence of causing a chain-reaction of further changes (voicing of voiceless intervocalics and fricatization/loss of voiced intervocalics).

It is certainly true that in VL there was a considerable increase in the incidence of geminates, as the result of a number of assimilations which affected certain common consonant groups. Of the following cases of assimilation (revealed by the spelling evidence quoted), not all affected all varieties of Romance; some were geographically widespread, others more limited, but all affected that variety of VL which gave rise to Spanish:

RS > /ss/	(e.g. DOSSUM for DORSUM; *Appendix Probi:* PERSICA NON PESSICA)
PS > /ss/	(e.g. ISSE for IPSE)
PT > /tt/	(e.g. SETTEMBRES for SEPTEMBRIS)
NF > /ff/	(e.g. *IFFANTE < INFANS, INFANTEM; not clearly attested in VL)
MN > /nn/	(e.g. ALUNNUS for ALUMNUS)
MB > /mm/	(e.g. *LUMMUS < LUMBUS; limited to central and S. Italy and to central and E. Spain; not attested until after the Latin period)

Note that the group NS was reduced to the simple consonant /s/ (e.g. *Appendix Probi*: ANSA NON ASA, MENSA NON MESA, TENSA NON TESA), not a geminate.

Following these changes (in the opinion of some, **because** of them), the intervocalic consonants of W. Romance underwent a series of interrelated modifications, which, in principle, take the following form. Geminates were reduced to simple intervocalic consonants (perhaps because geminates are expensive in terms of physical energy and the incidence of geminates had, as we have seen, increased); e.g. /kk/ > /k/. This simplification put pressure on pre-existing intervocalic consonants to change, causing the simple intervocalics (if they were originally voiceless) to become voiced (e.g. /k/ > /g/), in order to maintain, by other means, the original contrast between geminate and simple. In turn, the voicing of voiceless intervocalic phonemes threatened merger with the pre-existing voiced phonemes, and the latter (if originally plosive) became fricative (e.g. /g/ > [γ]) in order to avoid the merger. The chain-reaction was completed when, in order to avoid merger with the new voiced fricatives (< voiced plosives), the pre-existing voiced fricative /ǰ/ (the result of the palatalization of /g/ before front vowels, for which see 2.5.2.3) was eliminated from the words in which it occurred.

This chain-reaction can be summarized, still in principle, in the following table:

	Process	VL	OSp.	Example
1	Simplification	geminate	> simple	/kk/ > /k/
2	Voicing	voiceless	> voiced	/k/ > /g/
3	Fricatization	voiced plosive	> voiced fricative	/g/ > [γ]
4	Loss	voiced fricative	> zero	/ǰ/ > /zero/

In practice, it is important to know, in the case of Spanish, which of these processes were contemporary (and therefore mutually exclusive) and which were successive (allowing the output of one process to become the input of the next). Process 1 is contemporary with process 2; its output (a simple phoneme) never becomes the input of any of the other processes. Thus, VL /kk/, having been reduced to /k/ by simplification (1) (e.g. SICCU > *seco* 'dry'), remains a voiceless plosive and is not affected by voicing (2), fricatization (3) or loss (4).

Process 2 may (*viz.* in the case of the VL fricatives) stand alone. Thus VL -s-, having become /z/ (e.g. CASA = /kása/ > OSp. *casa* = /káza/ 'house'), suffers no further change. However, the output of process 2 may (*viz.* in the case of the VL voiceless plosives) become the input of process 3. Thus VL /k/ suffers both voicing and fricatization and appears in Old Spanish as [γ] (e.g. SECARE > *segar* 'to reap', where *g* = [γ], as in MSp.).

Process 3 may operate in isolation from the other processes, as can be seen in the treatment of VL -B-, fricatized (already in VL, see 2.5.3.1) but not lost (e.g. NŪBĒS > *nuves* 'clouds', where *v* represents the voiced fricative /β/, a word later respelt *nubes*). However, the output of process 3 may become the input of process 4. Thus, VL /g/, having been fricatized (process 3) is also, in a majority of cases, lost (e.g. REGĀLE > *real* 'royal', LIGĀRE > *liar* 'to bind').

Finally, process 4 may operate in isolation. This is what happens in the case of the VL voiced palatal fricative /ǰ/ (< G^{e,i}; see 2.5.2.3 [end]), which suffers loss (e.g. DIGITU > *dedo*, 'finger').

Full exemplification now follows of the effects of lenition on Spanish intervocalic consonants. The VL phonemes affected are organized into nine groups, on the basis of their distinctive features.

1 Labial plosives

VL	/-pp-/	>	OSp.	/p/	CUPPA > *copa* 'wine glass'
	/-p-/	>		/b/	CŪPA > *cuba* 'wine vat'
	/-b-/	>		/β/	CIBU > *cevo* 'food' (later 'bait')

We have seen (2.5.3.1) that Lat. /-b-/ merged with -v-, both giving OSp. /β/.

2 Labial fricatives

VL	/-f-/ (<-F-, NF) >	OSp.	/h/	DĒFĒNSA > *defesa* (later *dehesa*) 'unenclosed pasture'; CŌNFUNDERE > *cofonder* (Nebrija *cohonder*) 'to ruin' (later *confundir*)
	or		/β/	PRŌFECTU > *provecho* 'benefit'
/β/ (<-v-)	>		/β/	NOVU > *nuevo* 'new'

Internal /ff/ and /f/ are rare in VL and the effects of lenition are obscured here by the peculiar Castilian treatment of this phoneme (see 2.5.6). It will be noted that Old Spanish at first had no labiodental phonemes, /f/ being a late medieval development (see Penny 1972a and Penny 1990b), and that if VL indeed had a contrast between /ff/ and /f/ (see 2.5.1), this contrast was later largely lost (like the contrast between /mm/ and /m/, but unlike that between other geminates and simple consonants).

3 Labial nasal

VL	/-mm-/	>	OSp.	/m/	FLAMMA > *llama* 'flame' LAMBERE > *lamer* 'to lick' (for MB > /mm/, see above)
	/-m-/	>		/m/	RĒMU > *remo* 'oar'

This is the only contrast between geminate and simple consonant which is lost in the course of the development of Spanish.

4 Dental plosives

VL	/-tt-/	>	OSp.	/t/	GUTTA > *gota* 'drop' RUPTA > *roto* 'broken'
	/-t-/	>		/d/ (= [ð])	CATĒNA > *cadena* 'chain'
	/-d-/	>		/zero/	SEDĒRE > *seer* 'to sit, be'

In general, then, the threefold VL distinction between /tt/, /t/ and /d/ is maintained in Spanish in the form of a distinction between /t/, /d/ and

/zero/. However, there is a minority of cases in which VL /-d-/ survives as /d/ in Old Spanish and which therefore attest to occasional merger of VL /t/ and /d/ (CRŪDU > *crudo* 'raw', NŌDU > *nudo* 'knot', NŪDU > *desnudo* 'naked', VADU > *vado* 'ford', etc.). Some of these forms are attested in Old Spanish without /d/ (*crúo*, etc.), and I am inclined to see the /d/ of *crudo*, etc., as a case of the influence of Latin spelling (CRUDUS, etc.) on Spanish phonology, at a time when there was genuine vernacular hesitation between, say, *crudo* and *crúo*, leading to preference, in these cases, for the more conservative form of the two.

Note that the contrast between /t/ and /d/ operates only in syllable-initial position. Where these phonemes came to occupy syllable-final (including word-final) position, through loss of an intertonic or final vowel, the opposition is neutralized in Old Spanish, as indicated by the free variation between the spellings *t* and *d* in this position. For example, the -T- of words like PARIETE, voiced to /d/ through lenition and then becoming final through loss of /-e/, appears in Old Spanish as a phoneme whose voice is irrelevant, witness the spellings *paret ~ pared*, identical to *mercet ~ merced* (the semi-learned descendant of MERCĒDE).

5 Dental ~ alveolar fricative

VL	/-ss-/	>	OSp.	/s/	OSSU > *huesso* 'bone'
					URSU > *osso* 'bear'
					IPSŌS > *essos* 'those'
	/-s-/	>		/z/	ROSA > *rosa* 'rose'
					MĒNSĒS > *meses* 'months'
					(for NS > /s/, see above)

Thus, the VL contrast between geminate and simple phoneme persists into Old Spanish, but transformed into a contrast between voiceless and voiced consonant, a distinction maintained until the sixteenth century (see 2.6.2). The spelling contrast between *ss* (for /s/) and *s* (for /z/) was maintained, with hesitations in some texts, through the Middle Ages.

As in the case of /t/ and /d/, the contrast of voice between /s/ and /z/ is neutralized in syllable-final (including word-final) position, where only the spelling *s* occurs. Thus, e.g. MĒNSE, VL. MESE > *mes* 'month', -ĒNSE > *-és* (the adj. suffix seen in *cortés, montés*, etc.), where *s* represents VL /s/, show the same final unit as those words whose final consonant descends from VL /ss/, e.g. MESSE > *mies* '(ripe) corn'. It should be noted that when these words have added to them the plural morpheme /-es/, the opposition of voice between OSp. /z/ and /s/ (spelt *s* and *ss*) is reasserted, since the phoneme which was word-final (and therefore frequently syllable-final) in the singular form is syllable-initial in the plural form. Thus, *meses, corteses*, but *miesses*.

6 Dental ~ alveolar affricate

VL /-tts-/
(2.5.2.2[1])   >   OSp.   /ts/

PETTIA > pieça 'piece'
POST COCCEU > pescueço 'neck'
RUPTIĀRE > roçar 'to scrape, etc.'
COLLACTEU > collaço 'servant, etc.'
ASCIĀTA > açada 'hoe'
CRĒSCERE > creçer 'to grow' (see 2.5.2.3)

/-ts-/ (2.5.2.2[1])   >   /dz/

MINĀCIA > amenaza 'threat' (2.5.2.2.[1])
TRĪSTITIA > tristeza 'sadness' (id.)
LŪCĒS > luzes 'lights' (2.5.2.3)

As in the previous case, the VL distinction between geminate and simple consonant is maintained in Old Spanish as a contrast between voiceless and voiced consonant, spelt ç and z respectively. This contrast was lost in the sixteenth century (see 2.6.2).

Again similarly to the previous case, syllable-final neutralization takes place between /ts/ and /dz/, the result of the neutralization being spelt z. Thus words like *faz* 'bundle' (<FASCE), *pez* 'fish' (<PISCE), where z represents VL /tts/, have the same final unit as words like *paz* 'peace' (<PĀCE), *fez* 'lees (of wine), etc.' (<FECE) It should again be noted that when these words have added to them the plural morpheme /-es/, the opposition of voice between OSp. /dz/ and /ts/ (with separate spellings z and ç respectively) is reasserted, since the phoneme which was word-final (and therefore frequently syllable-final) in the singular form is syllable-initial in the plural form. Thus, *pazes, fezes*, but *façes, peçes*.

7 Palatal fricative

VL /-ĵĵ-/(2.5.2.2[4]) > OSp.   /ĵ/

RADIU > rayo 'ray, spoke'
PLAGIA > playa 'beach'
CŪIU > cuyo 'whose'

/-ĵ-/ (2.5.2.3)   >   /zero/

RĒGĪNA > reina 'queen'

The contrast between VL geminate and simple consonant for the most part survives into Spanish (as a contrast between simple consonant and /zero/), although when a front vowel precedes the contrast is lost, since, as noted in 2.5.2.2(4), under these circumstances the product of VL /ĵĵ/ was eliminated through assimilation (SEDEAM > sea, CORRIGIA > correa, PĒIŌRE > peor, etc.).

8 Velar plosives

VL	/-kk-/	>	OSp.	/k/	SICCU > *seco* 'dry'
	/-k-/	>		/g/ (=[γ])	SĒCŪRU > *seguro* 'sure'
	/-g-/	>		/zero/	LĒGĀLE > *leal* 'loyal'

The velar plosives have therefore evolved in precisely parallel fashion to the dental plosives. This similarity of treatment extends to the dual Old Spanish outcome of /-g-/; whereas /zero/ is the commoner result, in a few cases the VL phoneme survives (as [γ]): *LEGŪMINE > *legumbre* 'vegetable', PLĀGA > *llaga* 'wound', NĀVIGĀRE > *navegar* 'to sail'. As in the case of /d/, survival of /g/ may be due to the influence of Latin on early Old Spanish, at a stage when /g/ was in the process of elimination and vernacular words could appear either with or without the phoneme. Awareness that the corresponding Latin word was spelt with g (and read aloud with /g/) may have led in some cases (including the above) to preference for the vernacular form with /g/.

It should be noted that the /k/ of -QU- is subject to the same treatment as that spelt -C- (and occurring before A, O, U), whether or not the following glide [w] survives, as it does before /a/ but not before other vowels: AQUA > *agua* 'water', SEQUERE (CL SEQUĪ) > *seguir* 'to follow' (compare 2.5.7 [end]).

9 /n/, /l/ and /r/

VL	/-nn-/	>	OSp.	/ɲ/	PANNU > *paño* 'cloth' (2.5.2.5)
					DAMNU > *daño* 'harm' (for MN > /nn/, see above, this section)
	/-n-/	>		/n/	BONU > *bueno* 'good'
	/-ll-/	>		/ʎ/	GALLU > *gallo* 'cock' (2.5.2.5)
	/-l-/	>		/l/	MALU > *malo* 'evil'
	/-rr-/	>		/ř/	TURRES > *torres* 'towers'
	/-r-/	>		/r/	PIRA > *pera* 'pear'

In these cases, then, there is a departure from the general statement made about the operation of lenition (process 1) at the beginning of this section. The geminates /nn/, /ll/ and /rr/ are not reduced to the corresponding simple consonants (as is the case with all other VL geminates). In these three cases, simplification does take place, but the resulting phoneme differs in one of its features from the predicted phoneme. The reason for this difference of behaviour is probably that the VL simple consonants /n/, /l/, and /r/ do not qualify as the input of any of the four lenition processes (i.e. they are neither geminate, voiceless, voiced plosives, nor voiced fricatives) and therefore cannot undergo any lenition change. The consequence of this lack of change is that straightforward simplification of the corresponding geminates would automatically bring about merger of /nn/ with /n/, /ll/ with /l/, and /rr/ with /r/. No doubt in order to preserve these distinctions, simplification of these geminates leads to further change: /nn/ and /ll/ are simplified and made palatal, while /rr/ is simplified by changing the VL sequence of syllable-final /-r/ + syllable-initial /r-/ to the single syllable-initial vibrative /r̄/. It is acknowledged that this account begs the question of why /mm/ and /m/ were allowed to merge: the reason conceivably lies in the number of pairs which rested on the various contrasts of geminate vs single consonant, a number which it is now practically impossible to establish.

As noted in some previous cases, contrasts which function in syllable-initial position may fail to function in syllable-final position. This is true of the contrasts between /ɲ/ and /n/, /ʎ/ and /l/ and /r̄/ and /r/. This is witnessed, historically, by the fact that when, through loss of an intertonic or final vowel, VL /nn/, /ll/ or /rr/ came to occupy syllable-final position, their Old Spanish results are identical to those of VL /n/, /l/ and /r/, respectively, i.e. OSp. /n/, /l/ and /r/. Examples of this treatment of syllable-final geminates are the following:

VL	/nn/ > /n/:	JOHANNE > *Juan* 'John'
		VL DOMNE (CL DOMINE) > */dónne/ (see above) > *don*
VL	/ll/ > /l/:	MĪLLE > *mil* 'thousand' (but cf. *mill omnes*, where the lateral is syllable-initial)
		PELLE > *piel* 'skin' (cf. OSp. plural *pielles*, now restructured as *pieles*, and contrast *valle*, *valles* 'valley(s)', where the singular has been re-structured on the basis of the plural, as in the case of OSp. *cal*, pl. *calles* 'street(s)', now *calle(s)*)
		GALLICU > *galgo* 'greyhound'
		CABALLICĀRE > *cavalgar* (later *cabalgar*) 'to ride a horse'
VL	/rr/ > /r/:	CARRICĀRE > *cargar* 'to load' (contrast CARRU > *carro* 'cart')
		TURRE *C(R)EMATA > *Torquemada* (top. and surname; *torre* 'tower' is arguably restructured on pl. *torres*)

When an internal consonant is preceded by a vowel and followed by a glide, or vice versa, at the spoken Latin stage, the effects of lenition on the consonant are not self-consistent. In the case of Latin /p/, the glide (originally following but eventually preceding; see 2.5.2.2[6]) is evidently sufficient to prevent the consonant being treated as intervocalic (and thereby prevent its voicing): SAPIAM > *sepa* (pres. subj. of *saber* 'to know'), SAPUI > OSp. *sope* > MSp. *supe* (pret. of *saber* 'to know'). However, in the case of other consonants under these conditions, lenition (in the form of voicing) *does* occur: CAUSA > *cosa* 'thing' (with voiced /z/ in Old Spanish), PLACEAT > *plega* (obsolescent form of the pres. subj. of *placer* 'to please'), PLACUIT > OSp. *plogo* > MSp. *plugo* (obsolescent pret. of *placer* 'to please'), AQUA > *agua* 'water', EQUA > *yegua* 'mare', together with other cases in which -QUA- > -*gua*-.

2.5.3.3 *Further effects of lenition: consonant* + R *or* L

The first phoneme of certain Latin consonant groups was affected by lenition, in the same way as intervocalic consonants. Latin groups include those which had long been in existence in spoken and literary Latin (sometimes called CL groups) and those which came into existence in VL through loss of intertonic vowels (see 2.4.3.3), a loss which in VL was normally limited to vowels in contact with R or L. The groups under consideration here are precisely those whose second element is R or L, but excepting the groups TL, CL and GL, whose first consonant was palatalized to [i̯] (see 2.5.2.4) before the period of operation of the lenition process and so was exempt from the latter. All other such Latin groups show lenition of the first phoneme:

-PR- >	OSp.	/br/:	CAPRA > *cabra* 'goat'
-PL- >		/bl/:	DUPLU > *doblo* > *doble* 'double'
-FR- >		/br/:	AFRICU > *ábrego* 'south wind'
-TR- >		/dr/:	PATRE > *padre* 'father'
-DR- >		/r/:	QUADRĀGINTĀ > *quaraenta* (later *cuarenta*) 'forty'
	or	/dr/:	QUADRU > *quadro* (later *cuadro*) 'picture'
-CR- >		/gr/:	SOCRU > *suegro* 'father-in-law'
-GR- >		/r/:	PIGRITIA > *pereza* 'laziness'
	or	/gr/:	NIGRA > *negra* 'black'

2.5.3.4 *The Old Spanish voiced fricative series*

As a result of changes which began in VL and continued in subsequent centuries, studied in previous sections, Old Spanish came to have a series of voiced fricative phonemes, a series originally absent from Latin (see 2.5.1–2). There were four phonemes in this series, which are now given, together with the various sources of each phoneme.

OSp. phoneme	Latin sources	Examples	See
/β/	intervocalic B	CABALLU > *cavallo*	2.5.3.1
	intervocalic v	CLĀVE > *llave*	2.5.3.1
/z/	intervocalic s	CASA > *casa*	2.5.3.2(5)
	-NS-	MĒNSA > *mesa*	2.5.3.2(5)

OSp. phoneme	Latin sources	Examples	See
/ʒ/	L + [j]	MULIERE > *mugier*	2.5.2.2(2)
	(V)CL	NOVĀC(U)LA > *navaja*	2.5.2.4
	(V)GL	REG(U)LA > *reja*	2.5.2.4
/ĵ/	initial I (+ V)	IUGU > *yugo*	2.5.2.1
	intervocalic I	MĀIŌRĒS > *mayores*	2.5.2.2(4)
	initial Gᵉ·ⁱ	GYPSU > *yesso*	2.5.2.3
	G + [j]	EXAGIU > *ensayo*	2.5.2.2(4)
	D + [j]	PODIU > *poyo*	2.5.2.2(4)
	initial Ĕ	HERBA > *yerva*	2.5.2.3

2.5.4   *Final consonants*

Not all of the Latin consonants (2.5.1) could appear in word-final position. Of those that could, only /l/, /s/, /n/, and sometimes /m/ survive into Old Spanish in that position, while /r/ becomes internal and the remainder were eliminated:

/l/   FEL > *fiel* (later *hiel*) 'gall'
       MEL > *miel* 'honey'

/s/   MINUS > *menos* 'less'
       MONTĒS > *montes* 'mountains'
       TENĒS > *tienes* 'you have'

/n/   IN > *en* 'in' (but was eventually lost in NON > *non, no* 'no')

/r/   QUATTUŌR > *quatro* (later *cuatro*) 'four'
       SEMPER > *siempre* 'always'

/t/   as the marker of 3rd singular verbs survived to the twelfth century and then fell:
       SALĪVIT > *saliot, -d* (> *salió*) 'he left'
       POTE(S)T > *puedet* (> *puede*) 'he can'

/d/   AD > *a* 'to'
       ALIQUOD > *algo* 'something'

/m/   was eliminated by the 1st century BC:
       IAM > *ya* 'now'
       SUM > *so* (later *soy*) 'I am'
       CANTĀBAM > *cantava* (later *cantaba*) 'I sang'
       NOVUM > *nuevo* 'new',
       except in a few monosyllables, where it appears as /n/:
       QUEM > *quien* 'who'
       TAM > *tan* 'so'
       CUM > *con* 'with'

/k/   ILLĪC > *alli* 'there'
       DĪC > *di* 'say (imper.)'
       NEC > *ni* 'neither'

As anticipated in 2.5.3.3, in certain cases a dental or alveolar consonant which was internal in Latin became final in Old Spanish through the loss of a final vowel (usually /e/). Apart from the cases cited in 2.5.3.3 (/t/, /ts/, /s/), in which lenition is seen to operate before the consonants become final, such consonants suffer no change from Latin to Old Spanish:

/n/   PĀNE > *pan* 'bread'
      SINE > *sin* 'without'
/l/   FIDĒLE > *fiel* 'faithful'
      MALE > *mal* 'badly'
/r/   MARE > *mar* 'sea'
      SENTĪRE > *sentir* 'to feel'
/d/   under these circumstances was eliminated (2.5.3.2[4]) before the loss of /e/:
      FIDE > *fe* 'faith'
      PEDE > *pie* 'foot'

For final /nn/, /ll/, and /rr/, see 2.5.3.2(9).

2.5.5 Secondary consonant groups

Although the development of secondary consonant groups (sometimes called 'Romance consonant groups') involves the creation of no new phonemes, the incidence of phonemes is changed thereby, so that these clusters require some consideration. Secondary groups are those which came into existence, after the Latin period, through the loss of an internal (usually intertonic) vowel. It will be recalled (from 2.4.3.3) that there were two periods of loss of intertonics, the first in VL (which gave rise to VL groups, best regarded as primary, such as CL, GL; see also 2.5.2.4), and the second later. It is this second loss (e.g. SĒMITA > *senda* 'path', VINDICĀRE > *vengar* 'to avenge') which gave rise to the groups now under consideration.

An important chronological principle underpins the development of secondary consonant groups: the intertonic vowel is lost **after** the lenition processes (2.5.3.2) have taken place, so that the consonants concerned will have undergone simplification, voicing, etc., where appropriate, **before** they are brought together in new groups. Similarly, the palatalization processes discussed in 2.5.2.2–5 antecede the loss of intertonics. This chronological principle can be illustrated by means of a case like VL ACCEPTŌRE (CL ACCIPITER). The sequence of events was probably the following:

/akkeptóre/ > akkettóre/ (2.5.3.2)
/akkettóre/ > /attsettóre/ (2.5.2.3)
/attsettóre/ > /atsetóre/ (simplification of geminates; 2.5.3.2)
/atsetóre/ > /atstóre/ (2.4.3.3)
/atstóre/ > /atstór/ (loss of final vowel; 2.4.3.2)
/atstór/ > /atsór/ *açor* (later *azor*) 'goshawk' (secondary consonant group development; this section)

Similarly, in the following cases, we can see changes affecting internal consonants before the creation of secondary groups:

LITTERA > *letra* 'letter' (simplification)
SĒMITA > *senda* 'path' (voicing)
DOMĪNICU > *domingo* 'Sunday' (voicing)
FLACCIDU > *lacio* 'lank' (palatalization and simplification of -CCᵉˑⁱ-; fricatization and loss of -D-)
CŌGITĀRE > *cuidar* 'to think', later 'to take care of' (palatalization of -Gᵉˑⁱ-; loss of voiced fricative /ǰ/)

Where an intervocalic consonant of Latin, later grouped with preceding /l/ or /r/, shows no change (e.g. SOLITĀRIU > *soltero* 'unmarried'), this usually indicates that the groupings occurred in VL (i.e. before lenition).

The consonant groups formed in this way, probably in the tenth–eleventh centuries, sometimes posed no articulatory problems and have survived unchanged. This is the case in the following instances, in some of which it is impossible to determine whether the group was formed in VL or later, given that intertonics could be lost in VL when adjacent to R or L (and sometimes S or N; see 2.4.3.3) and given that consonants grouped (in VL) with following R or L were subject to lenition in the same way as intervocalic consonants (2.5.3.2[end]). Note that ' indicates the loss of an internal vowel and ć indicates that this consonant was followed by a front vowel (and was therefore palatalized; see 2.5.2.3).

R'M	EREMU > *yermo* 'wilderness'
R'T	VĒRITĀTE > *verdad* 'truth'
R'Ć	MAURICELLU > *morziello* (later *morcillo*) 'black (horse)'
MP'R	TEMPORĀNU > *temprano* 'early'
P'R	PAUPERE > *pobre* 'poor'
B'R	LĪBERĀRE > *librar* 'to set free' (OSp. /br/, rather than /βr/, suggests early formation of the group)
F'R	BIFERA > *bebra* (later *breva*) '(black) fig' (OSp. /br/ again suggests early grouping)
T'R	LATERĀLE > *ladral* (later *adral*) 'side-board (of cart)'
D'R	HEDERA > *yedra* (later spelt *hiedra*) 'ivy' (retention of /d/ may indicate VL grouping; cf. dialectal *yera*)
TT'R	LITTERA > *letra* 'letter'
L'D	SOLIDU > *sueldo* 'certain coin' (later 'salary') (for /d/, see HEDERA, above)
L'C	ALIQUOD > *algo* 'something'
P'L	POPULU > *pueblo* 'people, town'
MP'L	POMPELŌNE > *Pamplona* (top.)
B'L	NEBULA > *niebla* 'fog'
S'L	*ĪSULA (CL ĪNSULA) > *isla* 'island'
S'N	ASINU > *asno* 'donkey'
S'C	RESECĀRE > *resgar* (later *rasgar*) 'to rip'
Ć'M	DECIMU > *diezmo* 'tithe'
Ć'N	DŪRACINU > *durazno* '(kind of) peach'

In some cases, the bringing together of the consonants concerned requires a minor phonological adjustment. Thus, neutralization of syllable-final nasals determines that if the first consonant is a nasal its place of articulation will become identical to that of the following consonant, a principle which is most evident in the case of M'cons., but applies equally to all nasals:

M'T	SĒMITA > *senda* 'path', COMITE > *conde* 'count'
N'T	BONITĀTE > *bondad* 'goodness'
N'C	DOMĪNICU > *domingo* 'Sunday'

Likewise, where -LL-, -NN- or -RR- come to be grouped with a following consonant (and therefore become syllable-final), the phonological pattern of Spanish requires that they become /l/, /n/, and /r/ respectively, rather than /λ/, /ɲ/ or /r̄/, since the latter are regularly neutralized with the former in syllable-final position (see 2.5.3.2[9] for examples).

A further case of minor adjustment is that of R when grouped with preceding N. In this (post-consonantal, syllable-initial) position, the flap /r/ is impermissible in Spanish, so that R is here replaced by the vibrative /r̄/: HONŌRĀRE > *onrrar* (later spelt *honrar*) 'to honour'.

However, certain secondary groupings of consonants produced sequences which were contrary to the phonotactic rules of Spanish (i.e. such groups were hitherto unknown and therefore 'difficult') and necessitated some radical adjustment to bring them in line with these rules. The processes of adjustment employed are assimilation, dissimilation, metathesis, epenthesis (see 2.1.1 for these processes), etc., although it should be noted that the same group, occurring in different words, may be treated in more than one way.

Assimilatory adjustment can be seen in:

D'N > /n/:	FRIDENANDU > **Frenando* > *Fernando*
Ć'T > **/dzd/ > /dz/:	PLACITU > *plazdo* > *plazo* 'time limit'
D'Ć > /ddz/ > /dz/:	DUŌDECIM > *doze* (later *doce*) 'twelve'
PT'M > /tm/ > /m/:	SEPTIMĀNA > *setmana* > *semana* 'week'

In the case of the following groups, the assimilation takes the form of the devoicing of the third consonant (if the second is voiceless), followed by loss of the middle consonant (for details, see Penny 1983b):

ND'C > /ng/:	VINDICĀRE > *vengar* 'to avenge'
ND'Ć > /ndz/:	UNDECIM > *onze* (later *once*) 'eleven'
RD'Ć > /rdz/:	QUATTUŌRDECIM > *quatorze* (later *catorce*) 'fourteen'
NT'Ć > /nts/:	PANTICE > *pança* (later *panza*) 'belly'
MP'T > /nt/:	CŌMPUTĀRE > *contar* 'to count'
SC'P > /sp/:	EPISCOPU > *obispo* 'bishop'
SP'T > /st/:	HOSPITĀLE > *hostal* 'inn'
ST'C > /sk/:	MASTICĀRE > *mascar* 'to chew'

Dissimilatory change can be seen (between nasals) in:

N'M > /lm/:	ANIMA > *alma* 'soul',
or /rm/:	MINIMĀRE > *mermar* 'to lessen, shrink'
M'N > /mr/:	HOMINE > *omne* > **omre* (> *hombre*) 'man'
NG'N > /ngr/:	SANGUINE > *sangre* 'blood'
or /ngl/:	**ĪNGUINE* > *ingle* 'groin'
ND'N > /ndr/:	LENDINE (CL LENS) > *liendre* 'nit'

Metathesis is sometimes the solution to a 'difficult' secondary group:

T'N > /nd/:	CATĒNĀTU > *candado* 'padlock', RETINA > *rienda* 'reins'
T'L > /ld/	(in certain semi-learned words): CAPITULU > *cabildo* 'chapter (meeting)'
M'L > /lm/:	CUMULU > *colmo* 'height (fig.)'
N'R > /rn/:	GENERU > *yerno* 'son in law'
	VENERIS > *viernes* 'Friday' (see above, *honrar*, and below, *engendrar*)
F'C > *[βγ] > *[uɣ] > [ɣw]:	-ĪFICĀRE > *-iguar* (e.g. SANCTĪFICĀRE > *santiguar(se)* 'to cross (oneself)')

Epenthesis is also employed (usually between nasal and liquid) to resolve a problematical sequence:

M'R > /mbr/:	HUMERU > *(h)ombro* 'shoulder'
N'R > /ndr/:	in the semi-learned treatment of INGENERARE > *engendrar* 'to engender'
M'N > /mbr/ (via /mr/, see above):	
	FĒMINA > *hembra* 'female'
	HOMINE > *(h)ombre* 'man'
M'L > /mbl/:	TREMULĀRE > *temblar* 'to tremble'

A further process of adaptation of 'difficult' secondary groups, adopted by later Old Spanish, is to replace the first consonant by the glide [u̯], which was absorbed if the preceding phoneme was a homologous (i.e. back) vowel. This is the process adopted when a labial came to be grouped with a following dental and when /l/ was preceded by /a/ and followed by /dz/:

P'T	CAPITĀLE > *cabdal* > *caudal* 'capital (sum)'
P'D	CUPIDĪTIA > *cobdicia* > *codicia* 'covetousness'
B'T	CUBITU > *cobdo* > *codo* 'elbow'
V'T	CĪVITĀTE > *cibdad* > *ciudad* 'city'
B'D	DĒBITA > *debda* > *deuda* 'debt'
L'Ć	SALICE > *salze* > *sauce* 'willow'

When the first consonant of a secondary group was T or D, the Old Spanish result was at first the expected /d/ + cons. However, in later OSp., neutralization took place between syllable-final /d/ and /dz/, in favour of the latter, a process reflected in the replacement of the spelling *d* by *z*:

T'C	PORTĀTICU > *portadgo* > *portazgo* 'transit tax'
D'C	IUDICĀRE > *judgar* > *juzgar* 'to judge'
T'M	EPITHEMA > (semi-learned) *bidma* > *bizma* 'poultice'

Finally, note the treatment of CT, X, and GN when they constitute the first two consonants of a secondary group of three (2.5.2.4).

2.5.6   The development of Latin F

Modern Spanish words which descend orally from Latin words in F- reveal that there are two treatments of the Latin phoneme, as exemplified by the following:

1 FĪCU > *higo* 'fig'
   FĪLIU > *hijo* 'son'
   FĪLU > *hilu* 'thread'
   FARĪNA > *harina* 'flour'
   FACERE > *hacer* 'to do'
   FŌRMA > *horma* 'shoemaker's last'
   FORNU > *horno* 'oven'
2 FORTE > *fuerte* 'strong'
   FONTE > *fuente* 'spring'
   FRONTE > *frente* 'forehead'
   FOLLE > *fuelle* 'bellows'

In Old Spanish, all such words were spelt with *f* (*figo, fijo, filo, farina, fazer, forma, forno, fuerte, fruente, fuelle*), as were learned words drawn from Latin terms spelt with F- (*forma* 'shape', *falso* 'false', *fama* 'fame', *figura* 'image', etc). The modern spellings (*h* and *f*) reflect a phonemic split which will be discussed in 2.6.4, but it is arguable that until the late Middle Ages all the popular words concerned here had the same initial phoneme, with allophonic variation governed by the following phoneme.

The process by which Latin F- came to be eliminated from most popular Spanish words has been the subject of intense debate. An outline of this debate can be seen in Menéndez Pidal 1964a: 198–208, or in Baldinger 1972: 22–7. Discussion has been polarized between, on the one hand, accounts which appeal to substratum influence (exercised by Basque) on the Latin of Cantabria, and, on the other hand, those which seek purely intra-Latin explanations. The chief exponent of the former view is Menéndez Pidal (1964a: 198–233), who assembles data from medieval Hispanic documents, from modern Basque and from Gascon, to suggest that the absence of a labiodental phoneme /f/ from the pre-Roman language of N Central Spain and SW Gaul (i.e. Basque) had the consequence that, as speakers of Basque became bilingual in Latin, they replaced Lat. /f/ by means of sounds familiar in their native speech, of which the aspirate /h/ is the main survivor (in Gascon and Medieval Spanish, as in some modern Spanish dialects). The main objections to this theory are, firstly, that the development F- > /h/ is found in some (small) Romance territories where Basque influence is evidently impossible, and, secondly, that such a substratum account has difficulty in explaining why the words of group 2 (above) appear in Spanish with /f/. To expand on this second point, if Latin F- was replaced by /h/ in FARĪNA, etc., why was it not also replaced in FORTE, etc.? (The fact that rural dialects of Spain and America do indeed employ /huérte/ where the standard has *fuerte* does not answer the question why the standard shows /f/ in the words of group 2.) Adherents of substratum theory typically appeal to dialect mixing in order to explain the /f/ of *fuerte*, etc., seeing it as a phoneme borrowed from dialects spoken to the south of the area where Castilian originated (see 1.3.2), during the territorial expansion of Castilian which began in the early Reconquest.

Those who seek an internal Latin explanation for the loss of F- in Spanish have sometimes turned to regional Latin pronunciation (see, e.g., Penny 1972a and 1990b). It is possible that the spoken Latin of remoter areas (such as Cantabria) preserved a bilabial articulation (/φ/) of F-, which had earlier been normal in Latin but which had been replaced by labiodental /f/ in Rome and in those areas in closest contact with Rome. Such a bilabial articulation of F-, together with normal allophonic variation, governed by the nature of the following phoneme, may have led to a pattern like the following in the late VL of Cantabria:

> /φ/   realized as [ʍ] in words where the initial phoneme was followed by the
> glide [w], whose appearance was due to diphthongization (see 2.4.2.2);
> e.g. FŎRTE > [ʍwórte] or [ʍwérte];
> realized as [φ] elsewhere: [φrído] < FRĪGIDU, [φarína] < FARĪNA.

Through dissimilation of bilabial /φ/ to [h] before the (labial) vowels /o/ and /u/, the range of allophones was possibly increased, at an early period, to the following:

> /φ/:   [ʍ] before [w]: [ʍwérte];
> [h] before syllabic /o/, /u/ (i.e. not [w]): [hórno] < FURNU;
> [φ] elsewhere (includes other vowels, the glide [j], /r/, /l/): [φarína],
> [φrído]

As a result of a process of generalization of the allophone [h], which operated in such a way that [h] came to occur before all syllabic vowels (rather than only before back vowels, as hitherto), the following situation was reached (which was probably that of Old Spanish, until about the thirteenth century, and is certainly that of many rural dialects of Spanish today, e.g. Santander, Extremadura, W Andalusia, varieties of American Spanish):

> /φ/:   [ʍ] before [w]: [ʍwérte];
> [h] before all syllabic vowels and [j]: [hórno], [harína], [hjéro] < FERRU;
> [φ] before /r/ (FL- having been modified either to /ʎ/ (2.5.2.6) or to /l/):
> [φrío]

It is only in later OSp. that the allophones [ʍ] and [φ] were modified to labiodental [f], principally in urban Spanish (which forms the basis of the standard). This change may have been initiated by Frenchmen (speakers of French and Provençal) who entered Spain in large numbers in the twelfth and thirteenth centuries, sometimes occupying positions of great social prestige. Such people, as they learned Castilian, would have had difficulty imitating the labiovelar [ʍ] and the bilabial [φ], and may have replaced them with the most similar sound of their native language (namely [f]), a practice which arguably then spread to native speakers of Spanish, particularly those of educated, urban background, who would have been in closest contact with Frenchmen (Penny 1972a). Note that speakers of twelfth-century French would have no difficulty in adopting the allophone [h], since contemporary French included such an aspirate. Following such a change, late medieval urban Spanish would have included the following sounds (still perhaps best regarded as allophones of a single phoneme, which is here arbitrarily designated /h/):

/h/: [f] before [w] and /r/: [fwérte], [frío];
　　[h] elsewhere (i.e. before syllabic vowels and [j]): [harína], [hórno]

We shall see (2.6.4) that these two allophones were eventually phono-logized, providing Spanish with two distinct phonemes, /f/ and /h/, although the latter was being dropped from pronunciation in Old Castile in the later Middle Ages and this /h/-dropping continued to spread territori-ally and socially, until in the sixteenth century, /h/-less pronunciation became standard, a change which brought about the following pattern:

/f/:　　　　/fuérte/ *fuerte*, /frío/ *frio*, etc.
/zero/:　　/arína/ *harina*, /órno/ *horno*, /jéɾo/ *hierro*, etc.

It should be remembered that all the words considered in this section (i.e. all the words descended from Latin forms in F-) were spelt with *f*-throughout the Middle Ages, obscuring phonetic and phonological change. It was not until the late fifteenth and early sixteenth century that the spelling *h* came to be used in the case of those words which at that time had initial /h/. Thus OSp. *figo, fijo, filo, farina, fazer, forma, forno*, etc., were replaced by *higo, hijo, hilo, harina, hacer, horma, horno*, etc., while *fuerte, fuente, fruente, fuelle*, etc., continued with their traditional spelling. It should be noted that the graphical change (*f* replaced by *h*) is not contemporary with the phonological change F- > /h/, which occurred centuries earlier. The spelling change sprang from the need (felt in the late Middle Ages) to provide distinct spellings for what were for the first time two separate phonemes, i.e. to distinguish pairs like /hórma/ 'shoemaker's last' and /fórma/ 'shape', hitherto both spelt *forma*. Indeed, by the time the use of *h* had become normal in *horno, hablar*, etc., a substantial proportion of Spanish speakers no longer used any consonant at the beginning of such words.

For a medieval orthographical experiment to distinguish /h/ and /f/, by using *ff* for /f/, see Blake 1988a, 1988b.

The spread (social and territorial) of an innovation should always be carefully distinguished from the cause(s) of that innovation. Although the causes of the change by which Lat. F- becomes Sp. /h/ are by no means fully clarified, the spread of the articulation [h] is reasonably well established (see Menéndez Pidal 1964a: 219–33). Up to the period of the beginnings of Castilian expansion (early tenth century), [h] was limited to the area of origin, Cantabria (Santander, N Burgos, parts of the Basque country); other areas employed either [f] or [φ]. As Castile expands in the early Reconquest (tenth-thirteenth centuries), [h] comes to be used throughout Old Castile, begins to encroach upon León and perhaps begins to extend over the Guadarrama. In the later Middle Ages and early modern period (thirteenth–sixteenth centuries), [h] becomes part of standard (Toledan) pronunciation and is extended to S. Spain, with the Reconquest, except for Portuguese- and Catalan-speaking areas. It also expands vigorously into Leonese territory. At the same time as [h] was enjoying this success in the South and West, it was being replaced by /zero/ in Burgos and other areas of Old Castile. The sixteenth-century contrast between the Burgos pronunciation /ablár/, etc., and the Toledan pronunciation /hablár/, is well known. Following the establishment of the northern, /h/-less, pronunciation in Madrid in the 1560s, this style becomes the norm and is increasingly extended to all areas of Castilian speech, /h/ only surviving in remoter rural areas (W Santander, E Asturias, W Salamanca, Extremadura, W Andalusia, parts of America).

2.5.7   *Other initial consonants*

With the exception of /f-/ (2.5.6), and of the velars /k/ and /g/ when followed by front vowels (2.5.2.3), the Latin consonants in word-initial position were extremely stable, passing unchanged into Spanish in almost all instances. Only in the case of /r-/ and /k-/ (followed by non-front vowels) do we find departure from this norm.

It is observable that most initial consonants of Latin have an identical outcome in Spanish (and in other varieties of Western Romance) to that of their internal geminate counterparts. Thus initial /t-/ in TERRA and /tt/ in GUTTA both appear in Spanish as /t/ (*tierra, gota*) and both Latin /p-/ and /pp/ (PETRA, CUPPA) appear as Spanish /p/ (*piedra, copa*). However, in those instances where a Latin geminate is *not* reduced to its single correlate in

Spanish (i.e. in the case of -LL-, -NN-, -RR-; see 2.5.2.3.2[9]), there consequently arises a potential failure of this rule, and -LL- and -NN- do indeed have a different outcome in Spanish from L- and N-, despite some evidence in pre-literary Spanish (see Menéndez Pidal 1960: xcv–xcvii) of a move, ultimately thwarted, to palatalize initial L- and N- and thereby give them the same outcome as -LL- and -NN-. However, in the case of R- and -RR-, similarity of treatment of initial and geminate consonants *is* preserved, by changing the initial consonant's articulation from flap /r/ to vibrative /r̄/. This phonological change, which is masked by absence of any corresponding spelling change, has no exceptions in Spanish.

Initial /k-/ is the other phoneme which shows departure from the rule that the initial consonants of Latin are preserved unchanged in Spanish, although in this case the change is sporadic. Indeed, most cases of Latin /k-/ before non-front vowels show /k/ in Spanish: CUPPA > *copa* 'wine glass', CAPRA > *cabra* 'goat', CORNU > *cuerno* 'horn', etc. However, in a few cases we find voicing of /k-/ (i.e. the same treatment as in intervocalic position; see 2.5.3.2[8]): CATTU > *gato* 'cat', VL *COLOPU (CL COLAPHU) > *golpe* 'blow'.

Initial consonant groups were limited to /s/ + cons., cons. + /l/, cons. + /r/, and /kw/. The first of these types, /s/ + cons., remained unchanged, except for the addition of a preceding vowel (see 2.3.3), while PL-, CL-, FL- frequently produced palatal results (see 2.5.2.6), although in the case of FL- the ultimate result was occasionally /l/ (FLACCIDU > *llacio* > *lacio* 'lank'). Other initial combinations of cons. + /l/ are BL- and GL-, of which the first is retained unchanged in Spanish (BLANDU > *blando* 'soft'), while the second most frequently shows elimination of the first consonant (i.e. the /g/ receives the treatment it most frequently receives in intervocalic position [see 2.5.3.2(8)], as we have just seen occasionally occurs in the case of initial /k/): GLĪRE + suffix > *lirón* 'dormouse', GLATTĪRE > *latir* 'to throb, yelp', GLOBELLU > *luviello* > *ovillo* 'ball (of wool, etc.)' (with false separation of /l-/: *el luviello* > *el uviello*).

Cons. + /r/ is highly stable and rarely undergoes change. Only in the case of CR- do we find occasional instances of voicing to /gr/, similar to those seen in the case of ungrouped Latin /k-/ (above): CRĒTA > *greda* 'chalk', CRASSU > *graso* 'fatty'. However, these cases may not represent a regular change in Spanish; they may descend from VL forms which already displayed GR-, in cases like *greda* because of the frequent Latin adaptation of Gk. x as G-, and in the case of *graso* by analogical imitation of the initial group of GROSSU 'fat, stout' (whence *grueso* 'id.').

QU- (= [kw]) can be regarded in some sense as a group, consisting of the voiceless velar /k/ together with the opening glide [w]. Under almost all circumstances, the glide was lost (at a period prior to the appearance of written Spanish) and /k/ remained unchanged, although the digraph *qu-* was used before /e/ and /i/ in Old Spanish as well as in the modern language, and also sometimes before /a/ in Old Spanish:

> QUAERERE > *querer* 'to wish'
> QUĪNDECIM > *quince* 'fifteen'
> QUĪNGENTŌS > *quinientos* 'five hundred'
> QUATTUORDECIM > OSp. *quatorze* (*qu-* = /k/?) ∼ *catorze*, MSp. *catorce* 'fourteen'
> *QUASSICĀRE > *cascar* 'to crack'
> VL QUOMO (CL QUŌMODŌ) > *como* 'as, how'

However, where QU- is immediately followed by tonic /a/, the glide was retained as well as the /k/. Old Spanish spelling employs *qu-* also in this case; the spelling *cu-* dates from the nineteenth century.

> QUATTUOR > *quatro*, later *cuatro* 'four'
> QUĀLE > *qual*, later *cual* 'which'

2.5.8 The Old Spanish consonant system

As a result of the changes so far studied, the consonantal system of Latin (2.5.1) was transformed into the following Old Spanish system, character-istic of the literary period (twelfth–fifteenth centuries):

	labial	dental	alveolar	prepalatal	midpalatal	velar
voiceless plosive/affricate	/p/	/t/	/ts/	/tʃ/		/k/
voiced plosive/affricate	/b/	/d/	/dz/			/g/
voiceless fricative			/s/	/ʃ/		/h/
voiced fricative	/β/		/z/	/ʒ/	/ʝ/	
nasal	/m/		/n/	/ɲ/		
lateral			/l/	/ʎ/		
vibrative			/r̄/			
flap			/r/			

2.6 Phonological change since the Middle Ages

The phonological changes that have affected Spanish since the late Middle Ages all belong to the consonantal system and in many instances are cases of merger.

2.6.1 The merger of OSp. /b/ and /β/

This case was studied in 2.1.3.2 to exemplify the process of merger, but will here be considered in more detail.

Relative consistency of spelling in Old Spanish, and rhyme in Old Spanish verse, suggest a contrast, in many positions, between a voiced bilabial plosive /b/ (spelt *b*) and a voiced bilabial fricative /β/ (spelt *v*). In intervocalic position this contrast is certain:

/b/: *cabe* (pres. ind. *caber*; < CAPIT)
/β/: *cave* (pres. subj. *cavar*; < CAVET)

It is also likely that this contrast applied in initial position, at least when the word was preceded by a vowel or by certain consonants:

/b/: *bienes* 'possessions' (< BENE)
/β/: *vienes* 'you come' (< VENĪS)

Had the products of Latin B- and V- merged before the Old Spanish period, it is unlikely that Old Spanish spelling could have achieved such a high degree of consistency in the distinction of *b* (< B-) and *v* (< V-). After all, OSp. spelling makes no attempt to distinguish the products of Latin -B- and -V- (which had merged, in VL), but spells both with *v*.

However, in consonant clusters, confusion of spelling (e.g. *alba ~ alva* 'dawn') suggests neutralization, just as occasional hesitation between *b* and *v* in initial position suggests that, after certain phonemes, initial /b/ and /β/ were indistinguishable. To take the example of the *Cantar de mio Cid* (early thirteenth-century?), initial *b* and *v* are contrasted, in most cases, in the expected way, but there is a minority of cases (see Menéndez Pidal 1964b: 172–3) in which initial *b* and *v* are muddled: *vando ~ bando* (*b* expected), *bistades ~ vestidas*, *ban ~ van*, *boz ~ voz* (*v* expected), etc. Working with knowledge of the modern language, it is possible to suggest that neutralization of initial /b/ and /β/ occurred when they were preceded by a pause or when the preceding word ended in a nasal: *un buey* 'an ox', *un viento* 'a wind', and commands like *baxa* 'come down!' and *ven* 'come!' were probably all articulated with [b].

Neutralization took a further step when /b/ (like /d/ and /g/) took on fricative articulation in a wide number of environments, notably when preceded by a vowel. In later Old Spanish, it is likely that phrases like *no me baxo* 'I'm not coming down' and *no me voy* 'I'm not going' showed [β] at the beginning of both verbs. By the end of the fourteenth century, it is likely that initial /b/ and /β/ were neutralized in all environments and that the phonemic contrast survived only in intervocalic position. It is in the fifteenth century that the merger is completed. Some poets of this period allow words like *cabe*, *recibo*, *acaba*, *sabe* and *arriba* to rhyme with words like *suave*, *bivo*, *matava*, *grave* and *viva*, and although some sixteenth-century poets, such as Garcilaso (under Italian influence?), maintain the old distinction, such practice was by then no doubt out of touch with everyday (including educated) speech. No poet born after 1550 avoids rhyming *b* with *v*. The merger was by then complete in all varieties of Spanish.

For more detailed discussion of this topic, see Alonso 1967: 21–61, Alonso 1962: 155–209, Penny 1976.

Despite the merger of /b/ and /β/, Spanish spelling continues to use both the letters *b* and *v*. In initial position, the modern use of these letters is the same as the medieval practice, except for the occasional adjustment, made for etymological reasons, such as *bivo* and *boz* replaced by *vivo* and *voz*. In intervocalic position, the descendant of Latin -B- was spelt *v* until the late eighteenth century, but this letter was then replaced in the relevant words by *b*, again on etymological grounds. Medieval and modern use of intervocalic *b* and *v* can be summarized thus:

Latin	Sp. to 1800	Sp. from 1800
SAPIT	*sabe*	*sabe*
DĒBET	*deve*	*debe*
LAVAT	*lava*	*lava*

2.6.2 The Old Spanish sibilants

The term **sibilant** refers to fricative or affricate consonants articulated in the dental, alveolar and palatal areas; Old Spanish (see 2.5.8) had seven such phonemes, of which we shall disregard /tʃ/, since it passes unchanged into the modern language. The remaining six phonemes were organized in three pairs

	Voiceless	Voiced
Dental affricates	/ts/	/dz/
Alveolar fricatives	/s/	/z/
Prepalatal fricatives	/ʃ/	/ʒ/

for which the following spellings were used in intervocalic position:

/ts/ *c* or *ç*:	*decir* 'to descend', *alçar* 'to raise', *caça* 'hunt'
/dz/ *z*:	*dezir* 'to say', *pozo* 'well'
/s/ *ss*:	*espesso* 'thick', *passo* 'step'
/z/ *s*:	*espeso* 'spent', *casa* 'house'
/ʃ/ *x*:	*fixo* 'fixed', *dixo* 'he said', *caxa* 'box'
/ʒ/ *j* or *g*:	*fijo* 'son', *mejor* 'better', *mugier* 'woman'

It is possible that the phoneme /ʒ/, here described as fricative, was affricate in at least some of its realizations (e.g. after a pause or after certain consonants).

This sub-system underwent a series of three changes:

    1 The affricates /ts/ and /dz/ (together with any affricate realizations of /ʒ/) were weakened to fricatives. Similar changes affect most other W. Romance languages and may be regarded as cases of economy of effort, affricates being rather more 'expensive' in terms of energy than other

consonants. It is uncertain when this weakening occurred in Spanish, since, owing to the previous absence of dental fricatives from Spanish and the consequent impossibility of any merger resulting, it has no effect on the Spanish phonological system and is therefore not reflected in spelling. It seems likely, however, that the change was accomplished during the fifteenth century, so that by the end of the Middle Ages, the sibilant sub-system of Spanish comprised six fricatives:

	Voiceless	Voiced
Dental fricatives	/ş/	/ʑ/
Alveolar fricatives	/s/	/z/
Prepalatal fricatives	/ʃ/	/ʒ/

2 The three voiced phonemes came to be devoiced and therefore merged with their voiceless counterparts. Neutralization of voiced and voiceless phonemes in syllable-final position had probably always been the norm in Spanish (see 2.5.3.2(4–6)), a feature reflected in the fact that in this position there was no spelling contrast in Old Spanish between *c*/*ç* and *z*, between *ss* and *s* or between *x* and *j*/*g*; only *z*, *s*, and *x* were respectively used, e.g. *faz*, singular of *faces* (<FASCĒS) 'bundles', *cascar* (<*QUASSICĀRE) 'to split' (vs. *passo* 'step' <PASSU), *linax* (a variant of *linage*) 'lineage', *relox* (<OCat. *relotge*, where *tg* indicates a voiced phoneme) 'clock'.

In syllable-initial position, the contrast of voice is lost (in favour of voiceless values) in the standard Spanish of the sixteenth century. Absence of voiced sibilants had probably been a feature of extreme northern varieties of Castilian (and of other northern dialects) for some centuries and some scholars have seen influence from the neighbouring Basque language (which also lacks voiced sibilants) as the cause (e.g. Martinet 1974: 448–61, Jungemann 1955: 318–35). Now, with the establishment of Madrid as the capital of Spain in the 1560s and the influx of northerners into the new capital, the merger of the voiced sibilants with the voiceless spreads south and becomes the norm in the standard language (see Alonso 1967, 1969). Speakers in Toledo and further south for some time adhered to the older system, a territorial distinction which is referred to in the much-quoted statement of Fray Juan de Córdoba (published in Mexico in 1578, but referring to the linguistic situation in Spain several decades earlier): 'Los de Castilla la Vieja dizen haçer y en Toledo hazer, y (los de Castilla la Vieja) dizen xugar, y en Toledo (dizen) jugar', where the graphs *ç* and *x* represent the new voiceless articulation, typical then of the northern half of the Peninsula, by contrast with *z* and *j*, which reflect the traditional voiced pronunciation, still found from Toledo southwards.

Evidence also comes from misspelling. While most writers continue to make the graphical distinction set out at the beginning of this section, the more careless are betrayed by their pronunciation into confusion of *c*/*ç* with *z*, *ss* with *s* and *x* with *j*/*g*. Thus, Santa Teresa (b. Avila, 1515) spells *açer*, *reçar*, *deçir* (for the currently correct *hazer*, *rezar*, *dezir*), *tuviese*, *matasen*, etc. (for *tuviesse*, *matassen*, etc.), *dijera*, *ejerçiçio*, *teoloxia* (for *dixera*, *exercicio*, *teologia*).

As a result of the devoicing (and the consequent mergers) discussed here, the sibilant sub-system of sixteenth-century Spanish was reduced to three voiceless fricative phonemes:

Dental fricative   /ş/ e.g.   *caça* /káşa/ (previously /kátsa/)
                                  dezir /deşír/ (previously /dedzír/)

Alveolar fricative   /s/   *passo* /páso/ (no change)
                                  casa /kása/ (previously /káza/)

Prepalatal fricative   /ʃ/   *caxa* /káʃa/ (no change)
                                  mejor /meʃór/ (previously /meʒór/)

3 The dental and prepalatal phonemes changed locus, because of the great functional load placed upon the contrast of locus which separated /ş/, /s/ and /ʃ/. There had always been some interchange between alveolar and prepalatal fricatives (e.g. the Old Spanish competition between *tisera(s)* (<TŌNSŌRIĀS) and its replacement *tijeras* 'scissors'), but by the late sixteenth century there were many pairs (even triplets) of words whose meanings were distinguished by the locus of the relevant consonant. A case in point is provided by the words *caça* 'hunt', *casa* 'house', and *caxa* 'box'; meaning is now crucially dependent upon the correct production and perception of, respectively, the dental, alveolar and prepalatal locus of the intervocalic consonant. The potential confusion could only be avoided by making more perceptible the acoustic difference between the phonemes and this was achieved (for the most part) by exaggerating the contrasts of locus: /ş/ was moved forwards (away from /s/) and became interdental /θ/, while /ʃ/ was moved backwards (also away from /s/) and became velar /x/. Thus, words like *caça, alçar, dezir, pozo* achieved their modern pronunciation /θ/ and *dixo, caxa, hijo, mugier*, etc., acquired their current pronunciation, /x/ (although the modern spellings of such words only emerged as a result of eighteenth- and nineteenth-century reforms).

These changes of locus were spreading through society from the late sixteenth century and became normal by about the middle of the seventeenth (see Alonso 1967, 1969), although it is evident that the educated pronunciation of the early seventeenth century still preferred prepalatal /ʃ/, since the French and Italian adaptations of the name *Don Quixote* (*Don Quichotte*, and *Don Chisciotto*, respectively) show that the Spanish word was still pronounced /kiʃóte/ by at least some speakers.

The changes discussed in this section (2.6.2) can be summarized in the following way:

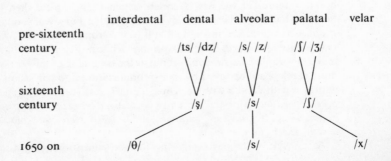

	interdental	dental	alveolar	palatal	velar
pre-sixteenth century		/ts/ /dz/	/s/ /z/	/ʃ/ /ʒ/	
sixteenth century		/ş/	/s/	/ʃ/	
1650 on	/θ/		/s/		/x/

2.6.3 The sibilants in Andalusian and American Spanish

In Seville and, as a result, much of Andalusia and all of America, the sibilants were affected by a slightly different sequence of changes from that just examined (2.6.2) in the standard language. In southern texts of the fifteenth and sixteenth centuries, *ss* and *s* are occasionally replaced by *ç* and *z* respectively (e.g. *paço* for *passo*, *caza* for *casa*) and vice versa. Contemporary observers, because of their preoccupation with spelling (rather than sound), gave the name **çeçeo** (i.e. 'abuse of the letter *ç*') to cases like *paço* for *passo* and used the term **zezeo** ('abuse of the letter *z*') for cases like *caza* for *casa*. Such spelling errors are motivated by phonological changes which were in progress in the south of Spain, namely the merger of the alveolar sibilants with the dentals, in favour of the dentals:

Although full merger of these pairs of phonemes begins, as we have noted, in the fifteenth century, neutralization of /ş/ and /s/, /ʒ/ and /z/ is observable in syllable-final position rather earlier, and not only in Andalusia, as can be seen in misspellings like *azno* for *asno*, *diesmo* for *diezmo*, and in the occasional standard form like *mezclar* 'to mix' (< OSp. *mesclar* < VL *MISCULĀRE).

Rather than by a change of locus of alveolar /s/ and /z/ to dental /ş/ and /ʒ/ this merger may have been motivated by the absence from medieval Andalusian speech of the alveolars /s/ and /z/. Corresponding to standard /s/ and /z/, southern speech may have had the dentals /ş/ and /ʒ/ (perhaps due to influence from Mozarabic or Arabic), so that the reduction of the (dental) affricates /ts/ and /dz/ to fricatives (see 2.6.2[1]) caused immediate merger with pre-existing /ş/ and ʒ/:

Whichever of these two accounts of the merger is correct, the two products of the merger (/ş/ and /ʒ/) were themselves merged in /ş/. This merger of voiced /ʒ/ with voiceless /ş/ occurs for the same reasons and at the same time as the general devoicing of sibilants in Spanish (see 2.6.2[2]), so that four medieval sibilants (/ts/, /dz/, /s/ and /z/) are reduced in most Andalusian (and all American) speech to a single phoneme (/ş/). Thus OSp. *caça*, *dezir*, *passo* and *casa* have come to share the phoneme /ş/ in the areas named (/káşa/, /deşír/, /páşo/, /káşa/), a process which has brought about a number of homonymic collisions such as those between *caza* 'hunt' and *casa* 'house', or between *cocer* 'to cook' and *coser* 'to sew'.

Since its emergence from /ts/, /dz/, /s/ and /z/ the phoneme /ş/ has come to be realized in two distinctive manners in Andalusian Spanish. In much of central Andalusia (including the cities of Seville and Córdoba) and also in the Canaries and throughout America, /ş/ is realized as a dental sibilant (not dissimilar to English or French /s/); this dental result of the merger is referred to as **seseo**. In other areas (particularly the coastal areas of Andalusia, including the cities of Huelva, Cádiz, Málaga and Granada), a fronted variety of /ş/ has come to be preferred. Although not identical to standard interdental /θ/, its acoustic effect is somewhat similar, and where this fronted variant is used, the local speech is described as showing **ceceo**. For *seseo* and *ceceo*, see Lapesa 1980: 283–4, 374–6, 508–9, 562–8.

The remaining sibilants behave in southern and American speech in a similar, but not identical, way to that seen in the standard. Devoicing of medieval /ʒ/ brings merger with /ʃ/ (see 2.6.2[2]), and this phoneme is then retracted to avoid confusion with /s/ (see 2.6.2[3]). However. whereas in the standard the result of this retraction is velar /x/, the process was more extreme in the regions now under consideration, resulting in laryngeal or glottal /ɦ/; thus, OSp. *caxa* and *mejor* (MSp. *caja, mejor*) are pronounced in these areas /káɦa/ and /meɦór/, a result which brings the consequence of merger with the /h/ descended from Lat. F- in areas where the latter survived (chiefly rural W Andalusia and rural American varieties). The Andalusian and American development of the sibilants can therefore be summarized as follows:

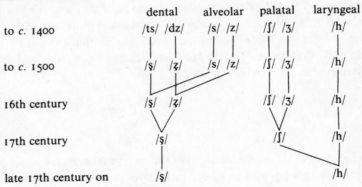

	dental	alveolar	palatal	laryngeal
to *c.* 1400	/ts/ /dz/	/s/ /z/	/ʃ/ /ʒ/	/h/
to *c.* 1500	/ş/ /ʐ/	/s/ /z/	/ʃ/ /ʒ/	/h/
16th century	/ş/ /ʐ/		/ʃ/ /ʒ/	/h/
17th century	/ş/		/ʃ/	/h/
late 17th century on	/ş/			/h/

2.6.4   *The phonologization of /f/ and /h/*

We have seen (2.5.6) that in the Middle Ages, Spanish lacked a phoneme /f/, although in urban (including standard) Spanish, the sound [f] had come into existence, as one of the allophones of a phoneme here arbitrarily designated /h/:

/h/: [f] before [w] and /r/: [fwérte], [frío];
 [h] elsewhere (i.e. before syllabic vowels and [j]): [harína], [hórno], [hjéřo]

all such words being written with a single letter (*f*), as befitted the monophonemic status of their initial consonant: *fuerte, frío, farina, forno, fierro.*

This case of complementary distribution of allophones was changed by the increasing introduction in Old Spanish of borrowings from Latin and Old Gallo-Romance. In the case of borrowings of words spelt *f* in the source-language, the Spanish sound [f] was used, in the first case because this was now the sound used in reading aloud Latin F and in the second case directly imitated from speakers of French or Provençal. In this way, [f] came to be used in environments from which it had previously been excluded (*viz.* before syllabic vowels and [j]) and could thereby come into meaningful contrast with [h]. Thus, the learned word *forma* 'shape', pronounced [fórma], contrasted with the popular word [hórma] 'shoemaker's last' (also spelt *forma*). From this stage onwards, Spanish is best described as having two phonemes /h/ and /f/, and at the very end of the fifteenth century, the spelling system of Spanish comes to reflect the phonological reality through the use, for the first time, of *h* to indicate /h/, leaving *f* to indicate the newly phonologized /f/; this spelling contrast is clearly seen in the works of Antonio de Nebrija, where words with /h/ receive their modern spelling (e.g. *horma* 'shoemaker's last') and only words with /f/ are spelt with *f* (e.g. *forma* 'shape'). For further discussion, see Penny 1990b.

2.6.5 Learned consonant groups

Many groups of consonants which had existed in Latin had been reduced to single phonemes during the development from Latin to Old Spanish. Thus the groups represented in Latin by the spellings CT, GN, X, MN, PT, PS, etc., had been resolved in the following ways:

CT > /tʃ/:	FACTU > *hecho* 'done'	see 2.5.2.4
GN > /ɲ/:	PUGNU > *puño* 'fist'	see 2.5.2.4
X > /ʃ/:	DĪXĪ > *dixe* (later *dije*) 'I said'	see 2.5.2.4
MN > /ɲ/:	SCAMNU > *escaño* 'bench'	see 2.5.3.2(3)
PT > /t/:	APTĀRE > *atar* 'to tie'	see 2.5.3.2(4)
PS > /s/:	IPSA > *essa* (later *esa*) 'that'	see 2.5.3.2(5)

However, many learned words borrowed in the late Middle Ages and (increasingly) in the Golden Age, were adaptations of Latin words which contained such groups, and these groups now posed a phonological problem for Spanish. At this stage of the language's development, velar consonants and /p/ were impermissible in syllable-final position; that is, the orally inherited word-stock showed no instances of such phonemes in this position. Similarly, syllable-final /m/ could not occur before /n/, and although syllable-final /b/ did occur in some words (only before /d/), it was already being replaced by /u/ or /zero/ (as in OSp. *cabdal > caudal*, OSp. *dubda > duda*; see 2.5.5 [end]). The problem posed by learned words containing impermissible groups was solved in two ways: by simplifying the group, usually through loss of the first consonant; or by attempting to pronounce both (or all three) consonants, thus introducing new phonotactic possibilities to Spanish. In the large majority of relevant learned words, both processes are applied, so that in late Old Spanish and in Golden Age Spanish, double forms (both in pronunciation and spelling) are frequent in such cases:

CT	*efeto*	*efecto*	< EFFECTU
CT (before I + vowel)			
	lición	*lección*	< LĒCTIONE
GN	*sinificar*	*significar*	< SIGNIFICĀRE
X	*examen* (/ʃ/)	*examen* (/ks/)	< EXĀMEN
	exercer (/ʃ/)	*exercer* (/ks/)	< EXERCĒRE
XC	*ecelente*	*excelente*	< EXCELLENTE
MN	*solene*	*solemne*	< SOLLEMNE
PT	*acetar*	*aceptar*	< ACCEPTĀRE
MPT	*pronto*	*prompto*	< PROMPTU
NST	*istante*	*instante*	< INSTANTE
BST	*astener*	*abstener*	< ABSTINĒRE

In the case of syllable-final /p/ and /b/ (and sometimes /k/), there was a third possibility in Golden Age Spanish: modification to the glide [u̯], like the treatment accorded to OSp. syllable-final /b/ (e.g. *cabdal > caudal*). Thus alongside *acetar* and *aceptar*, *afeto* and *afecto* we find spellings like *aceutar*, *afeuto*.

This variety of forms was eventually resolved (by the Academy in the late eighteenth century) in favour of the more latinate forms (those with the consonant group intact): *efecto*, *significar*, etc. As a result, the phonology of Spanish had come to accept syllable-final /k/, /g/, /p/ and /b/ (although with neutralization of /k/ and /g/, as of /p/ and /b/; see Alarcos 1965: 184–5). There are only two exceptions to this statement: on the one hand, non-standard Spanish has not accepted these syllable-final consonants and continues to prefer forms like *efeto* or *efeuto*, and, on the other hand, even in the standard there is a minority of individual learned words which have come through into the modern language in a simplified form (sometimes alongside an unsimplified form, with different meaning), e.g.

CT   *luto* 'mourning' < LŪCTU (cf. *luctuoso* 'mournful')
       plática 'chatter' < PRACTICA (cf. *práctica* 'practice')
       afición 'liking' < AFFECTIONE (cf. *lección* < LĒCTIONE)

GN	*sino* 'fate' < SIGNUM (cf. *signo* 'sign')
X	*ejercer* (NB /x/ < /ʃ/) 'to exercise' < EXERCĒRE (cf. *examen* (NB /gs/) 'examination')
PT	*setiembre* 'September' < SEPTEMBER (cf. *septiembre*, also pronounced without /p/)

2.6.6 *Yeísmo*

This term refers to the merger of the palatal lateral /λ/ and the midpalatal fricative /ĵ/, usually with non-lateral results:

The opposition between /λ/ and /ĵ/ was probably never very productive and the merger gives rise to few cases of homonymic collision (*pollo* 'chicken'/*poyo* 'stone bench', *mallo* 'mallet'/*mayo* 'May', *malla* 'mesh'/*maya* 'May Queen; Mayan', etc.). Although not attested in Spain until the eighteenth century, this merger probably began in late Old Spanish, since all varieties of Judaeo-Spanish (separated from Peninsular Spanish in 1492) and most varieties of American Spanish witness its accomplishment. Today, almost the whole southern half of the Peninsula lacks /λ/ and uses only /ĵ/; this includes the capital, where all but the oldest generation are *yeísta*. In the northern half of the Peninsula, most sizeable towns also show the merger, although intervening rural areas often maintain the traditional opposition.

Among speakers who have merged the two phonemes, various pronunciations are in use:

[dĵ] ~ [ĵ]	is usual in educated and urban Spanish in most areas of Spanish speech
[ʒ]	occurs in parts of Andalusia and America
[dʒ]	is associated with Extremadura, Argentina and Uruguay
[tʃ]	occurs in urban speech in the River Plate area
[ʃ]	appears in some varieties of Buenos Aires speech

2.6.7 *Weakening of syllable-final /s/ and /θ/*

Like *yeísmo*, this phenomenon is typical of the southern half of the Peninsula. However, although a few northern Peninsular districts are also affected (see Penny 1983a), weakening of /-s/ does not affect all American Spanish (most of Mexico and the Andean areas of South America are exempt) or any variety of Judaeo-Spanish. Note that in those Peninsular areas (such as New Castile, Extremadura, Murcia) where /θ/ exists as a separate phoneme from /s/ and where weakening of /-s/ takes place, syllable-final /-θ/ is similarly weakened.

The weakening process can be regarded as showing increasing degrees of intensity. These will be considered in turn, beginning with the least intense grade:

1 /-s/ is realized as fricative [ɹ], before /d/, a pronunciation typical of many northern rural areas: *desde*: [déɹðe], *desdeñar*: [deɹðeɲár].

2 A more intense degree of weakening affects most of the southern Peninsula, together with the northern areas mentioned and most (but not all) of Spanish America; it consists of the realization of syllable-final /s/ (and of /-θ/ where this is a separate phoneme) as an aspirate [h], whether before a consonant or a pause. It will be noted that this aspiration implies neutralization of syllable-final /s/ and /θ/ in the areas affected. E.g.: *este*: [éhte], *asno*: [áhno], *la tos*: [la tóh], *los viernes*: [loh βjérneh], *hazte acá*: [áhte aká], *diezmo*: [djéhmo], *la voz*: [la βóh].

3 The next most intense form of weakening of /-s/ is typical of Andalusia, but is also found in other areas where weakening occurs. It consists of various assimilations between the aspirate (see para. 2, above) and the following consonant. Usually the syllable-final phoneme takes on some of the features of the following phoneme, but when the second unit is /b/, /d/ or /g/ the latter is also affected, often becoming devoiced: *estos perros*: [é'toᵖ péřoh], *las botas*: [laφ φótah], *disgusto*: [dihú'to], *asno*: [áñno], *las manos*: [lañ mánoh].

4 The next most severe form of weakening, found especially in Western Andalusia and much of America (but also elsewhere, alongside less intense grades), consists of the total loss of final /s/ before a pause: *los hombres*: [loh ómbre], *las olas*: [lah óla].

5 Finally, the most acute form of weakening of /-s/, total elimination in all environments, may be heard in Eastern Andalusia: *las olas*: [la óla], *las manos*: [la máno].

This most intense form of weakening understandably has important phonological consequences, because of the hitherto vital grammatical role played by final /s/ (as the marker of plural number in nouns, adjectives, etc., and as the marker of the second person in the verb). In areas where final /s/ has been eliminated (i.e. in much of Eastern Andalusia), the grammatical functions of this phoneme have been transferred to other phonemes, namely the preceding vowel. A vowel which belongs to a syllable ending in a consonant (such as /s/) often in Spanish has a slightly different quality from a vowel which is syllable-final, the syllable-final vowel usually being a little more close than its non-final counterpart (see Navarro Tomás 1961: 46–64). This difference of quality has been exploited by some of the dialects concerned, in such a way that, as final /s/ was lost, the slightly open quality of the preceding (non-syllable-final) vowel was phonologized, so that such a vowel came into phonemic contrast with the corresponding word-final vowel, whose aperture had always been closer. In this way, the information originally carried by presence or absence of final /s/ comes to be carried by the open or close aperture of the preceding vowel (and often of the other vowels of the word), e.g.:

> *vienes*: [bjɛ́nɛ] vs *viene*: [bjéne]
> *bolos*: [bɔ́lɔ] vs *bolo*: [bólo]

In the case of the lowest vowels, it is not aperture which fulfils this role. The contrast is between fronted [æ] (where /-s/ previously followed) and [ɑ] (where the vowel was syllable-final):

> *las palas*: [læ pǽlæ] vs *la pala*: [lɑ pálɑ]
> *cantas*: [kǽntæ] vs *canta*: [kántɑ]

Since these vowel contrasts are evidently meaningful, one must conclude that in these (Eastern Andalusian) varieties of Spanish the vowel-system consists of at least the following eight phonemes:

/i/	/u/
/e/	/o/
/ɛ/	/ɔ/
/æ/	/ɑ/

2.7 Chronology of phonological change

An attempt has been made throughout this chapter to give a rough dating for each change considered. Such a dating has to be extremely approximate, since all change takes a very long period to spread through the society concerned, and we can usually only assign a change to a relatively extensive period (e.g. 'late Vulgar Latin', 'early Old Spanish', 'Golden Age', etc.). However, although an absolute chronology of each change cannot be achieved, it is possible to establish, with some precision, a relative chronology of change, indicating the order in which changes occur in a given language. Such a relative chronology is attempted here of the various phonological changes which, occurring in Vulgar Latin, in Western Romance generally, in Hispano-Romance, and specifically in Castilian, have produced the phonological system of modern Spanish. In some cases (e.g. metaphony), greater chronological precision is attempted here than in the relevant earlier section. For alternative approaches to the chronological sequence of phonological change in Spanish, see Menéndez Pidal 1958: 171–4, Hartman 1974, and Pensado Ruiz 1984.

1 Loss of final M (2.5.4) and initial H (2.5.2).
2 Pitch accent replaced by stress-accent (2.3.2).
3 Vulgar Latin vowel changes:
   (a) tonic

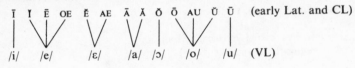

Ī Ĭ Ē OE Ĕ AE Ā Ă Ŏ Ō AU Ŭ Ū   (early Lat. and CL)

/i/   /e/   /ε/   /a/ /ɔ/   /o/   /u/   (VL)

   (b) atonic

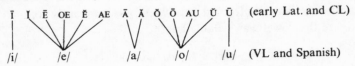

Ī Ĭ Ē OE Ĕ AE Ā Ă Ŏ Ō AU Ŭ Ū   (early Lat. and CL)

/i/   /e/   /a/   /o/   /u/   (VL and Spanish)

4 v fricatized to /β/ (2.5.3.1); non-syllabic I > /j/ (2.5.2.1).
5 Intervocalic B and V merge in /β/ (2.5.3.1).
6 Atonic E or I in hiatus with a following vowel > palatal glide [j] (2.4.3.4).
7 Palatalization of syllable-initial Cᵉ,ⁱ and Gᵉ,ⁱ (2.5.2.3).
8. VL loss of intertonic vowels (any, except A, in contact with R or L, sometimes S or N) (2.4.3.3).
9 Palatalization of syllable-final velars: CT > [it̯], X > [is̯], GN > [in̯], CL/GL > [i̯l̯] (2.5.2.4).
10 Assimilation of consonant groups: PT > /tt/, RS > /ss/, PS > /ss/, NS > /s/, MN > /nn/, MB > /mm/ (2.5.3.2).
11 Palatalization of T + [j] and C + [j] > /ts/ and of TT + [j], CC + [j], etc. > /tts/ (2.5.2.2[1]).
12 Raising of /o/ to /u/ when immediately followed by [i̯] or by N + [j]; raising of /e/ > /i/ and /o/ > /u/ when followed by M or B/V + [j] or by a group + [j] (2.4.2.1).
13 Raising of /ε/ > /e/ and /ɔ/ > /o/ by any following palatal glide (2.4.2.1).
14 Palatalization of L > /λ/ and N > /ɲ/ when followed or preceded by a palatal glide (2.5.2.2[2–3], 2.5.2.4) and of D + [j] and G + [j] > /ɟ͡ʝ/ (2.5.2.2[4]).
15 Diphthongization of /ε/ > /ie/ and /ɔ/ > /ue/ (2.4.2.2).
16 Palatalization of T > /tʃ/ and s > /ʃ/ when preceded by a palatal glide (2.5.2.4).
17 F- realized as [h] in many environments (could be placed earlier; 2.5.6).
18 Metathesis of R + [j] > [ir] and P + [j] > [ip] (2.5.2.2(6)).
19 /λ/ (resulting from 9 and 14) > /ʒ/ (2.5.2.2[2], 2.5.2.4).
20 Lenition (see 2.5.3.2 for the chronological relationship between (a), (b), (c) and (d)):
   (a) geminate > simple (and sonorants are additionally modified: LL > /λ/, NN > /ɲ/, RR > /r̄/);
   (b) voiceless > voiced (e.g. -T- > /d/, -S- > /z/, /ts/ > /dz/);
   (c) voiced plosives > fricatives (and are often eliminated);
   (d) /j/ > /zero/.

21 PL-, CL-, FL- > /ʎ/ (2.5.2.6).
22 Loss of surviving intertonic vowels (see 8), except /a/ (2.4.3.3); creates secondary consonant groups (2.5.6).
23 Metathesis s + [j] > [is] (2.5.2.2[6]).
24 /au/ > /ou/ > /o/ and /ei/ (from earlier /ai/ and /ei/, which arose through change 9) > /e/ (2.4.2.3, 2.4.2.4).
25 Merger of final /i/ and /e/ as /e/ (2.4.3.2).
26 Loss of final /e/ after ungrouped dental and alveolar consonants (except /t/) (2.4.3.2).
27 Modification of secondary consonant groups (see 22), by assimilation, dissimilation, etc. (2.5.6).
28 Loss of /h/ (except in SW, W and NW varieties of Peninsular Castilian and in some American varieties; 2.6.4).
29 OSp. /b/ and /β/ merge in /b/ (2.6.1).
30 Syllable-final /b/ > [u̯] (2.5.5 [end]).
31 Deaffrication of /ts/ > /ş/ and /dz/ > /ʐ/ (2.6.2).
32 Devoicing of voiced sibilants and merger with voiceless counterparts: /ş/ and /ʐ/ merge in /ş/, /s/ and /z/ merge in /s/, /ʃ/ and /ʒ/ merge in /ʃ/ (2.6.2).
33 Shift of locus /ş/ > /θ/ (except much of Andalusia and all America) and /ʃ/ > /x/ or /h/ (2.6.2).

3
Morpho-syntax

3.1   General concepts

Morphology studies the forms of words, and in particular the relationship between grammatical function and the various segments into which words can be divided from the point of view of such grammatical function. The basic units of morphological analysis are **morphemes**, segments which are capable of conveying grammatical function (such as 'plural', 'past', etc.). Morphemes may consist of one or more phonemes, but may not be subdivided without losing their ability to convey grammatical information. Thus, the word *pequeñitos* may be analysed into four morphemes: a root-morpheme *pequeñ-*, which carries the lexical meaning of the word, *-it-*, which conveys an affectionate or diminutive value, *-o-*, which indicates masculine gender, and *-s*, which is the exponent of plural number. Similarly, *cantaban* may be morphologically divided into four morphemes: a root-morpheme *cant-*, a conjugation-marker *-a-*, a tense/aspect/mood indicator (here, 'past' + 'imperfective' + 'indicative') *-ba-*, and a person/number morpheme *-n*.

Such morphological (or morphemic) analysis immediately reveals that the words of all languages are organized into closed sets (or **paradigms**). Two examples of paradigms in Spanish are

bueno	buenos
buena	buenas

(in which morphemes of gender and number are applicable to a large number of noun and adjective root-morphemes) and

canto	cantamos
cantas	cantáis
canta	cantan

(which groups morphemes of tense/mood/aspect and person/number which may be applied to a large class of verbal roots).

Syntax is concerned with discovering and stating the rules which govern the combination of words into sentences. However, since morphological and syntactical change are often intimately related, it is convenient, from a historical viewpoint, to consider morphology and syntax in conjunction. Such simultaneously morphological and syntactical analysis of language is termed **morpho-syntax**.

The interrelationship between morphological and syntactical change is best expressed by saying that information which at one stage is expressed by morphological processes may come at a later stage to be expressed by syntactical processes, and vice versa. In the course of the development from Latin to Spanish, morphologically expressed information has frequently come to be syntactically expressed, while the reverse is rare. For example, while such information as 'sentence subject', 'direct object', 'indirect object', etc., was expressed in the Latin noun, adjective and pronoun systems by means of morphemes of case (and number), bound to a root-morpheme, these notions came to be expressed in the descendants of Latin by syntactical means (word-order, number-agreement between subject and verb, presence or absence of prepositions, etc.). Languages like Latin, which have large numbers of bound morphemes (case-endings, verbal inflections, etc.) are sometimes categorized as **synthetic**, while languages like English, in which free morphemes (invariable words) predominate, be called **analytic**. While Spanish is more synthetic than English (particularly in its verbal system), it is less synthetic than its parent, so that the morpho-syntactical development from Latin to Spanish (and the other Romance languages) can be broadly characterized as one in which there has been a drift in favour of syntactical rather than morphological means of conveying the same information.

3.1.1

Morphological change is brought about principally by the operation of two forces, **phonological change** and **analogical adjustment**. Conditioned phonological change (the normal type) frequently has a disruptive effect upon paradigms, since some forms of a given paradigm may exhibit the conditions required for a change to occur, while other forms of the same paradigm may lack this conditioning factor. Thus the present indicative paradigm of the Latin verb DICERE 'say' has the same phoneme, /k/, at the end of the root-morpheme, whatever the following phoneme:

DĪCŌ = /di:ko:/
DĪCIS = /di:kis/, etc.

Now we have seen (2.5.2.3) that Lat. /k/ came to be palatalized before front vowels, but remained velar before non-front vowels. Bearing in mind other changes (see 2.5.3.2 and 2.6.2), we can therefore predict that the /k/ of DĪCŌ will yield Sp. /g/, while the /k/ of DĪCIS will give /θ/, a prediction which in this case proves accurate:

DĪCŌ > *digo*
DĪCIS > *dices*

Phonological change has in this case made the paradigm less coherent; it has introduced alternation between two phonemes where Latin showed a single phoneme, reducing the similarity between members of the same paradigm.

On the other hand, **analogy** often serves to restore or maintain the similarity between members of the same paradigm. Analogy is the process whereby forms which are related in grammatical function come to have a similar form. (Analogy also operates in the case of semantically related words, but this type of analogy does not concern us here.) Examples of grammatically motivated analogy can be seen in the present indicative paradigm of verbs like Lat. SENTĪRE 'feel, hear'. The tonic /ɛ/ of first person SENTIŌ, before the [j] of the final syllable, can be expected to provide Sp. /e/ (2.4.2.1), while, in the absence of [j], the tonic /ɛ/ of second person SENTĪS and third person SENTIT can be expected to yield Sp. /ie/ (2.4.2.2). Similarly, the /t/ + [j] sequence of words structured like SENTIO normally provides Sp. /θ/ (see 2.5.2.2), while such a result cannot arise in forms like SENTĪS, SENTIT, which lack [j]. In the development of SENTIŌ, neither of these two phonological changes took place (or, if they took place, they were reversed before the appearance of written Spanish) and the Spanish reflexes of the Latin forms are the familiar

SENTIO > *siento*
SENTĪS > *sientes*
SENTIT > *siente*

That is, owing to the similarity of function ('present indicative') between SENTIŌ and SENTĪS/SENTIT, the form of the first has remained similar, through analogy, to the form of other members of the paradigm and phonological change has been resisted or reversed. Similarly, analogy may operate between paradigms; the present subjunctive of verbs like PLICĀRE 'fold', later 'arrive' (PLICEM, PLICĒS, PLICET, etc.) does not show the otherwise expected palatalization of Lat. /k/ (contrast DĪCIS > *dices*, above), but maintains the velar phoneme, later voiced to /g/:

PLICEM > *llegue*
PLICĒS > *llegues*
PLICET > *llegue*

Morphological change, then, may be viewed as (in part) the result of competitive struggle between phonological change (which normally operates without regard to the meaning or function of the words it affects and leads to disruption of paradigms) and analogical adjustment (which maintains or restores phonological similarity between forms which have a related function). It is difficult to predict, in a given case of morphological development, which of these two forces will gain the upper hand, but it can be seen that the success of one force rather than the other is correlated (at least weakly) with the frequency of the words concerned. The more frequent a set of forms, the less likely it is to be affected by analogy, and (it follows), the more likely it is to show the disruptive effects of phonological change. Thus the present indicative paradigm *digo*, *dices*, etc., of the very frequent verb *decir* 'say' is morphologically 'irregular' (although 'regular' from the point of view of historical phonology), while the corresponding paradigm (*siento*, *sientes*, etc.) of the somewhat less frequent *sentir* 'feel' is morphologically more regular (although phonologically 'irregular' from a historical viewpoint). However, it cannot be argued that frequency is the only relevant factor here; frequency may be countered by other, less easily identifiable, factors.

Other types of morphological change are not excluded from the history of Spanish. Certain words may lose their independent status, be reduced to an auxiliary role and finally become inflectional morphemes. This is the case of HABĒRE, which came to be used with an infinitive to form a periphrastic future and conditional in spoken Latin (CANTĀRE HABEŌ/HABĒBAM). At a later stage, reduced forms of the auxiliary combined with the infinitive to form single words (*cantaré/cantaría*; see 3.7.7.4).

3.2 The noun

The Latin noun consisted of a root-morpheme followed by a single bound morpheme which indicated case and number (3.2.1). Gender (3.2.2) was in part indicated by the same (principally case/number) morphemes, but can be regarded as inherent in the root. The noun was originally organized into five form-classes (3.2.3).

3.2.1 Case and number

Each Latin noun had in principle twelve separate endings, by which were indicated the role of the noun in the sentence (i.e. its case) and its number. Using traditional terminology (where Nominative = Subject case, Vocative = case for direct address, Accusative = Direct Object case, Genitive = case indicating possession, etc., Dative = Indirect Object case, Ablative = case expressing a variety of sentence relations, often in combination with a preposition), such endings may be exemplified by means of an A-class noun such as MENSA 'table':

	singular	plural
Nominative	MĒNSA	MĒNSAE
Vocative	MĒNSA	MĒNSAE
Accusative	MĒNSĀM	MĒNSĀS
Genitive	MĒNSAE	MĒNSĀRUM
Dative	MĒNSAE	MĒNSĪS
Ablative	MĒNSĀ	MĒNSĪS

It will be seen that this noun has only seven distinct endings and in this it is typical of Latin nouns; none had more than eight distinct endings. As a result, form alone sometimes (perhaps often) did not unambiguously specify the role of the noun in a given sentence. In order to understand the function of, say, MĒNSAE, in a particular sentence, the hearer would need to have recourse to other clues such as word-order, verbal endings, the endings of other nouns, etc. This source of potential misunderstanding was compounded by another ambiguity inherent in the system: certain cases, especially the Accusative and Ablative, each had several different functions.

Although the system of case-endings described here could function reasonably well in written language, where re-reading will often resolve what is at first an ambiguity, this system was probably always inadequate at the spoken level, where immediate comprehension is required for communication to take place. Where the literary language (until about the first century AD) continued to rely on the unassisted case-endings, there is evidence that spoken Latin, from the earliest times, used additional devices, principally prepositions, to disambiguate the confusing noun-endings. Already in the popular drama of writers like Plautus (end of the third century BC) and even, occasionally, in the more 'serious' works of later writers, we find that certain noun-functions are not indicated by the noun-form alone, but by a combination of preposition and noun. The cases most frequently involved are the Genitive, Dative and Ablative. Instead of the Genitive, we occasionally find the preposition DE followed by an Ablative: DĪMIDIUM DE PRAEDĀ (Plautus), DE MARMORE TEMPLUM (Virgil), PAUCĪ DE NOSTRĪS (Caesar). This analytical construction is inherited directly by Spanish in the form of *de* + noun (*la mitad del botín, un templo de mármol, pocos de los nuestros*).

The indirect object in spoken Latin was often expressed by means of IN or AD together with the Accusative, while Classical Latin used an unqualified Dative. The same construction (eventually *a* + noun) was used in Spain and other areas to express a personal direct object, rather than the Accusative. Spanish (*lo dio*) *a su amigo*, and (*vio*) *a su amigo* are the linear descendants of VL AD + Accusative. In Old Spanish, this **personal a** construction was still not grammaticalized, but served to disambiguate propositions in which two nouns or pronouns were clustered with a verb of the same number (sing. or plur.). Under these circumstances, the relatively free word order of Spanish (which frequently allows the subject to follow its verb) could give rise to doubt as to which of the nouns was to be interpreted as the subject and which as the object, but the appearance of *a* before one of the (pro)nouns implied that the other was to be construed as the subject. This potential ambiguity most frequently arose in the case of *personal* nouns, since such nouns are more likely to function as the subject of the sentence. It was only at the end of the Golden Age that the 'personal *a*' became an obligatory particle, although frequent examples of its former disambiguating role can be seen in contemporary sentences like *mordió el perro al gato* 'the dog bit the cat', where neither noun is personal, but where, without the preposition, it is impossible to determine which of the nouns is the subject.

The CL 'Ablative of comparison' corresponded in VL to the construction DE + Ablative, a construction which continues into early Old Spanish (e.g. *De Iudas mui peor* (Berceo) 'much worse than Judas'), but was then ousted by the familiar *que* construction, one which has its roots in Latin QUAM. Similarly, the notion of the 'Instrumental Ablative' came to be expressed by means of expressions like *con* or *por medio de*. However, most values of the Lat. Ablative required the presence of a preposition even in the literary language. So, A(B) + Ablative was used to express 'the person by whom (an action is carried out)', a construction which persists into early Old Spanish (e.g. *Cantar de mio Cid* (*CMC*): *A los judios te dexaste prender* 'you let yourself be taken in by the Jews'), although it was then rapidly replaced by *de* + noun (e.g. *CMC: dexadas seredes de nos*, 'you will be abandoned by us'), the expression of agency which is normal until the sixteenth century, when *de* is largely, but not in all cases, replaced by *por* in this function; the older use continues after certain participles, e.g. *amado de todos*. The 'Ablative of company' also required the presence of a preposition (CUM), whose descendant is Spanish *con*.

This trend towards prepositional phrases was irreversible; although case-endings and prepositions perform the same function, the fact that the number of prepositions was larger than that of case-endings meant that prepositions performed this function more efficiently and the case-endings became mere redundant exponents of values better expressed by the accompanying prepositions. Such redundancy does not by itself imply that case-endings were bound to be abandoned (since all languages permit a large measure of redundancy), but it does mean that, should the case-endings be threatened with phonological convergence, such convergence is scarcely likely to be resisted. And phonological convergence is precisely what did overtake many pairs of endings. The relevant phonological convergences and their consequences for the case-system were the following:

1 Loss of final M (2.5.4) frequently caused the merger of Acc. sg. with Abl. sg. (e.g. Acc. MONTE(M) = Abl. MONTE).

2 Merger of Ā and Ă (see 2.4.1), together with loss of -M, made distinction impossible between Nom. MĒNSA, Acc. MĒNSAM and Abl. MĒNSĀ.

3 Merger of Ŭ and Ō, together with the other back vowels in final position (see 2.4.3.2), additionally made Accusative singulars like DOMINŬM indistinguishable from Dative/Ablative singulars like DOMINŌ.

4 Convergence of I and Ē, together with the other front vowels in final position (see 2.4.3.2), caused merger of Nom./Acc. pl. MONTĒS with Gen. sg. MONTĬS.

Note that it is not being argued here that phonological change caused morphological merger and the consequent replacement of case-endings by prepositions, as is often argued, but rather that the inadequate distinctions existing in early Latin between one case and another led to the use of prepositions in a disambiguating function, a development which made the case-endings largely redundant and allowed further merger, as a result of phonological change, to go ahead unchecked.

By the fourth or fifth centuries AD, the phonological changes just discussed led to a considerable reduction in the case-forms of all singular Latin nouns, while the plural forms were similarly reduced by analogy with the singular. In the East and in some parts of the West, there may have been as many as three surviving case-forms for some nouns (see Dardel 1964), but in most of the West (including Spain) by this period there was probably a maximum of two case-forms (a Nominative or subject-case, in contrast with an Oblique, which was used in all roles except that of subject) in both singular and plural. Even this distinction was no doubt lacking in some parts of the noun-system. In the late spoken Latin of Spain and other areas, then, the noun-system probably showed the following pattern (see Penny 1980):

		singular	plural
1	Nominative	/rósa/	/rósas/
	Oblique	/rósa/	/rósas/
2	Nominative	/ánnos/	/ánni/
	Oblique	/ánno/	/ánnos/
3a	Nominative	/léo/	/leónes/
	Oblique	/leóne/	/leónes/
3b	Nominative	/núβes/	/núβes/
	Oblique	/núβe/	/núβes/

The system posited here makes two assumptions which have not so far been discussed. Unimportant for present purposes is the assumption that in final syllables (see 2.4.3.2) /i/ (<Ī) and /e/ (<I, Ē, Ĕ) were still separate phonemes.

More significant is the statement that the Nom. plur. ending of A-class nouns was /-as/. There is good evidence (see Aebischer 1971) that in the spoken Latin of most areas this was the case from early times, by contrast with the literary dialect, which showed analogical -AE.

This two-case system survived, in French and Provençal, with minor changes, until the twelfth–thirteenth centuries. In other areas, there was an early further reduction to invariable sing. and plur. noun-forms, as the result of a series of analogical adjustments. It will be noted that A-class nouns already in late VL lacked any case-inflection, and that the same was true in the plural of the third VL declension. The fact that no case-distinction was possible in a large number of instances undoubtedly set the pattern for the obliteration of such distinction elsewhere. The analogical processes by which this obliteration was carried out were the following:

1 Final /s/ occurs in almost all plur. forms, but in only some sing. forms. This morpheme probably therefore came to be analysed as a marker exclusively of number and no longer of case. Crucially, this pattern (/-s/ = plur., /zero/ = sing.) was already established in the 1st VL declension. Analogical extension of this pattern no doubt led to the loss of /-s/ in those (usually Nominative) singular instances where it hitherto occurred, bringing immediate further convergence of Nom. sing. /ánno/, /núβe/ (previously /ánnos/, /núβes/) with the Obl. sing.

2 Many nouns of group 3a (imparisyllabic nouns; the Nom. sing. has one syllable fewer than the other forms) suffered analogical levelling by means of the expansion of their short Nom. sing. forms. The *Appendix Probi* condemns expanded GLĪRIS, GRŪIS and recommends traditional GLĪS, GRŪS, while in non-literary Latin we find MENTIS for MENS, CARNIS for CARŌ, BOVIS for BŌS, etc. This levelling was limited in VL to nouns with non-personal sense, but must have been extended to personal nouns in the following period. Taken together with the loss of sing. /-s/ just discussed, this change implies merger of Nom. sing. /leóne/ (< *LEŌNIS < LEŌ) with Obl. sing. /leóne/.

3 The operation of the previous two changes leaves morphological contrast between Nom. and Obl. only in the plural of o-class nouns (/ánni/ vs /ánnos/). Even leaving aside the universal constraint that plurals may not show a greater degree of morphemic contrast than the corresponding singulars, it is evident that the internal analogical pressures to level out the contrast between /ánni/ and /ánnos/ must have been practically irresistible. But which was to survive? In Spain and other Western areas, where the plural of most nouns was marked by the addition of /s/ to the same vowel as occurred in the singular, it is clear that /ánnos/ was bound to be preferred, and /ánni/ disappeared, perhaps after a period of free variation with /ánnos/ in both Nom. and Obl. roles. (In Central Italy and other Eastern areas, where /s/ was regularly lost and where most plurals differed from their corresponding singulars by means of a vowel alternation (sing. /rósa/, plur. /róse/), structural pressure would evidently lead to preference for /ánni/ over /ánno(s)/.)

As a result of these adjustments, all traces of case-distinction are lost from the system of three major form-classes that Spanish inherits: (1) *rosa/rosas*, (2) *año/años*, and (3) *león/leones, nube/nubes*. In the last category, the presence or absence of /-e/ is a matter of phonological history (see 2.4.3.2) rather than of morphology.

Traditional accounts of the development of the noun system (e.g. Menéndez Pidal 1958: 205–9) state that the Latin Accusative case-form survives at the expense of the other cases, taking over their functions. While it is true that the surviving Spanish noun-forms more closely resemble the CL Accusative than any other case, the traditional account cannot explain why a form (Accusative) which in Latin signals the direct object of a transitive verb should come to indicate also the subject of the sentence, as well as other functions. That is, the traditional argument, while morphologically adequate, is syntactically inadequate. The account given here, which depends upon phonological and analogical levelling of originally distinct endings, does not have to face this syntactical difficulty, since it argues that the Spanish (and other Romance) noun-forms inherit both the functions and (to a large extent) the forms of a wide variety of Latin cases.

3.2.2   Gender

In the development of the noun from Latin to Spanish, the category of gender undergoes two major modifications. On the one hand, there is the change from a three-gender system (masculine ~ feminine ~ neuter) to a two-gender system (masc. ~ fem.), with the consequent reassignment of surviving neuter nouns to one or other of the remaining genders. On the other hand, there were changes which brought about an increasingly close correspondence between gender and noun-endings.

3.2.2.1   Neuter nouns

It can be argued that the class of Latin neuter nouns was insufficiently distinctive both in form and semantic content and that this lack of distinctiveness ultimately caused its demise. The only formally distinctive characteristics of the neuters were the identity of Nom. and Acc. endings and the fact that the Nom. and Acc. plur. always ended in /a/. On the semantic side, although the neuters may once have exclusively indicated the class of 'inanimates' (while the masculines and feminines together indicated the 'animates'), by the first century BC this relationship had become extremely blurred; many inanimates had masc. or fem. gender, and some animates were to be found among the neuters. The result of this indeterminacy of the neuter class was a large measure of interchange, in VL, between neuters and (especially) masculines; neuters are frequently found with masc. endings and traditionally masculine nouns sometimes occur with the neuter plur. ending /a/. The general principle underlying the reallocation of the neuters is that, if the Latin noun had a back vowel in its final syllable it was assigned to the masc. class, although those (relatively few) neuters which evolved through their plur. form (in /-a/) acquired fem. gender. Where the final vowel was neither /-o/ nor /-a/ (that is, in those neuters with a final consonant or /-e/), the new gender appears to have been arbitrarily assigned, although in specific cases it appears that association of the neuter noun with a masc. or fem. noun of related meaning has been responsible for the assignment of masc. or fem. gender.

Latin neuters of the 2nd decl. (e.g. PRĀTUM, VĪNUM) differed in form from masc. nouns of the same class only in the Nom. sing. (-UM vs. -US), the Nom. plur. (-A vs. -Ī) and Acc. plur. (-A vs. -ŌS). Even this degree of distinction would eventually have been lessened, when the Nom. sing. /-s/ was lost from masc. nouns (see 3.2.1). However, even before this, such neuters had become identical with masc. nouns like ANNUS, DOMINUS, abandoning their plurals in /-a/ and adopting masc. endings. Such neuters therefore appear in Spanish as masc.:

> PRĀTUM, PRĀTA > *prado, prados* 'meadow(s)'
> VĪNUM > *vino* 'wine'

(It will be noted that VĪNUM and *vino*, as mass-nouns, do not have plural forms, except in the specialized sense of 'classes of wine'.)

Neuters of the 4th decl. merged in the same way with masculines of the same class and later became identical to the previous group (*prado, vino*, etc.) when the 4th decl. merged with the 2nd (see 3.2.3). Thus

> CORNU, CORNUA > *cuerno, cuernos* 'horn(s)'

Those neuters of the 3rd decl. whose Nom./Acc. sing. was in -US (TEMPUS, CORPUS, PECTUS, PIGNUS, OPUS; plur. TEMPORA, CORPORA, PECTORA, PIGNORA, OPERA; LATUS, plur. LATERA) were also eventually absorbed into the masc. class in -o, -os. However, there is some evidence that in pre-literary Spanish these nouns had an invariable /-os/ ending for both singular (where presence of /-s/ in the Acc. as well as the Nom. no doubt enabled the consonant to resist the analogical elimination which affected this consonant in masc. nouns [see 3.2.1]) and plural (where the ending was purely analogical). The evidence comes from early Old Spanish, where in certain phrases these nouns end in -os but have apparently singular meaning: *en tiempos de* 'in the time of', *en cuerpos* 'in body', *en pechos* 'on the breast', *huebos me es* 'it is necessary for me' (a continuation of the Latin phrase OPUS EST MIHI), *al lados de* 'beside'. But apart from such fossilized phrases, these nouns had by the Old Spanish period been fully assimilated to the masc. -o/-os group:

TEMPUS, TEMPORA > *tiempo, tiempos* 'time(s)'
CORPUS, CORPORA > *cuerpo, cuerpos* 'body, -ies'
PECTUS, PECTORA > *pecho, pechos* 'breast(s)'
PIGNUS, PIGNORA > *peño* 'pledge', later *empeño* 'id., etc.'
LATUS, LATERA   > *lado, lados* 'side(s)'

The plural PIGNORA had an independent development (> *prenda*), as did the plural OPERA; see below.

Neuters of the 3rd decl. were, in form, a somewhat heterogeneous group, but a substantial sub-group consisted of imparisyllabic nouns whose Nom./Acc. sing. ended in /n/ or /r/ (e.g. NŌMEN, pl. NŌMINA, RŌBUR, pl. RŌBORA). In Spain, these nouns were treated like other imparisyllabics (see 3.2.1 [end]), suffering expansion of the Nom. sing., and (since neuters had a short Acc. sing.) of the Acc. sing. too, in order to equalize the number of syllables in these forms with the number of syllables in the remaining forms of the paradigm. Since the expanded singular form ended in /e/ (e.g. NŌMEN > *NŌMINE, RŌBUR > *RŌBORE), these nouns were assimilated to the 3rd Spanish noun-class, replacing their -A plurals with /-es/. And since the class into which these nouns moved was shared by masc. and fem. nouns, the ultimate gender of the newcomers was arbitrarily assigned, although in some cases association of meaning with a pre-existing masc. or fem. noun may have played a role in assigning the new gender; thus LŪMEN becomes fem. (*lumbre*), perhaps by association with fem. LUX (> *luz*). The nouns belonging to this group are:

NŌMEN/NŌMINA	>	*NŌMINE/NŌMINA	>	*nombre(s)* m.	
VĪMEN/VĪMINA	>	*VĪMINE/VĪMINA	>	*mimbre(s)* m.	
AERĀMEN/AERĀMINA	>	*AERĀMINE/AERĀMINA	>	*alambre(s)* m.	
EXĀMEN/EXĀMINA	>	*EXĀMINE/EXĀMINA	>	*enjambre(s)* m.	
LEGŪMEN/LEGŪMINA	>	*LEGŪMINE/LEGŪMINA	>	*legumbre(s)* f.	
LŪMEN/LŪMINA	>	*LŪMINE/LŪMINA	>	*lumbre* f.	
CULMEN/CULMINA	>	*CULMINE/CULMINA	>	*cumbre(s)* f.	
RŌBUR/RŌBORA	>	RŌBORE/RŌBORA	>	*roble(s)* m.	
ŪBER/ŪBERA	>	*UBERE/ŪBERA	>	*ubre(s)* f.	
SULFUR	>	*SULFURE	>	*azufre* m.	

Similarly expanded (i.e. by analogy with Gen. LACTIS, Dat. LACTI, etc.) is:

LAC > LACTE > *leche* f.

Other 3rd decl. neuters were rather disparate in form, and either did not require expansion (because they were already parisyllabic) or (for various reasons, sometimes obscure) resisted it:

FEL	>	*hiel* f.
MEL	>	*miel* f.
RĒTE		(attested as f. RETIS in VL) > *red* f.
MARE	>	*mar* (m. or f. in Old Spanish, now usually m.)

COCHLEĀRE >	OSp. *cuchar* (m. or f.), with later preference for fem. gender and hypercharacterization (see 3.2.2.2) and movement to the *a*-class
CAPUT/CAPITA	with sing. /-o/ in VL, was drafted into the *o*-class (therefore m.), with analogical plur.: *cabo(s)*
VAS/VĀSA (CL)	had a VL competitor VASUM/VASA, which survives as Sp. *vaso(s)* m.
OS/OSSA (CL)	similarly was ousted by VL OSSUM/OSSA, whence *hueso(s)*

Although most neuters suffered analogical restructuring of their plurals, a number of neuter plurals (in -A) were transferred to the *a*-class, naturally becoming fem. sing. and acquiring a new plural in /-as/. Most such nouns were ones whose original plurals could be understood (sometimes loosely) as 'collective', a category in which the distinction between sing. and plur. becomes weakened. Thus, alongside CL neut. ARMUM/ARMA 'weapon(s)' (whose plural can be understood as a collective meaning 'weaponry' and therefore reinterpreted as a sing. noun) we find attested fem. ARMA/ARMAE, ancestor of Sp. *arma(s)* 'weapon(s)'. Similarly, alongside CL OPUS/OPERA 'work(s)', we find OPERA/OPERAE, whence *obra(s)* 'id.' (for OPUS > OSp. *huebos*, see above).

Some of the neuter plurals which have in this way passed to the fem. *a*-class retain vestiges of collective sense (some continuing as mass-nouns and having no Spanish plural):

BRACCHIA 'arms'	> *braza* 'fathom (the length of two outstretched arms)' (compare sing. BRACCHIUM > *brazo* 'arm')
FOLIA 'leaves'	> *hoja* 'leaf' (but also collective: '(dead) foliage')
LIGNA '(pieces of) wood'	> *leña* 'firewood'
OVA 'eggs'	> *hueva* 'roe (of fish)' (compare OVUM > *huevo* 'egg')
VŌTA 'vows'	> *boda* 'wedding'

Others have entirely lost such collective sense:

ARMA	> *arma* (see above)
MŌRA 'mulberries, blackberries'	> *(zarza)mora* 'blackberry, mulberry'
OPERA	> *obra* (see above)
PIGNORA 'pledges'	> *prenda* 'pledge; garment'
PIRA 'pears'	> *pera* 'pear'

Because of the amalgamation of the neuter nouns with masculines and feminines, there was a period of uncertainty in Latin over the gender of certain nouns, with the occasional effect that a masc. or fem. noun is found with the (originally neuter) plur. ending /-a/. Even more rarely, such

/a/-forms have survived, with fem. sing. status, like ARMA > *arma*, OPERA > *obra*, etc.:

> *fruta* '(piece of) fruit' < FRŪCTA 'fruit(s)' ('incorrect' plural of FRŪCTUS, whence *fruto* 'fruit, product')
>
> *rama* 'branch' < *RĀMA 'branches' ('incorrect' plural of RĀMUS, whence *ramo*, now only 'twig, bouquet, etc.')

It can be seen, then, that in the reclassification of neuter nouns as either masc. or fem., the form of the neuter noun determines its ultimate gender, with the rider that where form could not decide the matter (because the neuter noun ended in /e/ or a consonant), the ultimate gender is partly arbitrarily determined and partly determined by the gender of semantically related words.

3.2.2.2 Gender-marking of the noun

(1) masc. and fem. nouns in -US and -A.   There was already in CL a strong correlation between gender and noun-form; most nouns in -US (i.e. those of the 2nd and 4th declensions) were masculine (leaving aside the neuters of these declensions, which rapidly acquired masc. gender), while the large majority of those in -A (those of the 1st decl.) were feminine. In Vulgar Latin this correlation was strengthened (by the abandonment or by gender-switch of feminines in -US and masculines in -A) and by the Old Spanish period the correlation was almost absolute. At that stage, probably the only aberrant forms were the fem. *mano* and the masc. *día*. In reaching this position, three groups of words, in particular, had required adjustment: tree-names, gem-names, and kinship terms.

Tree-names, feminine in Latin, frequently ended in -US. The simplest solution to this 'anomaly', gender-switch, was adopted in numerous cases:

CERĀSIUS	>	*cerezo* 'cherry'	PŌPULUS	>	*chopo* 'black poplar'
FRAXINUS	>	*fresno* 'ash'	TAXUS	>	*tejo* 'lime, linden'
PĪNUS	>	*pino* 'pine'	ULMUS	>	*olmo* 'elm'

In other cases (especially, but not exclusively, where there was a need to distinguish between a tree-name and the name of the corresponding fruit), the tree-name continues to be fem., but acquires an /a/ ending through replacement of the original noun by a related adjective which agrees with fem. ARBOR:

> FĪCUS 'fig-tree' > (ARBOR) FĪCARIA > *higuera* 'id.' (NB FĪCUS 'fig' > *higo*)
>
> FĀGUS 'beech' > (ARBOR) FĀGEA > *haya*

This process was also sometimes applied to tree-names with other endings, again especially to provide distinction between tree-name and fruit-name:

> NUX 'walnut-tree' > (ARBOR) NUCĀLIS > *nogal*, or (ARBOR) NUCĀRIA > *noguera* (NB NUX/NUCE > *nuez* 'walnut')
>
> ĪLEX 'evergreen oak' > (ARBOR) ĪLICĪNA > *encina*

Gem-names are not in all cases popular words; some were introduced to Old Spanish from written sources. However, among those that may have a continuous oral history in Spanish are to be observed some which were (at least sometimes) fem. in Latin but ended in -US. They were slower than tree-names to find a settled form and Old Spanish hesitated wildly over their form, while adhering to the pattern /-a/ = fem., /-o/ = masc.:

> AMETHYSTUS > OSp. *ametisto/ametista*; from sixteenth century, *amatista*
> SAPPHĪRUS > OSp. *çafir*; *zafiro* from eighteenth century
> SMARAGDUS > OSp. *esmeragde/esmeralda*, MSp. *esmeralda*
> TOPAZIUS   > OSp. *estopaçio/estopaza/estopazo* (later remodelled as *topacio*)

The **kinship-terms** SOCRUS 'mother-in-law' and NURUS 'daughter-in-law' were of course feminine and therefore contravened the emerging VL rule of gender-marking. In this case, gender-switch is out of the question, so that change of form is the only available solution. That such change was already occurring in VL is attested by the *Appendix Probi* (NURUS NON NURA, SOCRUS NON SOCRA) and it is the condemned forms which have survived in Spanish as *nuera* and *suegra*.

There were, then, in Old Spanish perhaps only two exceptions (*mano* and *día*) to the rule that words in /-a/ were feminine and those in /-o/ masculine. However, from the late Middle Ages the force of this rule has been weakened and there are now large numbers of nouns which contravene it:

> masculines in /-a/, borrowings of Greek neuters (often fem. in OSp.): *profeta, planeta, clima*, etc.
> masculines in /-a/ originating, through metonymy (see 5.2.2), in fem. abstracts: *el cura* 'priest', *el corneta* 'cornet player', *guardia* 'policeman', *guarda* 'custodian', *centinela* (via Italian) 'sentinel', etc.
> feminines in /-o/, created through metonymy, abbreviation, etc.: *la modelo* 'model', *la moto* 'motorcycle', *la foto* 'photograph', *la dínamo*, etc.

(2) masc. and fem. nouns in /e/ or a consonant.   In these nouns there is, of course, no correspondence between gender and form. As a result, gender-switch from masc. to fem. and vice versa is easy and relatively frequent, and affects both popular and learned words. Change of gender, usually from fem. to masc., is particularly frequent in the case of nouns beginning with a vowel, since in Old Spanish the form of a preceding def. art. or indef. art. was identical for the two genders (*el amor*, f., *el origen*, f., *un árbol*, f.; see 3.5.3.2). In a minority of cases, the word may appear in Spanish with both genders, or there may be regional differences of gender. Examples of this hesitation of gender include:

> *amor, honor* fem. in Latin and Old Spanish, become masc. in later Old Spanish

calor, color change from fem. to masc. after the Golden Age; still fem. in regional speech; note that *labor* retains fem. gender even in the standard

árbol fem. in Lat.; often still fem. in Old Spanish; now masc.

arte fem. in Lat. and in Old Spanish (usually meaning 'skill, trick'); now masc. in sing., fem. in plur.

génesis fem. as a common noun; masc. as referring to the first book of the Bible

linde masc. in Lat.; fem. in Old Spanish; now fem. in sing., masc. in plur.

orden masc. in Lat.; gradually acquires fem. gender in some meanings (e.g. 'command')

origen fem. in Lat. and in Spanish until the Golden Age; now masc.

pirámide borrowed in the Golden Age as masc.; now fem.

sal masc. in Lat.; now fem. except in the NW of Spain

valle fem. in Lat.; often still fem. in Old Spanish (*la val*, etc.); now masc.

From the Latin period onwards, there has been a tendency to switch nouns from the category in which gender is not overtly marked (those in /e/ or a consonant) into the categories in which there is correspondence between gender and form (the *a*-class and the *o*-class). This process of providing nouns with an overt sign of their gender (/-a/ or /-o/) is sometimes referred to as **hypercharacterization** of gender; for the process whereby fem. nouns originally ending in *-or, -és, -e, -ón* came to end in *-ora, -esa, -a, -ona* in the later Old Spanish period, see England 1984, 1987. Examples of hypercharacterization of fem. nouns include:

AMITĒS > OSp. *andes* > MSp. *andas* 'stretcher'
GRŪE > OSp. *grua* 'crane' (later *grulla* in ornithological sense)
ĪNFĀNTE fem. > early OSp. *la infante* 'daughter of a noble family' > *infanta* 'princess'
PANTICE > *panza* 'belly'
PŪLICE > *pulga* 'flea'
PUPPE > *popa* 'poop, stern'
RESTE > *riestra* > *ristra* 'string (of onions), etc.'
SENIORE fem. > early OSp. *la señor* 'lady' > *señora* 'id.'
TURTURE > *tórtola* 'turtledove'

Examples of hypercharacterization of masculine nouns can be seen in:

CICERE > *chícharo* 'pea'
CORTICE > *corcho* 'cork'
CUCUMERE > OSp. *cogombro* > MSp. *cohombro* 'cucumber'
PASSARE (CL PASSER) 'sparrow' > *pájaro* 'songbird'
PULVERE > *PULVUS > early OSp. *polvos* > *polvo* 'dust'

3.2.3   Noun-classes

The five noun-classes of Latin were numerically unequal; the *a*-class (or 1st declension; e.g. MĒNSA, ROSA) was large, as were the *o*-class (or 2nd declension; e.g. DOMINUS, MAGISTER) and the class characterized by a consonant or /i/ (the 3rd declension; e.g. RĒX, NŪBIS), while the *u*-class (or 4th declension; e.g. MANUS, GRADUS) and the *e*-class (or 5th declension; e.g. DIES, RES) had few members. In addition, 4th-declension nouns shared many of their endings with those of the 2nd, while 5th-declension nouns were in many respects identical to 3rd-declension nouns. These similarities of structure were no doubt intensified as the system of case-endings was weakened (see 3.2.1), since the case-forms which survived were precisely the ones in which the similarities between declensions were greatest. As a result of these similarities and of the numerical imbalance between classes alluded to above, there was a reduction of form-classes, beginning in spoken Latin, from five to three. Before this merger, feminine nouns of the fifth declension generally moved to the first; thus MĀTERIĒS > MĀTERIA, RABIĒS > *RABIA. DIĒS, although only occasionally fem. in CL, and despite appearing in Spanish as masc., was also modified to first-declension form: *DIA.

Bearing in mind these convergences of noun-classes and previous discussion of the treatment of neuter nouns (3.2.2.1), Spanish comes to have three noun-classes, the main contributors to each of which are the following groups of nouns:

1 Nouns in /a/: nouns of the Lat. 1st decl. (e.g. *mesa, rosa*)
5th decl. feminines (e.g. *madera, rabia*)
neuter plurals of any declension (e.g. *hoja, boda*)
hypercharacterized fems. of the Lat. 3rd decl. (e.g. *señora, pulga*)

2 Nouns in /o/: masculines and neuters of the Lat. 2nd decl. (e.g. *dueño, vino*)
masculines and neuters of the Lat. 4th decl. (e.g. *paso*) and the single 4th decl. feminine *mano*
3rd decl. neuters whose Nom./Acc. sing. contained a back vowel (e.g. *cabo, tiempo*)
hypercharacterized 3rd decl. masculines (e.g. *pájaro, corcho*)

3 Nouns in /e/ or a consonant:
most Lat. 3rd decl. nouns (e.g. *nube, león*)
those Lat. 5th decl. nouns which did not pass to the *a*-class (e.g. *haz* 'face', *fe* 'faith')
a few 2nd decl. words, e.g. *cobre* 'copper' < CUPRU, *trébol* 'clover' < TRIFOL(I)U, whose endings were changed for obscure reasons

A very few Old Spanish nouns did not fit any of these declensional patterns. The main cases are *buei* 'ox' (< BOVE), *lei* 'law'(< LĒGE), *rei* 'king' (< RĒGE), whose plurals were at first phonologically regular (but morphologically irregular): *bueis* (< BOVĒS), *leis* (< LĒGĒS), *reis* (< RĒGĒS). During the course of the Middle Ages, these aberrant nouns were accommodated to the *e/cons*-class, through the remodelling of their plurals to *bueyes, leyes, reyes*.

3.3 The adjective

The function of the adjective remains unchanged in the course of the development of Latin to Spanish, and the syntactical rules governing its appearance remain essentially similar. Only position-rules appear to have been modified; whereas sub-classifying adjectives could appear before the noun in Latin, such adjectives now appear only after the noun, and only intensifying adjectives may precede. We shall therefore be concerned here only with the form of the simple adjective and with comparatives and superlatives.

3.3.1 Adjective endings

Latin had two major classes of adjectives. On the one hand, there were those like ALTUS, -A, -UM, in which there were separate sets of endings for all three genders, with endings identical to those of 1st and 2nd declension nouns, and, on the other hand, there were adjectives like FORTIS, -E, in which one set of endings served for both masc. and fem. reference and the other for reference to neuter nouns, the endings of FORTIS, etc., being similar to those of 3rd declension nouns. With the reclassification of neuter nouns between the other two genders (see 3.2.2.1), there was no longer a requirement for neuter endings in the adjective and they fell out of use. Similarly, as the case-endings of the noun were merged, first to two endings then to one (see 3.2.1), it followed that the case-endings of the adjective would be similarly reduced. Thus, from the multiplicity of forms that adjectives could assume in Latin, those of the ALTUS class emerge in Spanish with only four distinct endings (*alto, alta, altos, altas* 'high'), while those of the FORTIS class have only two (*fuerte, fuertes* 'strong').

The loss of the final vowel of a few masc. sing. adjectives (*buen, mal, primer, tercer*) and the reduction of *grande* to *gran* when these words immediately precede a noun referent is the result of the weakening process which affected intertonic and final vowels in pre-literary and early Old Spanish (see 2.4.3.2–3). Whereas analogy has ensured that this irregularity has been eliminated from the large majority of adjectives, the frequency of *bueno, malo, grande*, etc., has allowed them to preserve irregular sing. forms (see 3.1.1).

Another form of adjectival 'irregularity' which was eliminated during the Old Spanish period was that which originally existed in adjectives like (masc.) *antigo(s)*, (fem.) *antigua(s)* 'old, former', where differential phonological development of /kʷ/ before /o/ and /a/ (see 2.5.3.2[8]) leads to the Old Spanish alternation. However, by the late fifteenth century (Nebrija), this alternation has been levelled in favour of the fem. form: *antiguo, antigua*.

As in the case of nouns (see 3.2.2.2), VL showed a tendency to shift adjectives from the class in which masc. or fem. gender was not explicitly marked in the ending (e.g. FORTIS) into the class in which this distinction was formally marked (e.g. ALTUS). Such hypercharacterization of gender is condemned by the *Appendix Probi* (PAUPER MULIER NON PAUPERA MULIER, TRISTIS NON TRISTUS), but clearly gained ground in many varieties of Romance. The process was weaker in Spain than in most other areas (note that the descendants, *pobre* and *triste*, of the two Latin adjectives just quoted show no gender contrast, while Lat. FIRMUS, whence semi-learned *firme*, loses this contrast), but during the Old Spanish period certain groups of adjectives came to be affected (see Malkiel 1957–8 and England 1984, 1987):

1 **Adjectives in *-or*** were invariable for gender at first in Old Spanish (e.g. *alma sentidor, espadas tajadores*), but from the late fourteenth century gender-contrast is made overt by the introduction of fem. forms in *-ora: loadora, sabidora, traidora*, etc. This process does not extend to the comparatives *mejor, peor, mayor, menor, interior, inferior*, etc., unless nominalized (e.g. *superiora* 'mother superior'), although Old Spanish texts from the eastern area show examples of *menora*, etc., a tradition continued in modern Aragonese dialects.

2 **Adjectives in *-ón*** were, like the preceding group, unmarked for gender in early Old Spanish (e.g. *gentes españones*; cf. modern Judaeo-Spanish *lengua espaniol*). Adjectives of this class are found in later Old Spanish with fem. *-ona* (*ladrona, bretona*), as are those in *-ol* (*española*) and *-án* (*alemana, holgazana*, etc.).

3 **Adjectives in *-és*** show occasional hypercharacterized forms in early Old Spanish, although usually in adjectives functioning as nouns (e.g. *CMC: burgesas*, fem. of *burgeses*). In later Old Spanish, fem. *-és* is challenged by hypercharacterized *-esa*, first in the East (e.g. *cortesa* [*Razón de amor*, 1205]), although fem. *-és* can still occasionally be found in the sixteenth century (e.g. *la leonés potencia, la provincia cartaginés*). Thereafter, fem. *-esa* becomes obligatory in adjectives denoting national or regional origin (i.e. in *gentilicios: francesa, leonesa, cordobesa*, etc.). However, other adjectives generally preserve invariability of form: *cortés, montés* (beside rare *montesa*), *burgués*.

3.3.2 Comparison of adjectives

The system of comparison applied to most adjectives in CL was synthetic. (For this term, see 3.1):

FORTIS 'brave'
FORTIOR 'braver'
FORTISSIMUS 'bravest'/'very brave'

However, this system had an analytical competitor, at first applied only to adjectives whose final and penultimate vowels were in hiatus (for hiatus, see 2.4.3.4):

ARDUUS 'harsh'
MAGIS or PLŪS ARDUUS 'harsher'
MAXIME ARDUUS 'harshest'

In spoken Latin there was a clearly attested tendency to apply this analytical system to the large majority of adjectives; probably only the most frequent adjectives escaped. This tendency towards analysis was no doubt encouraged by the fact that the two senses (relative and absolute) of the superlative could thereby be distinguished:

FORTIS 'brave'
MAGIS or PLŪS FORTIS 'braver'
MAXIME FORTIS 'bravest'
MULTUM or VALDE FORTIS 'very brave'

It seems that in later spoken Latin the distinction between comparative and relative superlative (e.g. between 'braver [of two]' and 'bravest [of three or more]') was abandoned and the comparative form (e.g. MAGIS or PLŪS FORTIS) was used in both senses. This distinction was later reintroduced by different Romance languages (in Spanish, only partially) by the addition of the definite article in the case of the superlative. Thus Sp. *el más fuerte de todos* 'the strongest (man) of all', but *el hombre más fuerte* 'the stronger/strongest man'.

VALDE fell out of use, and MAGIS was preferred to PLŪS in most parts of Spain, so that in the late spoken Latin of these areas it is likely that the system of comparison was

FORTIS 'brave, strong'
MAGIS FORTIS 'braver, stronger; bravest, strongest'
MULTUM FORTIS 'very brave, very strong'

from which the Spanish system directly descends:

fuerte
(el) más fuerte
muy fuerte

Only the most frequent synthetic comparatives (and no synthetic superlatives) maintained their synthetic form. Thus MELIOR, PEIOR, MAIOR, MINOR (no doubt at some stage undergoing expansion of the Nom., like imparisyllabic nouns [see 3.2.1], which then merged with the reflexes of Oblique MELIŌRE, PĒIŌRE, MĀIŌRE, MINŌRE), having taken over the role of the relative superlatives OPTIMUS, PESSIMUS, MĀXIMUS, MINIMUS in addition to their comparative function, give Sp. *mejor, peor, mayor, menor*, although the last two compete with analytical *más grande* and *más pequeño*. Other apparently synthetic comparatives like *inferior, superior, interior, exterior, ulterior*, etc., are learned borrowings made from Latin in the medieval or post-medieval period.

The superlative ending -*ísimo* is also learned. Occasional instances of its use in Old Spanish (sometimes with the form -*ismo*) reveal relative sense. It was only in the sixteenth century that this form became usual in Spanish, henceforth only with absolute sense. The learned nature of this formation is revealed by the learned form adopted by some adjectives to which it is applied (*fuerte, fortísimo; antiguo, antiquísimo; cruel, crudelísimo*, etc.), although recent trends show a preference for a simpler form of derivation: *fuertísimo, buenísimo*, etc.

3.4 The adverb

CL derived adverbs from adjectives in a large variety of ways, of which the commonest were the following three: addition of the ending -E to adjectives of the BONUS type (e.g. MALE 'badly'), addition of the ending -ITER to adjectives of the GRANDIS type (e.g. FORTITER 'bravely'), and simple use of the Neuter sing. (Nom./Acc.) of the adjective (e.g. MULTUM 'much', FACILE 'easily'). There are few survivals in Spanish of these derivational types:

1 BENE > *bien* 'well', MALE > *mal* 'badly', TARDE > *tarde* 'late', LONGE > OSp. *lueñe* 'in the distance', RŌMĀNICĒ 'in the Roman manner', as in FĀBULĀRE RŌMĀNICĒ, whence OSp. *fablar romançe* 'to speak the vernacular (= Castilian, etc.)'; the adv. was then substantivized with the sense 'vernacular speech', eventually also 'vernacular writing (by contrast to Latin)', and 'verse composition in the vernacular').

2 -ITER leaves no descendants in Spanish.

3 MULTUM > *mucho*, and the comparatives LAXIUS 'more amply' > *lejos*, MAGIS > *más*. It is possible that constructions like *hablar fuerte, ver claro*, etc., contain adverbs descended from Latin neuter adjectives.

An additional, and informal, means of marking adverbial function in Old Spanish, as in other Romance languages, was by means of final /s/. This so-called 'adverbial s' has its origins in a number of Latin adverbs which, for a variety of reasons, ended in /s/: the comparatives MAGIS, LAXIUS, etc., just mentioned, FORAS (> OSp. *fueras* 'outside'), POS(T) (> *pues, después*), etc., together with a number which did not leave descendants, like GRĀTIS, ALIĀS. This /s/ was extended to other Old Spanish adverbs, although it does not survive further in all cases: NUMQUAM > *nunca(s)*, ANTE > *antes*, IN TUNC > *entonz* > *entonces*, DUM INTERIM > *domientre* > *demientre* > *(de)mientras*. The same element is also visible in the Old Spanish adverbs *c(i)ertas* 'certainly' and *primas* 'for the first time'. However, 'adverbial s' is at all times too irregularly applied to constitute a genuine derivational suffix.

A genuine adverbial suffix (for adverbs of manner) was created in VL, from the noun MENS, MENTIS 'mind'. The Latin expressions concerned were at first adverbial phrases in which the noun (in Ablative case) was accompanied by an agreeing adjective: DĒVŌTĀ MENTE 'in a devout frame of mind', i.e. 'devoutly'. It will be noted that the fem. gender of MENS requires a fem. form of the adjective. An indication that MENTE is moving towards the status of a derivational suffix comes in late Latin texts in which MENTE is accompanied by adjectives whose meaning is incompatible with the literal meaning of MENTE: LENTĀ MENTE, already at this stage, can only be glossed as 'slowly', the notion of 'mind' having been lost. The addition of MENTE to a fem. adjective remains the only productive means of creating adverbs in Spanish, although it will be noted that relics of the former independent status of *-mente* are to be found in the accentual pattern of the words concerned (these adverbs have two full stresses, unlike any other 'word') and in the fact that where more than one adverb, similarly formed, occur together, *-mente* appears only with the last: *lenta y cuidadosamente*.

In Old Spanish, the ending *-mente* alternated with *-miente* and *-mientre* (e.g. *fuertemiente, fuertemientre*), forms conceivably modified under the influence of *(do)mientre* (< DUM INTERIM; see above). A further, occasional, source of adverbial expressions in Old Spanish was the juxtaposition of a feminine adjective with the noun *guisa: fiera guisa* 'boldly'.

Other adverbs form a heterogeneous group, with varied forms and origins:

> *Aquí* < ECCUM HĪC, *ahi* < *a* + OSp. *y* 'there' < IBĪ (with loss of -B- under the influence of HĪC), *alli* < AD ILLĪC, *acá* < ECCUM HĀC, *allá* < AD ILLĀC, OSp. *end(e)* 'thence, for that reason' < INDE, OSp. *o* 'where' < UBĪ, *do* 'whence', later 'where' < *de* + *o*, OSp. *ond(e)* 'whence' < UNDE, OSp. *dond(e)* 'whence', later 'where' < *de* + *ond(e)*. *encima* < *en* + *cima* 'top', OSp. *suso* 'above' < SURSUM, *arriba* < *a* + OSp. *riba* 'riverbank', *debajo, abajo* < *de/a* + *bajo*, OSp. *(a)yuso* 'below' < DEORSUM (with the tonic vowel of SURSUM).

> *Ahora* < OSp. *agora* < HĀC HŌRĀ, *entonces*, OSp. *entonz, estonz* (see above), *luego* 'at once', later 'next', < (IN) LOCŌ, for ILICŌ, *aún* < ADHŪC (with the /-n/ of *sin, según*, etc.), *ya* < IAM, *jamás* < IAM MAGIS, *nunca* (see above), *cuando* < QUANDŌ, *hoy* < HODIĒ, *ayer* < *a* + HERĪ, OSp. *cras* 'tomorrow' < CRAS, *mañana* OSp. 'early', then 'tomorrow' < (HORA) *MĀNEĀNA, for MĀNE.

> *Asi* < *a* + OSp. *si* 'thus', later 'yes' < SĪC; *no*, OSp. *no(n)* < NŌN; *como*, OSp. *cuemo/como* < VL QUŌMŌ, CL QUŌMODŌ.

Note that the discussion above (3.3.2) concerning comparison of adjectives also applies, *mutatis mutandis*, to the comparison of adverbs. Thus, FORTITER – FORTIUS – FORTISSIME (as well as showing replacement of the simple adverbial ending by *-mente*; see this section) gives way to *fuertemente – más fuertemente – (lo) más fuertemente*. Again, only the commonest synthetic comparatives escape the analytical process. In the case of adverbs, there is only one surviving synthetic form: MINUS > *(lo) menos*.

3.5 The pronoun

The Latin pronouns had final morphemes which, like those of nouns and adjectives, indicated case and number, and which, like those of adjectives, indicated gender. These endings were for the most part phonologically the same as those of nouns and adjectives and were subject, in general, to the same processes of merger and loss (see 3.2.1–2, 3.3.1). However, personal and demonstrative pronouns have retained neuter singular forms (*ello, esto, eso,* etc.) separate from those of the masc. and fem.; these came to be used not to refer to the class of neuter nouns (which disappeared in spoken Latin), but to refer to ideas and propositions not reducible to a single noun. Likewise, although sentence-function ('case') is no longer signalled in the form of Spanish nouns, adjectives and most pronouns (as a result of the merger of the Latin case-endings), the personal pronouns have retained certain morphemes of case (e.g. Nominative or subject-case *ella,* vs Accusative or direct-object-case *la,* vs Dative or indirect-object-case *le*).

3.5.1 Personal pronouns

Latin had specifically personal pronouns only for the first and second grammatical persons; for the third person, Latin used any of the demonstratives (IS, HIC, ISTE, ILLE), although ILLE came to be preferred in this new role and provides the Spanish pronouns of the third person.

Except as the subject of a verb or as the object of a preposition, the Latin personal pronouns lost their stress (in cases where they had stress in Latin) and became clitics (i.e. they came to form a single phonological word together with some preceding or following stressed word, usually a verb). As a result of this change, the personal pronoun system of Spanish is best described as divided into stressed (or tonic) forms and unstressed (or atonic) forms:

	Tonic		Atonic	
	Subject	With preposition	Direct object	Indirect object
1 sg	EGŌ > *yo*	MIHĪ > *mí*	MĒ > *me*	MĒ > *me*
2 sg	TŪ > *tú*	TIBĪ > *ti*	TĒ > *te*	TĒ > *te*
3 sg m	ILLE > *él*	ILLE > *él*	ILLUM > *lo*	ILLĪ > *le*
f	ILLA > *ella*	ILLA(M) > *ella*	ILLAM > *la*	ILLĪ > *le*
n	ILLUD > *ello*	ILLUD > *ello*	ILLUD > *lo*	ILLĪ > *le*
1 pl	NŌS > *nos(otros)*	NŌS > *nos(otros)*	NŌS > *nos*	NŌS > *nos*
2 pl	VŌS > *vos(otros)*	VŌS > *vos(otros)*	VŌS > *(v)os*	VŌS > *(v)os*
3 pl m	ILLŌS > *ellos*	ILLŌS > *ellos*	ILLŌS > *los*	ILLĪS > *les*
f	ILLĀS > *ellas*	ILLĀS > *ellas*	ILLĀS > *las*	ILLĪS > *les*
3 sg/pl	(reflexive)	SIBĪ > *sí*	SĒ > *se*	SĒ > *se*

1 The subject forms of Spanish listed above descend in almost all cases from a Latin Nominative form (for popular Latin Nom. plur. fem. in -ĀS,

see 3.2.1 and Aebischer 1971). The exception is masc. pl. ILLŌS; in this instance, for similar reasons to those operating in the noun (preservation of /-s/ as a marker of plurality, etc.), originally Accus. ILLŌS additionally acquires Nom. role. The expanded form *vosotros*, introduced in late Old Spanish to distinguish the plural pronoun from frequently singular *vos*, will be considered in 3.5.1.1. The contemporary expansion *nos > nosotros* is an analogical imitation of the latter process.

It will be noted that those forms of the personal pronouns which retain their stress retain also the same number of syllables as their Latin antecedents (except for the regular loss of final -E in ILLE; see 2.4.3.2). Similarly, stressed forms alone show regular development of -LL- > /λ/; the apparent exception ILLE > *él* is accounted for in 2.5.3.2(9). Malkiel 1976 shows that EGŌ > EO > *yo* involves a regular development of the VL diphthong observable in this pronoun.

The pronouns *usted* and *ustedes* will be considered in 3.5.1.1.

2 The pronominal forms which follow prepositions descend for the most part from Latin Accus. forms, but can be seen to have become identical, in most cases, to the subject forms. Such identity already existed in Latin in some cases (ILLUD, NŌS, VŌS, probably also ILLĀS), or came about through phonological change (Accus. ILLAM, Abl. ILLĀ merge with Nom. ILLA), or through extension of Nom. function to an Accus. form (ILLŌS). Also implied is the same merger of Accus. and Abl. (and sometimes Dat.) forms we have observed in the development of the late VL Oblique case of the noun (see 3.2.1).

The 1st and 2nd sing. forms, like the 3rd pers. reflexive pronoun *sí* (< SIBĪ), descend from the Latin Dat. (with raising of tonic /e/ due to metaphony ascribable to final -ī; see 2.4.2.1). The use of the Dat. in this role (rather than Acc./Abl. MĒ, TĒ, SĒ) is an early innovation of obscure motivation. The fact that only in the 1st and 2nd sing. do the post-prepositional forms differ from the subject forms has led the non-standard speech of some areas (e.g. Aragon, parts of America) to use *yo, tú* after prepositions (*para yo, por tú*, etc.). Even in the standard, the contrast between reflexive *sí* and non-reflexive *él/ella/usted/ellos/ellas/ustedes* is often lost, usually in favour of the non-reflexive form (e.g. *por él* for *por sí*).

The appearance of a post-prepositional form (*él* < ILLE) descended from a Nom. (rather than the expected Acc./Abl.) is in part due to an extension of the substantial identity between subject and post-prepositional forms already commented on and in part to a need to preserve contrast between masc. and neut. forms, a problem we shall meet again in the case of the demonstrative (3.5.3).

The prepositional forms *conmigo, contigo, consigo* require special comment. Latin CUM, unlike other 'prepositions', followed certain personal pronouns (which took Abl. form): MĒCUM, TĒCUM, SĒCUM, NŌBĪSCUM, VŌBĪSCUM. Owing to the general convergence of Acc. and Abl. in spoken Latin, the latter two forms were replaced in VL by NŌSCUM, VŌSCUM (cf. *Appendix Probi*: NOBISCUM NON NOSCUM, VOBISCUM NON VOSCUM). The anomaly of post-posed CUM was then partially remedied, by anteposing CUM to the phrase, but (oddly) without deleting it from final position, so that the 'preposition' came to be expressed twice: CUM MĒCUM, CUM TĒCUM, CUM SĒCUM, CUM NŌSCUM, CUM VŌSCUM. These phrases are inherited directly by Old Spanish, but with raising by one degree of the tonic (in the sing. forms by analogy with *por mí, de ti*, etc., and in the plur. forms perhaps by analogy with the vocalic pattern of the sing. forms, namely /o/-/i/-/o/, but with retention of a high tonic back vowel appropriate to the plur. forms): *comigo, contigo, consigo, con(n)usco, convusco*. The two plur. forms were replaced before the end of the Middle Ages by restructured *con nos(otros), con vos(otros)*, but the sing. forms survive (with remodelling of *comigo > conmigo* on the basis of *contigo, consigo*).

3 As noted above, the direct object forms (which descend from the Latin direct object [i.e. Acc.] case-forms) have become atonic and, where not already so, monosyllabic. In addition, they come to form, together with a verb, a single phonological word (i.e. they become cliticized). It will be noted that because of the loss of tonicity of this class of words, direct (and, for that matter, indirect) object forms of ILLE show early reduction of -LL- to /l/ and escape the palatalization of -LL- > /ʎ/ which occurs, regularly, in subject and other tonic forms.

The forms listed here, including the late Old Spanish reduction of *vos > os*, continue with direct object function in many varieties of Spanish (principally Andalusian and American), but it will be noted that, in the Peninsular standard, certain interferences have taken place between direct and indirect object form (see comments on **leísmo** and **laísmo** in the following section).

4 The indirect object forms descend in part from Latin indirect object (i.e. Dat.) forms (ILLĪ, ILLĪS), but also show VL replacement of Dat. MIHĪ, TIBĪ, SIBĪ, NŌBIS, VŌBIS by Acc. MĒ, TĒ, SĒ, NŌS, VŌS, and therefore convergence in these instances with the direct object forms. The descendants of these forms have all become cliticized in the same way as the direct object forms have been. Like the latter, they have become monosyllabic and show early reduction of -LL- > /l/.

The form *le* is the first to show change of function. Already in early Old Spanish (e.g. *CMC* 655: *al bueno de mio Cid en Alcoçer le van çercar*), *le* is being used as a direct object form in the case of masc. personal referents (just as in the modern Peninsular standard). Northern dialects go further and use *le* as a direct object form for masc. countable referents (whether personal or non-personal; e.g. *esto vaso no hay que romperle*), but not for non-countable (or mass) referents (e.g. *heno, aire, machismo*). Such extension of the role of *le* is referred to as **leísmo**, while the retention of *lo* in its traditional, etymological function as a personal (as well as a non-personal) masc. pronoun is labelled **loísmo**. The latter term is also used for the very occasional extension of *lo* to indirect object function.

The counterpart of *leísmo* is **laísmo**, the use of *la* in (fem.) indirect as well as direct object role (e.g. *la di el papel a tu madre*). This (non-standard but frequent) usage perhaps represents a further step (beyond that represented by *leísmo*) towards a system of pronoun-reference in which case-distinctions are suppressed and gender-distinctions are enhanced.

Use of *les* for *los* (i.e. as [masc.] direct as well as indirect object) is less common than singular *leísmo*, and is today regarded as less than fully acceptable. Plural *laísmo* (*las* for *les*) is rare.

When a clause contained both a 3rd pers. indirect object pronoun (ILLĪ) and a 3rd pers. direct object pronoun (ILLUM, ILLAM, ILLUD, ILLŌS, ILLĀS), results different from those listed above are observable. After normal VL vowel-development and reduction of -LL- to /l/, the sequences ILLĪ ILLUM, ILLĪ ILLAM, etc., became /eljelo/, /eljela/, etc. Thereafter, normal Castilian treatment of the /l/ + /j/ cluster (see 2.5.2.2[2]) and elision of /e-/ (as in all other atonic personal pronouns) account for the appearance of the Old Spanish forms *gelo, gela*, etc. These forms also subsume the descendants of ILLĪS ILLUM, i.e. where the indirect object was plural and where the /s/ of ILLĪS might have been expected to prevent the formation of the glide [j] (only possible in cases of hiatus; see 2.4.3.2) and therefore of OSp. /ʒ/ (spelt *g*). That is, OSp. *gelo, gela*, etc., allow both sing. and plur. indirect object referents; *digelo* means 'I gave it to him/her/it/them'. This indeterminacy of number is inherited by the modern Spanish descendants of these words (*se lo, se la*, etc.), and since this *se* is often referentially equivalent to *le* (both mean 'to him, to her'), *le* may be found also with plur. value (e.g. *le di la carta* 'I gave them the letter') in modern non-standard usage.

The replacement of OSp. *gelo* by *se lo* is in part a phonological matter (confusion in the sixteenth century between /ʃ/ (</ʒ/, /ʃ/) and /s/; see 2.6.2[3]) and in part a syntactical one (merger of *gelo* with pre-existing OSp. and MSp. *se lo*, in which *se* is [quasi-]reflexive, so that *su amigo gelo tomó* 'his friend took it from him' becomes identical with *su amigo se lo tomó* 'his friend took it [for himself]').

In Old Spanish, the atonic personal pronouns were essentially enclitic (i.e. they normally formed a single phonological word with a preceding stressed word, usually but not exclusively a verb). As a result, the /e/ of *me, te, le, se* was subject to loss, like any other final /e/, when the preceding word ended in a vowel (see 2.4.3.2). This apocopation was most frequent in the case of *le* and *se* (e.g. *metiól en el mayor az, antes quel prendan, pagós mio Cid, nos van* 'no se van') and occasional examples are to be found still in the fifteenth century. Apocopation of *me* and *te* was always less frequent (e.g. *déxem ir en paz, nom lo aviedes rrogado, veot aguijar, éstot lidiaré aquî*) and does not survive the thirteenth century.

   The positioning of Old Spanish atonic pronouns followed rules different from those of the modern language, where such pronouns may follow only the infinitive, the gerund or a positive imperative. In Old Spanish, the pronoun(s) followed the verb (finite or non-finite), unless the verb was preceded, in the same clause, by another tonic word (noun, adverb, tonic pronoun, etc.). Thus: *e tornós pora su casa, ascóndense de mio Cid*, but *non lo desafié, aquel que gela diesse*. This position-rule does not give way to the modern rule until the Golden Age, when it is still observed by many seventeenth-century writers. It should be noted that if the first tonic word of an Old Spanish clause was a future or conditional verb or a compound verbal form consisting of participle + some form of *aver* (normally in this order under these circumstances), then any atonic pronoun(s) were positioned between the two elements which make up such verbal forms (for the compound nature of the fut. and cond., see 3.7.7.4.1): *dargelo he* (MSp. *se lo daré*), *dargelo ia/ie* (MSp. *se lo daría*), *dado gelo ha* (MSp. *se lo ha dado*), etc. The Old Spanish constituent order continues into the Golden Age, but apart from occasional seventeenth-century examples like Gracián's *escusarse ia* (see Lapesa 1980: 392), the two elements which comprise the future and conditional are inseparable from the end of the sixteenth century.

3.5.1.1   Forms of address

In the 2nd person of the pronoun system, Latin at first made distinctions only of number, TŪ being used whenever a single individual was addressed, whatever his or her status *vis-à-vis* the speaker, and VŌS used for addressing more than one person. In later Latin, vōs was used, in addition, for deferential address of a single person, apparently beginning with the Emperor, but then becoming extended to other circumstances where deference or formality of address was appropriate. This system, in which vōs has both singular (deferential) and plural (deferential and non-deferential) values continues in early Old Spanish, as it still does in modern French. In *CMC*, the king is addressed as *vos*, as is the Cid (by the king and others); the Cid addresses Ximena and most of his relatives as *vos*, but uses *tú* to his younger kinsmen. The young infantes de Carrión are always addressed as *tú*. At this stage, the system of forms of address can be described as follows:

	non-deferential	deferential
sing.	*tú*	*vos*
plur.	*vos*	*vos*

However, in later Old Spanish, it is evident that *vos* has widened its range of reference in such a way that it is used for many social relationships, and thus has lost much of its deferential value. By the fifteenth century, *vos* has become so close in value to informal *tú* that new deferential forms of address are experimented with, based on abstract nouns such as *merced* 'grace', *señoría* 'lordship', etc. Although occasional examples of *tu merced* are found, it was *vuestra merced* that found favour, together with *vuestras mercedes*, representing an entirely new plural deferential category. In the same (late Old Spanish) period, plural *vos*, restricted to non-deferential value by the creation of *vuestras mercedes*, was regularly expanded to *vosotros*. The combination *vos + otros* had previously been available with contrastive value (cf. Fr. *vous autres*), but now becomes the unmarked plural form, in opposition to singular *vos*. Perhaps by imitation of *vosotros*, *nos* is also regularly replaced by *nosotros* in the fourteenth and fifteenth centuries.

At the beginning of the Golden Age, the system of forms of address had therefore become:

	non-deferential	deferential
sing.	*tú ~ vos*	*vuestra merced*
plur.	*vosotros*	*vuestras mercedes*

During the Golden Age and the eighteenth century, the competition between *tú* and *vos* was resolved in favour of *tú* throughout the Peninsula and in those parts of America (Peru, Bolivia, Mexico) in closest contact with cultural developments in Spain. At the same time, the cumbersome form of address *vuestra merced* underwent a series of contractions, at first disallowed in cultured speech, which gave rise to *vuesarced, voacé, vucé, vuced, vusted*, etc., and finally *usted*. Likewise, *vuestras mercedes* was eventually reduced to *ustedes*. As a result, the modern system of pronominal address emerges:

	non-deferential	deferential
sing.	*tú*	*usted*
plur.	*vosotros*	*ustedes*

In Western Andalusia and in the whole of America, the distinction between deferential and non-deferential plural forms has again been lost, but in favour of the originally deferential form *ustedes*, which in these areas is now therefore the equivalent (in non-deferential cases) of standard Peninsular *vosotros*. Meanwhile, the competition in America between *tú* and *vos* for singular non-deferential use is differently resolved in different areas: we have seen that Mexico, Peru and Bolivia came to prefer *tú*, as did the Caribbean islands and most of Venezuela; it can now be added that in those areas most culturally 'distant' from Spain (e.g. Argentina, Uruguay, Paraguay, the central American states) *vos* came to dominate, while in other areas the two forms of address continue to compete, in complex sociolinguistic relationship (e.g. Chile, Ecuador, Colombia). Simplifying somewhat the complexity of the relationship between the two singular non-deferential forms, the forms of address used in American Spanish can be said to be:

	non-deferential	deferential
sing.	*tú ~ vos*	*usted*
plur.	*ustedes*	*ustedes*

It should be noted that whichever of the two subject pronouns, *tú* or *vos*, is used as the form of non-deferential address, the associated object pronoun (direct and indirect) is *te* and that the associated possessive forms are *tu* and *tuyo*. Where the expressed or unexpressed subject form is *vos*, we therefore find such constructions as the following: *(Vos) quedáte aquí* '(you) stay here (imper.)', *(Vos) te quedás aquí* 'you stay here (indic.)', *(vos) indicáme tu casa* '(you) show me your house', *(vos) siempre salís con lo tuyo* 'you always get your own way', etc. (For the verbal forms used in conjunction with *vos*, see 3.7.2.1–2.)

3.5.2 The possessive

Although the possessive functions not solely as a pronoun (it can also be adjectival), it will be considered at this point, since its similarities with other adjectives are more superficial than fundamental.

Latin had the following set of possessives:

	sing. possessor	plur. possessor
1st pers.	MEUS	NOSTER
2nd pers.	TUUS	VESTER
3rd pers. (refl.)	SUUS	SUUS

These forms were fully inflected (by means of endings identical to those of adjectives), each showing concordance with its noun referent in terms of case, number and gender.

The form VESTER had a VL competitor VOSTER. The latter was perhaps an older, undissimilated, form (displaced by VESTER in the standard); alternatively, it may have arisen through analogy with NOSTER, aided by the similarity of structure of the related personal pronouns NŌS, VŌS.

The form SUUS was used only when the possessor was the subject of the clause containing the possessive; it was therefore, at first, solely a reflexive form. When reference was to a possessor other than the clause-subject, Latin used invariable EIUS (lit. 'of him/her/it') or EŌRUM (lit. 'of them'). However, this distinction between reflexive and non-reflexive possessive was lost in VL, SUUS being used in both instances. By contrast, a distinction came to be made, in some varieties of spoken Latin, between the 3rd-pers. possessive appropriate to a sing. possessor and that used when the possessor was plural. In these varieties of VL, which did not include the Latin spoken in most of the Peninsula, SUUS was reserved for sing. possessors and ILLŌRUM (lit. 'of them') came to be used in the case of a plur. possessor.

Each of the forms listed above could function *adjectivally* (i.e. in connection with an expressed noun; e.g. FRĀTER MEUS 'my brother'), or *pronominally* (i.e. in isolation from a noun, whether expressed or not; e.g. NOSTRĪ 'our ones' [masc.]). As we shall see, this dual function is retained, in essence, by the Old Spanish possessive, but only partially by the modern language.

With the reassignment of neuter nouns to the masc. and fem. genders (see 3.2.2.1), the neuter endings of the possessive fell from use. Similarly, as distinctions of case came to be expressed by means other than word-endings (see 3.2.1), so the various case-endings of the possessive merged (or were lost), in exactly the same way as occurred in the noun. As a result, Old Spanish retains only four forms of each possessive: masc. sing., fem. sing., masc. plur., and fem. plur., which have descended in the following way into early Old Spanish:

		sing.	plur.
m.	MEU > *mio*		MEŌS > *mios*
f.	MEA > *mia/mie/mi*		MEĀS > *mias/mies/mis*
m.	TUU > *to*		TUŌS > *tos*
f.	TUA > *(tua)/tue/tu*		TUĀS > *(tuas)/tues/tus*
m.	SUU > *so*		SUŌS > *sos*
f.	SUA > *(sua)/sue/su*		SUĀS > *(suas)/sues/sus*
m.	NOSTRU > *nuestro*		NOSTRŌS > *nuestros*
f.	NOSTRA > *nuestra*		NOSTRĀS > *nuestras*
m.	VOSTRU > *vuestro*		VOSTRŌS > *vuestros*
f.	VOSTRA > *vuestra*		VOSTRĀS > *vuestras*

The forms in parentheses (*tua[s]*, *sua[s]*) are rare.

Whether their function was adjectival (either before or after a noun) or pronominal, all the Old Spanish forms appear to have been fully tonic, like their Latin antecedents, but unlike some of their modern descendants, e.g. *el mio fiel vassallo, mios yernos, la mi muger, mis fijas; se fará lo to, las tus mañas, el so* ('el suyo'), *fue so criado, todos los sos, a sus dueñas.*

Masc. *mio/mios* are the regular reflexes of MEU/MEŌS; this sequence of vowels normally produces /ió/ (see Malkiel 1976). These forms were at first monosyllabic (*mió/miós*), but rhyme and assonance reveal that they were gradually replaced by bisyllabic *mio/mios*, no doubt by analogy with the fem. forms, which almost always show forms with tonic /i/.

The fem. forms (sing. possessor) descend from VL forms in which raising of the tonic has taken place, by dissimilation from final /a/ in hiatus; thus MEA = /méa/ > /méa/, TUA = /tóa/ > /túa/, SUA = /sóa/ > /súa/, by contrast the masc. forms, where simple merger of like vowels takes place. Indeed, the 1st-pers. fem. form has undergone such dissimilation *twice*, since VL /méa/ has its tonic vowel further raised to /mía/. These fem. forms also reveal the beginnings of a separation of pronominal from adjectival forms. When used pronominally or as an adjective *following* a noun, there is a preference for forms in /-a/: *mia(s), tuya(s), suya(s)* (for the latter two forms, see below). By contrast, the forms *mie/mi*, etc., are almost exclusively used adjectivally before a noun.

Full separation into two sets of possessive forms takes place in the late Old Spanish period. When used adjectivally before a noun, the possessives lose their tonicity, shed their final vowels and (in the case of *to[s], so[s]*) suffer raising of their newly atonic vowels. In atonic position, as a result, the contrast of gender is lost. However, it should be noted that the forms *nuestro(s), -a(s), vuestro(s), -a(s)* escape this loss of stress and the consequent merger of masc. and fem. forms. To summarize these late Old Spanish changes in pre-noun position:

$$
\begin{array}{c}
\left.\begin{array}{l} mio(s) \\ mi(e)(s) \end{array}\right\} \quad > \quad mi(s) \\[1em]
\left.\begin{array}{l} to(s) \\ tu(e)(s) \end{array}\right\} \quad > \quad tu(s) \\[1em]
\left.\begin{array}{l} so(s) \\ su(e)(s) \end{array}\right\} \quad > \quad su(s)
\end{array}
$$

This loss of tonicity and reduction of form is accompanied by the loss of the definite article, which in Old Spanish frequently accompanied the possessive in pre-noun position (see examples above), so that such sequences as *la mi casa* are rare by the early sixteenth century.

When used pronominally or when adjectival after a noun, the possessives remain fully tonic, remain bisyllabic (in the case of *mio[s]*, become bisyllabic), and in some cases are reinforced with an intervocalic consonant:

mio(s)	>	*mio(s)*
mia(s)	>	*mia(s)*
to(s)	>	*tuyo(s)*
tua(s)	>	*tuya(s)*
so(s)	>	*suyo(s)*
sua(s)	>	*suya(s)*

This expansion begins early in the fem. forms. We have seen that *tua(s)* and *sua(s)* were rare in Old Spanish; they were rapidly replaced by *tuya(s)* and *suya(s)* partly for phonological reasons (to provide a sharper syllabic boundary than existed while /u/ and /a/ were in hiatus) and partly for analogical reasons (the possessives are in close semantic relationship with the interrogative pronoun meaning 'whose', i.e. OSp. *cuyo, -a* [e.g. *¿Cúyo es?* 'whose is it?'; see 3.5.4], and the form of the interrogative word influenced the form of its frequent [possessive] reply). Since this restructuring appears to have occurred first in the feminine, it follows that, for a time, the 2nd and 3rd person possessives showed the following alternation: masc. *to(s), so(s)*, fem. *tuya(s), suya(s)*. However, this alternation was levelled in the fourteenth century by the appearance of masc. *tuyo(s), suyo(s)*.

The lack of precision of the forms *su(s), suyo(s), -a(s)* has led to modifications, in the modern period, to many noun phrases containing a possessive. We have seen that Lat. SUUS was already appropriate to both sing. and plur. possessors and that this duality is inherited by Spanish; we have also seen that as well as being a reflexive possessive, SUUS additionally became non-reflexive in VL. With the late medieval appearance of *vuestra(s) merced(es)* (see 3.5.1.1), the forms *su(s), suyo(s), -a(s)* came to be used not just as 3rd-person, but as 2nd-person (deferential) possessives. This burden of values has come to be relieved by the optional addition of, or replacement by, genitive phrases (*de él, de ella, de ellos, de ellas, de Vd.*, etc.), so that, e.g. *su casa* may be clarified as *su casa de él, su casa de Vd.*, etc. (Note the similarity of this development with the Lat. use of EIUS, EŌRUM and, later in some areas, ILLŌRUM; see above.) Particularly in American Spanish, these genitive phrases may become obligatory, to such an extent that *su(s)* becomes redundant and is replaced by the definite article: *su casa de él* > *la casa de él*; similarly, phrases like *es suyo* are often entirely displaced by *es de él*, etc. The final step (replacement of other possessives by genitive phrases (e.g. *nuestra casa* > *la casa de nosotros*) has been taken only by some (non-standard) varieties of Spanish.

3.5.3   Demonstratives and articles

We shall see in 3.5.3.2 that the Spanish definite article descends from the Latin 3rd-person demonstrative, so that it is convenient to deal together with these categories, even though the indefinite article develops from a different category, the numeral (for which, see 3.6).

3.5.3.1   The demonstratives

The Latin demonstratives were fully inflected, like other pronouns and adjectives, in accordance with the case, number and gender of the referent concerned. Case-distinctions were merged or lost in the ways discussed in

3.2.1–2 and 3.3.1. However, whereas the neuter forms of most other adjectives and pronouns were lost (for lack of neuter referents, once neuter nouns had been reclassified as masc. or fem.), the demonstratives retain a separate neuter form (see 3.5, and below), used to refer to ideas and propositions not reducible to a single noun.

Latin used the same demonstrative forms in both adjectival and pronominal function. The CL forms concerned, HIC, ISTE and ILLE, constituted a three-place system, in which each demonstrative was related to one of the three grammatical persons. HIC was thus applied to referents near to or concerned with the speaker, ISTE to referents near to or concerned with the person spoken to, while ILLE was used in the case of referents near to or associated with neither the speaker nor the person addressed. This system has been inherited intact by Spanish, although the Spanish exponents of the system (*este, ese, aquel*) do not descend from the corresponding forms of the Latin system (except, partially, in the case of *aquel*). The Latin demonstratives (and certain related forms) underwent a series of changes of function which can be represented in the following way:

anaphoric	personal	demonstr 1	demonstr 2	demonstr 3	emphasis	identity
IS	ILLE	HIC	ISTE	ILLE	IPSE	ĪDEM
ILLE	ILLE	ISTE	IPSE	*ACCU ILLE	*MEDIPSISSIMUS	
el (que)	*él*	*este*	*ese*	*aquel*	*mismo*	

1 The phonological weakness of HIC, especially after the early loss of /h/ (2.5.2), is no doubt a major factor in its almost entire elimination from Latin speech, although there is evidence that, prior to its disappearance, it became a competitor of IS, in largely anaphoric role (i.e. it functioned mostly as the antecedent of a relative: IS QUI . . . 'he who . . .', etc.), a role from which both IS and HIC were anyway displaced by ILLE.

2 Loss of HIC was accompanied by transfer of ISTE from 2nd-person to 1st-person demonstrative role (the role still played by the Spanish descendant of ISTE, namely *este*). The Latin demonstrative system was in this way reduced from a three-place system to one of two places, a type which persisted into such Romance languages as Old French.

3 However, in more conservative areas such as Spain, the three-place system was restored by transfer of IPSE from its emphatic role (e.g. IPSE RĒX, originally 'the king himself') to 2nd-person demonstrative role. It is thus from IPSE that the Spanish 2nd-person demonstrative (*ese*) descends.

4 It will be seen from the chart above that ILLE was over-worked. Not only was it a 3rd-person demonstrative, but it also functioned as an anaphoric and as a personal pronoun (see also 3.5.1). Additionally, ILLE came to be used as a definite article (see 3.5.3.2). To avoid ambiguity, ILLE was reinforced, when it functioned as a demonstrative, by means of various deictic ('pointing') particles. VL ECCE ILLE, ATQUE ILLE, ECCU ILLE are attested in many areas; in Spain, the prefix took the form *ACCU (*ACCU ILLE > *aquel*).

5 When IPSE passed into the demonstrative system, its emphatic role was expressed by an expanded form *MEDIPSISSIMUS (a variant of attested METIPSISSIMUS), which additionally took over the role of IDEM; that is, *RĒX METIPSISSIMUS came to mean not only 'the king himself', 'the very king', but also 'the same king'. The Spanish descendants of *MEDIPSISSIMUS maintain this dual role, although the different senses may be distinguished by word-order: *el mismo rey* 'the king himself' or 'the same king', *el rey mismo* 'the king himself'. Spanish shows a number of competing descendants of *MEDIPSISSIMUS: in early Old Spanish, *meísmo* is found alongside *me(e)smo*, while from the fourteenth century *mesmo* is more frequent than *mismo* (<*meísmo*). This continues to be the case in the Golden Age, but by the seventeenth century *mismo* is the preferred form in the standard, and in the following century *mesmo* comes to be restricted to rural use.

In the phonological development of ISTE, IPSE and *ACCU ILLE, only the masc. sing. forms require comment, since it might be expected that, according to what we observe in the case of nouns and adjectives (see 3.2.1, 3.3.1), Nom. ISTE, Acc. ISTUM and Dat./Abl. ISTŌ would merge as *esto*, while *eso* and *aquello* would be the predicted outcomes of the 2nd- and 3rd-person masc. sing. demonstratives. The emergence of *este, ese, aquel* must be due to the need to distinguish the masc. sing. forms from neuter *esto, eso, aquello* (< ISTUD, IPSUM, *ACCU ILLUD). In Old Spanish, the masc. sing. forms often lose their final /e/ (*est, es*), in accordance with 2.4.3.2.

Although the distinguishing prefix *ACCU was strictly required only in the 3rd person, it was often applied to the other demonstratives, in medieval and Golden Age Spanish; *est(e)* and *es(se)* therefore alternated with *aquest(e)* and *aques(se)*, although the longer alternants were then rejected.

3.5.3.2 *The articles*

Latin originally lacked (and in its Classical form continued to lack) both definite and indefinite articles. Perhaps through the frequent bilingual use of Latin with Greek, both in Rome and in the East, speakers of Latin came to feel the need for such determiners and used pre-existing Latin particles to supply the newly felt need.

The essential function of the **indefinite** article is to refer to an individual (thing or person) not present before the participators in a dialogue and so far unknown to the hearer(s); e.g. 'Once upon a time there was a king....'. Since the singularity (not to say the uniqueness) of the individual is important in such a speech-situation, it is not surprising that VL should have used the numeral ŪNUS 'one' to fulfil this newly-required role.

Masc. ŪNUS loses its final /o/ (>*un*; see 2.4.3.2), while fem. ŪNA > *una*, except that in Old Spanish, final /a/ was elided when the following word began with a vowel (*un escoba, un onda*) and not solely before word-initial /á/, as happens in the modern language. The plurals *unos, -as* are not articles in any real sense, and are best considered together with other quantifiers.

The most basic function of the **definite** article is to refer to an individual or individuals (things or persons) not present before the participators in a dialogue but already known to the hearer(s); e.g. 'Once upon a time there was a king. **The** king had three daughters.' Under these speech-circumstances, it is understandable that an adjective of emphasis or emphasis/identity (IPSE RĒX 'the king himself') or a demonstrative appropriate to an absent individual (ILLE RĒX 'that king') should be pressed into service as a definite article by speakers of Latin. IPSE was preferred in this function in part of the Latin-speaking world (Sardinia, Balearic Islands, Costa Brava), but ILLE was elsewhere used as the VL definite article.

Just as happened when ILLE was used as an atonic personal pronoun (see 3.5.1), loss of tonicity on the part of ILLE, when used as an article, caused the reduction of -LL- to /l/ (rather than /λ/). However, the occasional medieval and early modern spelling *ell* of the masc. sing. and fem. sing. article, when the word it determined began with a vowel, suggests that the change -LL- > /λ/ *did* occur in this form of the article, perhaps at first only when -LL- was immediately followed by a tonic vowel (*ell omne, ell alma*), but later before atonic vowels too (*ell ermano, ell ermana*).

In pre-literary Spanish, the definite article was still bisyllabic (*ela* < ILLA, *elos* < ILLŌS, *elas* < ILLĀS, although the masc. sing. form is not unambiguously attested at the same stage), but lack of stress allowed elision of the initial vowel of the plural form (> *los, las*). In the singular forms, lack of stress led to the loss of one or other of the vowels (and, in some dialects, before a vowel, to loss of both). Thus masc. **elo* > *el* (and, in Old and early Modern Spanish, sometimes *ell* [see above] before a vowel, conditions under which N Castilian dialects today allow reduction to /l/). Pre-literary fem. *ela* is reduced, in Old Spanish, either to *la* (where the following word begins with a consonant) or to *el* (when the next word had vocalic onset). Fem. *el* competes with occasional *ell*. This distribution of fem. forms continues until the sixteenth century, when fem. *ell* is lost and *el* is replaced by *la* except before /á/ (*el arpa, el hambre*).

Like other medieval Romance languages, Old Spanish saw the extension of the use of the definite article from the circumstances described above to an increasingly wide range of other groups of nouns. Nouns used generically (in the singular) or collectively (in the plural) did not in Old Spanish normally carry an article (*miseria de omne, cristianos e moros*); nor did abstracts (*vedar compra*). The article also frequently did not appear in prepositional phrases where today it is present (*en campo, en mano*); nor did it appear with river-names (*cruzar Arlanzón*). In all these cases (and some others), the definite article only gradually came to be used, in most cases by the early Golden Age.

3.5.4   Relatives and interrogatives

The Latin interrogative QUIS merged entirely with relative QUĪ and three members of the merged paradigm survive in Spanish: QUĪ > *qui*, QUEM > *quien*, QUID > *que*, although it is possible that other forms of the Latin interrogative/relative (e.g. QUAE) contribute to the form of *que*.

In Old Spanish, *qui* alternates with *quien*, with personal reference, both as subject of the clause (interrogative or relative) and as the object of a preposition: *a qui...*, etc. *Qui* is also occasionally found in combination with certain determiners, e.g. *aquel qui*. In this latter instance, *que* was always commoner, and in its other functions, *qui* was entirely displaced by *quien* before the end of the Middle Ages, even though in the thirteenth and fourteenth centuries *qui* is extremely frequent in circumstances where the modern language requires *quienquiera que* or *cualquier persona que* (e.g. OSp. *qui lo fiziere* 'anyone who does so').

The diphthong /ie/ of *quien* (< QUĔM) suggests that this form emerged first in interrogative role only, where it would be fully tonic. However, even before the emergence of literary Old Spanish, *quien* had already acquired the relative value it still has (restricted then as now to personal reference), and had extended its role from Accusative to Nominative, as well as coming to be used as the object of a preposition (*a quien*, etc.), and as a plural (as well as a singular) form. Plur. *quienes* arises only in the Golden Age, although most writers prefer plural *quien* until at least the eighteenth century.

In interrogative function, *qué* has always been restricted to non-personal use, except in adjectival role, where its more frequent competitor is *qual* (< QUĀLIS; later *cual*), a form which has always been present in Spanish as an interrogative pronoun. However, relative *que* has always been capable of personal as well as non-personal reference, as subject or object of a relative clause, singular or plural. In other words, although *que* inherits its form predominantly from Neut. QUID, it inherits also the functions of Masc. Nom. QUI, Fem. Nom. QUAE, Masc. Acc. QUEM, and Fem. Acc. QUAM (as well as all the Nom. and Acc. plural forms QUĪ, QUŌS, etc.).

The pre-Classical Latin interrogative/relative adj. CŪIUS 'whose', although falling out of use in literary and non-literary Latin in the central parts of the Empire, continued to be used in the spoken Latin of Sardinia and Spain, where it survives as *cuyo* (cf. Ptg. *cujo*). In Old and early modern Spanish, this form could still function as an interrogative (e.g. *¿Cúyo es?*

'whose is it?'), a value it retains in the Spanish of the Canaries and parts of America (see Lapesa 1980: 587).

Lat. QUĀLIS 'of which kind?' loses its notion of 'quality' and provides the Spanish interrogative ¿*cuál*? and the relative *el cual*, although it is to be noted that in medieval Spanish relative *qual* was not normally accompanied by the definite article (e.g. *a qual dizen Medina* [*CMC* 2879]).

3.5.5   Indefinites

The Latin indefinite pronouns (and adjectives) were inherited by Spanish only in rare cases: TŌTUS (acquiring also the value of OMNIS) > *todo*; ALTER (combining the sense of ALTER and ALIUS) > *otro* (from which were derived OSp. *otri, otrie* and *otrien* 'somebody else'); *cierto* (< CERTUS) incorporates also the meaning of QUĪDAM; NŪLLUS > OSp. *nul, nulla* (ousted by *ningun[o]*, *-a*, see below); ALIQUOD > *algo*; pre-Classical ALID (CL ALIUD) > OSp. *al* 'something else'.

NĒMŌ was replaced by NEC ŪNUS (> *ningun[o]*, 'nobody' as well as 'none' in medieval and Golden Age Spanish) or by HOMINE NĀTU 'a man born', i.e. 'anyone at all', then 'nobody' (> early OSp. *omne nado*, whence later OSp. *nado*). OSp. *nado* competed with OSp. *nadi* (most probably *nado* modified under the influence of the OSp. interrogative *qui* [see 3.5.4], *pace* Corominas & Pascual 1980–, s.v. *nacer*), and later with *nadie*, whose final syllable arguably shows interference from *quien*. In parallel fashion, NIHIL was replaced by REM NĀTA(M), which gave the occasional OSp. *ren* (Berceo), but was more usually contracted to NĀTA(M), whence Spanish *nada*.

ALIQUIS was expanded to ALIQUIS ŪNUS, whence *algun(o)*, the normal Old Spanish expression for both 'some/any' and 'someone' until the fifteenth-century introduction of its competitor *alguién* (stressed thus) – a form of *alguno* modified under the influence of *quien* – which later displaced *alguno* in the sense 'someone' and suffered accent-shift to *alguien*, perhaps in imitation of the accentual pattern of *algo* 'something'.

QUISQUE gave way in Vulgar Latin to /káta/ (borrowed from Greek), whence *cada (uno)*.

QUĪLIBET, etc., were replaced by new constructions in which *quien, cual, cuando*, etc., were compounded with the pres. subj. of *querer*: *quienquiera, cualquier(a), cuandoquiera*, etc.

3.6   The numeral

3.6.1

The forms of the Latin **cardinal** numerals were invariable except in the case of ŪNUS, DUO, TRĒS, and the hundreds from DUCENTĪ to NONGENTĪ, and

MĪLLE pl. MĪLIA). With the merger of case-endings in the noun (3.2.1), distinction of case is also lost from ŪNUS, etc. Similarly, with the reassignment of neuter nouns to other genders (3.2.2.1), the neuter form of these numerals also had to be abandoned. However, distinction of gender does survive in the members of this group of numerals, except in the case of TRĒS, which already lacked distinction between masc. and fem. forms in Latin. The distinction between MĪLLE 'one thousand' and DUO MĪLIA, etc. 'two thousand', etc., was also abandoned, in favour of invariable MĪLLE.

Because each numeral obviously forms part of an extensive series of numbers, semantic analogy (see 3.1) is especially likely to affect the development of any member of the series. In the following list, predictable phonological change is accounted for by cross-reference to the appropriate discussion elsewhere, and only analogical and other similar changes are commented upon.

ŪNU > *uno/un* (2.4.3.2).

ŪNA > *una/un*. For the loss of final /a/ in *un espada, un onda*, etc., see 3.5.3.2

DUŌS = VL */dóos/ > *dos*

DUĀS = VL */dúas/ > OSp. *duas*, more usually *dues*. The raising of VL tonic /o/ > /u/ in hiatus with final /a/ appears to be a (minor) regular change of Spanish, similar to that which raises VL /é/ > /i/ under the same circumstances (e.g. DĪA > VL /déa/ > Sp. *dia*, and the regular imperfect endings of *-er* and *-ir* verbs (see 3.7.7.3.1).

TRĒS > *tres*.

QUATTUOR = VL */kʷáttor/ (2.4.3, with reduction of two adjacent identical vowels to one) > OSp. *quatro* (2.5.4), later respelled *cuatro*.

QUĪNQUE = VL CINQUE, through dissimilation (2.1.1.2) /kʷ/ ... /kʷ/ > /k/ ... /kʷ/. The final /o/ of OSp. and MSp. *cinco* is probably due to analogy with *cuatro*; Corominas & Pascual 1980–, s.v. *cinco*, quote cases of analogy between the numerals 'four' and 'five' in various languages.

SEX > *seis* (2.4.2.1). The final /s/ is not palatalized, in accordance with 2.5.2.4 (end), although the retention of the glide [i̯] (by contrast with FRAXINU > *fresno*) is unexplained.

SEPTEM > *siete* (2.4.2.2).

OCTO > *ocho*.

NOVEM > *nueve* (2.4.2.2), beside occasional OSp. *nuef* (2.4.3.2) with devoicing of /β/ in word-final position.

DECEM > *diez* (2.4.2.2, 2.4.3.2).

ŪNDECIM, also attested as ŬNDECIM, whence OSp. *onze* (2.5.5) > MSp. *once*.

DUODECIM = VL /dódeke/ (through analogy with the tonic /o/ of DUŌS, and reduction of two identical VL vowels to one) > OSp. *dodze/doze* (2.5.5) > MSp. *doce*, where retention of /-e/ is probably due to analogy with *once, catorce, quince*, whose final vowel must be retained because it follows a consonant group.

TREDECIM > OSp. *tredze/treze* > MSp. *trece* (for /-e/ see *doce*).

QUATTUORDECIM > OSp. *catorze* (2.5.5), with reduction of ŭŏ > /o/ probably on the pattern of *once, doce.*

QUĪNDECIM > OSp. *quinze* (2.5.5) > MSp. *quince.*

SĒDECIM > OSp. *sedze/seze,* replaced by analytical *dizeseis/diezeseis* whence MSp. *dieciséis/diez y seis.*

SEPTENDECIM, OCTŌDECIM, NOVENDECIM were early replaced by the analytical type *DECEM ET SEPTEM, etc., whence OSp. *dizesiete, dizeocho, dizenueve,* MSp. *diecisiete,* etc.

VĪGINTĪ > OSp. *veinte* (with dissimilation of initial /i/ from tonic /i/, whose close aperture is due to metaphony exercised by final ī; see 2.4.2.1) > MSp. *veinte* (with movement of accent from the higher to the lower of two vowels in hiatus; cf. REGĪNA > OSp. *reína* > MSp. *reina*).

TRĪGINTĀ > OSp. *treinta* (with /e/ analogical upon that of *tres* and /i/ on the pattern of OSp. *veínte*) > MSp. *treinta* (with accent-shift as in *veinte*).

QUADRĀGINTĀ = VL QUARAGINTA > OSp. *quaraenta.* After palatalization and loss of G^{e,i} (2.5.2.3 [end]) the accent in Hispano-Latin was retained on the /e/ (<ī) and was not retracted to the preceding /a/, as occurred in the majority of varieties of Romance; cf. Fr. *quarante,* It. *quaranta;* during the thirteenth century the ending *-aenta* was reduced to *-enta* (see Craddock 1985). Thus MSp. (respelled) *cuarenta.*

QUĪNQUĀGINTĀ = VL CINQUAGINTA, via the same dissimilation evident in CINQUE (> *cinco*), whence OSp. *cinquaenta,* MSp. *cincuenta.*

SEXĀGINTĀ > OSp. *sessaenta* (with /-s-/ due to analogy with *seis*) > MSp. *sesenta*).

SEPTUĀGINTĀ > OSp. *setaenta* (with loss of ŭ on the analogy of certain other tens [e.g. *ochaenta*], which can be analysed as 'simple numeral stem' [*och-*] + suffix, here with the reduction of /ie/ to /e/ appropriate to atonic syllables) > MSp. *setenta.*

OCTŌGINTĀ > OSp. *ochaenta* (with replacement of intertonic /o/ by /a/ on the pattern of the other numerals 40–90) > MSp. *ochenta.*

NONĀGINTĀ > OSp. *nonaenta,* beside *novaenta* (the result of an analogical restructuring based on *nueve,* with the replacement of /ue/ by /o/ appropriate to atonic syllables) > MSp. *noventa.*

CENTUM > *ciento,* reduced in Old Spanish before a noun or adjective to *cient* or *cien,* the latter especially where the following word began with a consonant. Only this (originally pre-consonantal) form could survive into the modern language, once the possibility of word-final consonant-groups was rejected by Castilian (see 2.4.3.2).

DUCENTŌS, -ĀS > OSp. *dozientos, -as,* with normal treatment of intervocalic C^{e,i} (2.5.2.3, 2.5.3.2[6]), replaced in early modern Spanish by *doscientos,* which, although written as a single word, reveals the treatment appropriate to initial C^{e,i} (2.5.2.3) and is therefore a compound of *dos* and *ciento(s)* which imitates *cuatrocientos, ochocientos,* etc.

TRECENTŌS > OSp. *trezientos,* replaced by *trescientos* at the same time and for the same reasons as in the case of *doscientos.*

QUADRINGENTŌS does not leave a descendant in Spanish, but was early replaced by a type *QUATTUOR CENTŌS, whence OSp. *quatrocientos,* later respelled *cuatrocientos.*

QUĪNGENTŌS survives in synthetic form as OSp. *quinientos/quiñentos*, showing one of the Castilian treatments of -NG^{e,i}- (>/ɲ/; the other produces OSp. /ndz/). However, the palatal glide of the diphthong [je] either causes dissimilatory depalatalization of /ɲ/>/n/, or is assimilated by it and is absorbed: [ɲj]>[ɲ]. Of the alternative forms thus produced, *quinientos* alone survives into the modern language, no doubt because its ending -*ientos* is shared by the remaining hundreds.

SĒSCENTŌS was already analytical in Latin, and remains so in Spanish: *seiscientos*.

SEPTINGENTŌS, OCTINGENTŌS, NŌNGENTŌS were all replaced, before the emergence of Old Spanish, by analytical *setecientos, ochocientos, novecientos*.

MĪLLE > OSp. *mil, mill*. Both forms must represent /míl/, at least before a consonant, since Old Spanish (like the modern language) did not permit palatals in syllable-final position (see 2.5.3.2[8]). However, it is conceivable that, before a vowel, *mill* indicated /míλ/ (e.g. *mill ombres*), even in the Golden Age. If this pre-vocalic pronunciation existed, it was analogically replaced by /míl/. No trace is found of the Latin plur. MĪLIA (e.g. DUO MĪLIA). In Old Spanish, we find only *dos mil(l)*, etc., or *dos vezes mil(l)*, etc., of which only the former survives beyond the Middle Ages.

The term *millón* is a late fifteenth-century borrowing from Italian. Until that time, only *cuento* was used in this sense.

3.6.2

Few of the Latin **ordinal** numerals have been inherited, as numerals, by Spanish, although rather more have survived in Spanish as nouns (e.g. SEXTA (HORA) > *siesta* 'siesta', DECIMU > *diezmo* 'tithe'). PRĪMUS (which survives as the noun *primo* 'cousin') was in much of W Romance replaced by PRĪMĀRIUS, originally 'of the first rank', whence *primer(o), -a*. SECUNDUS > *segundo*. TERTIUS was replaced by TERTIĀRIUS (> *tercer[o], -a*). QUĀRTUS > *quarto*, later *cuarto*. QUĪNTUS > *quinto*.

The remaining ordinals of Spanish are learned: *sexto, sétimo, octavo*, etc., although Old Spanish also possessed a series in -*eno* (*sesseno, seteno, ocheno*, etc.), of which only *noveno* (together with the nominalized *decena, docena, cuarentena*) survives. However, especially from 'eleventh' onwards, Spanish more frequently uses cardinal numerals in ordinal function.

3.6.3

The only Latin **multiple** numeral to be inherited by Spanish is *doble* (<DUPLUS, which Corominas & Pascual [1980–, s.v. *dos*] suggest was subject to dissimilation /ó/ ... /o/>/ó/ ... /e/). Other forms (e.g. *simple, duplo, triple, cuádruplo, múltiple/-o*) are learned.

Among the **partitive** numerals, only *mitad* (<MEDIĒTĀTE) is inherited.

Tercio is learned and in the remaining cases, Spanish uses an ordinal numeral, sometimes in combination with *parte* (*un cuarto, la cuarta parte*, etc.), although in technical language the denominator of a fraction is characterized by the suffix *-avo*: *dos dozavos*, etc.

3.7 The verb

By contrast with the noun-system (3.2), the Latin verbal system is well-preserved in the Romance languages, including Spanish. Although the Latin passive endings were entirely lost (see 3.7.1), the Latin morphemes expressing person/number (3.7.2), aspect (3.7.3), tense (3.7.4) and mood (3.7.5) have most frequently been inherited by Spanish. In certain regards (the creation of a 'perfect' tense beside the 'preterite' [3.7.3], the creation of a conditional tense [3.7.7.4.2], and the provision of a future subjunctive [3.7.7.4.3]), the Spanish verbal system has become more complex than that of Latin.

3.7.1 Voice

Latin had synthetic passive forms only for the present, imperfect, and future tenses, indicative and subjunctive (AMOR, AMĀBAR, AMĀBOR, AMER, AMĀRER); the passive of the so-called perfect-stem tenses was analytically formed from the participle (AMĀTUS) in combination with some form of the verb ESSE 'to be' (e.g. AMĀTUS EST 'he was/has been loved'). In spoken Latin, such analytical constructions came to be used for *all* tenses, through the reinterpretation of the auxiliary. Thus, AMĀTUS EST (by comparison with CĀRUS EST 'he is beloved', etc.) was assigned a present-tense value ('he is loved'), AMĀTUS ERAT 'he had been loved' was reinterpreted as 'he was loved', etc. New forms were consequently brought into use, such as AMĀTUS FUIT 'he was/has been loved', AMĀTUS FUERAT 'he had been loved', etc.

The fully analytical passive system of Vulgar Latin has been directly inherited by Spanish (*es amado, era amado, fue amado*, etc.), although alternative types of passive sentences (using quasi-reflexive *se*, the indefinite third person plural, etc.) have always been commoner in Spanish than the *ser* + participle construction. However, in recent centuries Spanish has come to specialize *ser* + participle as an 'action' passive, by contrast with *estar* + participle, which has 'resultant state' value. This contrast is intimately related to the early modern distinction of roles applied in all other circumstances to the verbs *ser* and *estar*.

3.7.2 Person/number

Apart from phonological change, the person/number markers applied to all Latin verbal paradigms except the preterite have undergone no modification. Leaving aside the preterite (until 3.7.7.5), the phonological changes involved are the following:

1st sing.	-Ō > /o/ (e.g. CANTŌ > *canto*)
	-M is lost (e.g. CANTĀBAM > *cantaba*)
2nd sing.	-S > /s/ (e.g. CANTĒS > *cantes*)
3rd sing.	-T survives until the twelfth century (e.g. VENIT > *vinet* [*Auto de los reyes magos* (*ARM*) 19; = *vienet*]), and is then lost (*viene*)
1st plur.	-MUS > /mos/ (e.g. CANTAMUS > *cantamos*)
2nd plur.	-TIS > OSp. /des/ (see below)
3rd plur.	-NT > /n/ (e.g. CANTABANT > *cantaban*)

Only the 2nd plur. forms, then, require comment. The /d/ of these forms was eventually eliminated (with consequential adjustments to the surrounding vowels), perhaps as a result of the markedly increased frequency of 2nd plur. verb forms consequent upon the increasingly wide use of *Vos* as a form of singular address (see 3.5.1.1). In considering the development of these verbal endings, it is necessary to distinguish between those cases in which OSp. /-des/ was immediately preceded by the stress (paroxytonic forms, e.g. *cantades, cantedes, cantaredes*) and those in which the stress fell on the antepenultimate syllable (proparoxytonic forms, e.g. *cantávades, cantárades, cantássedes, cantáredes*).

3.7.2.1

The first group of forms suffered loss of /d/ occasionally in the fourteenth and intensely in the first two thirds of the fifteenth centuries, and almost immediately the resulting hiatus was resolved to monosyllabic pronunciation, either via assimilation (e.g. *-aes > -ás*) or via dissimilation/reduction of hiatus (e.g. *-aes > -áis*). The endings affected were the following:

-ades (pres. ind. *-ar* verbs, pres. subj. *-er/-ir* verbs: e.g. *cantades* > *cantaes* > *cantáis/cantás*)

-edes (pres. ind. *-er* verbs, pres. subj. *-ar* verbs, future: e.g. *cantaredes* > *cantarees* > *cantaréis/cantarés*)

-ides (pres. ind. *-ir* verbs: e.g. *salides* > *salies > *salís*)

sodes (pres. ind. *se(e)r:* *sodes* > *soes* > *sois/sos*)

The following table summarizes the chronology of successive 2nd plur. verb forms of this (originally proparoxytonic) class:

Latin	early OSp.	1400–1470	1470–1550	1550–
CANTĀTIS	*cantades*	*cantades*	*cantaes*	*cantáis*
		cantaes	*cantáis*	
			cantás	

From the middle of the sixteenth century, Peninsular Spanish used only the dissimilated forms (*cantáis*, etc.), except where only an assimilated form was available (*salís*). However, in American areas of *voseo* (i.e. where historically 2nd pers. plur. verb-forms were used for non-deferential sing. address [see 3.5.1.1]), the assimilated forms *(Vos) cantás, (Vos) metés*, etc., came to predominate and are still current. For further details, see Dworkin 1988a.

The Latin 2nd plur. imperative forms were also penultimate-stressed, but the development of these forms is harder to trace, since they are less frequently attested in medieval texts. Pre-literary Spanish gives glimpses of forms like *cantade* (< CANTĀTE), which most frequently lost their /-e/ (see 2.4.3.2) and provided the predominant medieval and modern form *cantad*. However, pre-literary *cantade* was probably also the ancestor (via loss of /d/ and assimilation /áe/ > /á/) of the frequent Golden Age imperative *cantá* (similarly *meté, salí*). The latter forms survive into modern Peninsular use only when followed by reflexive *os* (e.g. *levantaos*), but have become the predominant imperative forms used in American areas of *voseo*.

3.7.2.2

The Old Spanish 2nd plur. verb-forms which were stressed on the antepenultimate syllable generally descend from Latin forms stressed on the penultimate but which were modified (in Vulgar Latin) to bring them accentually in line with the 1st–3rd sing. and the 3rd plur. forms, which were stressed on the syllable immediately following the stem; e.g. CANTABÁTIS > CANTÁBATIS. The Old Spanish forms concerned were the following:

imperf. ind. -*ar* verbs	*cantávades*
imperf. ind. -*er*/-*ir* verbs	*temíades* (also *temiedes, -iédes*, see 3.7.3.1)
conditional (all verbs)	*cantaríades* (also *cantariedes, -iédes*, see 3.7.4.2)
pluperf. -*ar* verbs	*cantárades*
pluperf. -*er*/-*ir* verbs	*temiérades*
imperf. subj. -*ar* verbs	*cantássedes*
imperf. subj. -*er*/-*ir* verbs	*temiéssedes*
fut. subj. -*ar* verbs	*cantáredes*
fut. subj. -*er*/-*ir* verbs	*temiéredes*

These forms maintained their /d/ until the Golden Age. Forms without /d/ (and subsequent modification of the vowels thus left in hiatus, via dissimilation [e.g. *cantavais*], or assimilation [e.g. *cantavas*]) begin to appear in the sixteenth century, but are less frequent than forms with /d/ until the end of the seventeenth century, when the latter disappear. Only dissimilated forms remain in use in the Peninsula, but in American areas of *voseo* the assimilated 2nd plur. forms (indistinguishable from 2nd sing. forms) were preferred and continue to the present. These preferences are readily understandable if one bears in mind that in the Peninsula the verb-forms concerned came to be used only with plural value (and therefore were required to contrast with existing 2nd pers. sing. forms), whereas in America the same verb-forms had only singular value and could therefore be allowed to merge, without damage, with the 2nd sing. forms inherited from Old Spanish (so that, for example, OSp. *cantavas* and *cantávades* were allowed to merge in American Spanish as *cantabas*). Alternatively, it might be argued that the lack of distinction between so many (historically) 2nd sing. and 2nd plur. verb-forms promoted the lack of distinction between the corresponding subject pronouns (*Tú* and *Vos*). See Lapesa 1970.

The development of the proparoxytonic 2nd plur. verb-forms can be summarized with the following examples:

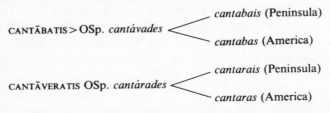

The 2nd plur. of the future subjunctive behaved slightly differently from the other proparoxytonic forms we have been examining. In addition to the expected Golden Age form *cantáredes*, and the occasional forms without /d/, *cantareis* and *cantares*, we find frequent forms in which /d/ has been retained but the post-tonic /e/ has suffered syncope: *cantardes*.

For further discussion of 2nd plur. verb-forms, see Blaylock 1986, Dworkin 1988b, Malkiel 1949, Mańczak 1976.

3.7.3   Aspect

In the Latin verbal system, the category of aspect was as important as that of tense. Indeed, it can be argued that aspect, the category which contrasts the various ways in which actions and events are perceived to be carried out, was **more** important than tense, the category which enables the time (relative to the moment of speaking) of the event to be indicated. The main aspectual contrast observable in the Latin verb was between **perfective** and **imperfective** verb-forms. Perfective verb-forms relate to actions and events which are perceived to involve some notion of commencement and/or completedness, while imperfective verb-forms relate to actions and events which are viewed as unlimited by such notions, that is, ones which are perceived as lasting for an undetermined period. Such an aspectual contrast has survived into Modern Spanish, but is now only available, in full form, with reference to past actions and events. Thus, actions and events which are anterior to the moment of speaking are also (obligatorily) marked as either perfective (e.g. *cantó*) or imperfective (e.g. *cantaba*), while, in the present and future, aspectual markers are optionally available. Thus, aspectually unmarked present *digo* may optionally be replaced by perfective *he dicho* 'I've finished speaking', or by imperfective *estoy diciendo que* ... 'the point I am in the process of making is that ...'. For the relationship between aspect and tense in Spanish, see Togeby 1963.

To return to Latin, but delaying detailed consideration of tense until 3.7.4, and of mood until 3.7.5, its verbal system can be described as follows:

	Indicative		Subjunctive	
	Imperfective	Perfective	Imperfective	Perfective
Anterior		CANTĀVERAM		CANTĀVISSEM
Past	CANTĀBAM	CANTĀVĪ	CANTĀREM	CANTĀVERIM
Present	CANTO	CANTĀVĪ	CANTEM	CANTĀVERIM
Future	CANTĀBŌ	CANTĀVERŌ		

The forms labelled 'anterior' express actions completed before some already established 'past' moment (that is, they correspond to what is traditionally labelled 'pluperfect'). It will be noted that the system established above has certain 'defects': the forms CANTĀVĪ and CANTĀVERIM functioned as both present perfective (equivalent to MSp. *he cantado, haya cantado*) and past perfective (equivalent to MSp. *canté* and *cantara/cantase*).

In the examples given above, it can be seen that perfectivity (by contrast with imperfectivity) is signalled by a stem increment -v-. In other verb-classes, perfectivity is signalled by other devices (see 3.7.7.5.2). With the increasing subordination of aspect to tense in the Latin verb, the exponents of perfectivity (here -v-) were often dropped, and there is evidence that, with growing frequency in spoken Latin, unincremented forms were becoming normal (e.g. CANTĀRAM for CANTĀVERAM, CANTĀSSEM for CANTĀVISSEM); such forms were also used with some frequency in writing (e.g. in Cicero's letters). Not only was there this unification of verbal stems in spoken Latin (i.e. the use of the same verbal stem [here CANT-], no matter what the aspect of the verb), but increasingly perfectivity came to be signalled in fundamentally different ways. In transitive verbs, this was achieved by the use of forms of HABERE 'have' together with a participle: e.g. HABEŌ CANTĀTUM for CANTĀVĪ 'I have sung'. At first, such constructions retained a notion of possession, and were therefore only available in cases where the subject was personal and where there was an overt direct object (the thing possessed), so that HABEŌ CULTELLUM COMPARĀTUM was probably a close equivalent of MSp. *el cuchillo lo tengo comprado*. However, weakening of the semantic component of 'possession' is evident when HABERE came to be used, as it did in spoken Latin, with participles whose meaning was incompatible with the notion of 'possession'; e.g. HABEŌ ILLUD AUDĪTUM. Such examples are already close in meaning to

MSp. *lo he oído* 'I have heard it', and the creation of the 'compound perfect' verb-forms is complete when we discover instances of HABERE + *participle* without a direct object (e.g. HABEŌ INTELLECTUM, with the sense of INTELLĒXĪ 'I have understood'). However, the sense of 'possession' originally inherent in the construction explains the fact that for centuries, well into the period of literary Old Spanish, the participle continued to agree in number and gender with the direct object. Thus, from VL HABEŌ VACCAM COMPARĀTAM, Old Spanish inherits *comprada he una vaca*. Such agreement gradually ceases, and the participle therefore becomes invariable, during the thirteenth–fifteenth centuries (see Menéndez Pidal 1964b: 360–1; Pountain 1985).

It should be noted that the HABĒRE + *participle* construction remained for centuries, in accordance with its origins, appropriate only to transitive verbs. Perfective forms of intransitive verbs (e.g. VĒNĪ 'I have come') were replaced in spoken Latin by forms of ESSE + *participle*, a process which perhaps represents a generalization of a structure originally appropriate only in deponent verbs (e.g. MORTUUS EST 'he has died') to other (eventually all other) intransitives (e.g. *VENĪTUS EST 'he has come'). Such an origin would account for the fact that throughout its history in Spanish (as in other Romance languages), this construction shows concord (in gender and number) of the participle with the subject: OSp. *venidos son* 'they have come'. Examples of *(h) an venido*, etc., are to be found occasionally in Old Spanish, but in the majority of cases, *ser* continues to be the auxiliary used in the perfective forms of intransitives until the sixteenth century. Examples such as *es llegado* 'he has arrived' are rare in the seventeenth century, and disappear by the middle of that century. For the use of perfective auxiliaries, see England 1982, Pountain 1985.

To return to spoken Latin, it should be made clear that, although the replacement of present perfective CANTĀVĪ by HABEŌ CANTĀTUM is the most frequent and probably the earliest case of restructuring of perfective verb-forms, this restructuring potentially affects **all** the perfective verb-forms listed at the beginning of this section. The evidence suggests that the structure HABERE or ESSE + *participle* was only gradually applied to the various tenses and moods, but by the thirteenth century the following replacements had taken place:

Class. Latin	Spoken Latin	Old Spanish
CANTĀVERAM	*HABUĪ/HABĒBAM CANTĀTUM	*ove/avía cantado*
CANTĀVĪ	HABEŌ CANTĀTUM	*he cantado*
CANTĀVERO	HABĒRE HABEŌ CANTĀTUM	*avré cantado*
CANTĀVISSEM	*HABUISSEM CANTĀTUM	*oviesse cantado*
CANTĀVERIM	*HABEAM CANTĀTUM	*aya cantado*

Class. Latin	Spoken Latin	Old Spanish
ĪVERAM	*ERAM ĪTUM	*era ido*
ĪVĪ	*SUM ĪTUM	*so ido*
ĪVERO	*ESSERE HABEŌ ĪTUM	*seré ido*
ĪVISSEM	*FUISSEM ĪTUM	*fuesse ido*
ĪVERIM	*SEDEAM ĪTUM	*sea ido*

Beside the spoken Latin forms listed above, it should be borne in mind that a 'conditional perfect' form probably existed, of the type *HABĒRE HABĒBAM CANTĀTUM, whence OSp. *avría cantado*. Similarly, a 'future perfect subjunctive' at some stage came into existence, based on a type *HABUERIM/HABUERŌ CANTĀTUM, with the Old Spanish form *ovier(e) cantado*; for futures and conditionals, see 3.7.7.4. For the development of auxiliaries in spoken Latin, see Vincent 1982.

Not all of the Latin perfective verb-forms were eliminated from use. CANTĀVERAM, CANTĀVĪ and CANTĀVISSEM continued in use, with perfective value:

1 CANTĀVERAM (whence *cantara*) continued in use as a 'pluperfect indicative' (alongside *avia cantado*) throughout the Old Spanish and Golden Age periods. However, in this value, *cantara* is now restricted to certain subordinate clauses in written registers only. In addition, *cantara* acquired conditional perfect (sometimes simple conditional) value, possibly in late Hispano-Latin, and appears with this value in Old Spanish and Golden Age Spanish; modern usage has restricted this value to a handful of verbs (*quisiera, debiera, hubiera*, and occasionally *pudiera*). For the various values associated at different times with *cantara*, etc. (see Wright 1932). For the subjunctive value of *cantara*, etc., see 3.7.5, 3.7.7.3.2.
2 CANTĀVĪ, although replaced by HABEŌ CANTĀTUM in its present perfective role, continued in use as a past perfective, providing OSp. and MSp. *canté* (see 3.7.5).
3 CANTĀVISSEM, reduced to CANTĀSSEM (see above), changed its role from 'pluperfect subjunctive' to 'past subjunctive' (without imperfective/perfective contrast), a process which probably began in conditional sentences, and provided OSp. *cantas(se)*, MSp. *cantase* (see 3.7.7.3.2).

As a result of the adjustments discussed in this section, the verbal system which emerged in Old Spanish was the following:

	Indicative		Subjunctive	
	Imperfective	Perfective	Imperfective	Perfective
Anterior		*cantara/ove cantado/ avía cantado*		*oviesse cantado*
Past	*cantava*	*canté*	*cantas(se)*	*cantas(se)*
Present	*canto*	*he cantado*	*cante*	*aya cantado*
Future	*cantaré*	*avré cantado*	*cantare*	*oviere cantado*
Conditional	*cantaria/-ie*	*avria/avrie cantado/ cantara*		

Between the thirteenth century and the present, modifications to the tense/aspect system of the Spanish verb have been relatively few and have not fundamentally altered the system:

1 'Pluperfects' of the *ove cantado* type (now *hube cantado*) have become restricted to certain temporal clauses and now belong only to written registers of the language.
2 The future subjunctive and future perfect subjunctive have, except in fossilized phrases, disappeared from the language. These tenses were fully functional throughout the Middle Ages and the Golden Age, but declined from the eighteenth century onwards, replaced most frequently by *cante* and *haya cantado*, but sometimes (i.e. in the protasis of conditional sentences) by *canto* and *he cantado* (see 3.7.7.4.3).
3 *Cantara* has moved from indicative to subjunctive role (see 3.7.5, 3.7.7.3.2), losing its 'pluperfect' and its conditional values (see above, this section).

As a result of these adjustments, the verbal system of the modern standard language emerges in the following form:

	Indicative		Subjunctive	
	Imperfective	Perfective	Imperfective	Perfective
Anterior		*(hube cantado)*		*hubiese cantado*
		había cantado		
Past	*cantaba*	*canté*	*cantase/*	*cantase/*
			cantara	*cantara*
Present	*canto*	*he cantado*	*cante*	*haya cantado*
Future	*cantaré*	*habré cantado*	*(cantare)*	*(hubiere cantado)*
Conditional	*cantaría*	*habría cantado*		

In American Spanish, as in some Western Peninsular varieties, certain differences from the Peninsular standard are observable. The main difference is that many speakers of American Spanish use *canté* not only as a past perfective (= 'preterite'), but also as a present perfective (i.e. as a 'perfect', in preference to *he cantado*) (see Harris 1982). Such varieties of Spanish therefore maintain, in *canté*, the dual function of its ancestor CANTĀVĪ.

As well as forms expressing perfective aspect, Spanish has acquired a set of forms expressing what is generally known as 'progressive' aspect, namely *estar* + gerund. Such forms are rarely obligatory and serve as optional alternatives to simple verb-forms, whenever the speaker wishes to emphasize that, in his or her view, an event is (or was, or will be) 'actually in progress'. Such a view of an event is not limited to events in progress at the moment of speaking, but to past and future events (*estuve esperando* 'I was waiting', *estará hablando* 'he will be speaking'). What is more, progressive aspect is compatible with both perfective and imperfective aspects, so that, for example, a past event seen as in progress between known or implied time-limits may be expressed by such statements as *estuvo esperando* 'he was waiting (from moment x to moment y)', while a past event seen as in progress but without any explicit or implied time-limits will be expressed by *estaba esperando* 'he was waiting (and may still be; when I saw him; etc.)'. Other Romance languages (Portuguese, Italian) partly coincide with Spanish, in having some progressive forms, but the development of a full set of such forms (independent of tense and of perfective aspect) appears to have occurred over recent centuries and exclusively in Spanish.

3.7.4   Tense

The tense system of Spanish is essentially similar to that of Classical Latin, and has already been referred to during discussion of aspect (3.7.3). Although the exponents of the various categories have in some cases changed with time, the categories themselves (Anterior, Past, Present, Future) have changed little (see the tables in section 3.7.3). The major differences between Latin and Spanish are the following:

1 The introduction of a conditional tense. This probably arose in spoken Latin at a time when the grammatical structure of indirect statements was undergoing fundamental change. Literary Latin, no doubt reflecting earlier oral practice, used the so-called 'Accusative + infinite' construction for indirect speech; e.g.

CRĒDŌ EUM VĒNTŪRUM ESSE	lit. 'I believe him to be about to come' = 'I think he will come'
CRĒDĒBAM EUM VĒNTŪRUM ESSE	lit. 'I believed him to be about to come' = 'I thought he would come'

However, in the first of these cases, spoken Latin came to use a future indicative verb, which in most areas (including Spain) took the form of an infinitive combined with the present indicative of HABERE (see 3.7.7.1.5)

CRĒDŌ QUOD VENĪRE HABET (> *creo que vendrá*)

Where the main verb was in a past tense, sequence of tense rules demanded that a past tense of HABĒRE should be used in the subordinate clause:

CRĒDĒBAM QUOD VENĪRE HABĒBAT (> *creía que* _vendría_)

Eventually, a conditional perfect was introduced, based upon the new conditional form of the perfective auxiliary (HABĒRE HABĒBAM, or, in the case of intransitives, *ESSERE HABĒBAM) + participle: *habría canta-do, sería venido* (later, *habría venido*).

2 The introduction of future subjunctives. The Latin 'future perfect indicative' (CANTĀVERŌ, often CANTĀRŌ) and the 'perfect subjunctive' (CANTĀVERIM, often CANTĀRIM) differed only in the 1st pers. sing.; in all other cases (e.g. CANTĀVERIS) the same forms were used for both paradigms. Although these forms were abandoned in most varieties of spoken Latin, they were preserved, in combined form, in the Latin of Spain and provided the Old Spanish future subjunctive:

> CANTĀVERO/CANTĀVERIM > *cantare*

At a later stage, a future perfect subjunctive was created, on the basis of the future subjunctive of the perfective auxiliary (*oviere*, < HABUERŌ/HABUERIM) + participle: *oviere cantado*. It has already been mentioned (3.7.3) that both the simple and the compound future subjunctive fell out of general use in the period after the Golden Age.

3.7.5   *Mood*

The categories of mood ('indicative' and 'subjunctive') have remained largely intact in the development from Latin to Modern Spanish. Although there are some constructions (e.g. indirect question, some temporal clauses [CUM VĒNISSET . . .]) which in Latin demanded the subjunctive mood and in Spanish require the indicative, there are others which in Latin required an indicative (e.g. temporal clauses referring to the future [UBI VENIET . . .]) and Spanish requires a subjunctive (*cuando venga* . . .), and the subjunctive (in its various tenses) retains full vitality in Spanish.

The various indicative and subjunctive paradigms will be discussed in section 3.7.7.1–5, where it will be noted that some Spanish paradigms are inherited from Latin paradigms which had the same function (e.g. present indicative, present subjunctive, imperfect indicative, preterite); others are descended from paradigms created in spoken Latin (e.g. future, conditional, the 'compound perfect' paradigms); and yet others are descended from paradigms familiar from Classical Latin, but with changed function (e.g. 'pluperfect subjunctive' CANTĀVISSEM > 'imperfect subjunctive' *cantase* [see also 3.7.3]). The only paradigm to have changed its mood is the Spanish descendant of CANTĀVERAM.

As noted in 3.7.3, the *-ra* form (e.g. *cantara, saliera*) has its origins in the Latin 'pluperfect indicative' (e.g. CANTĀVERAM, already reduced in VL to CANTĀRA[M]). OSp. *cantara* retains this value, but after the seventeenth century *-ra* with pluperfect value is rare, limited to certain subordinate clauses in written registers. The same paradigm occurs in Medieval and Golden Age Spanish in the main clause of conditional sentences expressing improbability or impossibility (i.e. with conditional or conditional perfect value; see 3.9), a role which the *-ra* form now plays only in the case of a few common verbs (*hubiera, debiera, quisiera,* sometimes *pudiera*). Change of mood (from indicative to subjunctive) began in the fourteenth century, when the first examples are found of -*ra* forms in the **subordinate** clause of the sentence-types just mentioned, a position thitherto occupied exclusively by -*se* forms. Although the -*ra* forms became more common than their -*se* competitors in these sentences in Golden Age Spanish, they were slower to compete with -*se* forms in other clauses requiring a past subjunctive. It is only after the seventeenth century that -*ra* forms become common in, say, final clauses (e.g. *para que saliera*...), although *cantara* is now more common in speech than *cantase* and in some varieties of Spanish (e.g. American Spanish) *cantara* has completely ousted *cantase*.

The Latin imperative ('imperative' is often considered to be a separate mood from 'indicative' and 'subjunctive') is well preserved in Spanish. Spanish preserves Latin imperatives (e.g. CANTĀ, CANTĀTE > *canta, cantad*) in just those circumstances where special forms existed (positive commands of the second person) and, like Latin, uses the subjunctive under all other circumstances (negative commands of the second person and all commands of the first and third persons). See 3.7.7.2.

3.7.6 Verb-classes

Latin verbs were distributed among four form-classes, exemplified by the four infinitive types -ĀRE, -ĒRE, -ĔRE, and -ĪRE. The first and last of these types remained fully productive, while -ĒRE and -ĔRE were rarely used as patterns for the creation of new verbs. By contrast with the Latin spoken in most areas, the Latin of most of Spain (including the area where Castilian developed) allowed the total convergence of the -ĒRE and -ĔRE types. reducing the number of verb-classes to three: -*ar*, -*er*, and -*ir*. This merger no doubt began in the present indicative paradigm, where the differences between the two classes rested upon two factors: (1) contrasting vowels in the final morpheme; and (2) certain differences of accentual pattern, e.g.:

-ĒRE	-ĔRE
DÉB(E)Ō	VÉNDŌ
DÉBĒS	VÉNDIS
DÉBET	VÉNDIT
DĒBÉMUS	VÉNDIMUS
DĒBÉTIS	VÉNDITIS
DÉBENT	VÉNDUNT

The 1st and 2nd plur. forms VÉNDIMUS and VÉNDITIS differed in their stress pattern from the corresponding pres. ind. and pres. subj. forms of all other verbs (and even from the present subj. forms of their own class: VĒNDÁMUS, VĒNDÁTIS). The strong analogical pressure thus induced accounts for the shift of stress to penultimate position in the 1st and 2nd pers. plur. of the

-ĔRE verbs (and ultimately, also, in the infinitive and in the plur. imperative, where the stress-pattern was originally also 'anomalous'). Taken together with the mergers of vowels in tonic and final positions (see 2.4.2.6, 2.4.3.2), these changes brought about the following typical forms for verbs of these classes, in the spoken Latin of much of Spain.

/déβo/	/βéndo/
/déβes/	/βéndes/
/déβet/	/βéndet/
/deβémos/	/βendémos/
/deβétes/	/βendétes/
/déβen/	/βéndon/

The now almost total identity of endings was sufficient to bring about identity in the one instance where different endings existed, so that /βéndon/ > /βénden/.

Similarly, infinitives of the type VÉNDERE became VENDÉRE (but after the merger of atonic Ĕ and Ē in /e/, so that no possibility arose of diphthongization of original Ĕ) and the plur. imperative VÉNDITE behaved like its indicative counterpart, becoming /βendéte/ and merging with /deβéte/. Since the endings of the other paradigms that survived were already common to these two classes of verbs, merger of the two sets was now complete and no distinction is observable between their Spanish descendants, *deber*, *vender*, etc.

The only 3rd-conj. verb-forms which, for a time, resisted stress-shift were FÁCIMUS, FÁCITIS and imper. FÁCITE, whose descendants *femos, feches, fech*, were found in early Old Spanish beside stress-shifted *fazemos, fazedes, fazed* and TRÁHITE, whence early OSp. imper. *tred* (see 3.7.7.1.5). Some would argue (e.g. Alvar & Pottier 1983: 229) that OSp. pres. ind. *vamos, vades* similarly descend from stem-stressed VÁDIMUS, VÁDITIS. However, the phonological difficulty of explaining VÁDITIS > *vades* makes it preferable to argue that *vamos* and *vades* were originally exclusively subjunctive forms (< VADÁMUS, VADÁTIS) which were attracted into the indicative paradigm because of their structural similarity to indicative *vas, va, van* (see 3.7.7.1.5).

All those -ĀRE verbs which survive in Spanish belong to the *-ar* class, a class whose numbers have been augmented by the addition of a few verbs from other Latin conjugations (e.g. TORRĒRE > *turrar* 'to roast', MINUERE > *menguar* 'to wane', MEIERE > *mear* 'to urinate'), usually for reasons of analogy with semantically related *a*-class verbs (e.g. *tostar*). To these verbs of Latin origin were added a number of Germanic borrowings (e.g. RAPÔN > *rapar* 'to crop [hair, etc.]', RAUBÔN > *robar* 'to rob, steal'), a very few arabisms (e.g. *recamar* 'to embroider', *(a)taracear* 'to inlay [furniture]'), and many borrowings from other sources, as well as the large majority of the many verbs created within Spanish by derivation from nouns, adjectives, etc.

Most surviving Latin verbs in -ĒRE and -ĔRE appear in Spanish as -*er* verbs, a class which has not proved productive in Spanish. Apart from a single accretion from other Latin conjugations (TUSSĪRE > *toser* 'to cough'), and a relatively small number of derived verbs in -*ecer* (e.g. *ensordecer* 'to deafen', from *sordo* 'deaf', *agradecer* 'to please', from OSp. *gradir* 'id.'), this verbal class has not grown; on the contrary, it has lost verbs, as we shall see, to the -*ir* class.

The -*ir* class, consisting principally of inherited Latin verbs in -ĪRE, at first proved a little more productive than the -*er* class, allowing a few additions from Germanic sources (e.g. WARNJAN > OSp. *guarnir* 'to provide, adorn, arm' [later *guarnecer*]), as well as considerable numbers of verbs which originally belonged to the Latin -ĒRE and -ĔRE classes. Those verbs which changed conjugation in this way were predominantly those whose 1st sing. pres. ind. ending was -EŌ or -IŌ, and whose pres. subj. endings were -EAM or -IAM, etc., since these endings were pronounced in spoken Latin in the same fashion ([jo] and [ja], etc.) as the corresponding endings of -ĪRE verbs, although not all such verbs moved into the -*ir* class (e.g. DĒBĒRE, DĒBEŌ > *deber* 'to be obliged to'). Some of the commonest verbs which changed conjugation in this way are the following:

-ĒRE > -*ir*:	COMPLEŌ, -ĒRE > *cumplir* 'to achieve'
	FERVEŌ, -ĒRE > *hervir* 'to boil' (beside non-standard *herver*)
	FLŌREŌ, -ĒRE > OSp. *florir* (later *florecer*) 'to bloom'
	IMPLEŌ, -ĒRE > *henchir* 'to stuff'
	LŪCEŌ, -ĒRE > *lucir* 'to shine'
	MONEŌ, -ĒRE > *muñir* 'to convene'
	PUTREŌ, -ĒRE > *pudrir* 'to rot'
	REPAENITEŌ, -ĒRE > *arrepentir(se)* 'to repent'
	RĪDEŌ, -ĒRE > *reir* 'to laugh'
-ĔRE > -*ir*:	CONCIPIŌ, -ĔRE > *concebir* 'to conceive'
	FUGIŌ, -ĔRE > *huir* 'to flee'
	MORIO(R), MORĪ > *morir* 'to die'
	PARIŌ, -ĔRE > *parir* 'to give birth'
	RECIPIŌ, -ĔRE > *recibir* 'to receive'
	SUCCUTIŌ, -ĔRE > *sacudir* 'to shake'

A further group of verbs was attracted from the -ĔRE class to the -ĪRE class despite the fact that their present tense endings lacked this similarity with the endings of the -ĪRE verbs:

-ĔRE > -*ir*:	*INADDŌ, - ĔRE > *añadir* 'to add' (beside OSp. *eñader*)
	CON-BATTUŌ, -ĔRE > *combatir* 'to fight' (beside OSp. *combater*)
	CONFUNDŌ, -ĔRE > *confundir* 'to confound' (beside OSp. *cofonder*)
	DĪCŌ, -ĔRE > *decir* 'to say'

EXCONSPUŌ, - ĔRE > *escupir* 'to spit'
PETŌ, -ĔRE > *pedir* 'to ask for'
REDDŌ, -ĔRE > *rendir* 'to render' (beside OSp. *render*)
SEQUO(R), SEQUĪ > *seguir* 'to follow'
SUFFERŌ, -E (probably expanded to SUFFERŌ, - ĔRE) > *sufrir*
'to suffer'

3.7.7   Verb paradigms

Following discussion of the major verbal categories of person/number,
aspect, tense and mood (3.7.1–5), we come now to an account of the
development of each of the paradigms of the Spanish verb.

3.7.7.1   Present indicative and subjunctive

These paradigms pose a number of problems, which will be dealt with in
turn: the palatal glide (yod) which in Latin occurred in the endings of
certain forms and its effect on preceding consonants (3.7.7.1.1); the
development of the endings (3.7.7.1.2); consonantal alternations at the end
of the verb-stem (3.7.7.1.3); and vocalic alternations of the stem (3.7.7.1.4).

3.7.7.1.1   The palatal glide [j] of the verbal endings   In spoken Latin, all
-ĒRE and -ĪRE verbs, together with some -ĔRE verbs, had a palatal glide
immediately following the stem in the 1st pers. sing. of the pres. ind. and
throughout the pres. subj.; e.g. DĒBĘŌ (DĒBĒRE), SALI̯Ō (SALĪRE), CAPI̯Ō
(CAPERE). Two sources of analogical pressure conspired to eliminate this
phoneme, in almost all cases. On the one hand, analogical influence was
exercised by the five other pres. ind. forms (e.g. DĒBĒS, SALĪS, CAPIMUS) and
by the large majority of other forms of these verbs, all of which lacked the
glide. On the other hand, pressure was exerted by the -ĔRE verbs, the large
majority of which had no glide in their present tense forms (e.g. VENDŌ,
TRAHŌ, CADŌ, etc.). This analogical loss of the glide evidently occurred
before the assimilatory changes which otherwise took place when certain
consonants were followed by [j] (see 2.5.2.2), since the /k/ of forms like
FACIŌ (analogically reduced to */fako/) was not palatalized but remained
velar, appearing in Old Spanish as /g/: *fago* (MSp. *hago*).

However, in a minority of the verbs whose present tense forms contained
a glide, this phoneme did survive long enough to combine with the
consonant at the end of the verbal stem, thereby producing a new phoneme.
For the phonological processes concerned, see 2.5.2.2. The verbs in which
such a combination took place belong to the following groups:

(a) those whose stem ended in -D-, -G- or (occasionally) -B-:

VIDEŌ   >   *veo*
RĪDEŌ   >   *rio*
AUDIŌ   >   OSp. *oyo* (later *oigo*)

> SEDEAM > *sea*
> FUGIŌ   > *huyo*
> HABEAM > *haya*

according to which pattern a number of other verbs, mostly displaying stem -D but lacking [j], came to be remodelled:

> CADŌ   > OSp. *cayo* (later *caigo*)
> RĀDŌ   > *rayo*
> RŌDAT > *roya*
> VĀDAM > *vaya*
> TRAHŌ > OSp. *trayo* (later *traigo*)

For the /g/ of *oigo, caigo, traigo*, see section (3) below.

In the case of OSp. *oyo* and *fuyo* (MSp. *huyo*), the consonant /ǰ/ was spread analogically from the 1st pers. sing. to the 2nd and 3rd pers. sing. and to the 3rd plur. (*oyes, oye, oyen, fuyes, fuye, fuyen*), no doubt to provide a sharper syllabic division than that previously existing between the stem-final vowel and the vowel of the ending (*/óes/ > /óǰes/). Although this pattern was adopted by the learned verbs in *-uir* (e.g. *distribuyes*, etc.), it did not affect the verbs whose stem ended in /a/ (thus, *caes, traes*, etc.).

(b) the two verbs whose stem ends in -AP-:

> CAPIŌ   > *quepo*
> SAPIAM > *sepa*

and one ending in -AC-:

> PLACEAT > *plega*

the last case conflicting with FAC(I)AT > *haga* and IAC(E)AT > OSp. *yaga* (MSp. *yazca*).

(c) verbs in -N- (VENIŌ, TENEŌ, REMANEAT). It is conceivable that in these verbs the [j] survived long enough to combine with -N- and produce an unprecedented consonantal alternation between /ɲ/ and /n/ (e.g. VENIŌ > *veño* vs VENĪS > *vienes*). If such an alternation existed (as is suggested by its appearance in Ptg. *venho, tenho* and OIt. *vegno, tegno*) it was replaced, before the Old Spanish period, by the alternation /ng/ ~ /n/: *vengo ~ vienes, tengo ~ tienes*, OSp. *remanga* (pres. subj. of OSp. *remanir*). To this pattern was adapted, from equally early times, the verb PŌNERE, which lacked [j] in Latin (PŌNŌ, PŌNAM): *pongo ~ pones*.

3.7.7.1.2 The present tense endings.

Reference to 3.7.7.1.1, to 3.7.2 and to 3.7.6 will show that the **indicative** endings of *-ar, -er* and *-ir* verbs develop, in almost all regards, in accordance with expected vowel and consonant evolution:

CANTŌ	>	*canto*
CANTĀS	>	*cantas*
CANTAT	>	*canta*
CANTĀMUS	>	*cantamos*
CANTĀTIS	>	OSp. *cantades* > MSp. *cantáis*
CANTANT	>	*cantan*

DĒB(E)Ō	>	*debo*
DĒBĒS	>	*debes*
DĒBET	>	*debe*
DĒBĒMUS	>	*debemos*
DĒBĒTIS	>	OSp. *devedes* > MSp. *debéis*
DĒBENT	>	*deben*
SAL(I)Ō	>	*salgo* (see 3.7.7.1.3)
SALĪS	>	*sales*
SALIT	>	*sale*
SALĪMUS	>	*salimos*
SALĪTIS	>	OSp. *salides* > *salís*
SAL(I)UNT	>	*salen*

The only further adjustment was in the 3rd plur. ending of -ĪRE verbs, where -UNT was replaced by *-ENT, no doubt by analogical extension to VL /sálet/–*/sálon/ of the pattern observable in /deβet/–/déβen/.

In Old Spanish, the final /e/ of many 3rd pers. sing. could be lost, depending on the nature of the preceding consonant (see 2.4.3.2). Thus, we find forms like *faz, diz, sal, pon, tien, vien, quier* in the Middle Ages, although in all such cases the modern language has preferred forms with /-e/, partially to maintain parity with those verbs which could not lose /-e/ because their stem ended in a consonant group or in /b/, /g/, etc. (e.g. *vuelve, rompe, debe, yergue*), and partially because the contrast of mood is specifically marked by the contrast, in the final syllable, of /e/ (indicative) with /a/ (subjunctive).

The development of the **subjunctive** endings is similarly transparent:

CANTEM	>	*cante*
CANTĒS	>	*cantes*
CANTET	>	*cante*
CANTĒMUS	>	*cantemos*
CANTĒTIS	>	OSp. *cantedes* > MSp. *cantéis*
CANTENT	>	*canten*
DĒB(E)AM	>	*deba*
DĒB(E)ĀS	>	*debas*
DĒB(E)AT	>	*deba*
DĒB(E)ĀMUS	>	*debamos*
DĒB(E)ĀTIS	>	OSp. *devades* > MSp. *debáis*
DĒB(E)ANT	>	*deban*
SAL(I)AM	>	*salga*
SAL(I)ĀS	>	*salgas*
SAL(I)AT	>	*salga*
SAL(I)ĀMUS	>	*salgamos*
SAL(I)ĀTIS	>	OSp. *salgades* > *salgáis*
SAL(I)ANT	>	*salgan*

For the /g/ of *salga*, etc., see 3.7.7.1.3.

3.7.7.1.3   Consonantal alternation of the stem.   Verbs whose stem in Latin ended with either of the velar consonants /k/ or /g/ can be expected, according to 2.5.2.3, to give rise to cases of consonantal alternation in their Spanish descendants, since these phonemes normally remain velar only when followed by back vowels or by /a/; when followed by front vowels, they can be expected to suffer palatalization and further fronting to dental position by the Old Spanish period. Thus, depending on the nature of the first (or only) vowel in the ending, stem-final /k/ or /g/ can be expected to give velar or non-velar results.

Verbs in *-ar* do not fulful this expectation; only a small minority of their endings (those of the pres. subj.) contained a front vowel, and in these cases the preceding velar consonant remained velar, under the analogical influence of the large number of forms in which the same velar consonant was followed by a back vowel or by /a/. Thus, on the model of PLICŌ > *llego*, PLICĀS > *llegas* (and no doubt of PLICĀRE > *llegar*, PLICĀBAM > *llegaba*, etc.), PLICEM, PLICĒS, etc., produce *llegue(s)*, etc. Similarly, PACŌ, PACĀS, etc. > *pago, -as*, etc., is the model according to which pres. subj. PACEM, PACĒS, etc. become *pague(s)*, etc. By contrast the noun PACE, -ĒS, not subjected to such analogical forces, produces the expected *paz, paçes*.

However, verbs in *-er* and *-ir* with stem-final velar often do show the predicted alternation. In these verbs, after the elimination of desinential [j] (see 3.7.7.1.1), the stem-final velar was followed by /a/ in six forms (those of the pres. subj.) and by /o/ in one instance (the 1st sing. pres. ind.), while in all other cases a front vowel followed. There are three groups of Latin verbs where this combination of phonemes can be expected to produce alternation of the stem-consonant: (a) those in which the stem ends in V(owel) + /k/; (b) those where the stem ends in /rg/ or /ng/; and (c) those in /sk/.

(a) Where the stem ends in V + /k/, we can make the following predictions:

V + /k/ + /o/ or /a/ > OSp. (and MSp.) V + /g/ + /o/ or /a/ (see 2.5.3.2[8])
V + /k/ + /e/ or /i/ > OSp. V + /dz/ + /e/ or /i/ (see 2.5.2.3 and 2.5.3.2[6]).

A number of verbs exhibit the expected pattern in Old Spanish:

1st sing. pres. ind.	all pres. subj.	2nd–3rd sing., 1st-3rd plur. pres. ind.	infin.
DĪCŌ > *digo*	DĪCAM > *diga*	DĪCIS > *dizes*	DĪCERE > *dezir* 'say'
FAC(I)Ō > *fago*	FAC(I)AM > *faga*	FACIS > *fazes*	FACERE > *fazer* 'do'

Similarly:

COQ(U)Ō > *cuego*	*cuega*	*cuezes*	*cozer* 'cook'
ADDŪCŌ > *adugo*	*aduga*	*aduzes*	*aduzir* 'lead'
IAC(E)Ō > *yago*	*yaga*	*yazes*	*yazer* 'lie'

(b) Where the stem of the Latin verb ends in /rg/ or /ng/, the following is the expected development (see 2.5.2.3[end]):

$$/rg/ + /o/ \text{ or } /a/ > /rg/ + /o/ \text{ or } /a/$$
$$/rg/ + /e/ \text{ or } /i/ > OSp. /rdz/ + /e/ \text{ or } /i/$$
$$/ng/ + /o/ \text{ or } /a/ > /ng/ + /o/ \text{ or } /a/$$
$$/ng/ + /e/ \text{ or } /i/ > OSp. /ndz/ \text{ or } /ɲ/ + /e/ \text{ or } /i/$$

Again, a number of Old Spanish verbs display this pattern:

SPARGŌ	>	*espargo*	SPARGAM > *esparga*
ER(I)GŌ	>	*yergo*	*yerga*
TANGŌ	>	*tango*	*tanga*
PLANGŌ	>	*plango*	*planga*
FRANGŌ	>	*frango*	*franga*

SPARGIS > *esparzes*	SPARGERE > *esparzir*
yerzes	*erzer* (also *erguir*) 'raise'
tanzes/tañes	*tañer* 'touch, play'
plañes	*plañir/plañer* 'lament'
franzes/frañes	*frañer/franzir* 'break'

Types (a) and (b) can be regarded as a single pattern in Old Spanish, a pattern characterized by the alternation, at the end of the stem, of /g/ (in the 1st sing. pres. ind. and the six forms of the pres. subj.) with another consonant (in the remaining forms). This pattern was sufficiently frequent and prominent to attract a large number of verbs which in Latin had not had /k/ or /g/ at the end of the stem. In some cases (*vengo, tengo, pongo*), the appearance of forms with /g/ is very early, before the emergence of Old Spanish (see 3.7.7.1.1[c]); in other cases, forms with and without /g/ are found in Old Spanish, the modern standard language only sometimes opting for the expanded form:

Lat. FER(I)Ō > OSp. *fier(g)o, -a* (inf. *ferir*) (now *hiero/herir*)
VEN(I)Ō > *vengo, a* (inf. *venir*)
TEN(E)Ō > *tengo, -a* (inf. *tener*)
PŌNŌ > *pongo, -a* (inf. *poner*)
SAL(I)Ō > OSp. *sal(g)o, -a* (inf. *salir*) (now only *salgo, -a*)
DOL(E)AT > OSp. *duel(g)a* (inf. *doler*) (*duelga* now only dialectal)
TOLLŌ > OSp. *tuelgo, -a* (inf. *toller*) (verb now obsolete)
SOL(E)Ō > OSp. *suel(g)o* (inf. *soler*) (*suelgo* now only dialectal)

In yet further cases, /g/ is not added to the verbal stem until the end of the medieval period. Where no further comment is made, the extended stem is accepted by the standard, but in other cases the /g/-forms have come to have restricted use:

Lat. VAL(E)Ō > OSp. *valo, -a* > GA Sp. *valgo, -a*
AUDIŌ > OSp. *oyo, -a* > GA Sp. *oigo, -a*
CADŌ > OSp. *cayo, -a* > GA Sp. *caigo, -a*
TRAHŌ > OSp. *trayo, -a* > GA Sp. *traigo, -a*
FUGIŌ > OSp. *fuyo, -a* > GA Sp. *huigo, -a* (now only dialectal)
VĀDAM > OSp. *vaya* > GA Sp. *vaiga* (now non-standard)
HABEAM > OSp. *haya* > GA Sp. *haiga* (now non-standard)
asa → OSp. *aso, -a* > GA Sp. *asgo, -a*

It can be seen that the pattern of consonantal alternation originating in groups (a) and (b) above has been particularly successful in spreading to other verbs. It is therefore paradoxical to note that the number of modern Spanish verbs which inherit this pattern from Latin (rather than acquiring it by analogy) is small. Only *digo/dices* and *hago/haces* continue the pattern direct from spoken Latin, while the remaining verbs of groups (a) and (b) have either been lost or have been adapted to other patterns. In most cases, the OSp. /g/ which appeared in the 1st sing. pres. ind. and throughout the pres. subj. has been replaced by the consonant with which it originally alternated:

OSp.			MSp.	
	cuego/cuezes	>		*cuezo/cueces*
	espargo/esparzes	>		*esparzo/esparces*
	tango/tañes	>		*taño/tañes*
	plango/plañes	>		*plaño/plañes*
	cingo/ciñes	>		*ciño/ciñes*

although in one case the /g/ has spread from the original seven forms to all forms of the verb:

> *yergo/yerzes* > *yergo/yergues* (inf. *erguir*).

In other cases, the alternation under consideration here has been replaced by the alternation to be considered in section (c) below:

yago/yazes	>	*yazco/yaces*
plego/plazes	>	*plazco/places*
lugo/luzes	>	*luzco/luces*
condugo/conduzes	>	*conduzco/conduces*

(c) Verbs in which /sk/ immediately preceded the ending were especially common in Latin, owing to the frequency of the inceptive infix -ESC- (e.g. FLŌRESCERE 'to [begin to] bloom'). The expected Old Spanish outcome of /sk/ was as follows:

/sk/ + /o/ or /a/ > /sk/ + /o/ or /a/
/sk/ + /e/ or /i/ > /ts/ + /e/ or /i/ (see 2.5.2.3)

Such a pattern of development is observable in a large number of Old Spanish verbs, e.g.:

MERĒSCŌ > meresco	*meresca*	*mere(s)çes*	*mere(s)çer*
COGNŌSCŌ > *conosco*	*conosca*	*cono(s)çes*	*cono(s)çer*
NĀSCO(R) > *nasco*	*nasca*	*na(s)çes*	*na(s)çer*

In late Medieval and early Modern Spanish (fifteenth–sixteenth centuries), this alternation was modified in the following way: the /s/ of *meresco, -a*, etc., was replaced by the /ts/ of *mere(s)çes*, etc., so that in the modern language, after change of /ts/ to /θ/ (see 2.6.2), the alternation has become /θk/ ∼ /θ/:

meresco/mere(s)çes	>	*merezco/mereces*
conosco/cono(s)çes	>	*conozco/conoces*, etc.
nasco/na(s)çes	>	*nazco/naces*

We have already seen in the previous section that some verbs which in Old Spanish exhibited /g/ in alternation with another consonant came to adopt the pattern under discussion here:

condugo/conduzes	>	*conduzco/conduces*, etc.

For the Romance background to the spread of stem-final /g/, see Malkiel 1974.

3.7.7.1.4   Vocalic alternation in the verb stem.   This kind of alternation is comparatively frequent in Spanish and can be seen in all three major verb-classes. Two phonological processes are involved: diphthongization of VL /ɛ/ and /ɔ/ when fully stressed (by contrast with their preservation as simple vowels when unstressed) (see 2.4.2.2); and the raising effect of [j] on the preceding tonic or atonic vowel (see 2.4.2.1 for this process and 3.7.7.1.1 for the incidence of desinential [j] in the verb).

In the case of *-ar* verbs, desinential [j] did not exist, and in the case of the verbs which provide the Spanish *-er* class, desinential [j] either did not appear (e.g. VENDŌ) or was eliminated early in spoken Latin (e.g. DĒBEŌ > *DĒBŌ). However, in the verbs which provide the *-ir* class, [j] persisted long enough in the ending to exercise the metaphonic effect on the tonic vowel discussed in 2.4.2.1. For this reason, it is necessary, when discussing stem-vowel alternations, to deal separately (a) with *-ar* and *-er* verbs, and (b) with *-ir* verbs.

It is also necessary to bear in mind that the Latin accent sometimes fell on the verbal stem and sometimes on the ending (see 3.7.6), so that the stem-vowel was sometimes tonic and sometimes atonic.

> (a) **-ar and -er verbs.** Where the stem of a verb of these classes contained Ĕ or Ŏ, we can make the following predictions about the development of these vowels (see 2.4.2.2, 2.4.3.1):

Ĕ (stressed) (= VL /ɛ/)	>	Sp. /ie/
Ĕ (unstressed) (= VL /e/)	>	/e/
Ŏ (stressed) (= VL /ɔ/)	>	/ue/
Ŏ (unstressed) (= VL /o/)	>	/o/

These predictions are fulfilled in a large number of verbs, e.g.:

Stressed stem	*Unstressed stem*
(1st–3rd sing., 3rd pers. plur.)	(1st–2nd plur.)
NĔGŌ (/négo/) > *niego*	NĔGĀMUS (/negámos/) > *negamos*
NĔGĀS (/négas/) > *niegas*	NĔGĀTIS (/negátes/) > *negáis*
NĔGAT (/négat/) > *niega*	
NĔGANT (/négant/) > *niegan*	
NĔGEM (/nége/) > *niegue*	NĔGĒMUS (/negémos/) > *neguemos*
NĔGES (/néges/) > *niegues*	NĔGĒTIS (/negétes/) > *neguéis*
NĔGET (/néget/) > *niegue*	
NĔGENT (/négent/) > *nieguen*	
MŎV(E)Ō (/mɔ́βo/) > *muevo*	MŎVĒMUS (/moβémos/) > *movemos*
MŎVĒS (/mɔ́βes/) > *mueves*	MŎVĒTIS (/moβétes/) > *movéis*
etc.	etc.

The many verbs which inherited this pattern shared the same stem-vowel (/e/ or /o/), in those cases where the stem was unstressed, with many other verbs whose unstressed /e/ or /o/ descended from Ē/Ĭ or Ō/Ŭ respectively. Thus *negamos, movéis*, etc., are identical in their vowel-pattern to *sembramos* (< SĒMINĀMUS), *coláis* (< CŌLĀTIS), etc. In a number of cases, this identity of atonic stem was extended to those cases where the stem was tonic, so that the stem alternations /e/ ~ /ie/ and /o/ ~ /ue/ came to appear in verbs whose Latin stem-vowel could not, by phonological change alone, lead to such alternation. Such analogical extension of vowel-alternation has affected different verbs at different stages of the history of Spanish:

> SĒMINĀRE > *sembrar/siembro* 'to sow' (cf. OSp. and dialectal *sembro*)
> PĒNSĀRE > *pensar/pienso* 'to think' (cf. non-alternating *pesar/peso*, from the same etymon)
> RĪGĀRE > *regar/riego* 'to water'
> FRĪCĀRE > *fregar/friego* 'to scrub' (cf. frequent dialectal *frego*)
> FĪNDĔRE > *hender/hiendo* 'to split'
> FOETĒRE > *heder/hiedo* 'to smell, stink'
> CŌLĀRE > *colar/cuelo* 'to filter'
> MŌNSTRĀRE > *mostrar/muestro* 'to show, display'
> CONSŌLARĪ > *consolar/consuelo* 'to console'

A number of verbs which earlier in their history showed the vocalic alternation under discussion have come to have their stems regularized, sometimes in favour of the simple vowel (/e/ or /o/) and sometimes in favour of the diphthong (/ie/ or /ue/). Examples of the first type are more numerous:

entregar, once	*entriego,* etc., now	*entrego*	'to hand over'
prestar	*priesto*	*presto*	'to lend'
templar	*tiemplo*	*templo*	'to temper'
vedar	*viedo*	*vedo*	'to forbid'
pretender	*pretiendo*	*pretendo*	'to aim to'
aportar	*apuerto*	*aporto*	'to contribute'
confortar	*confuerto*	*conforto*	'to comfort'
sorber	*suerbo*	*sorbo*	'to sip'

Where regularization has been in favour of the diphthong, this has occurred under the influence of a related noun or adjective which displays the diphthong concerned:

> OSp. *atesar/atieso* > *atiesar/atieso* 'to stiffen' (cf. *tieso* 'stiff')
> OSp. *dezmar/diezmo* > *diezmar/diezmo* 'to decimate, levy a tithe' (cf. *diezmo* 'tenth, tithe')
> OSp. *adestrar/adiestro* > *adiestrar/adiestro* 'to train' (cf. *diestro* 'skilful')
> OSp. *desossar/deshuesso* > *deshuesar/deshueso* 'to bone (meat)' (cf. *hueso* 'bone')
> OSp. *engrossar/engruesso* > *engruesar/engrueso* 'to fatten, become fat' (cf. *grueso* 'fat')

One verb, LĔVĀRE, has had an idiosyncratic history. In Old Spanish, the descendant of this verb (*levar* 'to carry') showed the expected /e/ ~ /ie/ alternation, but at the end of the Middle Ages one finds (stem-stressed) forms in which the sequence [ljé] is replaced by [ʎé] (as sporadically happened in the case of a few other words, e.g. *caliente* > *callente*, later only *caliente*). This change produced an unprecedented consonantal alternation between /ʎ/ (in stem-stressed forms) and /l/ (in forms with atonic stem), an alternation which was quickly levelled in favour of /ʎ/:

LĔVĀRE	>	*levar*	>	*levar*	>	*llevar*	
LĔVŌ	>	*lievo*	>	*llevo*	>	*llevo*	
LĔVĀS	>	*lievas*	>	*llevas*	>	*llevas*	
LĔVAT	>	*lieva*	>	*lleva*	>	*lleva*	
LĔVĀMUS	>	*levamos*	>	*levamos*	>	*llevamos*	
LĔVĀTIS	>	*levades*	>	*leváis*	>	*lleváis*	
LĔVANT	>	*lievan*	>	*llevan*	>	*llevan*	

(b) **-ir verbs.** As anticipated above, the [j] which occurred in certain endings of most verbs which contributed to the *-ir* class was preserved longer than the [j] which occurred in most of the verbs which contributed to the *-er* class, long enough for this glide to exercise metaphonic effect on the stem vowel of *-ir* verbs. Since metaphony (see 2.4.2.1) potentially affects all vowels (other than A, Ī, or Ū) which are followed by [j], we are here involved with the large majority of *-ir* verbs, and the phonological predictions which need to be made about the development of their stem-vowels are necessarily more complex than in the case of other verb-classes. The relevant phonological developments are the following:

CL	VL		Sp.	
Ī	/i/	(tonic or atonic, whether or not followed by [j])	>	/i/
Ē/Ĭ	/e/	(tonic, followed by [j])	>	/i/
		(tonic, not followed by [j])	>	/e/
		(atonic, followed by [j])	>	/i/
		(atonic, not followed by [j])	>	/e/
Ĕ	/ɛ/	(tonic, followed by [j])	>	/e/
		(tonic, not followed by [j])	>	/ie/
	/e/	(atonic, followed by [j])	>	/i/
		(atonic, not followed by [j])	>	/e/
Ū	/u/	(tonic or atonic, whether or not followed by [j])	>	/u/
Ō/Ŭ	/o/	(tonic, followed by [j])	>	/u/
		(tonic, not followed by [j])	>	/o/
		(atonic, followed by [j])	>	/u/
		(atonic, not followed by [j])	>	/o/
Ŏ	/ɔ/	(tonic, followed by [j])	>	/o/
		(tonic, not followed by [j])	>	/ue/
	/o/	(atonic, followed by [j])	>	/u/
		(atonic, not followed by [j])	>	/o/

In assessing the effect of these phonological changes on the stem-vowel of *-ir* verbs, we evidently need to consider four stem-types for each of the VL vowels:

1   tonic stem followed by [j] (i.e. 1st sing. pres. ind., 1st–3rd sing. pres. subj., 3rd plur. pres. subj.)
2   tonic stem without following [j] (i.e. 2nd–3rd sing. pres. ind., 3rd plur. pres. ind., sing. imperative)

3   atonic stem followed by [j] (i.e. 1st–2nd plur. pres. subj.)
4   atonic stem without following [j] (i.e. 1st–2nd plur. pres. ind., infin., plur. imperative)

Only one example of each type will be cited, respectively the 1st sing. pres. ind., 2nd sing. pres. ind., 1st plur. pres. subj., and the infinitive. Where the expected phonological outcome occurs, the forms will be cited in *italics*; where some analogical interference has occurred, forms will be cited in underlined characters; the source of the analogical restructuring is indicated by arrows between one section and another of the chart.

Stem-vowel	Tonic + [j]	Tonic (no [j])	Atonic + [j]	Atonic (no [j])
Ī	RĪDEŌ > *rio*	RĪDĒS > *ries*	RĪDEĀMUS > *riamos*	*RĪDĪRE > reir
Ē/Ĭ	MĒTIŌ > *mido*	MĒTIS > mides	MĒTIĀMUS > *midamos*	MĒTĪRE > *medir*
Ĕ	SĔRVIŌ > sirvo	SĔRVĪS > sirves	SĔRVIĀMUS > *sirvamos*	SĔRVĪRE > *servir*
	SĔNTIŌ > siento	SĔNTĪS > *sientes*	SĔNTIĀMUS > *sintamos*	SĔNTĪRE > *sentir*

Considering the 'tonic + [j]' forms, it can be seen that analogical stem /i/ has been spread from the Ī and Ē/Ĭ verbs to Ĕ verbs like *sirvo*, while other Ĕ verbs like *siento* have resisted this analogical restructuring. However, verbs of this last pattern do not show predicted stem /e/, but /ie/ extended from the tonic forms without [j].

In the case of tonic stems without [j], only Ī verbs can be expected to show /i/ in Spanish, but it can be seen that Ē/Ĭ verbs and many Ĕ verbs have also (analogically) adopted this vowel, while Ĕ verbs of the *sientes* pattern have retained the phonologically expected /ie/.

The 'atonic + [j]' forms show predicted stem /i/ (with the one exception of the verb *venir*) and this (near-)unanimity of stem-vowel was no doubt an important factor in the spread of stem /i/ through the tonic stems already examined. Exceptional *vengamos, vengades* (later *vengáis*) (< VĔNIAMUS, VĔNIATIS) are perhaps explained by attraction to the corresponding forms of *tener*, where stem /e/ is expected.

In the atonic stems without [j], only Ē/Ĭ and Ĕ verbs can be expected to have stem /e/. However, two forces have conspired to introduce this vowel into the Ī verbs also: analogy with the Ē/Ĭ and Ĕ verbs, on the one hand, and, on the other, the strong Spanish dissimilatory tendency of the type /i/ ... /í/ > /e/ ... /í/, also evidenced outside the verb (e.g. VĪCĪNU > *vecino*; see 2.1.1.2). This dissimilatory force was evidently weaker in Old Spanish than in the modern language, since one frequently encounters forms like *dizir* (< *DĪCĪRE < DĪCERE), alongside *dezir*, and even analogical *midir, sintir*, beside more usual *medir, sentir*. Occasionally, however, learned influences have overcome this dissimilatory force in the early modern period, since the most usual Old Spanish forms *escrevir* (< SCRĪBERE) and *bevir* (< VĪVERE) were replaced, in educated usage, in the Golden Age by *escribir* and *vivir*, forms no doubt felt to be in closer accord with their etyma. Similarly remodelled is one Ē/Ĭ verb, RECĬPERE, which in Old Spanish most frequently appeared as *recebir*, but which adopted the stem-vowel /i/ (*recibir*) in more recent times, in imitation of RECĬPERE.

One important effect of all these readjustments is that there has come to be no difference of stem-vowel among the ī verbs, the Ē/Ĭ verbs and many of the Ĕ verbs; all have /e/ or /i/ under equivalent circumstances. Some of the Ĕ verbs, alone, have remained aloof, retaining /ie/ in those forms where the stress fell on the stem. One Ĕ verb, *erguir* (the descendant of ĔR(I)GŌ 'I raise'), shows both treatments; on the one hand, we find *irgo, irgues*, with attraction to the ī and Ē/Ĭ paradigms, but, more frequently, modern Spanish shows *yergo, yergues*, forms which adhere to the autonomous Ĕ paradigm.

Stem-vowel	Tonic +[j]	Tonic (no [j])	Atonic +[j]	Atonic (no [j])
Ū	ADDŪCŌ > *aduzco*	ADDŪCIS > *aduces*	ADDŪCĀMUS > *aduzcamos*	*ADDŪCĪRE > *aducir*
Ō/Ŭ	SŪBEO > *subo*	SŪBĪS > *subes*	SŪBEĀMUS > *subamos*	SŪBĪRE > *subir*
Ŏ	MŎLLIŌ > *mullo*	MŎLLĪS > *mulles*	MŎLLIĀMUS > *mullamos*	MŎLLĪRE > *mullir*
	DŎRMIŌ > *duermo*	DŎRMĪS > *duermes*	DŎRMIĀMUS > *durmamos*	DŎRMĪRE > *dormir*

The behaviour of the back vowels, where the stress falls on the stem and [j] follows, is identical to that of the front vowels. The /u/ of ū and ō/ŭ verbs has been extended analogically to many ŏ verbs; in fact, the spread of the high vowel has here been more successful than in the case of verbs with a front vowel in the stem, since only two verbs (*duermo* and *muero*) have resisted the analogy. However, the /ue/ of *duermo* (like the /ie/ of *siento*) is due to intra-paradigmatic analogy, with *duermes*, etc. Note that there is no satisfactory example of a ū verb which is attested in Latin with desinential [j]; hence the necessity to cite ADDŪCŌ as an example here, although a form *ADDŪCIO may have briefly existed in Hispanic Latin, after ADDŪCERE moved to the -ĪRE class and before the general loss of [j] in this class.

Among the forms stressed on the stem but without following [j], the parallelism with the front-vowel verbs is again complete: the /u/ of the ū verbs has spread to the ō/ŭ verbs and to most of the ŏ verbs. Again, only *duermes* and *mueres* escape this pressure.

Where the stem is unstressed and followed by [j], the predicted outcome (/u/ in all verbs) is in fact observed. As with the front-vowel verbs, this unanimity of outcome no doubt vitally assists the generalization of /u/ in the two categories already examined.

Where the stem is atonic and no [j] follows, the back-vowel verbs differ from their front-vowel counterparts, principally because the dissimilatory force (/i/ . . . /i/ > /e/ . . . /i/) is necessarily lacking here. The /u/ of the ū verbs has been spread to almost all other back-vowel verbs (the only regular exceptions, again, are *dormir* and *morir*), but this adjustment (/o/ > /u/) is late: in Old Spanish, some ō/ŭ verbs (e.g. *escurrir, incurrir, bullir, urdir, confundir*) always have stem /u/, but the majority of ō/ŭ verbs and all ŏ verbs prefer stem /o/ (e.g. *sobir, sofrir, foir, recodir, complimos, mollimos, cobrides, escopir, nozir* 'to harm', etc.), although occasional forms like *subimos, cubrides, durmir* are found, as well as occasional cases of ū verbs with stem /o/ (e.g. *adozir*). Only in the early sixteenth century does /u/ become general in these forms (with the exception of *dormir, morir*), a change which is no doubt assisted by the standardization of /u/ in the 3rd sing. and plur. of the preterite and in the gerund of these verbs (e.g. *subió, cubrieron, huyendo*, earlier *sobió ~ subió, cobrieron ~ cubrieron, foyendo ~ fuyendo*, etc.; see 3.7.7.5.1 and 3.7.8.2). The only ō/ŭ verb to resist the spread of analogical /u/ is *podrir* (< PŬTRĒRE), which in the twentieth century is in the process of being replaced by its analogical competitor *pudrir*.

Finally, it should be noted that the probable motivation for the spread of high vowels /i/ and /u/ through the stems of the -*ir* verbs, which has been examined in the preceding paragraphs, lies in the need to provide a contrast of form between the -*er* and -*ir* classes, perhaps because the contrast of classes was perceived to correspond, at least in part, to a contrast between verbs of 'stative' sense (largely concentrated in the -*er* class) and verbs of 'dynamic' sense. Since no -*er* verb of Spanish has stem-vowel /i/ or /u/, and since it is very rare for -*ir* verbs to display tonic /e/ or /o/ in the stem (the only frequent exception is *oír*), preference for high vowels in the stem of -*ir* verbs serves to highlight the formal contrast between -*ir* and -*er* verbs, which is otherwise slight, limited as it is to only four verbal endings (-*emos*/-*imos*, -*éis*/-*ís*, -*ed*/-*id*, -*er*/-*ir*). For this differentiation of verb-classes, see Montgomery 1976, 1978, 1979, 1980, 1985, Penny 1972b, Wilkinson 1971.

3.7.7.1.5   Irregular present tense forms.   A few verbs, usually among the most frequent, show forms which are not accounted for by any of the alternations thus far examined (3.7.7.1.3–4). Such irregularity is 'explained' in a number of ways: (1) by the retention of forms which were already irregular in Latin; (2) by the operation of phonological change unchecked by analogy (see 3.1.1); and (3) by the analogical spread of an 'irregular' structural feature from one form to another or from one verb to another.

The pres. ind. of the verb *ser* descends in part from the Latin pres. ind.

SŬM	SŬMUS
ĒS	ESTIS
ĔST	SŬNT

a paradigm which suffered a number of modifications in the spoken Latin of Spain. In 1st sing., -M was lost (contrary to the normal treatment of -M in monosyllables; see 2.5.4), no doubt because this ending was otherwise

unprecedented in the pres. ind. With the simplification of word-final
-ST > -S (cf. POST > *POS > *pues* 'therefore'), the 2nd and 3rd sing. forms
became identical and in the Latin of Cantabria it seems that this ambiguity
was resolved by the introduction, into the 2nd pers. of originally future
ĔRIS. At the same time, in a wider area, 2nd plur. ESTIS was ousted by a form
*SŬTIS, analogically remodelled on SŬM, SŬMUS and SŬNT. Bearing in mind
regular phonological change, the forms used in C Northern Spain in early
times would therefore have been

/só/	/sómos/
/éres/	/sótes/
/és/	/són(t)/

In the subsequent development of this paradigm, /ɛ/ fails to diphthongize
(contrary to 2.4.2.2), perhaps because the forms of this paradigm, as well as
functioning as full verbs, sometimes functioned as auxiliaries (in the perfect
of intransitive verbs; see 3.7.3), in which case they received less than the full
stress necessary for diphthongization to take place. The result is the
following Old Spanish paradigm:

so	*somos*
eres	*sodes*
es	*son*

Apart from the regular development *sodes* > *sois* (see 3.7.7.1.2), the only
change to affect this paradigm in subsequent centuries was the late
medieval modification *so* > *soy*. This development also affects OSp. *do, vo*
and *estó* (> *voy, doy, estoy*) and is unsatisfactorily explained. It has been
speculated that the added element is the Old Spanish adverb *y* 'there' (see
3.4), a notion which is probably correct in the case of the contemporary
expansion of *ha* (< HABET) > *hay* 'there is/are', but which is less likely to be
true in the case of the verbs under consideration here. For discussion of this
problem, see De Gorog 1980, Müller 1963.

   Pres. subj. *sea*, etc., does not descend from the pres. subj. of ESSE 'to be',
but from that of SEDĒRE 'to sit, be seated'. This syncretism of the two Latin
verbs, producing in Spanish a single verb *se(e)r* capable of both meanings
at the medieval stage, but with specific tense-forms drawn from either
(sometimes both), must have occurred (at least in part) at the spoken Latin
stage, since other Romance languages provide evidence of the same merger
(e.g. Fr. *serai*, It. *sarò* 'I shall be' < SEDĒRE HABEŌ). For the phonological
development SEDEAM > *sea*, see 2.5.2.2[4]).

   The present tenses of *dar* and *estar*, apart from the forms *doy, estoy*
(< *do, estó*, see *ser*, above) are irregular only in the sense that they descend
from Latin paradigms most of whose members were monosyllabic (DŌ,
DEM, STŌ, STEM, etc.), so that the stress fell on syllables which in other verbs

constituted the (atonic) ending. In the case of STO, etc., this accent position remained unchanged even when /e/ was added, as it regularly was, before /st-/ (see 2.3.3).

DŌ	> *do*	> *doy*	STŌ	> *estó*	> *estoy*	
DĀS	> *das*		STĀS	> *estás*		
DAT	> *da*		STAT	> *está*		
DĀMUS	> *damos*		STĀMUS	> *estamos*		
DĀTIS	> *dades*	> *dais*	STĀTIS	> *estades*	> *estáis*	
DANT	> *dan*		STANT	> *están*		
DEM	> *dé*		STEM	> *esté*		
DĒS	> *des*		STĒS	> *estés*		
etc.			etc.			

The Old Spanish verb *veer* 'to see' had entirely regular present tenses, despite the occurrence of /d/+[j] in seven forms and /d/ alone in the remaining five in spoken Latin. This regularity is due to the fact that, after a front vowel, the reflex of /d/+[j] is *zero* (see 2.5.2.2[4] and 3.7.7.1.1), the same result as is normally expected from intervocalic /d/ (see 2.5.3.2[4]):

VIDEŌ	> *veo*	VIDEAM	> *vea*
VIDĒS	> *vees*	VIDEĀS	> *veas*
VIDET	> *vee*	VIDEAT	> *vea*
VIDĒMUS	> *veemos*	VIDEĀMUS	> *veamos*
VIDĒTIS	> *veedes*	VIDEĀTIS	> *veades*
VIDENT	> *veen*	VIDEANT	> *vean*

It was only with the late medieval contraction of /ee/ to /e/ that this verb came to have an 'irregular' structure (*veer* > *ver*, *vees* > *ves*, *veemos* > *vemos*, *veedes* > *veis*, etc.). Note that in the less frequent verbs *creer* and *leer* this contraction between stem-vowel and desinential vowel was resisted, in keeping with what we know about the generally more powerful effect of analogy in less frequent lexical items (see 3.1.1).

Haber (OSp. *aver*) receives dual treatment in its descent to Old Spanish. As a full verb (with the sense 'to possess'), it often retains its stem syllable (*av-*), while in its very frequent auxiliary use (in the perfect [3.7.3] and in the future [3.7.7.4.1]) it suffers contraction to tonic vowel + person/number marker. In principle, then, this verb has two contrasting paradigms in Old Spanish, although the contrast was never present in the 1st pers. sing., where the only form in use was *(h)e*, a form perhaps belonging originally only to the auxiliary paradigm but used from the earliest time also in the sense 'I possess'. The development of this form shows palatalization (as occasionally occurred in the development of Spanish; see 2.5.2.2[5]) of /β/+[j] > /ǰ/ (HABEŌ > **/aǰo/), followed by loss of final /o/ under conditions similar to those which allowed, e.g. *bueno* > *buen* (2.4.3.2). Since /ǰ/ cannot

occur in syllable-final position, the result of this loss is */ajo/ > /ai/, a stage
followed by the normal reduction of this diphthong to /e/ (2.4.2.4).

		full verb	auxiliary
HABEŌ	>	*(h)e*	*(h)e*
HABĒS	>	*aves*	*(h)as*
HABET	>	*ave*	*(h)a*
HABĒMUS	>	*avemos*	*(h)emos*
HABĒTIS	>	*avedes*	*(h)edes*
HABENT	>	*aven*	*(h)an*

However, some interchange between the two paradigms is evident even in
early Old Spanish texts. *Aves, ave* and *aven* are relatively rare and are
replaced, as full verbs, by originally auxiliary *(h)a(s)*, *(h)an*, while the full
forms *avemos, avedes* find their way into auxiliary use (in the perfect only;
not in the future). *Avedes* (now *habéis*) established itself permanently in the
perfect paradigm, while *avemos* (now *habemos*) was ousted from this
function in the standard language after the Golden Age and is now
restricted to non-standard use in the perfect. It must be remembered that
during the sixteenth century the verb *aver/haber* falls out of use as a full
verb, replaced by *tener*.

In the pres. subj. there is a single treatment of HABEAM, etc., whether used
as a full verb or as an auxiliary (in the perfect subjunctive). We observe the
same palatalization of /β/ + [j] as in HABEŌ:

HABEAM	>	*haya*
HABEĀS	>	*hayas*
HABEAT	>	*haya*
etc.		etc.

For non-standard *haiga*, etc., see 3.7.7.1.3.

The pres. ind. of *saber* is historically irregular only in the 1st sing., where
SAPIŌ might be expected to produce **sepo* (see 2.5.2.2), in the same way that
CAPIŌ > *quepo*. The form *sé* is best explained as an analogical imitation of *he*
(see above), due to the considerable structural similarity between the verbs
haber and *saber*, although it should be noted that in Old Spanish these verbs
had different stem consonants: *aver* with /β/ and *saber* with /b/.

The subj. of *saber* and *caber* is the historically regular (but synchronically
irregular) *sepa, quepa* < SAPIAM, CAPIAM, etc.; see 2.5.2.2.

Some present tense forms of the verb *ir* were inconveniently short in
Latin. EŌ, ĪS, IT, EUNT, EAM, EĀS, EAT, EĀMUS, EĀTIS, EANT lacked any stem
consonant. They were thus likely in speech to merge incomprehensibly with
surrounding words and were replaced by longer forms. These were drawn
from the semantically related VADERE 'to hasten', which supplied all present
tense forms in spoken Latin except the 1st and 2nd plur. pres. ind.:

VĀDŌ	ĪMUS		VĀDAM	VĀDĀMUS
VĀDIS	ĪTIS		VĀDĀS	VĀDĀTIS
VĀDIS	VĀDUNT		VĀDAT	VĀDANT

The indicative forms VĀDO, VĀDIS, VĀDIT and VĀDUNT suffered contraction, perhaps on the model of OSp. *do, das, estó, estás*, etc., while the subjunctive was remodelled (so far as its stem-consonant was concerned) on the pattern of verbs like AUDIŌ (see 3.7.7.1.1), although analogical *vayamos, vayades* alternated for a time with the historically regular subjunctives *vamos, vades*. Thus the Old Spanish paradigms were:

vo	imos		vaya	vamos/vayamos
vas	ides		vayas	vades/vayades
va	van		vaya	vayan

Because of their structure, *vamos, vades* must increasingly have been associated with the indicative paradigm. From the early Golden Age, *imos* and *is* (<*ides*) were restricted to dialectal use, while *vamos* and *vais* (<*vades*) lost their subjunctive value, although *vamos* (rather than *vayamos*) continued in imperative and optative function. Bearing in mind the change *vo > voy* (see *ser*, above), the result was the modern Spanish paradigms:

voy	vamos		vaya	vayamos
vas	vais		vayas	vayáis
va	van		vaya	vayan

For non-standard *vaiga*, see 3.7.7.1.3.

Oír is irregular in two ways. On the one hand, it is the only -*ir* verb which displays stem /o/ under the stress (see 3.7.7.1.4), no doubt because this /o/ developed from AU (e.g., OSp. *oyo* < AUDIŌ) too late to be affected by the [j] which originally occurred in the verbal ending. On the other hand, the consonant /j/ (<D+[j]) is found not only, as expected, in the 1st sing. pres. ind. and throughout the subjunctive, but also in *oyes, oye, oyen*, probably as an anti-hiatic consonant (i.e. to provide a sharper syllabic boundary than that provided by the pre-existing hiatus /ó-e/). It should be noted that /j/ could not be extended to *oímos, oídes*, since, except at the boundary between morpheme and derivational suffix (e.g. *ray-ita*), Spanish does not permit the sequence */ji/. The same pattern of development seen in the pres. indic. of *oír* also occurred, for similar reasons, in verbs whose infinitives ended in *uir*, whether popular (e.g. OSp. *fuyes, fuye, fuyen*, MSp. *huyes, huye, huyen*) or learned (e.g. *destruyes*, etc.). For the change *oyo > oigo*, see 3.7.7.1.3.

Hacer today conforms to the pattern in which stem-final /g/ alternates with /θ/ (*hago, haces*; see 3.7.7.1.3). In Old Spanish, in addition to this alternation, there were alternative 1st and 2nd plur. forms, one set of which showed the stress-shift normal in 3rd conj. verbs (FÁCIMUS, FÁCITIS > FACÍMUS, FACÍTIS > *fazemos, fazedes*; see 3.7.6), while the other retained the Latin stem-stress (FÁCIMUS, FÁCITIS > */fákmos/, /fáktes/ [2.4.3.3] > */fáimos/, /fáites/ [2.5.2.4] > *femos, feches* [2.4.2.1]). The phonologically regular (but morphologically anomalous) forms *femos, feches* were soon ousted by their morphologically regular counterparts *fazemos, fazedes* (see 3.1.1), from which the modern *hacemos, hacéis* descend.

Few of the verbs whose present tenses were irregular in Latin have survived into Spanish. Of those that did, *ser* and *ir* have been considered above, and the only remaining such verb is Lat. POSSUM. Because in some of its forms (e.g. PŎTĒS, PŎTUI) this verb was indistinguishable from regular -ĒRE verbs, it was eventually assimilated entirely to this class, suffering the appropriate restructuring of its present tenses (among others). The result was indic. *PŎT(E)O, PŎTĒS, *PŎTET, *PŎTĒMUS, etc., subj. PŎT(E)AM, etc., forms which produce the expected /ue/ ~ /o/ alternation (e.g. *puedo ~ podemos, pueda ~ podamos*), for which see 3.7.7.1.4. However, in the light of Fr. *puis*, It./Ptg. *posso* (< POSSUM), it may be argued that full regularization did not occur at the spoken Latin stage, but later (and not universally).

3.7.7.2   *The imperative*

As remarked in 3.7.7.1.3 and 3.7.7.1.4, the consonant and vowel alternations which affect the pres. ind. and the pres. subj. also affect the imperative forms. Since the sing. imperative is stressed on the stem and lacks desinential [j] (see 3.7.7.1.1), it manifests the same stem alternants as the 2nd–3rd sing. and 3rd plur. pres. ind. forms. Similarly, the plur. imperative, bearing its stress on the ending and having no [j] in its ending, shares the stem form of the 1st and 2nd pers. plur. pres. ind. The endings of the plural imperative have been discussed in 3.7.2.1, so that it remains to consider the singular endings.

The imperative sing. endings of the four Latin conjugations were respectively -Ā, -Ē, -Ĕ and -Ī. There is some evidence that the long -Ī of the 4th conjugation occasionally exercised metaphonic effect (see 2.4.2.1) on the stressed vowel; thus, VĔNĪ > *ven* (without diphthong /ie/). However, since the only other verb in which such an effect is visible belongs to the -ĒRE class and therefore lacks -Ī (TĔNĒ > *ten*), the explanation for the stem vowel of *ven* and *ten* cannot be said to be securely established.

Since Ĕ, Ē and Ī can be expected to merge in final syllables (see 2.4.3.2), only two distinct endings appear in Spanish (e.g. CANTĀ > *canta*; MŎVĒ > *mueve*, VOLVE > *vuelve*, APERĪ > *abre*). However, it should be noted that in the case of Old Spanish -*er* and -*ir* verbs whose stem ends in /e/ or /a/

(*creer, leer, seer, traer, veer*), the imperative ending is /i/: OSp. *crey, ley, sey, tray, vey*. The modern language has brought these imperatives in line with regular verbs of the same classes: *cree, lee, sé, trae, ve*).

The /-e/ of *-er/-ir* verbs was frequently lost in Old Spanish when the verbal stem ended in an ungrouped dental or alveolar consonant, in the same way as the /-e/ of the 3rd sing. pres. ind. (see 2.4.3.2 and 3.7.7.1.2). However, whereas in the pres. ind. there were strong analogical pressures leading to the eventual retention of final /e/ (3.7.7.1.2), such pressures were lacking in the imperative and a number of frequent singular imperatives have reached the modern language without final vowel: *pon, ten, ven, sal, val* (beside *vale*), *haz, yaz* (beside *yace*).

It can be seen that *haz* descends not from irregular FAC, but from regularized *FACE, since FAC would give *fa (see 2.5.4), just as irregular DIC gives *di*. Beside OSp. *faz* we find *fez*, whose vowel no doubt is due to analogical imitation of OSp. infin. *fer*, 1st plur. pres. ind. *femos*, etc. The imperative of *ser* descends not from ESSE but from SEDĒRE (as in the pres. subj.; see 3.7.7.1.5): SEDĒ > OSp. *sey* (see above) > MSp. *sé*, SEDĒTE > *sed*; while in the case of *ir*, imper. *ve* (beside occasional OSp. *va*) descends from VADE, perhaps via a form */vai/ displaying loss of -D- (3.5.3.2[4]) and dissimilation of resulting /áe/ > /ái/. *Está* and *oye* show the same irregularities as the corresponding indicative forms (see 3.7.7.1.5).

The only irregular plural imperatives to be observed in Spanish are OSp. *fech* (< FÁCITE, with preservation of 3rd-conjugation stress [see 3.7.6] and early loss of the post-tonic vowel, after which -CT- receives regular treatment [see 2.5.2.4]) and OSp. *tred* (< TRÁHITE, again with retention of 3rd-conjugation stress, and regular reduction of /ai/ to /e/). However, these two forms were soon replaced by regular alternatives, so that the modern language displays no irregular plural imperatives.

3.7.7.3 *Imperfect indicative and subjunctive*

3.7.7.3.1 The imperfect indicative. The endings of this tense in Latin can be exemplified by the following forms, one each from the four Latin conjugations: CANTĀBAM, TIMĒBAM, VENDĒBAM, AUDIĒBAM. However, there is evidence that in the -ĪRE verbs there was widespread use of the ending -ĪBAM, and such an ending appears to have been in use in the Latin of Spain. In the 1st and 2nd pers. plur., there was a retraction of the stress from penultimate to antepenultimate syllable, as in certain other tenses (see 3.7.7.3.2, 3.7.7.4.3), in order to regularize the position of the accent in relation to the stem. Thus, CANTABÁMUS, CANTABÁTIS, TIMEBÁMUS, VENDEBÁTIS, etc., became CANTÁBAMUS, CANTÁBATIS, TIMÉBAMUS, VENDÉBATIS, etc., to bring the stress onto the syllable immediately following the stem, in accordance with the remaining forms of the paradigm (e.g. CANTÁBAM).

Bearing in mind this stress-shift, verbs of the *a*-class evolve into Old and Modern Spanish in the phonologically expected way:

Latin	Old Spanish	Modern Spanish
CANTĀBAM	*cantava*	*cantaba*
CANTĀBAS	*cantavas*	*cantabas*
CANTĀBAT	*cantava*	*cantaba*
CANTĀBÁMUS	*cantávamos*	*cantábamos*
CANTĀBÁTIS	*cantávades*	*cantabais*
CANTĀBANT	*cantavan*	*cantaban*

However, verbs of other classes have lost the -B- from this paradigm, perhaps because a number of very frequent -ĒRE, -ĔRE, and -ĪRE verbs had -B- or -V- at the end of the stem, so providing the conditions for dissimilatory loss (see 2.1.1.2) of desinential -B-. In this way HABĒBAM would have been reduced to /aβéa/, and similar loss of -B- would have applied to verbs like DĒBĒBAM, BIBĒBAM, VIVĒBAM, etc. It is possible that, once the ending /-éa/ was established in these common verbs, it was extended to all other verbs of these classes.

The hiatus /éa/ was subject to dissimilation (> /ía/), just as occurred in the VL possessive /méa/ (whence *mía* 'my'; see 3.5.2), in the noun DĬA (VL /déa/ > *día* 'day'), etc. As a result, the ending of -ĒRE and -ĔRE verbs came to coincide with that of the -ĪRE class (where non-standard -ĪBAM > /ía/).

In final position, the sequence /ía/ was liable to sporadic modification in early Old Spanish to /íe/ and even /í/ (again, as in the possessive; cf. OSp. *mia/mie/mi*). The results of this modification appear in all forms of the imperf. ind., and for most of the Old Spanish period the forms with *-ie-* (sometimes stressed /ié/) were more frequent than the forms in *-ia-*, except in the 1st sing., where *-ia-* always predominated. However, in about the fifteenth century, the forms in *-ia-* were again preferred, perhaps due to analogical pressure from the *-ar* verbs, whose final/post-tonic /a/ had never been modified (see above). Leaving aside the relatively rare forms in *-i*, which appear to be limited to the 3rd sing. (e.g. *tení* 'he had'), the development of the imperf. ind. of *-er* and *-ir* verbs can be exemplified as follows:

Latin	Old Spanish	Modern Spanish
DĒBĒBAM	*devia, (-ie)*	*debía*
DĒBĒBĀS	*devias, -ies*	*debías*
DĒBĒBAT	*devia, -ie*	*debía*
DĒBĒBĀMUS	*deviamos, -iemos*	*debíamos*
DĒBĒBĀTIS	*deviades, -iedes*	*debíais*
DĒBĒBANT	*devia, -ien*	*debían*
AUDĪBAM	*oia, (-ie)*	*oía*
etc.	etc.	etc.

A further structural feature of the Old Spanish imperf. ind. was the variability of the stem-vowel of -*ir* verbs. As in the corresponding forms of the present tenses (i.e. those in which the stem was unstressed and no [j] appeared in the ending; see 3.7.7.1.4[b]), Old Spanish hesitated between stem /e/ and /i/ (e.g. *sentia/-ie ~ sintia/-ie* 'he felt') and between stem /o/ and /u/ (e.g. *sofria/-ie ~ sufria/-ie* 'he suffered'), irrespective of whether the Latin stem-vowel was Ī, Ĭ, Ē or Ĕ, in the first case, or Ū, Ŭ, Ō or Ŏ, in the second. As in the present, this variation was resolved, in the late Middle Ages, by preference for /e/ in the first case (where, once desinential /ía/ had ousted its rival /ie/, there was strong dissimilatory pressure of the type /i/ . . . /í/>/e/ . . . /í/, whence MSp. *sentía*), and for /u/ in the second *MSp. *sufría*, etc.). Note that, as in the present, this stem-vowel variation did not occur in -*er* verbs, whose stems have never permitted the appearance of /i/ or /u/. A further parallel with the present is that *oía* 'to hear' is the only -*ir* imperfect whose stem /o/ never suffered competition from /u/, while *oía* and *podría* 'it rotted' are the only two imperfects to pass into the modern language with the shape /o/ . . . /í/, although the latter is now being ousted by its long-standing competitor *pudría*.

The verb HABĒRE provides two imperf. ind. paradigms in Old Spanish. On the one hand, when it functioned as a full verb (i.e. with the meaning 'I possessed', etc.), we note the regular development HABĒBAM > *avia/-ie*, a form also used, together with the participle, in one of the Old Spanish pluperfect paradigms (see 3.7.3. and 3.7.7.3.2). On the other hand, when HABĒBAM functioned, together with the infinitive, as part of the conditional paradigm (see 3.7.4[1] and 3.7.7.4.2), it was dramatically shortened, losing its entire stem: *(h)ia/(h)ie, (h)ias/(h)ies*, etc. This short form still constitutes the ending of the conditional (e.g. *cantaría*).

Only two irregular Latin imperf. ind. paradigms have survived into Spanish. ĪBAM, unlike other verbs of its class, retains desinential -B- (OSp. *iva*, MSp. *iba*), thereby avoiding the fate (replacement) of other verbal forms which lacked a consonant. The imperf. ind. of ESSE, ĔRAM (whence *era*), shows no diphthongization of tonic /ɛ/, for reasons no doubt similar to those which gave rise to undiphthongized *eres, es* (<ĔST, ĔRIS) (see 3.7.7.1.5). Old Spanish had a competing imperf. ind. *se(d)ia, -ie* <SEDĒBAM 'I was sitting', which in some contexts was equivalent to *era*, but which alternatively could retain the Latin sense.

3.7.7.3.2 *The imperfect subjunctive.*

As anticipated in 3.7.3, the Latin imperf. subj. (e.g. CANTĀREM) did not survive in Spanish (or in most other varieties of Romance). The type CANTĀREM was replaced by CANTĀVISSEM, originally pluperf. subj., in the spoken Latin of most areas. This replacement seems to have begun in past conditional sentences of improbability or impossibility, where the original temporal remoteness of

CANTĀVISSEM would help to emphasize the unlikeliness that the condition expressed would be fulfilled. Thus, for example, SI POSSEM, FACEREM 'if I could, I would do it' was replaced by SI POTUISSEM, FĒCISSEM or FĒCERAM (for FĒCERAM, see below), which had earlier meant only 'if I had been able to, I would have done it' (see 3.9.2 and Lausberg 1966: 302–5). In Old Spanish, *cantas(se)* (<CANTĀVISSEM) can still indicate both improbability and impossibility, so that *si pudies(se), fizieralo/ferlo ia* could mean 'if I were to be able...' and 'if I had been able...'. However, this form had long since extended its functions to become the [+ past] counterpart of the pres. subj. For the successive values of *cantas(se)*, see Harris 1971 and 1986, Marcos Marín 1982, Mendeloff 1960, Pountain 1983, Rojo & Montero 1983, and Väänänen 1968: 260.

As sketched in 3.7.3, the infix -v(I)- of the Latin perfective verb-forms came to be omitted in spoken Latin, so that CANTĀVISSEM was contracted to CANTĀSSEM. In addition, the accent-position of the 1st and 2nd plur. forms was retracted in the same way as in the imperf. ind. (3.7.7.3.1). In Old Spanish, the final /e/ of the 1st and 3rd sing. forms was subject to frequent loss, like any other /-e/ (see 2.4.3.2), although analogical pressure from the remaining forms of the paradigm was eventually to lead to preference for the forms with final /e/. The development of the imperf. subj. can therefore be set out as follows:

CL	Hispano-Latin	Old Spanish	Modern Spanish
CANTĀVISSEM	CANTĀSSEM	*cantas(se)*	*cantase*
CANTĀVISSĒS	CANTĀSSĒS	*cantasses*	*cantases*
CANTĀVISSET	CANTĀSSET	*cantas(se)*	*cantase*
CANTĀVISSÉMUS	CANTÁSSEMUS	*cantássemos*	*cantásemos*
CANTĀVISSÉTIS	CANTÁSSETIS	*cantássedes*	*cantaseis*
CANTĀVISSENT	CANTĀSSENT	*cantassen*	*cantasen*
DORMĪVĪSSEM	DORMĪSSEM	*dormies(se)* ~	*durmiese*
etc.	etc.	*durmies(se)*	etc.
		etc.	

It is likely that the /ié/ (rather than expected /í/) of the Spanish -*ir* verbs was borrowed from the paradigm of the -*er* verbs, where /ié/ originated in the pluperfect subjunctive of verbs like VENDERE, e.g. *vendies(se)* <*VENDĒDISSEM, perhaps via a haplological form *VENDĚ(DI)SSEM (see 3.7.6, 3.7.7.5.1).

Since the Sp. imperf. subj. descends from a Latin paradigm (the pluperf. subj.) which has the same stem irregularities as the perfect, Spanish verbs which are irregular in the preterite (the descendant of the perfect) display the same irregularity in the imperf. subj. For these stem irregularities, e.g. OSp. *fizies(se), ovies(se)*, MSp. *hiciese, hubiese*, etc., see 3.7.7.5.1.

The stem-vowel of otherwise regular *-ir* verbs was subject in Old Spanish to the same variability as we have seen in the imperf. ind. (3.7.7.3.1). Thus, whether the Latin stem-vowel was Ī, Ĭ, Ē, or Ĕ, the Old Spanish stem may display /i/ or /e/ (e.g. *midiesse, sirviesse* vs *mediesse, serviesse*). Similarly, irrespective of whether the Latin stem-vowel was Ū, Ŭ, Ō or Ŏ, Old Spanish *-ir* verbs may show either stem /u/ or /o/ (e.g. *aduziesse, durmiesse* vs *adoziesse, dormiesse*). However, unlike the imperf. ind., the imperf. subj. of *-ir* verbs eventually preferred the high vowel in all cases (with the usual exception of *oyese*). The cause of this divergence between the imperf. subj. and the imperf. ind. perhaps lies in the fact that in the former paradigm the glide [j] (which often raises preceding vowels) is always present, whereas, in the imperf. ind., forms with [j] (e.g. *sentié ~ sintié*) alternated with (more frequent?) forms in which the desinential /i/ bore the stress (e.g. *sentía, -e ~ sintía, -e*). In the latter case, we can also witness the additional dissimilatory force /i/ . . . /í/ > /e/ . . . /í/, the conditions for which are lacking in the imperf. subj.

Until the end of the Middle Ages, the only imperf. subj. paradigm at the disposal of Spanish speakers was the one just discussed in *-se*. However, from that time onwards, the *-se* form has had a competitor in *-ra*, whose origins lie in the Latin pluperf. ind. paradigm and whose morphological development was in all ways parallel to that of the *-se* form:

CL	Hispano-Latin	Old Spanish	Modern Spanish
CANTĀVERAM	CANTĀRAM	*cantara*	*cantara*
CANTĀVERĀS	CANTĀRĀS	*cantaras*	*cantaras*
CANTĀVERAT	CANTĀRAT	*cantara*	*cantara*
CANTĀVERÁMUS	CANTÁRAMUS	*cantáramos*	*cantáramos*
CANTĀVERÁTIS	CANTÁRATIS	*cantárades*	*cantarais*
CANTĀVERANT	CANTĀRANT	*cantaran*	*cantaran*
DORMĪVĔRAM	DORMĪRAM	*dorm-, durmiera*	*durmiera*
etc.	etc.	etc.	etc.

The remark made above concerning the replacement of Hispano-Latin Ī of DORMĪSSEM by /ié/ also applies to the Ī of DORMĪRAM; /ié/ probably originates in the Ĕ of forms like *VENDĔ(DE)RAM, which first provided the regular ending of *-er* verbs and then were imitated by *-ir* verbs.

This identity of morphological development between the *-se* and *-ra* paradigms extends to the survival of irregular stems (e.g. OSp. *fiziera, oviera*, MSp. *hiciera, hubiera*, for which see 3.7.7.5.1) and to the Old Spanish variability of stem-vowels (see above).

OSp. *cantara* frequently preserves the pluperf. ind. value of its Latin ancestor. However, analytical competitors (*avia cantado* and *ove cantado*) were in existence throughout the Old Spanish period (see 3.7.3), and the former of these has all but ousted *cantara* from this role. It survives, only in written registers, in certain adjectival clauses (e.g. *el libro que empezara en 1920...* 'the book he had begun in 1920...').

A second value of the *-ra* form, conditional value, was acquired in the late Latin of some areas. In the main clause of conditional sentences expressing improbability or impossibility of outcome, it became possible to use the type CANTĀVERAM instead of imperf. subj. CANTĀREM or pluperf. subj. CANTĀVISSEM (see 3.9; for the replacement of CANTĀREM by CANTĀVISSEM, see above). Thus, for standard SI POTUISSEM, FĒCISSEM (and for earlier SI POSSEM, FACEREM; see above), we find SI POTUISSEM, FĒCERAM 'if I were to be able to, I would do (it)', or 'if I had been able to, I would have done (it)'. This latter construction remains the normal one in Old Spanish and a frequent one in Golden Age Spanish for the expression of 'improbable' or 'impossible' conditions: *si pudiesse, lo fiziera* (later *hiciera*) (alongside less frequent *si pudiesse, ferlo ia* [later, *lo haría*]). However, since the Golden Age, the possibility of using the *-ra* form with this conditional (or conditional perfect) sense has been severely restricted, while there has been a consequent increase in frequency of the type *si pudiese, lo haría*. Conditional perfect sense has been entirely lost from the *-ra* form and simple conditional sense is now possible only with a limited range of very frequent verbs: *hubiera, debiera, quisiera* (= *habría, debería, querría*). Additionally, *pudiera* is still sometimes found with this value (that is, *pudiera* may be equivalent to *podría*).

The imperf. subj. value of the *-ra* form is the value it acquired last. This change of value again probably began in conditional sentences expressing improbability or impossibility of outcome. It is well known from many languages that the verb form used in the principal clause of such sentences may come to be used also in the subordinate clause, and this phenomenon is attested in Spanish, rarely at first, from the fourteenth century. From that time, we find sporadic examples of the construction *si pudiera, fizieralo*. In this way the *-ra* form, until then an exponent of the indicative mood, comes to be an alternative to the *-se* form, and therefore acquires subjunctive value. The type *si pudiera, hiziéralo* remains the favourite Golden Age construction (alongside *si pudiese, hiziéralo*) to express the notion 'if I could, I would do it/I would have done it', a notion expressed in modern Spanish, as we have seen, by the type *si pudiera/pudiese, lo haría* or by the type *si hubiera/hubiese podido, lo hubiera/habría hecho*.

Having established itself as an alternative to the *-se* form in the subordinate clause of conditional sentences, the *-ra* form gradually becomes more frequent as an alternative to the *-se* form in other clauses (e.g. *para que volviera/volviese*). Full acceptance of this interchangeability is slow to be reached and Golden Age Spanish has an overwhelming preference for *-se* forms over *-ra* forms in non-conditional clauses requiring a past subjunctive. In more recent times, the *-ra* forms appear to have been gaining the upper hand, becoming more frequent than *-se* forms and entirely ousting the latter from some spoken varieties of Spanish.

For the history of the *-ra* forms, see Wright 1932, Klein-Andreu forthcoming, Pountain 1983, Ridruejo 1982.

3.7.7.4 *The future and conditional*

3.7.7.4.1 *The future indicative.*
The Latin future forms do not survive into Spanish. These forms, which can be exemplified, for each of the Latin verb-classes, by the types CANTĀBŌ, TIMĒBŌ, VENDAM, SENTIAM, suffered from a number of deficiencies, of which the most important were the following:

1. There was little formal similarity of ending among the various classes; the future marker of -ĀRE and -ĒRE verbs was tonic and displayed the consonant /b/, while that of the -ĔRE and -ĪRE classes was atonic and lacked any consonant.
2. The 1st sing. future ending of -ĔRE and -ĪRE verbs was identical to that of the pres. subj. (VENDAM, SENTIAM).
3. The phonemic merger in spoken Latin of intervocalic -B- and -V- (see 2.5.3) had the effect of making certain pairs of verbal forms indistinguishable; the 3rd sing. future CANTĀBIT and 1st plur. future CANTĀBIMUS became identical to the corresponding perfect forms CANTĀVIT and CANTĀVIMUS.
4. When Ĕ, Ē and Ĭ merged in final syllables (see 2.4.3.2), one of the consequences was that 2nd and 3rd sing. future forms of most -ĔRE verbs (VENDĒS, VENDĔT) became indistinguishable from the corresponding pres. ind. forms (VENDĬS, VENDĬT).

Given that special future forms are not indispensable (many languages lack them), since an adverb of time together with, say, a pres. ind. verb may often adequately express the notion of 'future' (e.g. CRAS VENIT, *viene mañana*, 'he is coming tomorrow'), it is not surprising that the Latin future forms, with their various inadequacies, were entirely abandoned in speech. However, spoken Latin did not entirely dispense with special future verb-forms, but created new paradigms on the basis of existing structures whose meaning was in some way related to that of the future. These structures were expressions of 'wish', 'obligation', 'intention' etc., and included such phrases as VOLŌ 'I wish' + infin., DĒBEŌ 'I must' + infin., VENIŌ 'I come' + AD + infin., HABEŌ + infin. The last of these phrases came to be used as the normal expression of the future in much of the Latin-speaking world, including Spain. The meaning of HABEO in isolation was of course 'I have, I possess', but combined with an infinitive it appears at first to have indicated intention, then obligation, and finally simple futurity. These semantic developments are visible in written Latin, although they no doubt took place more slowly there than at the spoken level. Thus we find, in Cicero (first century BC), sentences like DĒ RĒ PUBLICĀ NIHIL <u>HABEŌ</u> AD TĒ <u>SCRĪBERE</u>, where the notion of possession is almost entirely absent and that of intention is uppermost ('I don't propose to say anything in this letter about politics'). Seneca's question (first century AD) QUID <u>HABUI</u> <u>FACERE</u>? expresses obligation ('What should I have done?') and implies the existence of phrases like *QUID <u>HABEŌ FACERE</u>? ('What must I do?'). When this expression is found with inanimate subjects, as in St Augustine's TEMPESTĀS ILLA <u>TOLLERE HABET</u> TŌTAM PALEAM DĒ ĀREĀ (fourth–fifth centuries AD), it is evident that notions of intention and obligation are absent and that simple futurity is the appropriate interpretation ('The storm will carry all the straw from the threshing-floor').

The structure combining HABEŌ with an infinitive did not at first have a fixed order (as can be seen from the examples above) and it is likely that HABEŌ + infin. and infin. + HABEŌ competed in spoken Latin with HABEŌ AD or DE + infin. Of these possibilities, infin. + HABEŌ became the main exponent of futurity in Spain, although HABEŌ DE + infin. also survives, to express intention or simple futurity: *he de hacerlo mañana* 'I plan to do it tomorrow', or 'I shall do it...'.

The development of HABEŌ, in its auxiliary function, has been discussed in 3.7.7.1.5. The evolution of the Spanish future tense can now be summarized as:

Spoken Latin	Old Spanish	Modern Spanish
CANTĀRE HABEŌ	cantaré	cantaré
CANTĀRE HABĒS	cantarás	cantarás
CANTĀRE HABET	cantará	cantará
CANTĀRE HABĒMUS	cantaremos	cantaremos
CANTĀRE HABĒTIS	cantaredes	cantaréis
CANTĀRE HABENT	cantarán	cantarán

For the history of the HABEŌ + infin. construction, see Coleman 1971, Lausberg 1966: 310–16, Valesio 1968.

Until the sixteenth century, it was possible for an atonic pronoun (see 3.5.1) to fall between the two components (infinitive and auxiliary) which historically comprise the future forms. Indeed, if the future verb was the first tonic word of its clause, this component order was obligatory (e.g. *Ferlo he amidos, Doblarvos he la soldada*, etc., by contrast with *Conseio nos dará, amidos lo faré*, etc.). However, this separation of infinitive and auxiliary is already rare in the seventeenth century (when, at the beginning of a clause, *harélo, doblaréos*, etc., would exemplify normal practice) and thereafter each future verb-form is viewed as a single unit, with single word-stress.

Unless separated by a pronoun in the way just described, the two components of the future forms constituted, already in Old Spanish, a single word, with single stress (on the auxiliary). Thus, for example, AUDÍRE HÁBEŌ became OSp. *oyré*. The consequence of the loss of the stress which earlier fell on the infinitive is that the previously stressed /a/, /e/, or /i/ now found itself in pretonic position, and was subject to the treatment normally accorded to pretonic vowels. It will be remembered from 2.4.3.3 that, in intertonic position, almost all vowels other than /a/ were effaced in the immediate pre-literary period of Spanish. Among the few exceptions were cases like OSp. *oyré, caeré, fuyré* (beside *odré, cadré, fudré*, see below), *traeré*, in which the previously stressed vowel was in contact with the preceding vowel. All other *-er* and *-ir* verbs were liable to lose the /e/ or /i/ of the infinitive ending, resulting in contraction of the verbal stem:

> DĒBÉRE HÁBEO > *devér hé* > *deveré* > *devré*.

In cases like the one just quoted, the consonants brought into contact by the loss of the intertonic vowel (/β/ . . . /r/) form a group which was already familiar in Spanish. The same is true in the following instances of future stem contraction in Old Spanish:

/r/ . . . /r/	*querrá*	'he will wish'
	morrá (now *morirá*)	'he will die'
	ferrá (now *herirá*)	'he will strike, wound'
	parrá (now *parirá*)	'she will give birth to'
/b/ . . . /r/	*concibrá* (now *concebirá*)	'he will conceive'
	recibrá (now *recibirá*)	'he will receive'
/β/ . . . /r/	*avrá* (now *habrá*)	'he will have'
	bevrá (now *beberá*)	'he will drink'
	bivrá (now *vivirá*)	'he will live'
	subrá (now *subirá*)	'he will rise'
/d/ . . . /r/	*pidrá* (now *pedirá*)	'he will ask'
	recudrá (now obsolete)	'he will reply'
	podrá	'he will be able'
	comidrá	'he will ponder'
	perdrá (now *perderá*)	'he will lose'
	prendrá	'he will take'
/g/ . . . /r/	*consigrá* (now *conseguirá*)	'he will succeed in'
/t/ . . . /r/	*partrá* (now *partirá*)	'he will depart'
	consintrá (now *consentirá*)	'he will consent'
	repintrá (now *se arrepentirá*)	'he will repent'
	vistrá (now *vestirá*)	'he will dress'
/ts/ . . . /r/	*creçrá* (now *crecerá*)	'he will grow'
	pareçrá (now *parecerá*)	'he will seem'
/dz/ . . . /r/	*yazrá* (now *yacerá*)	'he will lie'

However, as in the case of all secondary consonant groups (see 2.5.5), the loss of an intervening vowel sometimes produced a sequence of consonants which was phonotactically unacceptable in Old Spanish, so that some adjustment of the group was required. Sometimes, the adjustment consisted of the replacement of one of the phonemes by a related phoneme. This is what often occurred in the sequences /l/ ... /r/ and /n/ ... /r/, where /r/ was replaced by /r̄/: *salrrá* (also spelt *salrá*; now *saldrá*) 'he will go out', *valrrá* (also spelt *valrá*; now *valdrá*) 'he will be worth', *ponrrá* (also spelt *ponrá*; now *pondrá*) 'he will put'.

In other cases, more fundamental readjustment of the sequence may take place, such as epenthesis, metathesis, or assimilation (see 2.1.1.1–4):

Epenthesis	/m/ ... /r/	*combrá* (now *comerá*)	'he will eat'
	/n/ ... /r/	*pondrá*	'he will put'
		vendrá	'he will come'
		remandrá	'he will remain'
	/l/ ... /r/	*moldrá* (now *molerá*)	'he will grind'
		doldrá (now *dolerá*)	'it will hurt'
		saldrá	'he will go out'
	/ʎ/ ... /r/	*toldrá* (now obsolete)	'he will take away'
	/dz/ ... /r/	*yazdrá* (now *yacerá*)	'he will lie'
	/ts/ ... /r/	*falleztrá* (now *fallecerá*)	'he will die'
Metathesis	/n/ ... /r/	*porná* (now *pondrá*)	'he will put'
		verná (now *vendrá*)	'he will come'
Assimilation	/n/ ... /r/	*porrá* (now *pondrá*)	'he will put'
		verrá (now *vendrá*)	'he will come'
	/dz/ ... /r/	*dirá*	'he will say'
		adurá (now *aducirá*)	'he will bring forward'

It can be seen that the same sequence may be treated in a number of competing ways, as is generally the case with secondary consonant groups (see 2.5.5).

The Old Spanish future forms of *caer* and *oír* often differ from the pattern so far observed in this section. Whereas the infinitives lack /d/ (see 2.5.3.2[4]), this consonant often appears in the future and conditional: *cadrá, odrá*. The development of these forms was presumably the following:

CADERE HABET > *caderá*	> *cadrá* (beside *caerá*)	'he will fall'
AUDĪRE HABET > *odirá*	> *odrá* (beside *oirá*)	'he will hear'

a pattern presumably extended to cases like *fudredes* 'you will flee' (< FUGERE HABĒTIS), beside *fuyrá*. However, in the case of other verbs whose etyma displayed -D- (*creer, seer, veer* < CRĒDERE, SEDĒRE, VIDĒRE), the Old Spanish future is formed without this consonant (*crerá, será, verá*), although it is notable that the stem of these forms is usually monosyllabic, and does not show the *ee* spelling of the corresponding infinitives.

It should be noted that the stem-vowel of *-ir* verbs often contrasts with that of *-er* verbs. Whereas in the infinitive of *-ir* verbs (and in other forms in which the ending displays tonic /i/, e.g. the imperf. ind.) there is hesitation between stem /e/ and /i/, and between stem /o/ and /u/ (e.g. *sentir ~ sintir, adozir ~ aduzir* [see 3.7.7.1.4]), in contracted future and conditional forms only stem /i/ or /u/ is normally permitted: *bivrá, comidrá, concibrá, (con)sintrá, dirá, pidrá, recibrá, repintrá, (con)sigrá, vistrá; adurá.* This obligatory high vowel no doubt serves the purpose of identifying the class to which the verb concerned belongs, bearing in mind that high stem-vowels are excluded from the *-er* class, and that in the contracted future it is precisely the class-identifying vowel that is deleted. The only exceptions to this rule are the contracted *-ir* futures in which the stem-vowel is followed by /r̄/ or by /r/+consonant, phonological circumstances in which vowel-lowering is attested in many languages: *ferrá, verrá/verná, morrá.* The Old Spanish form *vendrá* also fails to conform to the rule established here, but may be explained by analogy with *verrá/verná* and with *tendrá.* It should be remembered that other forms of *venir* also show irregular stem /e/ (pres. subj. *vengamos, vengáis* [see 3.7.7.1.4]), an irregularity usually assigned to the mutual attraction exercised between this verb and *tener.*

All of the contracted future (and conditional) forms of Old Spanish coexisted with uncontracted forms (even in the case of verbs which appear in the modern language with contracted futures; e.g. OSp. *averá, salirá*). In most cases the uncontracted form was eventually preferred, probably on the pattern of the *-ar* verbs, where contraction could never occur. Thus, for example, OSp. *concibrá* has given way entirely to *concebirá* by the sixteenth century. Golden Age Spanish allowed a few more contracted forms than the modern language (e.g. *debrá*), but current usage permits only the following, which belong (as expected) to some of the most frequent verbs: *habrá, sabrá, cabrá, querrá; vendrá, pondrá, tendrá, saldrá, valdrá; dirá.*

The descendants of FACERE HABET pose special problems. There were three descendants of the infinitive FACERE in Old Spanish (*fer, far,* and *fazer* [see 3.7.8.1]), and each can be used to form the future (*ferá, fará, fazerá*), although the last type was rare except where a pronoun intervened (e.g. *fazerlo ha,* beside *ferlo ha, farlo ha*). Of the various Old Spanish forms, it was the type *fará* which survived into the modern language, as *hará.*

3.7.7.4.2 The conditional. The creation of the conditional (a paradigm which did not exist in literary Latin) was discussed in 3.7.4(1). It will be recalled that the new set of forms consisted of infinitive + imperf. ind. of HABĒRE. Bearing in mind the treatment of HABĒBAM when used in this auxiliary role (see 3.7.7.3.1), it will be seen that the development of the conditional from spoken Latin to Old and modern Spanish was as follows:

Spoken Latin	Old Spanish	Modern Spanish
CANTĀRE HABĒBAM	*cantaría/-ie*	*cantaría*
CANTĀRE HABĒBĀS	*cantarías/-ies*	*cantarías*
CANTĀRE HABĒBAT	*cantaría/-ie*	*cantaría*
CANTĀRE HABĒBĀMUS	*cantaríamos/-iemos*	*cantaríamos*
CANTĀRE HABĒBĀTIS	*cantaríades/-iedes*	*cantaríais*
CANTĀRE HABĒBANT	*cantarían/-ien*	*cantarían*

What is said in 3.7.7.4.1 about the separability of the two components of the future, about the contraction of the future stem, and about the (almost complete) absence of the vowels /e/ and /o/ from contracted future stems, applies also, in every detail, to the conditional. A single example may suffice: OSp. *vestirlo ie el rey* alternates with *el rey lo vistrie*.

3.7.7.4.3 The future subjunctive.

The introduction of a future subjunctive into the verbal system was seen in 3.7.4(2). The source of this new tense was a double one: the Latin 'future perfect indicative' (CANTĀVERŌ) and the 'perfect subjunctive' (CANTĀVERIM). These two paradigms differed only in the forms quoted (1st sing.); in the remaining cases (CANTĀVERĪS, CANTĀVERIT, etc.), Latin used identical forms to express the two functions. As in other perfective verb-forms of this class, the marker of perfectivity (here -VE-) was lost in spoken Latin (see 3.7.3), and in the 1st and 2nd plur. the stress was retracted to the vowel immediately following the stem (to match the stress-pattern of the remaining forms of the paradigm), just as happened in many other cases (imperf. ind. [3.7.7.3.1], imperf. subj. [3.7.7.3.2], -*ra* form [3.7.7.3.2]). The development of the fut. subj. of -*ar* verbs can therefore be summarized as follows:

CL	Hispano-Latin	Old Spanish	Modern Spanish
CANTĀVERŌ, -IM	CANTĀRŌ, -IM	*cantaro, -r(e)*	*cantare*
CANTĀVERĪS	CANTĀRĪS	*cantares*	*cantares*
CANTĀVERIT	CANTĀRIT	*cantar(e)*	*cantare*
CANTĀVERÍMUS	CANTÁRIMUS	*cantáremos*	*cantáremos*
CANTĀVERÍTIS	CANTÁRITIS	*cantáredes*	*cantareis*
CANTĀVERINT	CANTĀRINT	*cantaren*	*cantaren*

The endings appropriate to -*ir* verbs were also applied to -*er* verbs, both classes behaving in parallel fashion to the -*ar* verbs:

DORMĪVERŌ, -IM	DORMĪERŌ, -IM	*durmiero, -r(e)/*	*durmiere*
etc.	etc.	*dormiero, -r(e)*	etc.
		etc.	

For the 2nd plur. ending (OSp. and Golden Age Spanish *cantáredes, durmiéredes, cantardes, durmierdes,* etc.), see 3.7.2 (end).

The fut. subj., originating as it does in tenses which in Latin shared the same stem as the perfect, the pluperf. subj. and the pluperf. ind., shares the same stem irregularities as the Spanish pret. (3.7.7.5.1), the imperf. subj., and the *-ra* form (3.7.7.3.2), e.g. OSp. *fezier(e)*, *ovier(e)*, *dixier(e)*, etc., MSp. *hiciere, hubiere, dijere*, etc. Similarly, the stem-vowel in the fut. subj. of regular *-ir* verbs shows the same variation between /e/ and /i/, /o/ and /u/ as the *-se* and *-ra* forms (e.g. OSp. *sentier(e)* ~ *sintier(e)*, *dormier(e)* ~ *durmier(e)*, MSp. *sintiere, durmiere*).

Until its relatively recent demise, the fut. subj. was fully integrated into the Spanish verbal system (see 3.7.3). It frequently occurred in a number of clause-types, for example, in the subordinate clause of conditional sentences whose principal verb was future ind. (e.g. *si viniere, se lo daré* 'if he comes, I'll give it to him'), in adjectival clauses whose antecedent was indefinite (including negative) (e.g. *los que quisieren hacerlo* 'those who (in the future) wish to do it'), and in temporal clauses dependent upon a main verb which is pres. or fut. (e.g. *cuando llegare, se lo daré* 'when he arrives, I'll give it to him'). However, in these and other cases, the fut. subj. alternated (apparently freely) with other verb-forms: in conditional sentences, with the pres. ind.; in adjectival and temporal clauses, with the pres. subj. (see Menéndez Pidal 1964b: 347, 357). During the Golden Age, there was a decline in the frequency of the fut. subj., and after the eighteenth century it was restricted to literary use (now very infrequent) and to a few set phrases (e.g. *venga lo que viniere* 'come what may'), where the fut. subj. form alternates with the pres. subj. (*venga lo que venga*).

Spanish also displayed, until recent times, a fut. perf. subj. This tense had its origins in a combination of the fut. subj. of the auxiliary (e.g. OSp. *ovier(e)*, *-o* < HABUERIM, -ō) and the participle. In recent centuries, the descendant of this perfective structure (*hubiere cantado*) has suffered the same fate as its imperfective counterpart, being replaced by the perf. ind. or perf. subj. See Blase 1898.

3.7.7.5 *The preterite*

It has been seen in 3.7.3 that the Latin 'perfect' functioned in two ways, as a 'present perfect' indicating actions and events occurring in a period of time including the moment 'now', and as a 'preterite', indicating actions and events which occurred in a period of time which terminated before the moment 'now'. It was also seen that in the first of these functions the Latin forms were replaced by analytical expressions (HABEŌ CANTĀTUM, etc.) which provide the Spanish perfect (*he cantado*, etc.). In the second function, the Latin forms continued in use and gave rise to the Spanish preterite forms (*canté*, etc.), which are the subject of this section.

The Latin perfect forms were distributed between two broad classes, 'weak' and 'strong'. Weak perfects are those which bore the stress, in all six forms, on the ending (e.g. CANTÁVĪ, CANTĀVÍSTĪ, etc.), while the strong perfects are those which, in some forms of the paradigm, bore the stress on the stem (e.g. FÉCĪ, FÉCIMUS, etc., HÁBUĪ, HÁBUIT, etc.).

3.7.7.5.1   The weak preterite.   Almost all -ĀRE verbs had weak perfects in Latin (e.g. CANTĀVĪ), as did the large majority of -ĪRE verbs (e.g. DORMĪVĪ) and a small number of -ĒRE verbs (e.g. DELĒVĪ). In addition, it will be seen that many other -ĒRE verbs, together with many -ĔRE verbs, came to have weak accentuation in spoken Latin, as a result of the extension of the type *VENDÉDĪ (< VÉNDIDĪ).

As seen in 3.7.3, the Latin marker of perfectivity (-V[Ī]-) was abandoned in spoken Latin. Indeed, it was frequently absent from the perfect of -ĪRE verbs even in Classical Latin (e.g. DORMĬĬ beside DORMĪVĪ). However, in the spoken Latin of Spain, it appears that the 3rd sing. endings -ĀVIT, -ĪVIT were reduced to -AUT (= /áu̯t/), -ĪUT (= /íu̯t/), rather than to -A(I)T, -ĪT, as occurred elsewhere (see Väänänen 1968: 227). Additionally, in the 2nd sing., 1st plur. and 2nd plur. forms of the Old Spanish -*ir* preterite paradigm, beside inherited forms with tonic /i/ *(dorm-, durmist(e)(s), dorm-, durmimos, dorm-, durmistes)*, there were frequent forms in /ié/ *(durmiest(e)(s), durmiemos, durmiestes)*. These /ié/ endings, which do not survive beyond the Middle Ages, probably have their origin in the -*er* paradigm (for which, see below), as does the /ié/ of 3rd plur. *durmieron*, which entirely ousted from Old Castilian any descendant of late Latin DORMĪRUNT (viz. **dormiron*).

Bearing in mind the normal treatment AI > OSp. /e/ and AU > OSp. /o/ (see 2.4.2.4), the development of most -ĀRE and -ĪRE verbs from Latin to Old Spanish can be stated as follows:

CL	Hispano-Latin	Old Spanish
CANTĀVĪ	CANTÁĪ	*canté*
CANTĀVISTĪ	CANTÁSTĪ	*cantast(e)(s), -est(e)(s)*
CANTĀVIT	CANTÁUT	*cantó*
CANTĀVIMUS	CANTÁMUS	*cantamos, -emos*
CANTĀVISTIS	CANTÁSTIS	*cantastes, -estes*
CANTĀVĒRUNT	CANTÁRUNT	*cantaron*
DORMĪVĪ	DORMÍ	*dormí, durmí*
DORMĪVISTĪ	DORMÍSTĪ	*dormist (e)(s), durmist(e)(s)* *(beside dormiest[e][s], durmiest[e][s])*
DORMĪVIT	DORMÍUT	*dormió, durmió*
DORMĪVIMUS	DORMÍMUS	*dormimos, durmimos (beside dormiemos, durmiemos)*
DORMĪVISTIS	DORMÍSTIS	*dormistes, durmistes (beside dormiestes, durmiestes)*
DORMĪVĒRUNT	DORMÍRUNT	*dormieron, durmieron*

It can be seen that there was a great deal of variation in the Old Spanish endings, most of it created at the pre-literary stage, through phonological change (e.g. loss of /-e/ in 2nd sing. [see 2.4.3.2]), or through intra- and extra-paradigmatic analogy. The forms *cantest(e)(s)*, *cantemos*, *cantestes* are probably to be accounted for by extension of the /é/ of *canté*, on the pattern /-í/, /-íst(e)(s)/, /-ímos/ /-ístes/ frequently visible in the *-ir* verbs (e.g. *dormí, dormist(e)(s), dormimos, dormistes*), while the sporadic appearance of /-s/ in the 2nd sing. is undoubtedly owed to imitation of the 2nd sing. of all other paradigms of the language, where /-s/ was universally found.

The variation of stem-vowel in the *-ir* preterites (e.g. *dormí ~ durmí, sentimos ~ sintimos*) was identical in Old Spanish to that observed in those *-ir* present-tense forms in which the stem-vowel was unstressed and not followed in Latin by [j] (e.g. *subís ~ sobís, medimos ~ midimos* [see 3.7.7.1.4(b)]). In the OSp. *-ir* preterite, there was free variation between /o/ and /u/ and between /e/ and /i/ in all members of the paradigm, although /o/ and /e/ were more frequent where the ending contained /i/, while /u/ and /i/ were more frequent when the ending contained [j]. This variation was resolved in early Modern Spanish in much the same way as in the present tenses: (1) /u/ was preferred over /o/ in all forms of all verbs except *dormir* and *morir*, where /o/ survives before /í/ but /u/ is preferred where the ending contains [j] (*durmió, murieron*); and (2) /e/ came to be preferred, in almost all verbs, in all cases where the ending eventually chosen contained /í/ (e.g. *sentí, sentiste, sentimos, sentiste(i)s*), while /i/ was preferred where the ending contained [j] (e.g. *sintió, sintieron*). It should be noted that the probable motivation for this choice of stem-vowels was the desire to distinguish, by means of their stem-vowels, verbs which belonged to the otherwise very similar *-er* and *-ir* classes.

So far, we have considered the development of -ĀRE and -ĪRE verbs, but it has to be borne in mind that the majority of Spanish verbs which descend from the -ĒRE and -ĔRE classes have displayed the same endings as the -ĪRE verbs. A possible explanation for this fact (see, for example, Lausberg 1966: 345–8) can be found in a frequent subset of -ĔRE verbs, namely CRĒDĔRE 'to believe', PERDĔRE 'to lose', REDDĔRE 'to give back', VENDĔRE 'to sell', etc. The perfect of these verbs was originally of the strong reduplicative type (CRÉDIDĪ, PÉRDIDĪ, RÉDDIDĪ, VÉNDIDĪ, etc. [see 3.7.7.5.2]), but since these verbs were perceived to be related to DARE 'to give' (perf. DÉDĪ), they were restructured in spoken Latin, thereby becoming weak (*CREDÉDĪ, PERDÉDĪ, *REDDÉDĪ, VENDÉDI, etc.). This pattern was then extended to other -ĒRE and -ĔRE verbs, and eventually to all but a handful (which preserved other strong perfects; see below). The 1st and 2nd sing. forms of this paradigm probably developed endings, via haplology (see 2.1.1.2), in which the tonic vowel was /i/:

*VĒNDĔ(D)Ī > */βendéi/ > */βendiéi/ > *vendí*

*VĒN(DE)DĬSTĪ > *vendiste* (where /é/ > /i/ through metaphony; see 2.4.2.1).

Since in these cases, the endings of -*er* verbs coincided with the inherited endings of the -*ir* verbs, it is unsurprising that there should have been mutual influences between the remaining forms of the two paradigms. We have already seen that the /ié/ (which originated in such forms as *VENDEDIMUS > */vendeémos/ > vendiemos) spread to the corresponding forms of the -*ir* paradigm. The reverse analogy, the spread of /í/ to most forms of the -*er* paradigm, is equally evident, as is the development of 2nd sing. forms with /ié/ in both paradigms (*vendiest[e][s], dorm-, durmiest[e][s]*) by imitation of the frequent /ié/ forms in the remainder of the paradigms. Similarly, the 3rd sing. -*ió* is probably spread from *durmió* to create *vendió*, although it has been argued (Malkiel 1976) that the ending of *vendió*, etc., descends from -ĒU < -ĒVIT.

As a result of these mutual influences, all Old Spanish verbs of the -*er* and -*ir* classes share an identical range of endings. However, it should be noted that the stem-vowel variation we have observed in -*ir* verbs did **not** occur in the -*er* preterite; the high vowels /i/ and /u/ are as rigorously excluded from the weak pret. of -*er* verbs as from all other tenses of these verbs.

The weak preterite forms in use in Old Spanish, and their modern descendants, can therefore be summarized as follows:

Old Spanish		Modern Spanish	
-ar verbs		-ar verbs	
canté		*canté*	
cantast(e)(s), -est(e)(s)		*cantaste*	
cantó		*cantó*	
cantamos, -emos		*cantamos*	
cantastes, -estes		*cantasteis*	
cantaron		*cantaron*	

-er verbs	-ir verbs	-er verbs	-ir verbs
vendí	*sentí, sintí*	*vendí*	*sentí*
vendiest(e)(s)	*sentiest(e)(s), sintiest(e)(s)* ⎫	*vendiste*	*sentiste*
vendist(e)(s)	*sentist(e)(s), sintist(e)(s)* ⎭		
vendió	*sentió, sintió*	*vendió*	*sintió*
vendiemos	*sentiemos, sintiemos* ⎫	*vendimos*	*sentimos*
vendimos	*sentimos, sintimos* ⎭		
vendiestes	*sentiestes, sintiestes* ⎫	*vendisteis*	*sentisteis*
vendistes	*sentistes, sintistes* ⎭		
vendieron	*sentieron, sintieron*	*vendieron*	*sintieron*
bolví	*dormí, durmí*	*volví*	*dormí*
bolviest(e)(s)	*dormiest(e)(s), durmiest(e)(s)* ⎫	*volviste*	*dormiste*
bolvist(e)(s)	*dormist(e)(s), durmist(e)(s)* ⎭		
bolvió	*dormió, durmió*	*volvió*	*durmió*
bolviemos	*dormiemos, durmiemos* ⎫	*volvimos*	*dormimos*
bolvimos	*dormimos, durmimos* ⎭		
bolviestes	*dormiestes, durmiestes* ⎫	*volvisteis*	*dormisteis*
bolvistes	*dormistes, durmistes* ⎭		
bolvieron	*dormieron, durmieron*	*volvieron*	*durmieron*

although it should be remembered that in the modern language only two verbs (*dormir* and *morir*) continue to show alternation between /o/ and /u/; in all other verbs, the Old Spanish alternation has been resolved in favour of /u/ throughout the paradigm.

It can be seen that the Old Spanish variations of ending have been eliminated. The occasional /-s/ of the 2nd sing. has been rejected by the standard, although non-standard varieties of Spanish continue to mark the 2nd sing. in this way, and final /e/ became normal from the late thirteenth century (see 2.4.3.2). The types *canteste, cantemos, cantestes* have been abandoned by the standard (despite the resulting homonymy between pres. ind. and pret. *cantamos*), although pret. *cantemos* continues in rural use. The variation between /ié/ and /í/ in the 2nd sing., 1st and 2nd plur. of *-er* and *-ir* verbs has been resolved in favour of the latter, perhaps because in the 1st plur. the ending *-iemos* appeared also in the Old Spanish imperf. ind. paradigm of these verbs (see 3.7.7.3.1). Preference for /í/ rather than /ié/ enabled this ambiguity to be avoided, and was perhaps then spread from the 1st plur. to the 2nd pers. forms.

In the 2nd plur. of all verbs, the ending continued to be /-stes/ until the seventeenth century. However, by that time (but not before) all other 2nd plur. verb-forms, except pres. ind. *subís*, etc., displayed a diphthong in their final syllable (see 3.7.2), and the corresponding preterite forms were analogically modified: *cantastes > cantasteis, volvistes > volvisteis*, etc.

3.7.7.5.2   The strong preterite.   As anticipated in 3.7.7.5, the 'strong' perfects of Latin do not bear the stress on the stem of **all** members of the paradigm; the 2nd pers. forms are always stressed on the ending (e.g. FĒCÍSTĪ, FĒCÍSTIS), while the 3rd plur. forms are frequently stressed in this way (e.g. HABUÉRUNT). In the spoken Latin of Spain, only the 1st and 3rd sing. forms remained strong (e.g. FÉCĪ, FÉCIT), while the 1st and 3rd plur. became weak in all cases (so that, for example, FÉCIMUS > FĒCÍMUS, FÉCERUNT > FĒCÉRUNT), although it is convenient to continue to refer to such (mixed) preterite paradigms as 'strong'.

It should be noted that this change of accentual type affects not only the Latin perfect paradigm. Latin verbs whose perfect was strong were strong also in the tenses related to the perfect (e.g. FÉCERAM, FÉCISSEM, FÉCERO, FÉCERIM), but in all these cases the stress was shifted to the ending (OSp. *fe-/fiziera, fe-/fiziesse, fe-/fiziere*, MSp. *hiciera, hiciese, hiciere*). All these accentual changes were no doubt due to analogy with the weak preterites (3.7.7.5.1) and with the *-ra, -se* and *-re* forms of the regular *-er* and *-ir* verbs (see 3.7.7.3.2 and 3.7.7.4.3).

The influence of the weak forms upon the strong was not limited to accentual pattern; the endings themselves were very frequently transferred from the weak paradigms of *-er* and *-ir* verbs to the various strong paradigms. In the following list (which is representative of all Spanish strong preterites and related tenses), the endings of the <u>underlined</u> forms were borrowed in this way from the weak *-er/-ir* paradigm:

Latin	Old Spanish	Modern Spanish
FĒCĪ	*fiz(e)*	hice
FĒCĬSTĪ	*fizist(e)*	hiciste
	fezist(e)	
	fiziest(e)	
	feziest(e)	
FĒCIT	fezo	
	fizo	hizo
FĒCĬMUS	fizimos	hicimos
	fezimos	
	fiziemos	
	feziemos	
FĒCĬSTĬS	fizistes	hicisteis
	fezistes	
	fiziestes	
	feziestes	
FĒCĔRUNT	fizieron	hicieron
	fezieron	
FĒCĔRAM	fiziera	hiciera
	feziera	
FĒCĬSSEM	fizie(se)	hiciese
	fezie(se)	
FĒCĔRIM, -O	fizier(e), -o	hiciere
	fezier(e), -o	

Only in the case of *hice, hiciste* do we observe the phonologically expected ending (see 2.4.2.1 for the effect of final ī). In *hizo*, /o/ is borrowed from weak *cantó, vendió*, etc., perhaps in part to provide distinction between the 3rd sing. and the 1st sing. In *hicimos, hicisteis*, tonic /i/ is phonologically unexpected, as is OSp. /ie/, since Lat. Ĭ, even after it receives the stress, can only give Sp. /e/ (see 2.4.2.6). In *hicieron, hiciera, hiciese, hiciere*, /ie/ is the expected Spanish outcome of Lat. Ĕ, but only after the stress was shifted onto this vowel (see 2.4.2.6).

There is yet another manner in which the weak preterites (and related tenses) influenced the strong. Many verbs which were strong in Latin (and had a perfect stem which differed from that of the present, infinitive, etc.) appear in Old Spanish with entirely weak accentuation (and the same stem in the preterite as in the present). Thus, ÁRSĪ (perf. of ARDEŌ) 'I burnt' appears in Old Spanish as *ardí*. Further examples of this analogical process will be given during discussion of each of the four types of strong preterites.

Latin strong perfects can be divided into four types, each of which has representatives in modern Spanish, although there are now few verbs in two of the four classes. The type which ended in -UĪ (e.g. HABUĪ [HABĒRE]) was found most frequently in -ĒRE verbs, but was analogically extended to some verbs in -ĔRE; The type ending in -sī (spelt -xī in combination with stem-final /k/ or /g/) occurred mainly in -ĔRE verbs (e.g. scrīpsī [scrīběre], dīxī [dīcěre]) but also had representatives in the 2nd conj. (e.g. mansī [manēre]); perfects in -ī, in which the stem-vowel often showed modification when compared with the present, were similarly distributed (e.g. fēcī [facěre], vīdī [vidēre]), but with an occasional representative in the -īre class (vēnī [venīre]); finally, reduplicative perfects, in which a stem consonant which occurs once in the present appears twice in the perfect (with an intervening vowel), are found mainly in the -ĔRE class (e.g. vēndidī [vēndĕre]), to which dāre and stāre (perf. dedī, stetī) originally belonged. Each of these types will be discussed in turn:

1 The -uī perfects which survive into Old Spanish had either stem a or stem ŏ. In the former case, the desinential u, articulated in spoken Latin as a glide (see 2.4.3.4), was transferred to the end of the preceding syllable (through metathesis; see 2.1.1.4), eventually combining with the stem /a/ to produce OSp. /o/ (see 2.4.2.4). The commonest verb of this type was

habuī > */áuβi/ > OSp. *ove* 'I had',

and this preterite was analogically imitated by a number of verbs whose Latin perfects were differently structured: *tove* (Lat. tenuī) 'I had', *estove* (Lat. stetī) 'I was', *andove* (Lat. ambitāvī) 'I went', *sove* (Lat. sēdī) 'I sat, I was' (therefore sometimes an equivalent of *fui* < fuī [see below]), *crove* (Lat. crēdidī) 'I believed', *atrove* (Lat. attribuī) 'I dared', of which the first three survive into Golden Age and Modern Spanish and the remainder were lost or remodelled (*crove* as *creí*, *atrove* as *atreví*).

The same vocalic development, but with different internal consonant, can be seen in

sapuī	>	OSp. *sope* 'I knew'
iacuī	>	OSp. *yogue* 'I lay'
placuī	>	OSp. *plogue* 'I pleased'

of which the first was analogically imitated by *cope* 'I fitted'. A further strong pret. of this type (OSp. *troxe* 'I brought') reveals attraction to this vocalic pattern, while retaining the consonant /ʃ/, which descends from the -x- which occurred in its Latin perfect ancestor (traxī).

Where the stem-vowel of the Latin -uī perfect was ŏ, the vocalic development was more complex. Through metathesis of the glide and diphthongization of tonic ŏ (2.4.2.2), it is likely that a triphthong was produced, which at the stage /uóu/ was reduced to /ú/ by assimilatory raising of the tonic, under the attraction of the surrounding glides. There are two perfects which show this development,

pŏsuī > */puóusi/ > OSp. *puse* 'I put'
pŏtuī > */puóuti/ > OSp. *pude* 'I was able'

The first serves as the model for analogical OSp. *respuse* (Latin perf. respondī) 'I replied', while the second is the model for the following Old

Spanish restructured preterites: *estude* 'I was', *andude* 'I went', **tude* (implied by OSp. fut. subj. *tudiere*) 'I had'. For independent reasons, occasional OSp. *conuve* (<COGNŌVĪ, perhaps via *COGNOVUĪ) 'I knew' showed the same vocalic pattern as all these verbs.

Old Spanish, then, displayed two strong preterite paradigms which descended from the Latin -UĪ perfect, one with stem /o/ and the other with stem /u/ (e.g. *ove* vs *pude*). The distinction began to be blurred when /o/ was occasionally raised to /u/ in forms where the ending contained [j]. In later Old Spanish, forms like *uvieron, tuviera, supiesse, pluguiere* begin to compete with traditional *ovieron, toviera, sopiesse, ploguiere*, etc. It will be noted that this vowel raising, although similar to that observed in weak -*ir* preterites (3.7.7.5.1), is not limited to strong preterites of the -*ir* class, but is just as frequently observed in -*er* verbs. By the sixteenth century, /u/ has ousted /o/ from forms of the type just quoted and is then rapidly extended to those forms whose ending had never contained [j], so that *ove* > *uve*, *sopiste* > *supiste, tovimos* > *tuvimos*, etc. As a result of this replacement of stem /o/ by /u/, the two Old Spanish paradigms typified by *ove* and *pude* become indistinguishable (MSp. *hube, pude*).

Many verbs which in Latin displayed a -UĪ perfect passed to the weak paradigm before the emergence of Old Spanish. Thus TIMUĪ, MOLUĪ, DĒBUĪ, APERUĪ, etc., leave no Spanish descendants, but were replaced by the ancestors of *temi, moli, debi, abri*, etc. Similarly, a number of the Old Spanish strong preterites noted above had weak competitors, which eventually displaced them entirely, e.g. *crei, atrevi, yazi, respondi* beside *crove, atrove, yogue, respuse* (although occasional MSp. *repuso* 'he replied', may be a descendant of OSp. *respuso* 'id.', curiously influenced by the pret. of *reponer* 'to replace'). It will also be seen that where Old Spanish displayed two competing strong preterites for the same verb (e.g. *tove* ~ **tude, estove* ~ *estude, andove* ~ *andude*), only one survives into the modern language. OSp. *troxe*, which competed with *traxe* (see 2, below), survived into the Golden Age as *truxe/truje*, but has now been restricted to dialectal use. OSp. *sove*, one of the preterites of *seer*, was completely ousted by *fui* (see 3, below).

2 Latin perfects in -SĪ (sometimes called sigmatic perfects) are well represented in Old Spanish:

> AD-, CONDŪXĪ > *a-, condux(e)* 'I led' (inf. *a-, conduzir*)
> COXĪ > *coxe* 'I cooked' (inf. *cozer*)
> DESTRŪXĪ > *destruxe* 'I destroyed' (inf. *destroir*)
> DĪXĪ > *dix(e)* 'I said' (inf. *dezir*)
> MĪSĪ > *mise* 'I put' (inf. *meter*)
> REMANSĪ > *remase* 'I remained' (inf. *remanir*)
> RĪSĪ > *rise* 'I laughed' (inf. *reir*)
> SUBRĪSĪ > *sonrise* 'I smiled' (inf. *sonrreir*)
> SCRĪPSĪ > *escrise* 'I wrote' (inf. *escrevir*)
> TRAXĪ > *trax(e)* (with /á/ analogical on inf. *traer*, etc.) 'I brought'

Because of the frequency of this type of preterite, a number of other verbs were attracted to it, of which the following are the most notable:

> *(d)espise* (inf. *(d)espender* 'to spend', Latin perf. DISPENDĪ)
> *fuxe* (inf. *foir* 'to flee', Latin perf. FUGĪ)

prise (inf. *prender* 'to take', Latin perf. PREHENDĪ)
aprise (inf. *aprender* 'to learn', Latin perf. APPREHENDĪ)
quise (inf. *querer* 'to wish', Latin perf. QUAESĪ(V)Ī)
tanxe (inf. *tañer* 'to touch, play', Latin perf. TETIGĪ)
cinxe (inf. *ceñir* 'to gird on', Latin perf. CINXĪ)
tinxe (inf. *teñir* 'to dye', Latin perf. TINXĪ)

Note that OSp. *cinxe* and *tinxe* cannot be directly inherited from CĬNXĪ
and TĬNXĪ, since (quite apart from the fact that stem Ĭ would give Sp. /e/)
the development of /ʃ/ from Lat. /ks/ (=-x-) demands that /k/ be in
syllable-final position, where it is modified to [i̯] and then palatalizes
following /s/ (see 2.5.2.4); if a consonant precedes -x-, the appearance of
[i̯], which requires a preceding vowel, is impossible. We would therefore
predict that CINXĪ, TINXĪ (even with tonic /i/ analogical on *rise*, etc.) would
give **cinse*, **tinse* or **cise*, *tise*; cf. PUNCTU > *punto*, etc.).

The occasional Old Spanish strong pret. *visque* 'I lived' (beside weak
bevió ~ *bivió*) may owe its origin to borrowing from Lat. VĪXĪ, perhaps
read aloud in the Middle Ages as /βiksi/, rather than /βíksi/. In imitation
of *visque*, Old Spanish also created *nasque* 'I was born' (beside *nasci*), and
trasqui 'I brought' (beside *troxe/traxe*).

It can be seen that the stem-vowel of the Old Spanish sigmatic preterites
was almost always /i/ (only *coxe, destruxe, remase, traxe* and *fuxe* are
exceptions), whether the verb belonged to the *-er* or to the *-ir* class; the
prohibition on high stem-vowels we have observed in tenses other than the
strong preterite (see 3.7.7.1.4, 3.7.7.5.1) therefore does not apply here,
perhaps a sign that the 'strong preterite' class is perceived as overriding
the division between *-er* and *-ir* classes. The frequency of stem /i/ is due to
the fact that most of the Latin perfects concerned displayed stem Ī, while
in other cases /i/ was adopted for analogical reasons (*quise*, etc.).
Variation between stem /i/ and /e/ was relatively rare (by contrast with
fize, vine, to be considered in the next section), although occasional
instances are found of *dexist(e), presieron*, etc.

Very few of the Old Spanish preterites of this group have survived into
the modern language (*conduje, dije, traje, quise*), while the remainder were
either replaced by weak formations (most of which were already in use in
the medieval period: *coci, destroi/destrui, meti, rei, sonrei, escrevi/escribi,
foi/hui, (a) prendi, respondi, tañi, ceñi, teñi*) or have been lost along with the
infinitives to which they belonged (*remase, (d)espise*).

As in other categories of strong perfect, many Latin perfects in -SĪ were
replaced by 'regular' (i.e. weak) alternatives before the appearance of Old
Spanish: ARSĪ (*ardi*), SPARSĪ (*esparzi* [now *esparci*]).

3 Only four strong perfects belonging to the class characterized by -Ī
(together with stem-vowel change) have survived into Spanish. The Old
Spanish paradigm descending from FĒCĪ is set out near the beginning of
this section, and the paradigm of OSp. *vin(e)* (< VĒNĪ) is in all respects
similar. It can be seen that whereas the 1st sing. form has stem /i/ (*fiz(e),
vin(e)* > FĒCĪ, VĒNĪ) due to metaphonic raising of tonic Ē by final Ī (see
2.4.2.1), the 3rd sing. in early texts shows stem /e/ (*fezo, veno* < FĒCĬT,
VĒNĬT), since the final vowel in this case is Ĭ, a phoneme which has no
metaphonic effect. However, by the end of the thirteenth century, *fezo,
veno* had given way to *fizo, vino*, in part under the influence of the 1st sing.

forms and in part through analogy with the sigmatic preterites, where
tonic /i/ was the most frequent stem vowel (*miso, dixo*, etc.) and stem /é/
was entirely lacking, as we have seen (section 2, above). In the remainder
of the paradigms, stem /e/ coexisted with /i/, although the latter was
considerably more frequent.

Because the stem-vowel of VĪDĪ was already high, the Old Spanish
descendant of this strong perfect shows no vowel other than /i/ in its stem.
However, the variable fate of -D- (2.5.3.2[4]) gives rise to alternative Old
Spanish forms. The most frequent medieval forms are:

VĪDĪ > *vide, vi*	VĪDĪMUS > *vimos*
VĪDISTĪ > *vist(e)*	VĪDISTIS > *vistes, viestes*
VĪDIT > *vido, vio*	VĪDĒRUNT > *vieron*

although occasional *viest(e)*, *viemos*, *vidiest(e)*, *vidiemos*, *vidiestes*,
vidieron are found, particularly in early and non-central texts. The form
vio was at first stressed *vío* (as revealed by assonating verse), but this
pattern rapidly gave way to *vió*, under the influence of the weak *-er/-ir*
verbs. The alternatives *vide/vi* and *vido/vio* continue to coexist in the
standard until the Golden Age, but thereafter *vide* and *vido* are confined to
non-standard (including non-standard American) use. At the same time
as in the weak paradigm (see 3.7.7.5.1), the /ie/ forms *vieste, viemos, viestes*
were abandoned in favour of their (already more frequent) counterparts
viste, vimos, vistes, the latter form expanded to *visteis*, like all other 2nd
plur. forms, in the seventeenth century.

Lat. FUĪ (which in the Latin of Spain also took on the role of Ī[V]Ī and
became the pret. of *ir* as well as of *se[e]r*) provides a multiplicity of
competing forms in early Old Spanish. This was due, on the one hand, to
the survival of both standard forms with ŭ (whence Sp. /o/, unless ŭ was
followed by final ī, or unless it was in hiatus, in which cases it gave /u/ [see
2.4.2.1, 2.4.3.4]) and popular Latin forms with ū (which always provides
/u/). On the other hand, variation was due to loss or retention of the post-
tonic vowel in cases like FU(Ī)MUS (whence *fomos* and *fumos*). Analogy
among the various outputs of these processes accounts for yet further
forms. The processes outlined here are responsible for the following Old
Spanish forms, among which those underlined are analogically arrived at,
either through intra-paradigmatic influences (e.g. *fueste* in imitation of
fue) or under influence from the weak *-er/-ir* paradigm (e.g. *fui, fuimos,
fuistes*, in imitation of *dormí, dormimos, dormistes*, etc.):

FŪĪ FŬĪ	} >	*fue/fu*			<u>fui</u>
FŬĪSTĪ FŬĪSTĪ	} >	*fuist(e)*			<u>fuest(e), fost(e), fust(e)</u>
FŪĪT FŬĪT	} >	*fue*	FŬ(Ī)T	> *fo*	
FŪĪMUS FŬĪMUS	} >	*fuemos*	FŪ(Ī)MUS FŬ(Ī)MUS	> *fumos* > *fomos*	<u>fuimos</u>
FŪĪSTIS FŬĪSTIS	} >	*fuestes*	FŪ(Ī)STIS FŬ(Ī)STIS	> *fustes* > *fostes*	<u>fuistes</u>
FŪĒRUNT FŬĒRUNT	} >	*fueron*			<u>furon, foron</u>

The forms listed above were not equally frequent. *Fu, fost(e), fust(e), fo, fumos, fomos, fustes, fostes, furon, foron* are attested up to the thirteenth century (sometimes only in a form reconstructed on the basis of assonance or rhyme), but thereafter only forms with stem /ui/ or /ue/ are found, except in dialectally flavoured texts. At the end of the fifteenth century, Antonio de Nebrija (1492: 238) recommends the following forms: *fue, fueste, fue, fuemos, fuestes, fueron,* but it is evident that the forms *fui, fuiste, fuimos, fuistes* had not been lost, since they emerge (with modification *fuistes > fuisteis*) as the standard forms in Golden Age and modern Spanish.

Other Latin perfects of this type were remodelled according to the weak paradigm before the emergence of Old Spanish: CONCĒPĪ (*concebí*), LĒGĪ (*leí*), MŌVĪ (*moví*), VĪCĪ (*vencí*), etc.

4 Only two reduplicative perfects survive into Old Spanish, DĔDĪ and STĔTĪ. After normal loss of -D-, DĔDĪ was substantially remodelled (perhaps in imitation of the pret. of *veer*, since the 2nd pers. forms *dist(e), distes*, from earlier **deíst(e), *deístes*, were similar in structure to *vist(e), vistes*):

di	*dimos*
dist(e)(s)	*distes*
dio	*dieron*

a paradigm directly inherited by the modern language, with the usual seventeenth-century modification *distes > disteis*.

STĔTĪ provides OSp. *estide*, etc., a paradigm influenced in its stem-vowel by the many other strong preterites which displayed /i/ (*dixe, mise*, etc.). *Estide* was sufficiently influential to cause the occasional remodelling of the preterites of a number of other verbs, all of which are -*ar* verbs which, like *estar*, show a dental consonant at or near the end of the stem: *andide, demandide, entride, catide. Estide* and its imitators all had more frequent competitors (*estove/estude, andove/andude, demandé, entré, caté*), among which the ultimate survivors are to be found.

Reduplicative perfects of other surviving verbs were replaced by weak forms at an earlier stage: CECIDĪ *(caí)*, CUCURRĪ *(corrí)*, MOMORDĪ *(mordí)*.

For further detailed discussion of strong preterites, see Wilkinson 1973–5.

3.7.8 Non-finite verbal forms

3.7.8.1 The infinitive

The four infinitive types of Latin (e.g. CANTĀRE, DEBĒRE, VENDĔRE, AUDĪRE) were reduced to only three in Spanish (*cantar, deber/vender, oír*), as a result of stress-shift in the 3rd-conj. forms (e.g. VÉNDERE > VENDÉRE), a consequence of the merger of the present tense forms of the 2nd and 3rd conjugations (see 3.7.6). The only 3rd-conj. infinitive which in Spain retained, for a while, the Latin accentual pattern was FÁCERE, which (via */fákre/*) produced OSp. *fer* (see 2.4.3.3, 2.5.2.4), a form which competed with regularized (i.e. stress-shifted) *fazer* and with *far*, a form which probably descends from a VL contracted infinitive *FĀRE, modelled on DĀRE.

Apart from stress-shift of the 3rd-conjugation infinitive and the general loss of final /e/ (see 2.4.3.2), the form of the infinitive has remained essentially stable. A sporadic medieval assimilation between the final /r/ of the infinitive and the following /l/ of an enclitic pronoun (e.g. *perder + lo > perdello* rhyming with *ello*, etc.) became common in the sixteenth and seventeenth centuries, at that stage forming part of elegant usage but subsequently declining. For the loss of infinitival /e/ and /i/ in the formation of the future and conditional tenses, see 3.7.7.4.1–2.

The stem-vowel of *-ar* and *-er* infinitives has been stable throughout their history, apart from occasional cases like OSp. *jogar* > MSp. *jugar* 'to play'. It should also be noted that high vowels /i/ and /u/ have never been permissible in the stem of *-er* verbs. However, the stem-vowel of *-ir* infinitives was subject in Old Spanish to certain free variations. Although stem /a/ was not subject to variation (e.g. *salir* 'to go out', *partir* 'to depart'), stem /e/ varied freely with /i/ in Old Spanish, while /o/ varied with /u/, irrespective of the Latin vowel which underlies each Old Spanish vowel. Thus, OSp. *dizir* 'to say', *escrivir* 'to write' alternate with OSp. *dezir, escrevir* (where the origin of the stem-vowel is Ī: DĪCERE, SCRĪBERE), just as OSp. *midir, sintir* alternate with OSp. *medir* 'to measure', *sentir* 'to feel, hear' (in which the Latin stem-vowel is respectively Ē [MĒTĪRĪ], and Ĕ [SĔNTĪRE]). Similarly, OSp. *aduzir* alternates freely with OSp. *adozir* (Latin stem-vowel Ū: ADDŪCERE), as OSp. *subir, cumplir, durmir*, although less frequent, appear alongside OSp. *sobir* 'to go up', *complir* 'to fulfil', *dormir* 'to sleep' (i.e. whether the Latin stem-vowel is Ŭ [SŬBĪRE], Ō [CŌMPLĒRE], or Ŏ [DŎRMĪRE]). That is to say, the stem-vowel of OSp. *-ir* infinitives behaves identically with that of all other *-ir* verb-forms in which the stem is unstressed and whose ending did not include the glide [j] (see 3.7.7.1.4[b]). As in the case of other similarly structured verb-forms, this variation of stem-vowel was abandoned in the sixteenth century. Variation between /e/ and /i/ was at that time largely resolved in favour of /e/, at least in part due to the dissimilatory interaction between stem-vowel and infinitival vowel (which can be expressed thus: /i/ ... /i/ > /e/ ... /i/), whence MSp. *decir, medir, sentir*, but with infrequent exceptions like MSp. *escribir, recibir* (OSp. also *escrevir, recebir*) due to learned interference stemming from the form of corresponding Latin verbs (SCRĪBERE, RECIPERE, etc., read aloud with stem /i/). Variation between stem /o/ and /u/ was similarly resolved, in the sixteenth century, this time in favour of the higher vowel /u/ (thus, MSp. *aducir, subir, cumplir*, etc.), except in the case of the verbs *dormir* and *morir*, where /o/ was preferred, no doubt owing to the fact that these are the only two *-ir* verbs which display /ue/ when they receive the stress on the stem, and to the awareness among Spanish-speakers of all periods that tonic /ue/ 'ought to' alternate with atonic /o/, not with /u/.

The only infinitives which were irregular in Latin and which belonged to verbs which survived in Spanish are ESSE, POSSE, and compounds of FERRE. ESSE was regularized in Vulgar Latin by expansion into 'normal' 3rd-conjugation shape, becoming *ÉSSERE, which in the Latin of Spain must have suffered the usual accent-shift (see 3.7.6) to *ESSÉRE. It is likely that this form merged (through elision of initial /e/) with the outcome of Lat. SEDĒRE 'to seat' (for loss of -D-, see 2.5.3.2[4]). Such a merger of infinitives is in line with the general merger of these two verbs in Hispano-Romance (certain tenses of the Spanish verb 'to be' are supplied by SEDĒRE, e.g. pres. subj. *sea* < SEDEAM; and the OSp. verb *se[e]r* means both 'to be' and 'to be seated') and also accounts for the fact that in Old Spanish monosyllabic *ser* alternates freely (i.e. in a way unrelated to meaning) with bisyllabic *seer*. We can therefore say that OSp. (monosyllabic) *ser* is the formal descendant of *ESSERE, while *seer* is the formal descendant of SEDĒRE, but both Old Spanish forms inherit the sense of both Latin verbs. Note that OSp. *creer* (< CRĒDERE) is always bisyllabic, and that although we find both OSp. *ver* and *veer* (< VIDĒRE) this variation may be due to imitation of OSp. *ser/seer*.

POSSE was also regularized in Vulgar Latin, this time to *POTĒRE, no doubt because certain forms of PŎSSE (e.g. the perfect POTUĪ) displayed the same endings as regular 2nd-conjugation verbs (e.g. DĒBUĪ, perf. of DĒBĒRE). *POTĒRE evolves normally to produce Sp. *poder* 'to be able'.

SUFFERRE was similarly expanded in Vulgar Latin, usually to *SUFFERĪRE, whence OSp. *sof(f)rir/su-*, MSp. *sufrir* 'to suffer'. OFFERRE was similarly restructured to *OFFERĪRE, giving OSp. *of(f)rir* 'to offer', but in this case the OSp. infinitive, like other *-ir* forms, was challenged by an alternative infinitive in *-ecer* (*ofrecer*) and was quickly replaced by the newcomer.

3.7.8.2   The gerund

The Spanish gerund descends from the Ablative of the Latin gerund (e.g. CANTANDŌ > *cantando*, DĒBĔNDŌ > *debiendo*, VENIENDŌ > *viniendo*); in the process, it can be seen that there is a merger between the descendant of the 2nd and 3rd conjugation ending -ĔNDŌ and the descendant of the 4th conjugation ending -IENDŌ. The remaining forms of the Latin gerund (Accusative, Genitive, Dative) were replaced by infinitive constructions, but the surviving Spanish gerund has acquired some of the functions carried out by the Latin present participle (CANTANS, CANTANTIS, etc.).

Spanish adjectives and nouns in *-nte* (e.g. *cantante, amante, sirviente*) do not appear to be popular descendants of Latin present participles, some of whose functions, as we have just seen, were absorbed by the Spanish gerund. Forms like *cantante* do not have the verbal function of their Latin counterparts (CANTANS, -TIS, etc.) and appear to be learned additions to the vocabulary of medieval and modern Spanish. Occasional verbal function of *-nte* forms can be observed in Old Spanish (e.g. *Un sabado esient, domingo amanezient,/ ui una grant uision en mio leio dormient: [Disputa del alma y el cuerpo* 3–4]), but such usage reveals the influence of Latin syntax on Spanish and is not found after the Middle Ages.

As in the case of other verbal categories, the stem-vowel of *-ir* gerunds shows variation in Old Spanish, unlike that of *-ar* and *-er* gerunds, from the latter of which the stem-vowels /i/ and /u/ are excluded. In the stem of *-ir* gerunds, /a/ is stable, but /i/ alternates with /e/ and /u/ with /o/ (e.g. *viniendo ~ veniendo, sintiendo ~ sentiendo, durmiendo ~ dormiendo, subiendo ~ sobiendo*). Forms with stem /e/ or /o/, although not infrequent, are less common than forms with high stem-vowels and barely survive to the sixteenth century. Preference for the high stem-vowels /i/ and /u/ cannot be due to the presence of the glide [j] in the end of the *-ir* gerund, since the same ending [-jéndo] occurs in the *-er* gerund, which, as we have seen, *never* permits high stem-vowels (except in the case of *pudiendo*; see below); preference for /i/ and /u/ must be due (here as elsewhere; see 3.7.7.1.4 [end]) to the need to provide a formal differentiation between gerunds of the *-er* and *-ir* classes.

Verbs whose Old Spanish infinitives display the hiatus /ee/ between stem-vowel and infinitival vowel (*creer, leer, seer, veer*) normally maintain the stem-vowel in forming their gerunds (*creyendo, leyendo, seyendo, veyendo*), although in a minority of cases one finds forms without stem-vowel (*liendo, siendo, viendo*). The mixture of forms inherited by the modern language (*creyendo, leyendo, siendo, viendo*) is evidently related, in each particular verb, to the loss or retention of the stem-vowel in other verb-forms.

Finally, it should be noted that occasionally in Old Spanish (as currently in the Leonese and Aragonese areas) the gerund of verbs with an 'irregular' preterite is formed by adding /-iendo/ to the preterite stem (e.g. *dixiendo, toviendo, sopiendo, pusiendo*, etc., beside much more frequent *diziendo, teniendo, sabiendo, poniendo*, etc.). These forms are best regarded as dialectal or otherwise non-standard already in the medieval period, but it is notable that one such form (*pudiendo*, beside more frequent OSp. *podiendo*) has become part of the modern standard.

3.7.8.3   *The participle*

The Latin participle retained in Spanish its verbal and adjectival values, and we have seen (3.7.3) that its perfective aspectual value led to its use in the formation of a wide range of new 'compound' verb-forms.

In Latin, most -ĀRE and -ĪRE verbs had weak participles (i.e. with stress on the ending: CANTÁTU, AUDÍTU) and the Spanish descendants of these verbs display the historically expected endings *-ado* and *-ido*. Verbs of the -ĒRE and -ĔRE classes mostly had strong participles (i.e. stressed on the stem:

MÓNITU [MONĒRE], DÍCTU [DĪCERE], MÍSSU [MITTERE], etc.), although a small group (none of which survived) showed weak -ĒTU, and a further small group (those with perfect in -UĪ; see 3.7.7.5.2) displayed the weak ending -ŪTU. Already in Old Spanish, most descendants of -ĒRE and -ÉRE verbs had come to have weak participles, either by adopting the -*ido* ending inherited by -*ir* verbs (e.g. *metido, corrido, avido*, replacing respectively MÍSSU, CÚRSU, HÁBITU) or by adopting the ending -*udo* (< ÚTU) (e.g. *metudo, defendudo, vençudo*, replacing MÍSSU, DEFÉNSU, VÍCTU). The two endings -*ido* and -*udo* alternated freely in the participles of -*er* verbs during the thirteenth century, but thereafter -*udo* declines in frequency and does not survive into the modern period, leaving the field to -*ido*.

With regard to the stem-vowel of weak participles in Spanish, the same remarks are in order as in the case of the infinitive (3.7.8.1). The variation observable in -*ir* verbs (e.g. *venido* ~ *vinido, sobido* ~ *subido*), but not in -*ar* or -*er* verbs, is resolved in the same way as in the infinitive, and at the same period (the sixteenth century).

Occasional Old Spanish weak participles are found in which the stem is not that of the infinitive but that of the (irregular) preterite: *ovido, quesido*, the latter with dissimilation /i/ ... /í/ > /e/ ... /í/. Such forms were always rare and have been entirely lost from the standard.

Verbs whose Old Spanish infinitives showed the hiatus /ee/ between stem and ending also display hiatus in their participles in Old Spanish: *creydo* [kreíðo], *leydo* [leíðo], *seydo* [seíðo]. Eventual loss of the stem vowel in *seydo* (> *sido*) is related to the eventual rejection of other forms of this verb which displayed stem /e/ (e.g., *seer/ser* > *ser*).

A small number of frequent verbs inherit participles stressed on the stem:

> APERTU > *abierto*
> COPERTU > *cubierto*
> DICTU > *dicho*
> FACTU > *hecho*
> FRĪCTU > *frito*
> MORTUU > *muerto*
> POSITU > VL *POSTU > *puesto*
> RUPTU > *roto*
> SCRĪPTU > *escrito*

On this pattern a few other participles were remodelled:

> *suelto* (CL SOLŪTU) (now found as a participle only in compounds: *resuelto*, etc.)
> *visto* (CL VĪSU)
> *vuelto* (CL VOLŪTU)

Old Spanish had a number of other strong participles, either inherited directly (*aducho* [*aduzir*] 'to lead' < ADDUCTU, *cocho* [*cozer*] 'to cook' < COCTU, *defeso* [*defender*] 'to forbid, defend' < DEFĒNSU, *espeso [espender]* 'to spend' < EXPĒNSU, *mis[s]o [meter]* 'to put' < MĬSSU, *nado [nasçer]* 'to be born' < NATU, *preso [prender]* 'to take' < PRĒNSU, *trecho [traer]* 'to bring' < TRACTU), or analogically remodelled (*repiso [(ar)repentirse]* 'to repent', *cinto [ceñir]* 'to gird' < CINCTU, *tinto [teñir]* 'to dye' < TINCTU [with the /i/ of *frito, escrito*], *tuelto [toller]* 'to take away'). These forms normally had weak competitors (*nasçido* beside *nado*, etc.), which either ousted them entirely during the medieval period, or restricted them to purely adjectival use (*tinto, [mal]trecho*, etc.). Similar competition is observable in the modern period between strong *frito, impreso, provisto, roto* and weak *freido, imprimido, proveido, rompido*.

It can be observed that the strong participles of *-ir* verbs do not permit the appearance in their stems of the monophthongs /e/ and /o/. Besides the occasional diphthong (*abierto, cubierto, muerto*) and one case of /a/ (*nado*), only high vowels occur in these forms (*aducho, escrito, frito*). It is probably in order to adhere to this pattern that the participle of OSp. *dezir* acquired the form *dicho* rather than the expected *decho < DĬCTU (cf. *estrecho* < STRĬCTU), although a contributory factor must be analogy with the stem-stressed forms (in /i/) of the present and preterite. A similar case is that of *cinto, tinto* (< CINCTU, TINCTU), which adopt the tonic vowel of *escrito, frito*.

The forms *conquisto* 'conquered' and *suelto* 'loose(ened), free', originally participles of OSp. *conquerir* and *solver* respectively, served as the basis for the creation in Old Spanish of the verbs *conquistar* and *soltar*, and for some time served as the participles of the new verbs, alongside the eventually successful competitors *conquistado* and *soltado*. The appearance of this pattern in Old Spanish (*conquistar*, part. *conquisto, soltar*, part. *suelto*) was made possible by the existence of occasional 'short' participles of *-ar* verbs (e.g. *canso, pago*, participles of *cansar, pagar*), possibly inherited from Latin but now restricted to adjectival use (e.g. *estoy canso* 'I'm tired') in certain regions (e.g. the Leonese area).

3.8 Other word-classes

3.8.1 The preposition

The prepositions of Spanish, like those of other languages, have values which are organized in a way which is much looser than that observable in the case of other categories (for example, the categories of gender in the noun, or tense in the verb). Prepositions are 'organized' in open systems which are similar to those found in the lexical component of languages, but since their function can be described as primarily grammatical (e.g. they have much in common with other, purely grammatical, markers of 'case';

see 3.2.1), and only secondarily lexical, it is convenient to consider them here, rather than in the section on lexis (chapter 4).

Historically, prepositions have a close relationship with adverbs, in the sense that adverbs (either in combination with pre-existing prepositions [e.g. Sp. *más allá de, fuera de*], or alone [e.g. Sp. *bajo*]) may come to have prepositional value; for the adverbs concerned, see 3.4. Certain nouns too have contributed to the creation of prepositions (e.g. *frente a, arriba de, al lado de*), and it is evident that there is a close relationship between many prepositions and conjunctions (e.g. *para/para que, después/después (de) que*).

It can be seen from some of the above examples that no attempt will be made to distinguish, in this discussion, between simple prepositions (*con, por, de*, etc.) and prepositional phrases (i.e. groups of words which function in the same way as a simple preposition: *alrededor de, cerca de, detrás de*, etc.).

For a fuller account of the development of prepositions in Spanish, see Alvar & Pottier 1983: 285–319.

AD 'to' was inherited by Spanish as *a*, although *para* (see PER, below) in part also expresses this concept. In the sense 'towards' (also expressed by VERSUS), AD (like VERSUS) was replaced by expressions derived from FACIE 'face': preliterary OSp. *faz a*, later *faza, fazia* (now *hacia*). In the same sense, Old Spanish occasionally used the form *cara a* (based on *cara*, also 'face'), often modified to *carra* and *carria* (under the influence of *fazia*); however, forms based on *cara* now survive only in non-standard Spanish. In the sense 'as far as' (also conveyed by TENUS), AD was superseded by Ar. *hátta*, borrowed in various guises (*adta, ata, hata, fata, fasta*) by early Old Spanish. From the thirteenth century, we find only *fasta*, eventually respelt *hasta*. For *a* as a marker of indirect objects and of personal direct objects, see 3.2.1.

AB 'away from' could scarcely survive, since it would have become identical to the product of AD. Its content came to be expressed by *de* or *desde*. We have seen (3.2.1) that to express the agent of a passive verb, Latin AB did survive tenuously into Old Spanish, as *a*, but was soon replaced entirely by *de*, the preposition used until the early modern period, when it was largely replaced by *por*.

DĒ 'away from, after' expanded its range of reference (absorbing the values of AB and EX) and survived as *de*. It could be combined with EX in the OSp. *des* (e.g. *des allí*), a form later found only in the further expanded *desde*.

CUM '(together) with' > *con*.

SINE 'without' > *sin*. The expected form is *sen*, which occurs only rarely in the medieval period. *Sin* (together with occasional OSp. *sines*) may owe its form to influence from OSp. *nin* or *sino*, perhaps to avoid confusion with *en* after words ending in /s/.

IN 'to, into, in, at' > *en*, which continued in Old Spanish to be compatible with expressions of movement (e.g. *allá las subie en el más alto logar* [*CMC* 1611]) as well as with 'static' expressions. The former pattern is now almost entirely restricted to *entrar en (casa*, etc.), and the preposition *a* (< AD) has replaced *en* in almost all cases where motion is involved.

EX (and its variant Ē) 'away from, out of' has left little trace in Spanish. Combined with DĒ (DĒ + EX), it survives in OSp. *des*, later *desde* (see DĒ, above), but it has been generally replaced by DĒ alone (e.g. *salir de casa*), or by expressions based on FORĀS (an adverbial variant of FORĪS 'outside', used in spoken Latin already as a preposition), whence *fuera de*, as in *llevar a alguien fuera de su país*. It can be seen that as well as replacing EX, *fuera de* also replaces Lat. EXTRĀ 'outside'.

INTER 'between, during' survives as *entre* (for metathesis of -R, see 2.5.4), although the Spanish form retains only some of the meanings of its ancestor ('between', 'among', occasionally 'during', e.g. *entre tanto* 'meanwhile'). To express 'within', it has been replaced by *dentro de* (see INTRŌ), and the meaning 'during' is now most commonly expressed by *durante*, originally a present participle, used in absolute phrases like *durante la comida*, whose literal sense was at first 'while the meal lasted'.

INTRŌ 'within' survives only as part of the originally compound form *dentro* (< DĒ + INTRŌ). *Dentro* could function in Old Spanish as a simple preposition (e.g. *dentro la villa*), but was more frequently found in combination with *en* (e.g. *dentro en Sevilla*). Later, it entered into combination with *de* (*dentro de*), the only prepositional form now used by Spanish.

EXTRĀ 'beyond, outside of' is largely replaced by *fuera de* (see EX, above).

PER 'through, during, by means of' coalesces, probably in spoken Latin, with PRŌ 'in front of, on behalf of, in place of', providing OSp. *por*, a form which expresses almost all the senses of the two Latin prepositions, together with those of OB and PROPTER 'because of', although 'in front of' was already at that stage expressed by the descendants of ANTE (see below). As an alternative to *por*, in some of its senses, Old Spanish used the combination *por a*, more usually written *pora*, which is normal (in the senses today expressed by *para*) until the late thirteenth century, when it is replaced by the modern form, *para*. This change is unsatisfactorily explained, but may be due to influence from an independent Old Spanish descendant of PER, namely *par*, used only in oaths and exclamations (e.g. *par Dios*). *Para* has increased its range of reference over the centuries, and has encroached on the territory of other prepositions, for example *hacia* (see AD, above), coming to mean 'towards'. On the other hand, *por* has suffered competition, in some senses, from new creations, including *a través de* 'through, across', first recorded in the Golden Age (in the form *al través de*).

TRANS 'across, beyond' retains this sense only in certain place-names (*Trasmiera*, etc.). When used in expressions of movement, it is replaced by *por* (<PER/PRŌ) and by *a través de*; in static expressions (where it competed with ULTRA (see below), TRANS was superseded by *más allá de, del otro lado de*, or, in Old Spanish only, *allén de* (<ILLINC 'from there'), later felt to be a single word, *allende* (e.g. *allende mar* 'beyond the sea') which could suffer loss of its final vowel: *allend ~ allent ~ allén*. TRANS is retained, as *tras*, only in the (static) sense 'behind'.

SUPER 'over, above, during, besides' > *sobre*, a form almost entirely restricted to locative sense, in which it is in close relationship with *en* and expressions derived from nouns such as *arriba de* (<RĪPA '[river-]bank), *encima de* (<late OSp. *cima* 'summit' <CỸMA 'shoot [of a plant]'). In temporal sense, *sobre* conveys only 'at about' (e.g. *sobre las seis*) and has otherwise been replaced by *durante* (see INTER, above). The sense 'besides' came eventually to be expressed by the compound preposition *además de*.

SUB 'under' > *so*, the commonest form in Old Spanish, but antiquated by the sixteenth century. Its competitors, *baxo de* (later *bajo de*, and *bajo* only since the seventeenth century) and *debaxo de*, are adaptations of the adjective *baxo* 'low' <BASSUS, with internal consonant modified under the influence of *baxar* 'to go down, to lower' < *BASSIĀRE.

RETRŌ 'behind' and POST 'id.' (for the temporal sense of POST, see below) are replaced by descendants of TRANS (originally 'across, etc.'; see above): *tras, detrás de*. For the descendant of RETRŌ, see CIRCĀ, below.

ANTE 'before, in front of, faced with' provides OSp. *ante*, a form which continues all the Latin meanings (of time, place, etc.). A competitor *(antes [de])* with 'adverbial s' (see 3.4) is only gradually preferred in temporal sense, while in locative sense *ante* had competitors derived from combinations of ANTE with other prepositions: *desante* <DĒ EX ANTE, *enante* <IN ANTE, *denante* <DĒ IN ANTE. From the last of these descends *delante*, through dissimilation /n/ ... /n/ > /l/ ... /n/, and non-standard *delantre*, with addition of /r/ perhaps through influence from OSp. *mientre* 'while', etc. Descendants of ANTE have therefore absorbed the values of PRAE 'in front of'.

Other prepositional expressions of place are created in Spanish on the basis of nouns: *al lado de, enfrente de, frente a*.

POST 'after, behind' does not survive in simple form, except as an adverb *(pues)*. In temporal sense, it is expanded to OSp. *empués, empós* (<IN POST), *depués* (<DĒ POST), *después* (<DĒ EX POST), and *después de*, of which only the last survives into the modern language, or is replaced by *desde* (see

DĒ and EX, above). In locative sense, POST is replaced by descendants of TRANS (see above): *tras, detrás de*.

ULTRĀ 'on the far side of' does not survive, and its values are expressed by descendants of TRANS (*tras, detrás de*, see above), by new creations based on LATUS 'side' (*del otro lado de*, etc.), and by originally adverbial *más allá de, allén de* (see TRANS, above).

CITRĀ 'on this side of' is likewise lost, its content expressed by *de este lado de, más acá de*, or, in Old Spanish only, by *aquén de* (< *ACCU HINC 'from here'), which, like *allén de* (see TRANS, above) could be treated as a single word, *aquende*.

SECUNDUM 'following, next to, in accordance with' survives, with the last sense only, as *según* (OSp. also *segund, segunt*).

CONTRĀ 'against, contrary to, opposite' appears in Old Spanish in a variety of forms, occasionally displaying diphthongization (*cuentra*), or combining with other prepositions (*escontra, encontra*), most usually in what is now its only shape (*contra*).

CIRCĀ 'around, near' maintains the second of these senses (also expressed in Latin by PROPE, which does not survive) in its descendant *cerca*, at first found in simple form (e.g. OSp. *cerca el pueblo*), later only in combination with *de*. The same meaning is also expressed by OSp. *cabo, cab(e)* (abbreviations of *[al] cabo de* 'beside', an expression based on *cabo* 'extremity' < CAPUT 'head') and by *junto a* (< IŪNCTU, part. of IUNGERE 'to join'). In the sense 'around', CIRCĀ is replaced by descendants of RETRŌ (see above): OSp. *redor (de)*, later combining with other prepositions (*aderredor, enderredor (de)*). *Aderredor* was modified to *alderredor* (perhaps because at this stage *-derredor* was interpreted as a noun), and finally, through metathesis, to *alrededor*.

LONGE 'in the distance, far away' functioned in Latin only as an adverb (which survives as OSp. *lueñe* 'id.'). *Lueñe* is ousted, in later Old Spanish, by its competitor *lexos* (< LAXIUS 'more broadly, more separately'), and it is from this adverb that Spanish derives its most frequent preposition meaning 'far from': *lejos de*.

3.8.2 *The conjunction*

The coordinating conjunctions of Spanish are largely inherited from Latin.

ET 'and', being atonic, is generally represented in Old Spanish by *e*, although *i/y* also appears in early texts. The latter form probably arose in cases where the conjunction preceded a vowel (*e esto > y esto*), but both forms are found in all environments until the early sixteenth century, when *e* gives way to *y* except before /i/, even though some writers use *y* before /i/ until the eighteenth century. The common OSp. spelling *et* is an imitation of Latin ET and reflects the pronunciation /e/, just as *e* does.

AUT 'or' > *o*. The form *u* probably arose in pre-vocalic position, and has only in the modern period come to be restricted to use before words beginning with /o/ (e.g. *uno u otro*).

NEC 'and not, nor' appears in Old Spanish as *ni*, or as *nin* (until the fifteenth century), a form arrived at by imitation of the Old Spanish alternation between *no* and *non*. The vowel /i/ is difficult to explain, and cannot be due simply to development in pre-vocalic position (as applies in the case of *y* < ET [see above]) since *ne* is very rare in medieval Spanish. Corominas & Pascual (1980–, s.v. *no*) postulate primitive **nei*, in which the final glide is the product of -C before a consonant (see 2.5.2.4), with subsequent reduction to *ni*.

Lat. SED 'but' was generally replaced in VL by MAGIS, whence early OSp. *maes*, quickly replaced by its competitor *mas*. The synonym *pero* descends from post-Classical PER HOC, which, especially in negative clauses, came to mean 'nevertheless', a sense still attached to OSp. *pero*, but eventually weakened to that of 'but', after which *pero* succeeded in restricting *mas* to literary registers. *Pero* could be used after negatives until the seventeenth century, but thereafter is entirely replaced by *sino*. The latter form represents a coalescence of *si* and *no* (OSp. variant *sinon*) whose medieval meaning was 'except' (e.g. *nadi, sinon dos peones* [*CMC* 686]), from which the modern value (already occasionally visible in Old Spanish: *non se faze assi, sino* ..) then emerges.

Few subordinating conjunctions are inherited by Spanish from Latin. *Si* (occasionally *se* in early Old Spanish) continues SĪ 'if', although its negative counterpart NISI leaves no descendant, but is replaced by *si . . . no* or by new creations based on MINUS 'less': *a menos que*. Apart from SĪ, the only frequent survivor is the prime marker of subordination *que*, < VL QUID (the replacement of CL QUOD), which clearly already had this subordinating role (amongst other functions; for its relative value, see 3.5.4). It is likely that *que* (alongside an Old Spanish variant *ca*) also descends from an atonic variant of QUIA 'because' (although loss of -A is difficult to account for), since OSp. *que* frequently has this value. Similarly, *que* has acquired the value of QUAM 'than' (again, beside *ca*, although *ca* with this meaning is rare and restricted to early texts). Another descendant of a Latin subordinating conjunction is *quando*, later *cuando* < QUANDŌ.

OSp. *que* expressed a wide range of meanings, now associated with other conjunctions: 'in such a way that', 'in order that', 'because', etc. This multivalency, which marks early texts, continues at least until the fourteenth century. Until well after Spanish began to be used as the vehicle of history, science, philosophy, etc., kinds of writing in which complex subordination is used, *que* is used with multiple values, provided the context makes it sufficiently clear which particular value is intended.

However, during this time and earlier, Spanish was enriched with a new range of conjunctions, from a variety of sources, sometimes used in combination with the subordinator *que*, sometimes without.

An addition to the stock of Vulgar Latin conjunctions was the Greek borrowing μαχάριε (Voc. of μαχάριος 'happy, fortunate'), whence OSp. *maguer(a)*. At first this form functioned only as an adverb, with a similar sense to that of *enhorabuena*. Lapesa (1980: 62) exemplifies the change of sense by noting the approximate equivalence of meaning between a phrase such as *hágalo enhorabuena; no lo aprobaré* and others such as *no lo aprobaré aunque lo haga*. *Maguer(a)*, sometimes combined with *que*, declines in the face of *aunque, puesto que* during the fourteenth and fifteenth centuries and is rarely found in the sixteenth. A later addition, this time found only in Peninsular Romance, is OSp. *oxalá*, now *ojalá* < Ar. *wa šā lláh* 'and may God will'.

Other subordinating conjunctions are created from words belonging to other classes. Adverbs are a frequent source. VL DUM INTERIM 'while' > early OSp. *domientre* (whose diphthong results from the influence of the OSp. adverbial ending *-mientre* < MENTE; see 3.4). *Domientre* was modified to *demientre* (since many other conjunctions, adverbs and prepositions had *de-* as their first syllable (*de[s]pués, debajo, detrás*, etc.) and then to *mientre* for similar reasons (the fact that *de-* often functioned as a detachable prefix: *debajo, detrás*, beside *bajo, tras*, etc.). The change of the final syllable, to *mientra(s)*, comes about through attraction exerted by other OSp. particles ending in *-a(s)* (*fuera(s), nunca(s), contra*, etc.). From earliest times, *mientras* appears either with or without *que*, and it is only in recent times that the form without *que* has come to be preferred in temporal sense ('during the time that'), while the form with *que* is now preferred where a contrastive sense ('whereas') is required. Other conjunctions created from adverbs include *aunque, ya que* (frequent from the Golden Age), and *como* < VL QUŌMŌ (CL QUŌMODŌ) 'in what way'. In Old Spanish, *como* competed with *cuemo/quemo*, a form which probably arose where the word was used under conditions of full stress, by analogical extension of the frequent Castilian pattern in which /ue/ was the tonic counterpart of atonic /o/.

Conjunctions created from prepositions include *pues* (< POST, already used in late Latin in place of POSTQUAM 'after, since'; in the latter sense *pues* was later challenged by *puesto que*, originally 'although' [see below]), *pues que, antes que, porque* (which in Old Spanish meant both 'because', when followed by an indicative verb, and 'in order that', when followed by a subjunctive, a duality which persists into Golden Age Spanish), *para que* (the form which has almost entirely replaced *porque* to introduce final clauses).

Subordinating conjunctions are sometimes created from nouns. Such new formations include *de manera que, de modo que*, OSp. *de guisa que* (based upon a medieval synonym [<Gmc wīsa] of *manera* and *modo*), *a pesar de que*.

Additionally, conjunctions have been formed from other classes of words: OSp. *como quier(a) que* 'although', *puesto que*, which also meant 'although' until the seventeenth century, when the modern sense 'since' emerges, perhaps because of the similarity of form between *puesto que* and *pues*.

3.9   Conditional sentences

Conditional sentences require special consideration owing to the fact that the relationship between the two clauses of such sentences is far closer than the relationship between 'principal' and 'subordinate' clause in other types of complex sentences. The unitary nature of conditional sentences is demonstrated in particular by the fact that the principal clause (or **apodosis**) and the subordinate clause (or **protasis**) of such sentences frequently display verbs with the same tense/mood marker, a parallelism which frequently involves the use of subjunctive verb-forms in the principal clause, a characteristic which is rare outside conditional sentences.

Conditional sentences in Latin and in Spanish can be conveniently divided into three types. Firstly, there are those sentences in which the speaker leaves open the question of whether or not the condition stated will be or will not be fulfilled (or was or was not fulfilled); these sentences will be labelled **open** conditional sentences. Secondly, the speaker may wish to imply that the condition stated is (or was) unlikely to be fulfilled; these sentences will be called **improbable** conditional sentences. Finally, the sentence may express the fact that the condition definitely was not (or could not) be fulfilled; such sentences will be called **impossible** conditional sentences.

It is implied in the foregoing discussion that it is often necessary to distinguish between conditions which arose in the past, on the one hand, and those which arise in the present or will arise in the future, on the other. This sixfold system can be illustrated by means of the following Classical Latin conditional sentences, to which an English gloss (together with other explanatory detail) is added:

	past	non-past
1 (open)	SĪ FĒCIT, IMPRUDENS FUIT (pret. + pret.) If he did that (and I don't know), he was unwise	SĪ POTEST ~ POTERIT, FACIET (pres. ind. ~ fut. + fut.) If he can, he will do it SĪ POTEST, FACIT (pres. ind. + pres. ind.) If he can, he does it

	past	non-past
2 (improbable)	SĪ POSSET, FACERET (imperf. subj. + imperf. subj.) If he was able (but I don't think he was), he would have done it	SĪ POSSIT, FACIAT (pres. subj. + pres. subj.) If he were to be able (but I don't think he is/will be), he will/would do it
3 (impossible)	SĪ POTUISSET, FĒCISSET (pluperf. subj. + pluperf. subj.) If he had been able to (but he wasn't), he would have done it	SĪ POSSET, FACERET (impf. subj. + imperf. subj.) If he were to be able (but he definitely isn't/won't be), he would do it

3.9.1   Open conditional sentences

These sentences are characterized, in Latin and in Spanish, by the indicative verb-forms which appear in both the apodosis and the protasis, in sentences which refer both to past and non-past time. In past open conditions, Latin and Spanish can employ any past indicative verb-form, such as the preterite (SĪ FĒCIT, IMPRUDENS FUIT > *Si lo hizo, fue imprudente*), the imperfect (SĪ POTERAT, FACIĒBAT > *Si podía, lo hacía*), etc. Where reference is to present time, the Latin present indicative of both apodosis and protasis is directly inherited by Spanish (SĪ POTEST, FACIT > *Si puede, lo hace*), but in the case of future conditions, where Latin allowed a future indicative (POTERIT) or a present indicative (POTEST) in the protasis, Spanish allows only the present, while at both stages the verb of the apodosis is in the future indicative (although at a colloquial level Spanish allows a present indicative here too: *Si viene, se lo doy* 'if he comes, I'll give it to him'). Thus SĪ POTEST ~ POTERIT, FACIET > *Si puede, lo hará*. It should of course be noted that the exponents of 'future indicative' differ widely between Latin and Spanish; for the replacement of FACIET by FACERE HABET (whence *hará*), see 3.7.7.4.1.

An exception to the statement that open conditional sentences allow only indicative verb-forms can be seen in those that refer to future time. Throughout the medieval and Golden Age periods, such sentences often displayed a future subjunctive (alternating apparently freely with the present indicative) in the protasis (*Si pudiere, ferlo ha*, later *Si pudiere, lo hará*). This tense, whose form represents an amalgam of the Latin future perfect indicative (POTUERŌ) and the perfect subjunctive (POTUERIM) (see 3.7.7.4.3), has been ousted in recent centuries from these sentences by its present indicative competitor, just as in other sentences it was ousted by the present subjunctive (see 3.7.7.4.3).

3.9.2   *Improbable and impossible conditional sentences*

These types of sentences need to be discussed jointly because, for much of its history, Spanish has shown no distinction between the two types, and there continues to be identity (as in Latin) between past improbable conditions and non-past impossible conditions. From the table above, it can be seen that Latin improbable and impossible conditional sentences are characterized (in contrast to open conditional sentences) by the presence of subjunctive verb-forms, in both protasis and apodosis, whether present (SĪ POSSIT, FACIAT), imperfect (SĪ POSSET, FACERET), or pluperfect (SĪ POTUISSET, FĒCISSET).

In late spoken Latin (see Harris 1978: 239), the difference between impossible and improbable conditions, and between past and non-past types, was obscured, perhaps obliterated, by the incursion of the type SĪ POTUISSET, FĒCISSET into non-past impossible sentences and into all improbable sentences. As a result of this change, the present subjunctive (as in non-past improbable sentences of the type SĪ POSSIT, FACIAT) everywhere ceases to be used in conditional sentences. We have already noted (3.7.7.3.2) that the general replacement of the imperfect subjunctive by the pluperfect subjunctive probably began in the types of sentences now under scrutiny (SĪ POSSET, FACERET giving way to SĪ POTUISSET, FĒCISSET), perhaps because the temporal remoteness of a pluperfect form was felt to enhance the notion of improbability of outcome, even at the expense of removing the distinction between impossible and improbable conditions. To summarize these changes in late spoken Latin, we can say that at that stage the commonest exponents of improbable and impossible conditional sentences were as follows:

	past	non-past
(improbable)	SĪ POTUISSET, FĒCISSET	SĪ POTUISSET, FĒCISSET
	If he was able (but I don't think he was), he would have done it	If he were to be able (but I don't think he is/will be), he will/would do it
(impossible)	SĪ POTUISSET, FĒCISSET	SĪ POTUISSET, FĒCISSET
	If he had been able to (but he wasn't), he would have done it	If he were to be able (but he definitely isn't/won't be), he would do it

A further Latin change, which was not to become universal, but which was fully accomplished in Spain, was the replacement of FĒCISSET (in the apodosis of improbable and impossible conditional sentences) by FĒCERAT. This use of the 'pluperfect indicative' for the 'pluperfect subjunctive' was at first, naturally, limited to past impossible conditions (e.g. Cicero, PRAECLARE VICERAMUS, NISĪ (. . .) LEPIDUS RECĒPISSET ANTONIUM 'We should

have won a famous victóry, if Lepidus had not recaptured Antony'), but, as
FĒCISSET moved into the apodosis of other impossible and all improbable
conditional sentences, so FĒCERAT accompanied it, and, in Spain, completely ousted FĒCISSET from this niche, giving rise to the following system in
the Latin of Spain (and some other areas):

	past	non-past
(improbable)	SĪ POTUISSET, FĒCERAT	SĪ POTUISSET, FĒCERAT
	If he was able (but I don't think he was), he would have done it	If he were to be able (but I don't think he is/will be), he will/would do it
(impossible)	SĪ POTUISSET, FĒCERAT	SĪ POTUISSET, FĒCERAT
	If he had been able to (but he wasn't), he would have done it	If he were to be able (but he definitely isn't/won't be), he would do it

Bearing in mind the regular changes associated with the development in
Spanish of the 'pluperfect subjunctive' and 'pluperfect indicative', this
system evolves directly into the main early Old Spanish (pre-fourteenth
century) system, a system which still, therefore, lacked distinction between
improbable and impossible conditional sentences and between past and
non-past types:

	past	non-past
(improbable)	*Si pudies(se), fizieralo*	*Si pudies(se), fizieralo*
	If he was able (but I don't think he was), he would have done it	If he were to be able (but I don't think he is/will be), he will/would do it
(impossible)	*Si pudies(se), fizieralo*	*Si pudies(se), fizieralo*
	If he had been able to (but he wasn't), he would have done it	If he were to be able (but he definitely isn't/won't be), he would do it

It should be noted that those cases of Old Spanish conditional sentences
which are quoted (e.g. by Harris 1978) with -*se* forms in both clauses are not
descendants of the Latin type SĪ POTUISSET, FĒCISSET. In every case I have
examined of such Old Spanish sentences the -*se* form of the apodosis
appears there because the apodosis is in turn subordinated to another verb
which requires a past subjunctive, e.g. *CMC* 163–4: *Ca assil' dieran la fe e ge
lo avien iurado/ que si antes las catassen que fuessen periurados*, where the
form *fuessen* is determined by the expression *dieran fe que* 'they had sworn
that'.

   The main competitor of this early Old Spanish type is that in which the
Romance conditional tense (developed from infin. + HABĒBAT, e.g. *feria,
~ie, faria, ~ie*, or with inserted pronoun *fer~farlo ia~ie*; see 3.7.7.4.2)
replaces the verb-form of the apodosis. This innovation undoubtedly
began in late spoken Latin, and is occasionally attested in writing (e.g. St

Augustine, *Serm. app.* 253, 4: SANĀRE TE HABĒBAT DEUS, SĪ (. . .) FATERERIS 'God would cure you, if you confessed'). As a result, we find in early Old Spanish, alternating with the type already discussed (*Si pudies[se] fizieralo*), the following sentence-type:

	past	non-past
(improbable)	*Si pudies(se), ferlo ie ~ ia* If he was able (but I don't think he was), he would have done it	*Si pudies(se), ferlo ie ~ ia* If he were to be able (but I don't think he is/will be), he will/would do it
(impossible)	*Si pudies(se), ferlo ie ~ ia* If he had been able to (but he wasn't), he would have done it	*Si pudies(se), ferlo ie ~ ia* If he were to be able (but he definitely isn't/won't be), he would do it

It will be noted that in past contexts, the 'conditional' verb-form has what would now be regarded as 'conditional perfect' sense.

From the fourteenth century, a further element of variation is introduced into the sentences under consideration, namely the introduction into the protasis of the *-ra* form. The motive was no doubt the (possibly universal) tendency, already observed in Latin, for the same verb-form to appear in both the apodosis and the protasis of conditional sentences. As a result, in all the categories of conditional sentences under consideration here, we find the type *Si pudiera, fizieralo*. Although never the exclusive late Old Spanish type (as already seen, we also find the types *Si pudies(se), fizieralo* and *Si pudies(se), ferlo ia ~ ie*, as well as innovatory *Si pudiera, ferlo ia ~ ie*), the type *Si pudiera, fizieralo* was the commonest form observed in this period and continues to be the most frequent in the Golden Age (then superficially changed to *Si pudiera, lo hiziera*).

It has been noted above that, throughout the Old Spanish period, there was normally no distinction made between improbable and impossible conditional sentences, nor between conditions which arose in the past and those which arise in the present of future. However, with the spread of compound verb-forms (consisting of *aver* or *ser* + participle) from one tense to another and from one mood to another (see 3.7.3), the means were increasingly available to introduce (more precisely, to reintroduce) a more subtle discrimination between conditional sentence types. The notion of completion expressed by the participle of compound verb-forms was particularly appropriate to past impossible conditions, where, by definition, the speaker knows that the possibility of the condition being fulfilled has come to an end. Perhaps for this reason, we find occasional cases in Old Spanish of compound verb-forms occurring in one or both of the clauses of past impossible conditional sentences. The verb-forms concerned are *ovies(se) podido* or (from the fourteenth century) *oviera podido* in the protasis, and *oviera fecho* or *avria ∼ -ie fecho* in the apodosis. For late Old Spanish, then, the complete range of conditional clause types can be stated as follows:

	past	non-past
(improbable)	*Si pudies(se)/pudiera, fizieralo/ferlo ie ∼ ia* If he was able (but I don't think he was), he would have done it	*Si pudies(se)/pudiera, fizieralo/ferlo ie ∼ ia* If he were to be able (but I don't think he is/will be), he will/would do it
(impossible)	*Si pudies(se) pudiera/ ovies(se)/oviera podido, fizieralo/ferlo ie ∼ ia/ovieralo fecho/avria ∼ -ielo fecho* If he had been able to (but he wasn't), he would have done it	*Si pudies(se)/pudiera, fizieralo/ferlo ie ∼ ia* If he were to be able (but he definitely isn't/won't be), he would do it

This system remains fundamentally unchanged during the sixteenth and seventeenth centuries, although with minor changes of spelling, phonology and morphology. Thus, to use typical Golden Age spelling, the forms appropriate to past impossible conditional sentences were as follows: *Si pudies(s)e/pudiera/huvies(s)e podido/huviera podido, lo hiziera/lo haria/lo huviera hecho/lo havria hecho.*

However, during the Golden Age and in the eighteenth century we can perceive the two changes which were to bring about the modern system. On the one hand, simple forms are gradually excluded from both clauses of past impossible sentences, leaving only compound forms. On the other hand, -ra verb-forms are increasingly excluded from the apodosis of all types of conditional sentences. This exclusion appears to operate verb-by-verb, so that in current Peninsular Spanish, only in the case of a handful of common verbs does the -ra form have 'conditional' sense (i.e. can appear in the apodosis of conditional sentences): *hubiera, quisiera, debiera,* and occasionally *pudiera.* As a result, the verb-forms which can occur in the various types of Modern Spanish conditional sentences are the following:

	past	non-past
(improbable)	*Si pudiese/pudiera, lo haria* If he was able (but I don't think he was), he would have done it	*Si pudiese/pudiera, lo haria* If he were to be able (but I don't think he is/will be), he will/would do it
(impossible)	*Si hubiese podido/hubiera podido, lo hubiera hecho/lo habria hecho* If he had been able to (but he wasn't), he would have done it	*Si pudiese/pudiera, lo haria* If he were to be able (but he definitely isn't/won't be), he would do it

The occasional appearance, in the modern language, of compound -*se* forms (e.g. *hubiese hecho*) in the apodosis of past impossible conditional sentences would appear to be a hypercorrection, due to the fact that in many varieties of spoken Spanish the -*se* is declining in frequency while the -*ra* form increasingly becomes the only 'spontaneous' form of the past subjunctive. Under these circumstances, the -*se* form is felt to be a more prestigious or more literary variant than -*ra* and may therefore replace the latter in pretentious styles, even in the case of clauses (the apodosis of past impossible conditional sentences) from which the -*se* form has traditionally been excluded in Spanish.

For further discussion of conditional sentences in Spanish, see Harris 1971, 1978: 234–46, 1986, Mendeloff 1960, Pountain 1983, Wright 1932.

4
Lexis

By contrast with phonological, morphological and syntactical systems, the lexical systems of language are inherently open-ended, and it is not intended here to attempt an exhaustive treatment of the Spanish lexis (such a treatment is, in any case, by definition impossible) or to account in detail for the cultural conditions which were responsible for borrowings from various sources. Partial discussion of these matters will be found in the various sections of the Introduction (1.1–5); in the sections that follow, the intention is to examine in outline the main sources of the vocabulary of Spanish, using a minimum of exemplification.

4.1 Vocabulary inherited from Latin

The core vocabulary of Spanish, including many hundreds of the most frequent words, as well as many less frequent items, has descended from spoken Latin, passed on orally in unbroken succession from generation to generation, and undergoing the various phonological changes detailed in chapter 2. Such words have already been defined (see 2.2.1) as **popular** words.

However, it should be noted that **semi-learned** words (see 2.2.3), over which there has been much controversy, are here regarded also as orally inherited, differing from popular words only to the extent that semi-learned words have undergone one or more modifications of form due to the influence exerted upon them by the pronunciation with which related Latin words were read aloud at various periods, either as part of the offices of the Church or in legal/administrative circles.

4.2 Words of pre-Roman origin

As the use of Latin spread across the Peninsula, in the centuries following the first Roman involvement in Spain (218 BC), Latin came to be used bilingually with other, pre-existing, languages. Since the linguistic map of pre-Roman Spain was complex, the nature of this bilingualism differed from area to area, but it is evident that the conditions existed for the borrowing of lexical items by the Latin of Spain from a variety of other languages. Such borrowing does not appear to have been extensive, since the languages spoken bilingually with Latin mostly enjoyed low prestige and no doubt exhibited the more restricted vocabulary associated with the less-developed cultures they served. However, in some instances there would be no Latin term to express some concept (usually related to local flora or fauna, to local life-styles or techniques) and the remedy was to borrow the local term for the concept. On other occasions, despite the prior existence of a Latin word, the borrowing of a local word (to replace its Latin counterpart) could remedy some Latin lexical defect. Such a defect might be that the Latin term had acquired in some contexts a negative value (e.g. SINISTER 'sinister'); borrowing of a non-Latin word (in this case, the Basque word which gives rise to *izquierdo*), to replace the Latin term in its primary sense ('left'), solved a problem of potential ambiguity.

Celtic was widely spoken in central and western parts of the Peninsula in pre-Roman and Roman times and has provided a number of loans to the Latin of Spain. The following can be included among such borrowings, with varying degrees of certainty: *álamo* 'poplar', *berro* 'watercress', *bota* 'leather wine-bottle', *brezo* 'heather', *brío* 'verve', *engorar* 'to addle', *gancho* 'hook', *greña* '(greasy) lock of hair', *lama* 'silt', *légamo* 'slime', *losa* 'flagstone', *serna* 'ploughed field'. However, rather more words of Celtic origin were borrowed outside the Peninsula (mostly from the Gaulish speech of France) and became part of the word-stock of popular Latin wherever it was used, including Spain. Spanish words arguably inherited in this way from Celtic have cognates in other Romance languages and include *abedul* 'birch', *alondra* 'lark', *arpende* 'unit of land-measurement', *braga* 'breeches', *cabaña* 'shack', *camino* 'road, path', *camisa* 'shirt', *carpintero* 'carpenter', *carro* 'cart', *cerveza* 'beer', *legua* 'league', *saya* 'skirt', *vasallo* 'vassal'.

Basque provides a number of borrowings in Spanish, many of which were no doubt introduced into the Latin of Spain in the period following the Roman conquest of the northern Peninsula. However, since Basque, alone among the pre-Roman languages of Spain, has continued to be spoken down to the present, this language has at all times constituted a potential source of borrowing. Especially frequent are personal names (e.g. *García, Íñigo, Javier, Gimeno, Sancho*), but a certain number of other words (especially nouns) are of Basque origin, including: *aquelarre* 'witches' sabbath', *boina* 'beret', *(caer) de bruces* '(to fall) headlong', *cachorro* 'whelp', *cencerro* 'animal bell', *chaparro* 'dwarf oak', *izquierdo* 'left', *laya* 'spade', *legaña* 'rheum', *narria* 'sledge', *pizarra* 'slate', *socarrar* 'to scorch', *urraca* 'magpie', *zurdo* 'lefthanded'.

In addition to the preceding cases, Spanish has a number of words which in all probability were borrowed from some unidentified pre-Roman source (in some cases, perhaps Basque). Cognates of these words are sometimes to be found in Portuguese and/or Gascon, but do not appear to be related to any known Latin or Celtic word. The following should be included (with varying degrees of certainty) in this portion of the Spanish vocabulary: *abarca* 'sandal', *aliso* 'alder', *alud* 'avalanche', *arroyo* 'stream', *ascua* 'live coal', *balsa* 'pool', *barro* 'clay, mud', *becerro* 'calf', *bruja* 'witch', *cama* 'bed', *chamorro* 'close-cropped', *charco* 'puddle', *garrapata* 'tick', *gazapo* 'young rabbit', *gusano* 'maggot, caterpillar', *madroño* 'strawberry tree', *manteca* 'lard', *nava* 'marshy valley', *páramo* 'moor', *pestaña* 'eyelash', *sapo* 'toad', *sarna* 'scabies', *sarro* 'plaque (on teeth)', *vega* 'river-plain', *zarza* 'bramble'.

4.3 Latinisms

Throughout its history, Spanish has made borrowings from the vocabulary of Latin; these are the so-called **learned** words of Spanish (see 2.2.2), which have been transferred to Spanish essentially through writing, and with minimal change (usually limited to the final syllable, to fit the latinism to the morphological patterns of Spanish). The requirement which Spanish has continually had for new vocabulary (chiefly, but by no means exclusively, relating to non-material aspects of life) could often be met by borrowing from Latin, whether from the Latin of the Church, the law or administration, or from Classical Latin sources. Because of the prestige associated with the Latin language, over the centuries and still today, the Latin lexicon has usually been the first source to which Spanish speakers and writers have turned to provide labels for new concepts.

Latinisms have been continually introduced into Spanish, and although a proportion of those introduced were subsequently abandoned, it has been calculated (Alvar & Mariner 1967: 21–22) that latinisms comprise between 20 and 30 per cent of the vocabulary of modern Spanish.

Before the development of reasonably consistent vernacular spelling (in about the twelfth century), it is impossible to distinguish latinisms from archaically spelt popular or semi-learned words. Thus, an early spelling like *desiderio* (San Millán gloss 132) may be interpreted as a rendering of a learned borrowing */desidério/ (which later fell out of use) or (more probably) of popular /deséo/. However, from the twelfth century onwards, latinisms can be clearly distinguished from inherited vocabulary, so that, for example, we are safe in interpreting *vision* (*Disputa del alma y el cuerpo*, 4) as a learned borrowing pronounced [βizjón] (< vīsiō, vīsiōnis), later pronounced [bisjón]. And from this point on, borrowings from Latin can be identified in each century, in greater or lesser quantities according to the cultural climate. In periods of literary development in which translation from Latin or adherence to Latin literary models is frequent (as in the later thirteenth century, the fifteenth century, much of the Golden Age and the eighteenth century), latinisms are numerous. Similarly, borrowing from Latin has satisfied part of the requirement for new scientific and commercial terminology, especially in the nineteenth and twentieth centuries, although a large proportion of the latter borrowings were probably not made directly from Latin, but via other modern European languages.

A small selection of Latin borrowings made by Spanish at various periods can be made as follows:

> By the thirteenth century: *argumento, condición, confortar, contrición, criatura, diluvio, crucificado, alva* (later *alba*), *actoritat* (later *auctoridat, autoridad*), *ascensión, bendiçión, caridat* (later *-dad*), *castidat* (later *-dad*), *claridat* (later *-dad*), *comendaçión*.
>
> By the fourteenth century: *adversario, ánima, apellido, cotidiano, defender, e(n)mendar, herencia, manifestar, patrimonio*.
>
> By the fifteenth century: *cóncavo, epitafio, férrea, fulgente, húmido* (later *húmedo*), *inclita, ingénte, mente* (plus many subsequently abandoned: *nubífero, vaníloco*, etc.).
>
> By the sixteenth century: *ambición, decoro, dócil, ecepción* (later *excepción*), *objeto, purpúreo, superstición* (again together with some latinisms later abandoned, such as *flamígero, horrísono*, etc.).
>
> By the seventeenth century: *aplausos, cándido, capacidad, cerúleo, cólera, concepto, crepúsculo, ejecución, emular, erigir, esplendor, evidencia, exhalación, fábrica, funesto, inmóvil, instante, mísero, nocturno, ostentar, prodigio, rústico, trémulo*.
>
> By the eighteenth century: *amputación, caries* 'tooth decay', *conmiseración, excavación, excreción, proyección, undulación*.

In the case of the latinisms of the nineteenth and twentieth centuries, it is often the case that the words concerned entered Spanish through the medium of some other modern language, at first usually French, now usually English. Such words should therefore be regarded strictly as gallicisms or anglicisms. At all events, we are dealing here with forms it would be pointless to list, since they have cognate forms (usually with identical meaning) in a variety of other languages.

For the problem of phonological adaptation posed by some latinisms, and the resolution of this problem in the Golden Age, see 2.6.5. For the definition and general discussion of latinisms in Spanish, see the introduction to Castro 1936.

4.4 Hellenisms

Apart from a handful of place-names, the language spoken in the Greek settlements along the east coast of the Peninsula in pre-Roman (and possibly in Roman) times has left no legacy in Spanish. All the hellenisms in

Spanish found their way into the language as a result either of being first incorporated into the Latin of Rome or of being borrowed directly from literary Greek. Three separate strands of such Greek borrowings can be recognized in Spanish.

Firstly, popular Latin borrowed a considerable number of words from Greek, owing to contact between Greek-speakers and Latin-speakers at all levels of Roman society and over a period of several centuries. Such borrowings became part of the popular Latin word-stock and in many cases were inherited orally by Spanish (that is to say that, once borrowed by Latin, such words are treated identically to words of native Latin origin and in the process of their inheritance they undergo all the changes which affect orally inherited Latin words, although a number have been subjected to semi-learned remodelling, again in the same way as many inherited Latin words). The hellenisms of this first stratum typically refer to aspects of everyday life, and include names of tools and domestic items (*ampolla* 'flask', *ancla* 'anchor', *baño* 'bath', *cesta* 'basket', *cuévano* 'basket [carried on the back]', *cuchara* 'spoon', *cuerda* 'rope', *espada* 'sword', *espuerta* '[non-rigid] basket', *estopa* 'tow', *lámpara* 'lamp', *linterna* 'lantern', *sábana* 'sheet', *saco* 'bag'), items referring to the house and to building (*bodega* 'wine-cellar', *cal* 'lime', *cámara* 'chamber', *mármol* 'marble', *piedra* 'stone', *plaza* 'square', *torre* 'tower', *yeso* 'plaster'), terms relating to the land (*greda* 'chalk', *yermo* 'wasteland'), botanical names (*ajenjo* 'absinth', *caña* 'cane', *cáñamo* 'hemp', *cereza* 'cherry', *cima* '[tree]top', *cizaña* 'darnel', *codeso* 'laburnum', *espárrago* 'asparagus', *esparto* 'esparto', *olivo* 'olive tree', *rábano* 'radish', *regaliz* 'liquorice', *tallo* 'stem [of plant, etc.]'), animal names (*concha* 'shell', *esponja* 'sponge', *morena* 'moray [eel]', *ostra* 'oyster', *perdiz* 'partridge', *pulpo* 'octopus', *púrpura* 'purple [originally extracted from the murex]'), words related to man (*golpe* 'blow', *huérfano* 'orphan', *lágrima* 'tear', *pena* 'grief', *talento* 'talent', *tío, -a* 'uncle; aunt'), as well as a small number of grammatical particles (*cada* 'each' [see 3.5.5], OSp. *maguer* 'although' [see 3.8.2]).

Secondly, since the language of the Church, even in the Western Empire, was at first Greek, ecclesiastical Latin was full of hellenisms, many of which have passed into Spanish. However, since ecclesiastical Latin (with its Greek lexical component) continued to be heard in church down to the twentieth century, vernacular Spanish words of Greek origin relating to Christianity and the Church (like their purely Latin-derived counterparts) were especially open to latinizing influences, so that, on the one hand, much of the vocabulary concerned reveals semi-learned transmission, while, on the other, some ecclesiastical hellenisms are fully learned. Words of this group include: *abismo* 'abyss', *bautismo* 'baptism', *bautizar* 'baptize', *biblia* 'bible', *blasfemar* 'blaspheme' (and, via a modified VL form of the same hellenism, *lastimar* 'harm, pity'), *canónigo* 'canon', *cátedra* '(bishop's) chair', later also 'university chair', *catedral* 'cathedral', *católico* 'catholic', *celo* 'zeal', *cementerio* 'cemetery', *cisma* 'schism', *clérigo* 'cleric', *coro* 'choir, chorus', *diablo* 'devil', *diácono* 'deacon', *ermita* 'hermitage', *himno* 'hymn', *iglesia* 'church', *lego* 'lay(man)', *limosna* 'alms', *mártir* 'martyr', *misterio* 'mystery', *monaguillo* 'altar boy', *monasterio* 'monastery', *palabra* orig. 'parable', then 'word', *papa* 'pope', *paraíso* 'paradise', *parroquia* 'parish (church)', *Pascua* 'Easter, Christmas', *patriarca* 'patriarch', *profeta* 'prophet', *salmo* 'psalm'.

Thirdly, Greek has served, throughout the history of Spanish, as a source of technical and scientific vocabulary. Most such words are ones which have first passed into Latin, as Latin expanded its own lexical resources, and should therefore be regarded as a subset of the learned words discussed in 4.3. However, a number of words from this stratum (especially medical terms) passed sufficiently early into everyday speech to undergo the phonological changes typical of the vernacular and must therefore be regarded as popular words, while other hellenisms of this stratum which passed into the vernacular were subject to partial remodelling (particularly from the period of the humanists onwards) and therefore constitute examples of semi-learned transmission.

As in the case of latinisms, a small selection of technical and scientific borrowings from Greek is given, organized by approximate period of adoption.

By the thirteenth century: *anatomía* 'anatomy', *apoplejía* 'apoplexy', *catarro* 'catarrh', later 'common cold', *cólera* 'bile, anger', *estómago* 'stomach', *flema* 'phlegm', *lepra* 'leprosy'; *alabastro* 'alabaster', *diamante* 'diamond', *esmeralda* 'emerald', *jaspe* 'jasper', *tesoro* 'treasure', *topacio* 'topaz' (see 3.2.2.2[1]); *carta* 'charter, letter', *crónica* 'chronicle', *escuela* 'school', *filosofía* 'philosophy', *gramática* 'grammar', *historia* (at first also *estoria*) 'history', *lógica* 'logic', *pergamino* 'parchment', *poeta* 'poet', *teatro* 'theatre', *teología* 'theology'; *caramillo* 'flute', *música* 'music', *órgano* 'organ', *zampoña* 'Pan pipes'; *aire* 'air', *aritmética* 'arithmetic', *astrólogo* 'astrologer', *astrónomo* 'astronomer', *astronomía* 'astronomy', *clima* 'climate', *átomo* 'atom', *esfera* (at first also *espera*) 'sphere', *geometría* 'geometry', *hora* 'hour, time', *planeta* 'planet', *ballena* 'whale', *búfalo* 'buffalo', *cocodrilo* 'crocodile', *dragón* 'dragon', *elefante* 'elephant', *gigante* 'giant', *grifo* at first 'griffin', later 'gargoyle', now 'tap'.

By the fifteenth century: *arteria* 'artery', *cardíaco* 'cardiac', *cólico* 'colic', *diarrea* 'diarrhoea', *epilepsia* 'epilepsy', *gangrena* 'gangrene', *pronóstico* 'prognosis', *tísico* 'consumptive'; *academia* 'academy', *alfabeto* 'alphabet', *armonía* 'harmony', *biblioteca* 'library', *coma* 'comma', *comedia* 'comedy, play', *diptongo* 'diphthong', *etimología* 'etymology', *melodía* 'melody', *metro* 'metre', *ortografía* 'orthography', *prólogo* 'prologue', *ritmo* 'rhythm', *sintaxis* 'syntax', *tragedia* 'tragedy'; *ártico* 'Arctic', *caos* 'chaos', *cilindro* 'cylinder', *cono* 'cone', *cubo* 'cube', *eclipse* 'eclipse', *matemáticas* 'mathematics', *océano* 'ocean', *período* 'period', *polo* 'pole', *trópico* 'tropic', *zona* 'zone'; *acacia* 'acacia', *celidonia* 'celandine', *narciso* 'daffodil', *peonía* 'peony'; *arpía* 'harpy', *bisonte* 'bison', *delfín* (at first also *dolfín*) 'dolphin', *hiena* 'hyena', *lince* 'lynx', *sátiro* 'satyr', *sirena* 'mermaid', *tigre* 'tiger'.

By the seventeenth century: *antídoto* 'antidote', *ántrax* 'anthrax', *cráneo* 'cranium', *disentería* 'dysentery', *dosis* 'dose', *embrión* 'embryo', *epidemia* 'epidemic', *erispela* 'erysipelas', *esqueleto* 'skeleton', *laringe* 'larynx', *náusea* 'nausea', *síntoma* 'symptom', *terapéutica* 'treatment', *tráquea* 'trachea'; *catálogo* 'catalogue', *crítico* 'critic(al)', *dialecto* 'dialect', *drama* 'drama', *enciclopedia* 'encyclopaedia', *epigrama* 'epigram', *epíteto* 'epithet', *escena* 'stage', *filología* 'philology', *frase* 'phrase, sentence', *hipótesis* 'hypothesis', *idea* 'idea', *idioma* 'language', *metáfora* 'metaphor', *museo* 'museum', *paradoja* 'paradox', *paréntesis* 'parenthesis', *problema* 'problem', *símbolo* 'symbol', *sinónimo* 'synonym', *teoría* 'theory', *tesis* 'thesis', *tomo* 'volume'; *ábaco* 'abacus', *catástrofe* 'catastrophe', *cometa* 'comet', *diámetro* 'diameter', *elipse* 'ellipse', *éter* 'ether', *fósforo* 'phosphorus', *geografía* 'geography', *horizonte* 'horizon', *máquina* 'machine', *meteoro* 'meteor', *paralelo* 'parallel', *topografía* 'topography'; *achicoria* 'chicory', *crisantemo* 'chrysanthemum', *menta* 'mint', *mirto* 'myrtle', *opio* 'opium'; *anfibio* 'amphibious', *fénix* 'phoenix', *foca* 'seal', *hipopótamo* 'hippopotamus', *rinoceronte* 'rhinoceros'; *anarquía* 'anarchy', *aristocracia* 'aristocracy', *democracia* 'democracy', *déspota* 'despot', *economía* 'economy', *monarca* 'monarch'; *esfinge* 'sphynx', *quimera* 'chimera'; *ateo* 'atheist', *místico* 'mystic'.

By the eighteenth century: *asfixia* 'asphyxia', *autopsia* 'autopsy', *hemorragia* 'haemorrhage', *miope* 'shortsighted'; *antología* 'anthology', *bibliografía* 'bibliography', *criterio* 'criterion', *heterodoxo* 'heterodox', *homónimo* 'homonym(ic)', *lema* 'motto', *parodia* 'parody', *sinfonía* 'symphony', *sistema* 'system', *táctica* 'tactic(s)'; *base* 'base', *ciclo* 'cycle', *farmacia* 'pharmacy', *fase* 'phase', *hélice* 'helix', later also 'propeller', *magnético* 'magnetic', *periferia* 'periphery', *prisma* 'prism', *simetría* 'symmetry'; *autonomía* 'autonomy', *crisis* 'crisis', *dinastía* 'dynasty'.

The words borrowed from Greek during the nineteenth and twentieth centuries are almost all international words (and in many cases probably reached Spanish from other modern European languages, rather than directly from Greek or Latin). They include a number of words which combine Greek lexemes in ways not observed in Greek. Only a small selection of the many recent hellenisms will be given: *anemia* 'anemia', *anestesia* 'anaesthesia', *clínico* 'clinical', *neumonía* 'pneumonia', *psiquiatría* 'psychiatry', *quirófano* 'operating theatre', *quiste* 'cyst', *raquitismo* 'rickets'; *autógrafo* 'autograph manuscript', *biografía* 'biography', *fonética* 'phonetics', *taquígrafo* 'stenographer'; *asteroide* 'asteroid', *cosmos* 'cosmos', *cráter* 'crater', *sismo* 'earthquake'; *arcaico* 'archaic', *arqueología* 'archeology', *laico* (beside *lego*, see above) 'lay', *programa* 'programme'.

For Greek words which passed to Spanish via Arabic, see 4.6, and, for further discussion of hellenisms in general, see Fernández Galiano 1967 and Eseverri Hualde 1945.

4.5   Germanic borrowings

Words of Germanic origin, from which we arbitrarily exclude recent anglicisms (discussed in 4.10), constitute a relatively small proportion of the Spanish vocabulary, although a few members of the groups have quite high frequency. Like some other groups of borrowings, loans from Germanic languages have reached Spanish by a number of routes.

Firstly, a certain number of germanisms entered spoken Latin as a result of the centuries-long contact between Latin-speakers and speakers of Germanic languages along an extensive frontier. A proportion of such loans became part of the normal vocabulary of spoken Latin and were used in all the territories where Latin was established as the vernacular, although usually with the exception of Dacia, which was largely cut off from the spread of western neologisms after it was abandoned by Rome in AD 271. The borrowings of this group were made, by definition, before the political fragmentation of the Empire, probably in the fourth and fifth centuries, and it follows that the Spanish words which descend from these loans have cognates in other Western Romance languages, but not usually in Rumanian. Examples of Spanish words descended from this first stratum of Germanic loans include: *banco* 'bench', *brasa* 'ember', *espuela* 'spur', *fresco* 'fresh, cool', *guadañar* 'to scythe', *guarda* 'watchman', *guardar* 'to keep', *guarir* (later *guarecer*) 'to protect', *guarnir* (later *guarnecer*) 'to adorn', *guerra* 'war', *guiar* 'to guide', *guisa* 'manner', *jabón* 'soap', *rico* 'rich', *robar* 'to steal', *tapa* 'lid, cover', *tejón* 'badger', *tregua* 'truce', *yelmo* 'helmet'.

Secondly, a number of terms of Germanic origin can be observed to occupy only the Peninsula and Southern France, or the Peninsula alone. These borrowings were taken from the Gothic language of the tribe (the Visigoths) who were allowed by the Roman authorities to settle in SW Gaul in the early fifth century and who established there a semi-autonomous kingdom, with its capital at Toulouse. During the fifth century, the Visigoths expanded their territory to embrace considerable portions of the Iberian Peninsula, so that the earliest loans from Gothic are to be found not only in Occitan, but also in Catalan, Spanish and Portuguese. Examples of Spanish words which descend from Gothic borrowings made in this early period include: *arenga* 'harangue', *banda* 'group of soldiers, etc.', *bramar* 'to roar', *brote* 'bud', *escullirse* 'to overflow', *espía* 'spy', *espiar* 'to spy', *estaca* 'stake', *guadaña* 'scythe', *hato* 'clothing; herd', *parra* (?) 'climbing vine', *rapar* 'to crop (hair)', *ropa* 'clothing', *rueca* 'distaff', *sacar* 'to extract', *sera* 'esparto basket', and perhaps *sitio* 'place'. However, the Visigoths were driven out of Southern France by the Franks in the later fifth century, and the final borrowings made by Romance from Visigothic survive only in the Peninsular languages. e.g. Spanish *ataviar* 'to adorn', *casta* (?) 'breed', *cundir* (?) 'to be abundant', *espeto* 'roasting spit', *escanciar* 'to pour wine', *esquilar* 'to shear', *frasco* 'bottle', *gana* 'desire', *ganar* to earn', *ganso* 'goose', *gavilán* 'sparrow hawk', OSp. *taxugo/texugo* 'badger', *triscar* 'to stamp, gambol'.

Thirdly, the vocabulary passed to Spanish from French and Occitan (especially in the twelfth and thirteenth centuries, but also in subsequent periods [see 4.8]), and also from Catalan (see 4.11), contained a considerable proportion of words which in turn had earlier been borrowed from varieties of Germanic (principally Frankish). Such loans include the following cases: *adobar* 'to prepare', *afanar* 'to harrass', *albergue* 'hostel', *ardido* 'bold', *arenque* 'herring', *arpa* 'harp', *bala* 'bale', *banda* 'strip', *bando* 'edict', *barón* 'baron' and *varón* 'male', *blanco* 'white', *blandir* 'to brandish', *botar* 'to bounce, launch' (orig. 'throw'), *bruñir* 'to burnish', *buque* 'ship', *cañivete* 'small knife', *dardo* 'spear', *desmayar* 'to faint', *escarnir* (later *escarnecer*) 'to scorn, mock', *esgrimir* 'to fence', *esmalte* 'enamel', *esquila* 'cattle-bell', *esquina* 'external corner', *estandarte* 'banner', *estribo* 'stirrup', *falda* 'skirt', *fieltro* 'felt', *flecha* 'arrow', *flete* 'charter price', *fruncir* 'to gather (fabric)', *gerifalte* 'gerfalcon', *guante* 'glove', *guinda* 'morello cherry', *hucha* 'chest', *jardín* 'garden', *marta* 'pinemarten', *orgullo* 'pride', *sala* 'room', *toldo* 'awning'.

The processes of phonological adaptation of Germanic loans differ according to the period of borrowing. Borrowings of the third group suffer most of the phonological changes typical of French and/or Occitan before passing into Spanish, at which stage the modification required is relatively slight, since the phonemic systems of Old French/Occitan and Old Spanish were considerably more similar than those of their modern descendants. Thus, for example, Frankish *HERIALD > OFr. *hiraut/héraut*, in which the initial aspirate is maintained. The second of these forms (/heráut/) was borrowed by Old Spanish, again maintaining the aspirate, but with addition of /e/ after the now-impermissible final /t/: *faraute* 'ambassador, interpreter'. It will be noted that the initial letter of *faraute* is merely the normal medieval Spanish spelling of /h/ (thus *faraute* = /haráute/), while Golden Age *faraute* (where *f-* = /f/) indicates that the Old French word may have been transmitted to Spanish also via a second channel, namely Occitan or Catalan, where OFr. /h/ was replaced by /f/.

Germanic loans made in the Vulgar Latin and Visigothic periods were apparently readily adapted to the phonology of the recipient language and occurred sufficiently early for them to be subject to all the regular phonological changes typical of spoken Latin, Hispano-Romance and Spanish. Only in the case of a few Germanic phonemes was there no near equivalent in Latin, a situation requiring more radical processes of adaptation; thus Germanic /h/, /w/ and /θ/, and the intervocalic plosives /p/, /t/, /k/ gave rise to certain problems.

Since Latin /h/ had been eliminated by the first century BC (see 2.5.2), Germanic /h/ was problematic for Latin speakers and words containing it were adapted by simply dropping the /h/: HARPA > *arpa* 'harp', HELM > *yelmo* 'helmet', *HRAPÔN > *rapar* 'to crop (hair, etc.)', *SPAIHA > *espía* 'spy'. Similarly, since spoken Latin had no syllable-initial [w] (early [w], spelt v, had rapidly become [β] or [v]; see 2.5.3.1), Germanic /w/ was replaced by [gw] (which was familiar in traditional Latin words like LINGUA, by this stage pronounced [léŋgwa]). This adapted pronunciation has survived in Spanish where the following vowel is /a/, but, where a front vowel followed, [gw] was later reduced to /g/, although the same spelling (*gu-*) continues to be used with both values: WAITH- (+ suffix) > *guadaña* 'scythe', WARDÔN > *guardar* 'to guard, put away'; WERRA > *guerra* 'war', WĪSA > OSp. *guisa* 'manner, way'.

Latin and its successors had no /θ/ (Spanish /θ/ arises only in the seventeenth century; see 2.6.2), and in Germanic words containing this phoneme, /θ/ is replaced by /t/: THRISKAN > *triscar* 'to gambol', *THAHSUS > late Latin TAXŌ, -ŌNIS > *tejón* 'badger'. Similarly, it seems likely that the Germanic intervocalic voiceless plosives differed from their nearest Latin counterparts, perhaps in that the Germanic phonemes were aspirated (like English initial /p/, /t/, /k/: [pʰ], [tʰ], [kʰ]), and were sometimes equated with Latin /pp/, /tt/, /kk/, rather than with /p/, /t/, /k/. As a consequence (see 2.5.3.2), Germanic intervocalic /p/, /t/, /k/ often appear in Spanish as /p/, /t/, /k/, rather than as /b/, /d/, /g/: *RAUPA > *ropa* 'clothes', SPITU > *espeto* '(roasting) spit', REIKS (whence *RĪCUS) > *rico* 'rich'.

4.6   Arabisms

From the eighth to the fifteenth century, Arabic was the official language of a considerable (but eventually shrinking) portion of the Peninsula, and within this area (i.e. within Al-Andalus) all inhabitants would have at least some familiarity with that language, whether as native speakers or as second-language users. However, the multilingual nature of Al-Andalus cannot by itself explain the host of arabisms incorporated into the Spanish lexicon, since the forms of Romance (the Mozarabic dialects) spoken bilingually with Arabic in Islamic Spain were, of course, not forms of Castilian, but independent descendants of spoken Latin, which became extinct in the later Middle Ages. The Castilian dialect, from which standard Spanish descends, originated outside Al-Andalus, so that the loans it made from Arabic (the large majority of which were made in the period up to the tenth century, before the substantial expansion of Castile and its dialect into Arabic-speaking territory) were loans made from a neighbour rather than from a language spoken in the same territory. The reasons for the heavy borrowing of Arabic words by Castilian must therefore be sought in factors other than extensive bilingualism, and can probably be reduced to two: firstly, the need for names applicable to the many new concepts (both material and non-material) which reached Castile from Al-Andalus and which it was most convenient to name by means of words borrowed from the dominant language used in that area, and secondly, the very high prestige associated with Arabic in the early Middle Ages, owing to the fact that Arabic was the vehicle of a culture which was considerably more 'advanced' than that of Christian Spain, and indeed than that of the rest of Christian Europe. The first of these factors is responsible for the numerous **additions** to the Spanish vocabulary from Arabic sources, while the second factor is responsible for the less frequent **replacement** of existing Castilian words by Arabic synonyms. However, other factors must be borne in mind in conjunction with those just mentioned. On the one hand, even in the period up to the tenth century, there was a certain influx into Castile (as into other Christian territories) of southern Christians (Mozarabs) already familiar with Arabic and perhaps speakers of it. On the other hand, from the tenth century on, through the southward expansion of Castile and the movement of Castilian-speaking population into newly reconquered Arabic-speaking territory, there would have come into existence for the first time a certain body of bilingual Castilian-Arabic speakers, who would have been responsible for the borrowing of at least some Arabic lexical items.

A very high proportion of the arabisms in Spanish are nouns, an even higher proportion than that observable in other cases of heavy interlingual borrowing, where nouns normally predominate. These loans very frequently begin with the syllable *a(l)-*, owing to the fact that the Arabic definite article *al*, etc. (which was invariable for gender and number) was interpreted by speakers of Romance (where the definite article varied in form) as an integral part of the noun and therefore borrowed together with the noun it accompanied. The Spanish vocabulary contains many hundreds of arabisms, some of which are among the most frequently used words of the language, spread across most semantic fields. The semantic fields selected for discussion here are those in which borrowing from Arabic was particularly frequent, usually because of the large number of new concepts, introduced to Spanish-speakers, which belonged to those fields.

As Castilian-speakers adopted Moorish weaponry and tactics during the Reconquest, they often adopted the associated Arabic terminology: *adarga* 'shield', *alfanje* 'scimitar', *alférez* 'second lieutenant', *alforjas* 'saddlebag', *alarde* 'review, display', *almirante* 'admiral', *jinete* 'horseman', *rehén* 'hostage', *tambor* 'drum', *zaga* 'rearguard'. Closely related are terms relating to fortification: *alcaide* 'governor of fortress', *alcázar* 'citadel', *almenas* 'battlements', *atalaya* 'watchtower'.

Civil life too was affected by new arrangements, borrowed from Moorish Spain together with the necessary vocabulary: *alcalde* 'mayor', *aldea* 'village', *alguacil* 'bailiff', *almacén* 'warehouse, department store', *arrabal* 'suburb', *barrio* 'district (of town)'.

The development of commerce and trade which took place in medieval Spain under the influence of the Moors is likewise reflected by Castilian borrowings: *aduana* 'customs', *ahorrar* 'to save (money)', *almoneda* 'auction', *alquiler* 'renting, rental', *maravedí* 'former coin', *tarifa* 'tariff'. Until the introduction of the metric system (and still in rural areas in Spain and Spanish America), the names of weights and measures were mostly arabisms: OSp. *adarme* 'dram', *arroba* '11·5 kilos', *azumbre* '2·016 litres', *cahíz* '666 litres; 690 kilos', *fanega* '1·58 bushels; 1·59 acres', *maquila* 'multure', *quilate* 'carat', *quintal* '46 kilos'. Similarly, the names of certain trades are borrowed from Arabic: OSp. *alarife* 'architect', *albañil* 'builder', *albardero* 'packsaddle-maker', *albéitar* 'veterinary surgeon', *alfarero* 'potter'; as are certain names of tools and instruments: *alfiler* 'pin', *alicates* 'pliers', *almadía* 'raft', *almohaza* 'currycomb'.

As a result of the imitation of building styles and techniques, Castilian acquired considerable numbers of arabisms related to house-building and decoration: *adobe* 'sun-dried brick', *albañal* 'drain', *alcantarilla* 'sewer', *alcoba* 'bedroom', *aldaba* 'bolt, doorknocker', *andamio* 'scaffolding', *azotea* 'flat roof', *azulejo* 'ceramic tile', *rincón* '(interior) corner', *zaguán* 'vestibule'. For similar reasons, the contents of the house often have Arabic-derived names: *ajuar* 'household furnishings', *alacena* 'larder', *alfombra* 'carpet', *almirez* 'mortar', *almohada* 'pillow', *jarra* 'jug, mug', *jofaina* 'washbasin', *taza* 'cup'.

The introduction by the Moors of new techniques and sometimes new species of plants revolutionized the agriculture of the Peninsula. New products (and some already known) which reached the Castilian north often brought their Arabic names: *aceite* '(olive) oil', *aceituna* 'olive', *acelga* 'chard', *albaricoque* 'apricot', *albérchigo* '(clingstone) peach', *alcachofa* '(globe) artichoke', *alfalfa* 'alfalfa', *alfónsigo* 'pistachio tree', *algarroba* 'carob bean', *algodón* 'cotton', *alubia* 'kidney bean', *arroz* 'rice', *azafrán* 'saffron', *azúcar* 'sugar', *berenjena* 'aubergine', *chirivía* 'parsnip', *limón* 'lemon', *naranja* 'orange', *zanahoria* 'carrot'. As Castilian came to be spoken in territories previously cultivated by the Moors, it adopted some words related to agricultural techniques (*almazara* 'oil-mill', *almocafre* 'hoe'), and the majority of its vocabulary relating to irrigation (e.g. *acequia* 'irrigation channel', *alberca* 'reservoir', *aljibe* 'cistern', *azuda* 'sluice', *noria* 'chain pump'), although these words remain typical only of the southern half of the Peninsula.

Gardening (including the herb-garden) was a further area of skill in which the Moors had much to offer, and as Castilians became familiar with Moorish gardens, they adopted many names of plants and related notions: *albahaca* 'basil', *alerce* 'larch', *alhelí* 'wallflower', *alheña* 'privet, henna', *alhucema* 'lavender', *almáciga* 'seedbed', *almez* 'nettle tree', *almoraduj* 'marjoram', *altramuz* 'lupin', *arrayán* 'myrtle', *azahar* 'orange blossom', *azucena* 'white lily'.

Words referring to the natural world which were borrowed by Castilian from Arabic are not numerous, but a small number of such terms has remained frequent: *alacrán* 'scorpion', *alcaraván* 'stone curlew', *alcatraz* 'gannet', *bellota* 'acorn', *garra* 'claw', *jabalí* 'wild boar'.

A number of new foods found their way into the Spanish diet, bringing their Arabic names: *albóndiga* 'meat ball', *alfeñique* 'sugar paste', *almíbar* 'syrup', *fideos* 'vermicelli', *jarabe* 'syrup', *mazapán* 'marzipan'.

Because Arabic science, during much of the Middle Ages, was considerably more advanced than that of Christian Spain (and indeed of Europe generally), Castilian-speakers acquired almost the whole of their scientific vocabulary from Arabic. A good number of these medieval scientific terms persist in Spanish: *alambique* 'retort', *alcanfor* 'camphor', *alcohol* 'alcohol', *álgebra* 'algebra', *almanaque* 'almanac', *alquimia* 'alchemy', *azogue* 'quicksilver', *cénit* 'zenith', *cero* 'zero' (via Italian; see 4.1.3), *cifra*, orig. 'zero', now 'figure', *nadir* 'nadir'.

It has already been said that arabisms have penetrated almost all fields of the Spanish lexicon. In addition to those considered above, the following terms may serve to illustrate the degree of penetration of the Spanish vocabulary by Arabic and the persistence there of the Arabic-derived words: *ajedrez* 'chess' (and the related *alfil* 'bishop'), *albornoz* 'bathrobe', *alcurnia* 'ancestry', *alhaja* 'jewel', *alquitrán* 'tar', *añil* 'indigo', *asesino* 'murderer', *ataúd* 'coffin', *azafata* 'stewardess', *azul* 'blue', *dado* (?) 'dice', *fonda* (?) 'inn', *fulano* 'what's-his-name', *gandul* 'good-for-nothing', *hasta* 'as far as; even', *hazaña* 'feat', *joroba* 'hunchback', *marfil* 'ivory', *melena* 'mop (of hair)', *mezquino* 'wretched; paltry', *mengano* 'what's-his-name', *mezquita* 'mosque' (together with *alminar* 'minaret', *almuédano* 'muezzin'), *nuca* 'nape', *ola* 'wave', *ojalá* 'I hope so!', *recamar* 'to embroider (in relief)', *tabaco* (?) 'tobacco', *tarea* 'task', *zagal* 'youth'.

With the decline in prestige of Arabic culture in the late Middle Ages and in the Spanish Golden Age, some losses did occur from among the arabisms of Castilian. In a number of cases, an arabism was replaced by a borrowing from a source at that stage perceived as more prestigious, or by a term created by means of the derivational resources of Spanish. Thus *albéitar* gave way to *veterinario* (from Latin), *alfageme* 'barber' disappeared in the face of *barbero* (a derivative of pre-existing *barba* 'beard'), *alfayate* 'tailor' was replaced by *sastre* (from Occitan), *alarife* was displaced by *arquitecto* (from Greek, via Latin).

Not all of the arabisms which appear in Spanish are borrowings of words which belong to the native Arabic word-stock. Because Arabic, after the seventh century, was the language of a cultural zone which stretched from India to the Atlantic, it was in contact with many other languages, some of which had great prestige, and from which Arabic consequently borrowed numbers of words. Such words were in some cases passed on to Spanish (and to other European languages). Examples of such complex transmission include Sp. *ajedrez* and *alcanfor* (from Sanskrit), *alfalfa, alfeñique, almíbar, añil, azul, jazmín, naranja* (from Persian), and *acelga, adarme, alambique, alquimia, arroz* (from Greek). In addition, before its expansion out of the Arabian peninsula, Arabic came into contact with Latin, sometimes directly, sometimes via Greek, and borrowed from that source a number of words which were subsequently passed to Spanish. These include *albaricoque* (Lat. PRAECOQUU '[early] peach'), *albérchigo* (Lat. PERSICU, whence also Sp. *prisco* 'apricot', by normal descent), *alcázar* (Lat. CASTRU, from a diminutive form of which, CASTELLU, descends *castillo*, by direct transmission), *almud* (Lat. MODIU).

The incorporation of arabisms into the Spanish vocabulary posed considerable problems of phonemic adaptation (unlike the incorporation of Germanic loans; see 4.5). At the time of intense borrowing from Arabic (eighth–tenth centuries), and later, Arabic contained a fair number of phonemes with no near equivalent in Romance. These phonemes were for the most part velar and laryngeal consonants, but the Arabic dental fricatives and Arabic /w/ were also problematical for Romance-speakers. In addition, there were problems of distribution (phonemes similar to those of Romance but in unfamilar positions in the word) to be overcome.

The Arabic velars and laryngeals were occasionally replaced by Castilian /h/ (spelt *f*), as in *ḥinna > alfeña* (later *alheña*) 'privet, henna', *ḥanbal >* OSp. *alfamar*, later *alhamar* 'carpet'. However, the Spanish velars /k/ and /g/ were also used as replacements for the 'difficult' Arabic phonemes: *'arabiya > algarabía* 'hubbub', *manâ ḥ > almanaque* 'almanac', *šaix >* OSp. *xeque*, modern *jeque* 'sheik', *ḥuršûfa > alcachofa* 'artichoke', *ḥarrûba > algarroba* 'carob bean'. A further solution was to omit the Arabic phoneme: *'aqrab > alacrán* 'scorpion', *'arif > alarife* 'architect', *'ard > alarde* 'display', *'az'ár > alazán* 'chestnut(-coloured)', *ḥáula > ola* 'wave', *ṭaríḥa > tarea* 'task'. Where /f/ appears in modern Spanish in correspondence with an Arabic velar or laryngeal (e.g. *xorǧ > alforja* 'saddlebag'), it is probably the case that the Arabic word was first borrowed by a non-Castilian variety of Romance (where no /h/ was available as a replacement for the problematic phoneme) and that the word was then passed to Castilian at a relatively late date (see Penny 1990b).

The Arabic dental fricatives /ṣ/ and /z̧/ (whether velarized or not) did not correspond closely to Romance /s/ and /z/, which were apico-alveolar. The

Arabic phonemes were consequently replaced by the nearest Romance *dental* phonemes, the affricates /ts/ and /dz/, which were spelled *ç ~ c* and *z* respectively in Old Spanish, and which provide /θ/ in the modern language (see 2.6.2): *sékka > ceca* 'mint', *ṣifr > cifra* 'figure', *safunariya > OSp. çahanoria > MSp. zanahoria* 'carrot', *sâqa > zaga* 'rearguard'. A special problem arose in the case of the Arabic group /ṣt/. The sibilant was first replaced, as we have seen, by Romance /ts/, and then the resulting group /tst/ was simplified to /ts/ (/θ/) since the seventeenth century): *'usṭuwân > OSp. açaguán > modern zaguán* 'vestibule', *musta'rib > moçarabe > mozárabe* 'Mozarab'.

Arabic syllable-initial [w] is modified in more than one way during the borrowing process. On the one hand, it is sometimes replaced by /g/+[w] (just as happened in the case of Germanic words in [w]): *'usṭuwân > zaguán* 'vestibule', *wazîr > alguacil* 'constable, etc.', *sarāwîl > zaragüelles* 'wide-legged breeches', *wadî > Guad(-iana, -alquivir, -arrama,* etc.) 'river'. Secondly, [w] may be interpreted as Romance [β] (OSp. *v*): *karawân > alcaraván* 'stone curlew', *muġâwir > almogávar* 'frontier-soldier', *waṣîya > alvacea > albacea* 'executor'. A further treatment of [w] is retention, when, through loss of a preceding vowel, [w] comes to occupy second position in a syllable: *šuwâr > ajuar* 'trousseau', *diwân > aduana* 'customs (house)'.

Words borrowed from Arabic which ended in a single labial or velar consonant or in /t/, /tʃ/ or /dʒ/ offered a structure which was impermissible in Spanish (at least, in Spanish before the twelfth and after the thirteenth century; see 2.4.3.2). The solution was to add a final /e/, replace the impermissible consonant with a dental or alveolar, or to omit it. Examples of these three adaptation processes can be seen in: *a'rab > árabe* 'Arab', *'arîf > alarife* 'architect', *'anbiq > alambique* 'alembic, retort', *laqqâṭ > alicate(s)* 'pliers', *zabâġ > azabache* 'jet'; *'aqrab > alacrán* 'scorpion', *muḥtasáb > almotacén* 'inspector of weights and measures', *rabâb > rabel* 'rebec', *muqaddam > almocadén* 'commander'; *rabâb > rabé* 'rebec'.

Arabic words ending in a consonant cluster are adapted either by adding a final /e/ or by anaptixis (addition of a vowel between the consonants): *'ard > alarde* 'display', *ṭumn > azumbre* 'liquid measure'; *qaṣr > alcázar* 'fortress', *quṭn > algodón* 'cotton', *rahn > rehén* 'hostage', *baṭn > badén* 'furrow drain'.

Medieval Spanish had few if any nouns and adjectives ending in a tonic vowel, so that Arabic words with this pattern (or ones which had lost a final consonant following a tonic vowel) were sometimes modified when borrowed by Spanish, usually by addition of one of the permissible word-final consonants: *waqî > aloquín* 'mould', *kirâ' > alquiler* 'rent', *qabâ' > gabán* 'overcoat', *bannâ' > albañil* 'builder'. However, in other instances the final tonic was retained, thus extending the phonemic possibilities of Spanish: *ḥairî > alhelí* 'wallflower', *qarmazî > carmesí* 'crimson', *ǧabalî > jabalí* 'wild boar'.

In other respects, arabisms usually appeared early enough in Hispano-Romance to undergo the same phonological changes undergone by words of Latin origin. Thus, the intervocalic voiceless phonemes of Arabic are subject to lenition (see 2.5.3.2): *quṭn >* Hispano-Arabic *quṭún > algodón* 'cotton', *sâqa > zaga* 'rearguard'. Similarly, Ar. /ll/ and /nn/ underwent palatalization: *ġulla > argolla* '(metal) hoop', *ḥinna > alheña* 'privet, henna', *bannâ' > albañil* 'builder'. Likewise, /ai/ and /au/ were reduced to /e/ and /o/ (*ḍáị'a > aldea* village', *máịs > almez* 'lotus', *háụla > ola* 'wave', *sáụṭ > azote* 'blow, lash'; see 2.4.2.3–4), although there is a residue of arabisms in which the first diphthong survives, as /ai/ or /ei/: *ǧufáịna > jofaina* 'washbasin', *qâ'id > alcaide* 'prison governor', *záịt > aceite* 'oil', *báịṭar > albéitar* 'vet'. The latter forms may be suspected of being passed from Mozarabic to Castilian (having earlier been borrowed by Mozarabic from Arabic) only after the termination of the processes /au/ > /o/ and /ai/ > /e/.

It is clear that the palatalization of syllable-initial velars (see 2.5.2.3) had ceased to occur before the incorporation of arabisms into Spanish, since Arabic velars before front vowels remain velar in Spanish: *miskîn > mezquino* 'poor, wretched'.

4.7 Mozarabisms

Castilian displays a number of borrowings from Mozarabic, the vernacular speech of Christians (but also of many Muslims and Jews) in Al-Andalus, that is, in those areas of medieval Spain which were under Islamic rule. With reference to language history, the term 'Mozarabic' indicates a series of descendants of Latin, spoken until at least the thirteenth century (and perhaps as late as the fifteenth in Andalusia) in the southern two thirds of the Peninsula. These southern Hispano-Romance varieties were eventually replaced by Catalan, Castilian and Portuguese, as the latter, northern, varieties of Hispano-Romance expanded in the wake of the Christian Reconquest of Islamic Spain. In New Castile, Murcia, and Andalusia, Castilian was spoken alongside Mozarabic, no doubt often by the same individuals, for considerable periods of time after the conquest of each city. It is known, for example, that in the case of Toledo, reconquered in 1085, Mozarabic still enjoyed some use in the early thirteenth century (see González Palencia 1926–30, Galmés 1983), in part because its speakers were often more cultured than the incoming Castilian-speakers, owing to their ancestors' participation in the culture of Al-Andalus, which until the eleventh century was considerably more developed than that of the Christian north. Until the creation of literary Castilian (beginning in the late twelfth century) and until Castilian came to be used as a national language of administration (in the later thirteenth century), Mozarabic no doubt enjoyed considerable social prestige in reconquered areas and was therefore in a position to exert influence upon Castilian. This influence, as we have seen (4.6), often resulted in the transmission to Castilian of arabisms previously adopted by Mozarabic, but also accounts for the borrowing by Castilian of certain Mozarabic words of Latin origin (in some cases, perhaps, replacing traditional Castilian forms). Among such borrowings, words referring to agriculture and the living world were particularly frequent, as can be seen from the following selection of probable mozarabisms in Spanish: *cagarruta* '(animal) dropping', *campiña* 'area of cultivated land', *cangilón* 'jug, bucket of chain-pump, etc.', *capacho* '(shopping) basket', *capuz* 'hood, hooded cloak', *corcho* 'cork', *chícharo* 'pea' (in Andalusia, Galicia, Cuba, Mexico, etc.), *chinche* 'bedbug', *chirivía* 'parsnip', *fideos* 'noodles', *gazpacho* 'id.', *guisante* 'pea', *habichuela* 'bean', *jibia* 'cuttlefish', *judía* 'bean', *macho* 'mallet', *marisma* 'salt marsh', *mastranzo* 'variety of mint', *muchacho* 'boy', *muleto* 'young mule', *nutria* 'otter', *pleita* 'plaited esparto', *rodaballo* 'turbot', *semilla* 'seed', *testuz* 'forehead'.

For further treatment of mozarabisms, see Corominas & Pascual 1980–, Galmés 1967: 316–23, 1983.

4.8   Gallicisms and occitanisms

Although there are arguably a few gallicisms which passed into Spanish in the early Middle Ages, almost all have entered the language since the eleventh century. The reasons for the very frequent medieval borrowing from French and Occitan lie, naturally, in the cultural importance of northern and southern France in the later Middle Ages, and can be seen to be related, in particular, to four spheres of life, political, religious, literary and commercial.

The involvement of Frenchmen in the Reconquest and in the settlement of reconquered areas is well known, as is their role (particularly that of the monks of Cluny and Cîteaux) in monastic and other religious reform and in the pilgrimage to Santiago (the majority of pilgrims were French and many Frenchmen were permanently established along the pilgrim routes). The indebtedness of medieval Spanish literature to French and Occitan writing is well established, as is the growing commercial importance of France from the late Middle Ages. Many of these general motives for borrowing have persisted into the modern period (although religious influence has perhaps been slight in recent centuries).

In some cases, it is difficult to establish whether a borrowing has been taken from French or from Occitan, and this will not be attempted here. However it should be noted that occitanisms are almost entirely restricted to the medieval period, since by the end of that period Occitan culture was in severe decline, dominated by that of northern France. For Germanic words passed to Spanish via French, see 4.5.

In the following discussion, mention will be made only of words which have survived to the present (sometimes with changed meaning); we shall pass over the many borrowings, some of them very frequent in their day, which have become obsolete.

Contacts with territories north of the Pyrenees became increasingly important from the eleventh century, owing to the greater political stability of the Christian kingdoms of Spain. This increased stability attracted French and Occitan immigrants both of a temporary kind, such as pilgrims, and of a more permanent kind, like monastic reformers and settlers of newly-reconquered territories. In this first period of frequent borrowings from French and Occitan (11th–13th centuries), we observe the most remarkable loan of all, *español* 'Spanish', replacing native *españón*. Borrowed military terms, reflecting French participation in the Reconquest, include *aliar* 'to ally', *blandir* 'to brandish', *corcel* 'steed', *dardo* 'spear', *esgrimir* 'to wield', *estandarte* 'banner', *flecha* 'arrow', *galopar* 'to gallop', *maestre* 'master (originally of a chivalric order)', *malla* 'chainmail', *trotar* 'to trot', together with the more general *emplear* 'to use'. Religious terminology is also well represented: *capellán* 'chaplain', *capitel* 'capital (of a column)', *deán* 'dean', *fraile* 'friar, monk', *hereje* 'heretic', *hostal* 'hostelry (originally a religious foundation)', *mesón* 'inn', *preste* 'priest' (archaic). Terms related to the feudal system and to a leisured lifestyle are relatively frequent: *bachiller* 'holder of certificate of secondary education' (originally 'young knight'), *doncel* 'squire', *doncella* 'maiden', *duque* 'duke', *homenaje* 'homage', *linaje* 'lineage'; *bailar* 'to dance', *danzar* ' to perform a dance', *rima* 'rhyme', *trobador* 'poet, troubadour', *vihuela* 'viol', *deleite* 'pleasure', *vergel* 'orchard'; *joya* 'jewel', *granate* 'garnet', *estuche* 'small box, case', *cascabel* 'small bell (on clothing, a hawk's leg, etc.)', *polaina* 'gaiter', *palafrén* 'palfrey'. A number of words refer to the household and to food: *arenque* 'herring', *jamón* 'ham', *jengibre* 'ginger', *manjar* '(fine) food', *vianda* 'food'; *antorcha* 'torch', *chimenea* 'chimney', *jaula* 'cage', *mecha* 'wick'. A few terms belong to the natural world: *baya* 'berry', *laurel* 'laurel', *papagayo* 'parrot', *ruiseñor* 'nightingale'. Others, including abstracts, cover a wide field: *desdén* 'contempt', *desmayar* 'to faint', *enojar* 'to annoy', *esquila* 'handbell, cattle-bell', *gris* 'grey', *jornada* '(period of a) day', *jornal* 'day's wage', *ligero* 'light (in weight)', *mensaje* 'message', *tacha* 'blemish'.

In the fourteenth and fifteenth centuries, borrowing from French and Occitan had passed its apogee but was still reasonably frequent. In this period we continue to find military and related (including naval) terms: *baluarte* 'bastion', *botín* 'booty', *heraldo* 'herald', *pabellón* 'pavilion; flag'; *amarrar* 'to moor', *cable* 'cable', *quilla* 'keel'. The courtly life continues to be reflected, for example in: *dama* 'lady', *paje* 'pageboy', *gala* 'elegant dress; elegance', *galán* 'gallant', *jardín* 'garden', *patio* 'courtyard'; *balada* 'ballade', *chirimía* 'shawm', *flauta* 'flute', *refrán* 'refrain; proverb'. The material and natural worlds are reflected in : *cordel* 'cord, rope', *correo* 'courier; post', *despachar* 'to dispatch, settle', *forjar* 'to forge', *maleta* 'suitcase', *perfil* 'outline, profile', *pinzas* 'pincers', *trinchar* 'to carve'; *avestruz* 'ostrich', *faisán* 'pheasant', *salvaje* 'wild'. Other borrowings of this period include: *ardite* 'farthing', *burdel* 'brothel', *desastre* 'disaster', *embajada* 'mission; embassy', *jerigonza* 'gibberish', *lisonja* 'flattery', *parlar* 'to chat'.

In the Golden Age, the conflict between France and Spain led to many borrowings in the military and naval spheres, including: *arcabuz* 'arquebus', *asamblea* 'assembly', *barricada* 'barricade', *batallón* 'battalion', *batería* 'battery', *bayoneta* 'bayonet', *brecha* 'breach', *calibre* 'calibre', *carabina* 'carbine', *cartucho* 'cartridge', *coronel* 'colonel', *jefe* 'head, leader', *marchar* 'to march', *piquete* 'picket', *rancho* 'communal meal', originally 'billet, etc.', *trinchera* 'trench', *tropa* 'troop'; *babor* 'port side', *estribor* 'starboard', *borde* 'edge', originally 'side (of ship)', *convoy* 'convoy', *izar* 'to hoist', *pilotaje* 'pilotage', *(echar) a pique* 'to sink'. Words concerning elegant living continue to be borrowed: *banquete* 'banquet', *billete* 'note, ticket', *carmín* 'crimson', *conserje* 'porter', *damisela* 'damsel', *etiqueta* 'etiquette; label', *galón* 'braid', *moda* 'fashion', *ocre* 'ochre', *parque* 'park', *peluca* 'wig', *servilleta* 'napkin', *sumiller* 'chamberlain'. Words concerning the house, including food, are also frequently represented among these borrowings: *barrica* 'barrel', *baúl* 'trunk', *claraboya* 'skylight', *dintel* 'lintel', *hucha* 'chest', *marmita* 'cooking pot', *paquete* 'packet', *taburete* 'stool'; *bacalao* 'cod', *clarete* 'rosé wine', *crema* 'cream', *fresa* 'strawberry'. Other gallicisms of this period include: *farándula* 'wandering theatre company', *frenesí* 'frenzy', *peaje* '(road) toll', *placa* 'plate, plaque', and *tacha*, later *tachuela* 'hobnail'.

The eighteenth century is usually regarded as the period of most intense borrowing from French, but many eighteenth-century gallicisms failed to establish themselves permanently in the language, partly as a result of purist reaction among certain prestigious Spanish writers. This period can nevertheless be seen as one in which particularly large numbers of French words passed into Spanish. Military and naval terms continue to form a significant proportion of loans: *brigada* 'brigade', *brigadier* 'brigadier', *cadete* 'cadet', *comandar* 'to command', *desertar* 'to desert', *fusil* 'rifle', *obús* 'shell', *retreta* 'retreat; tattoo'; *corbeta* 'corvette', *equipar* 'to fit out'. Loans relating to fashion and to dress are particularly frequent: *bisutería* 'dress jewellery', *boga* 'fashion', *bucle* 'ringlet', *corsé* 'corset', *jade* 'jade', *modista* 'dressmaker', *pantalón* 'trousers', *satén* 'sateen', *tisú* 'lamé'. Words concerning the house, domestic activities, and food, are well represented: *chalé* 'detached house', *hotel* 'hotel'; *botella* 'bottle', *buró* 'bureau', *cacerola* 'saucepan', *sofá* 'sofa'; *croqueta* 'croquette', *frambuesa* 'raspberry', *galleta* 'biscuit', *grosella* '(black)currant', *merengue* 'meringue'. Words relating to the practical world, to work, etc., are present for the first time: *bisturí* 'scalpel', *control* 'check', *engranaje* 'gear(s)', *hulla* 'coal', *lingote* 'ingot', *resorte* 'spring', *útiles* 'tools'. The natural world is represented by: *avalancha* 'avalanche', *chacal* 'jackal', *pingüino* 'penguin'. Other borrowings of this period include: *abonar* 'subscribe', *billar* 'billiards', *coqueta* 'coquette', *detalle* 'detail', *esternón* 'breastbone', *favorito* 'favourite', *galante* 'gallant', *galimatías* 'nonsense', *interesante* 'interesting', *intriga* 'intrigue', *rango* 'rank', *silueta* 'silhouette'.

During the nineteenth and twentieth centuries, borrowing from French has continued apacé, slackening in frequency only in the last few decades, in the face of the onslaught of anglicisms (see 4.10). Words relating to the financial and commercial world were borrowed in this period: *bolsa* 'stock exchange', *cotizar* 'to quote', *cupón* 'coupon', *endosar* 'to endorse', *explotar* 'to exploit', *ficha* 'counter, filing card', *financiero* 'financial', *finanzas* 'finance(s)', *garantía* 'guarantee', *letra de cambio* 'bill of exchange', *lote* 'lot, share', *postal* 'postal'. Technical vocabulary was frequently drawn from French: *aterrizaje* 'landing', *aviación* 'aviation; air force', *avión* 'aircraft', *bicicleta* 'bicycle', *biela* 'connecting rod', *bloque* 'block', *bobina* 'bobin', *bujía* 'candle; spark plug', *camión* 'lorry', *cremallera* 'rack; zip fastener', *descapotable* 'convertible (car)', *garaje* 'garage', *rodaje* 'running-in (of car)'. We also find words referring to political and related matters: *burocracia* 'bureaucracy', *comité* 'committee', *complot* 'conspiracy', *debate* 'debate', *parlamento* 'parliament', *patriota* 'patriot', *personal* 'staff', *reportaje* 'report', *rutina* 'routine', *tomar acta* 'to take notes'. Words concerning clothes and personal appearance are frequent, as in previous periods: *babucha* 'slipper, mule', *beige* 'beige', *blusa* 'blouse', *canesú* 'bodice, yoke', *chaqueta* 'jacket', *frac* 'dress coat', *levita* 'frock coat', *maquillaje* 'makeup', *maquillarse* 'to put on makeup', *marrón* 'brown'. Vocabulary related to domestic life and food continues to be borrowed from French in this period: *bidé* 'bidet', *damajuana* 'demijohn', *ducha* 'shower', *parqué* 'parquet', *quinqué* 'oil lamp', *somier* 'spring mattress', *vitrina* 'display cabinet'; *besamel(a)* 'béchamel sauce', *consomé* 'consommé', *coñac* 'cognac', *cruasán* 'croissant', *champán* 'champagne', *champiñón* 'button mushroom', *escalope* 'escalope', *flan* 'caramel custard', *paté* 'paté', *restaurant(e)* 'restaurant', *suflé* 'soufflé'. Borrowings in the field of entertainment include: *acordeón* 'accordeon', *clisé* 'photographic negative', *debut* 'début', *debutar* 'to make one's début', *doblaje* 'dubbing', *film* 'film', *filmar* 'to film', *ruleta* 'roulette'. Borrowings reflecting urban life include: *boutique* 'boutique', *bulevar* 'boulevard', *quiosco* 'kiosk'. Words concerning nature include: *begonia* 'begonia', *buganvilla* 'bougainvillea', *chimpancé* 'chimpanzee', *morsa* 'walrus'. However, gallicisms are found which belong to a wide variety of other spheres: *bebé* 'baby', *braza* 'breaststroke', *camuflaje* 'camouflage', *carné* 'card, licence', *entrenar* 'to train', *esquí* 'ski(ing)', *gripe* 'flu', *pelotón* 'squad', *turismo* 'tourism', *turista* 'tourist'.

For further details of borrowing from French and Occitan, see Colón 1967a, Lapesa 1980, Pottier 1967.

4.9   Amerindianisms

The first European contact with the New World (as a result of Columbus's voyages of discovery) took place in the West Indies and the major West Indian islands became an indispensable staging-post for the later conquest of the northern and southern continents. The first contact of Spanish with Amerindian languages was thus with the languages of the Caribbean (Carib and Arawak, the latter including Taíno, the variety of Arawak spoken in the major Caribbean islands), followed by contact with the main language of Mexico (Nahuatl) and that of the Inca empire (Quechua). The majority of loans to Spanish were made from these languages, although numbers of borrowings were made (and continue to be made) from other Amerindian sources, including Maya (Southern Mexico and the northern Isthmus), Chibcha (Ecuador, Colombia and the southern Isthmus), Tupí-Guaraní (the major river-basins of the southern continent, including Paraguay), Araucanian or Mapuche (Central Chile and the Pampa area of Argentina). However, very few words borrowed from languages other than Carib, Arawak, Nahuatl and Quechua have become universal in Spanish or have even become general in American Spanish.

There follows a selection of words which Spanish has borrowed from a variety of Amerindian sources. The words selected are those which show a significant geographical spread, having become universal in the Spanish-speaking world, or being used throughout Spanish America or in several major Spanish American countries. The origin of the words indicated with (?) is still the subject of dispute, either as to the precise Amerindian source-language or as to whether they are Amerindian borrowings at all.

Borrowings from Arawak (including Taíno) comprise, among others, *ají* 'chilli', *batata* 'sweet potato', *bejuco* 'liana, rattan', *bohío* 'cabin, hut', *cacique* 'Indian chief, local political boss', *canoa* 'canoe', *caoba* 'mahogany', *cayo* 'low island, key', *comején* 'termite', *enaguas* 'petticoat', *guacamayo* 'macaw', *hamaca* 'hammock', *huracán* 'hurricane', *iguana* 'iguana', *maguey* 'agave', *maíz* 'maize', *maní* 'peanut', *sabana* 'savannah', *tuna* 'prickly pear', *yuca* 'cassava'.

Loans from Carib include *batea* (?) 'flat pan for separating gold from sand', *butaca* '(easy) chair', *caníbal* 'cannibal', *curare* 'curare', *loro* 'parrot', *mico* 'monkey', *piragua* 'wooden canoe'.

A few amerindianisms borrowed in the Caribbean area may be from Arawak or from Carib: *aje* 'kind of yam', *guasa* 'joke', *guateque* 'party', *guayaba* 'guava'.

Among the many loans made to Spanish by Nahuatl are *aguacate* 'avocado', *cacahuete* 'peanut', *cacao* 'cocoa', *coyote* 'prairie wolf', *chicle* 'chewing-gum', *chile* 'chilli', *chocolate* 'chocolate', *galpón* 'shed', *guajolote* 'turkey', *hule* 'rubber', *jícara* 'cup (for chocolate)', *nopal* 'prickly pear', *ocelote* 'ocelot', *petaca* 'tobacco pouch, cigarette case', *petate* 'palm matting', *sinsonte* 'mockingbird', *tiza* 'chalk', *tocayo* (?) 'namesake', *tomate* 'tomato', *zopilote* 'buzzard'.

Loans from Quechua include *alpaca* 'alpaca', *cancha* 'open space; (tennis) court, etc.', *coca* 'coca', *cóndor* 'condor', *guanaco* 'guanaco', *guano* 'guano', *llama* 'llama', *mate* 'Paraguayan tea', *palta* 'avocado', *pampa* 'pampas', *papa* 'potato', *puma* 'puma', *puna* 'high plateau, altitude sickness', *soroche* 'altitude sickness', *vicuña* 'vicuña'.

From Tupí-Guaraní have been borrowed *ananá(s)* 'pineapple', *cobaya, -o* (?) 'guineapig', *jaguar* 'jaguar', *mandioca* 'manioc', *ñandú* 'rhea, American ostrich', *petunia* 'petunia', *tapioca* 'tapioca', *tapir* 'tapir', *tiburón* 'shark', *tucán* 'toucan', *zarigüeya* 'opossum'.

In addition, there are a number of frequent words, like *caucho* 'rubber', whose origin is Amerindian but whose precise linguistic source is unknown.

When speakers of Spanish travelled or settled in the New World, their new experiences were often interpreted as we have just seen, by means of words borrowed from native languages. The earliest of these (*canoa, cacique* and the disputed borrowing *niames* 'yams') are recorded in Columbus's shipboard log of 1492–3. However, it should not be forgotten that borrowing is not the only means of giving linguistic labels to new concepts; a pre-existing word may extend its sense to encompass the new experience. Thus, the jaguar, the puma, and the pineapple were at first named by means of the Old World terms *tigre, león* and *piña*, words which eventually came to have competitors of Amerindian origin (*jaguar, puma, ananá[s]*), and this competition may survive through the centuries. In the cases mentioned, *jaguar* and *puma* became part of the Old World Spanish, while *tigre* and *león* continue in use (at least in popular speech) in much of the area where these animals have their habitat; on the other hand, the borrowing *ananá(s)* is not used in Peninsular Spanish or in large regions of Spanish America (where only *piña* occurs).

On other occasions, a New World concept may be labelled by competing amerindianisms. A well-known case is that of the avocado; the term *aguacate* (from Nahuatl, as noted above) is used in Spain, in North and Central America and in the Northwestern region of the southern continent (Colombia and Venezuela), while in territories further south (Ecuador, Peru, Bolivia) the Quechua loan *palta* is used.

For further discussion of Amerindian loans, including those whose distribution is limited to part of the American continent, see Buesa 1967.

4.10 Anglicisms

Until the middle of the twentieth century, almost all English words borrowed by Spanish were of British English origin, and were usually transmitted through writing, often via French. From the 1950s onwards, the main source of such borrowing has been American English, and anglicisms have been transmitted partly through written media (especially newspapers, translation of scientific works, etc.), but increasingly through the oral media (dubbing of American films, TV programmes, etc.).

The term 'anglicism', like others referring to interlanguage borrowing, is poorly defined. The definition adopted here is that of Pratt 1980 (from whom many examples are taken); 'anglicisms' are loans whose immediate etymon is an English word or expression, irrespective of the source of the English word (whose ultimate etymon is often a word or expression of a third language). By this criterion, it is appropriate to include among the anglicisms of Spanish such items as the following, whose ultimate etymolgy is indicated in parentheses: *té* (Chinese), *anorak, kayak* (Eskimo), *kinder-garten* (German), *kimono~quimono, judo, karate* (Japanese), *géiser* (Islandic), *gongo* (Malay), *caqui, pijama* (Persian). Similarly, it will be necessary to exclude from the list of anglicisms in Spanish such terms as the following, whose ultimate etymon is an English word, but which have reached Spanish through the medium of another language (usually French): *auto-stop* 'hitch-hiking', *camping* 'campsite', *dáncing* 'dance-hall', *footing* 'jogging', *parking* 'car-park', *recordman* 'record-holder', *(espejo) retrovisor* 'rear-view (mirror)', *smoking* 'dinner jacket', *en directo* 'live (e.g. TV programme)'. The items quoted should be considered to be gallicisms, since they are attested earlier in French than in Spanish and often reveal French processes of semantic adaptation.

The most frequent (but by no means the only) manifestation of the influence of English upon Spanish is lexical loan. Anglicisms of this kind generally reflect the need to label new concepts (although some are introduced for non-linguistic reasons such as snobbery) and affect a very wide range of semantic fields. The language of almost every aspect of urban, sophisticated life reveals borrowings from English, but the language of the media, fashion, business, science and sport are particularly affected. In the vocabulary of the communications media, which naturally intersects with the terminology of the technological world, we find: *bestséller, cámera, cameraman, cassette, cinemascope, clip, copyright, disc-jockey, fading, film(e), flas(h), hit, interviewar ~ interviuvar, interviú, LP ~ elepé, mass-media, monitor, offset, off* (e.g. *una voz en off*), *pick-up, playback, pop, póster, rol, scriptgirl, show, sketch, speaker ~ espíquer* 'newsreader', *spot* 'advertising spot', *suspense, trailer, transistor, video, videocassette.* Lexical borrowings from English in the field of fashion and cosmetics and clothing include such items as: *anorak, bikini, coldcream, cosmético, champú, cheviot, eslip ~ slip, jersey, jumper, kilt, kimono ~ quimono, loción, mini-falda, nylon ~ nailon, overol, panty, pijama, pullover, raglán, rímel, shetland, shorts, suéter ~ sweater, tweed.* The language of commerce and finance provides examples such as: *actuario, balance, boom, boutique, broker, cartel, chárter, deflación, devaluación, dumping, factoring, holding, inflación, leasing, manager, marketing, self(-service), stock, ténder, turismo.* In the world of science and technology (including medicine) we note many anglicisms, including: *acrílico, aeropuerto, aerosol, ameba, analgesia, baquelita, cibernética, ciclamato, colesterol, coma, container, cracking, detergente, ecología, esquizofrenia, fobia, fuel-oil, gasoil, polución, quántum, quark, rádar, robot, síndrome, spray* 'aerosol', *stress ~ estrés, trolebús.* Sporting language has long shown a particular openness to anglicisms, which can be exemplified by: *bantam, béisbol, bob, bobsleigh, boxeo, bunker, caddie, córner, crawl ~ crol, croquet, cross country, chutar, doping, dribbling, fútbol, gol, golf, groggy ~ grogui, handicap, hockey ~ jóquey, jockey, judo, júnior, karate, karting, kayak, knock-out ~ nocaut, lob, match, offside, par, penalty, ping-pong, pony, récord, ring, round, rugby, set, slam, smash, sparring, sprint, tándem, tenis, volleyball ~ volibol, wélter.*

English can also be seen to have affected the morphology and syntax of Spanish (see Pratt 1980). The semantic influence of English upon Spanish, extending the sense of pre-existing Spanish words, has also been considerable; this latter phenomenon is examined and exemplified in 5.1.5.

4.11   Catalanisms

Considerable numbers of words have passed from Catalan to Castilian, especially in a number of fields in which the inhabitants of Catalonia, Valencia and the Balearic Islands were perceived by Castilian speakers to be preeminent. In some cases, these words were earlier borrowed from other sources, including Occitan, Old French, Italian, Arabic.

Food is one semantic field in which such borrowing is common. We find names of fish, such as *anguila* 'eel', *calamar* 'squid', *jurel* 'horse mackerel', *mújol* 'mullet', *rape* 'monkfish', together with many other culinary terms including *manjar* 'dish (of fine food)', *anís* 'aniseed', *butifarra* 'Catalan sausage', *entremés* 'hors d'œuvre; short comedy', *escalfar* 'to poach (eggs)', *escarola* 'endive', *horchata* (?) 'drink made of almonds or chufas', *paella* 'id.', *sémola* 'semolina', *vinagre* 'vinegar', *vinagreta* 'vinaigrette'.

Other domestic terms borrowed from Catalan are not infrequent: *barraca* 'cabin, stall', *delantal* 'apron', *fogón* 'kitchen range, stove', *patio* 'courtyard', *picaporte* 'doorlatch, -knocker', *reloj* 'clock, watch', *retrete* 'lavatory', *convite* 'invitation, banquet'. Much of the terminology of card-playing is also of Catalan origin, including *naipe* 'playing card', *sota* 'knave (in cards)'.

The Catalans were the predominant sea-faring group in the Peninsula until the end of the Middle Ages and this predominance is reflected in the many Castilian borrowings belonging to this semantic field, such as *aferrar* 'to grapple, anchor, grasp', *betún* 'bitumen', *buque* 'ship', *calafatear* (?) 'to caulk (a ship)', *esquife* 'skiff', *galera* 'galley', *gobernalle* 'helm', *golfo* 'gulf', *muelle* 'dock, pier', *nao* 'sailing ship', *socaire* 'lee', *surgir* 'to anchor', *timonel* 'helmsman'. Closely related are catalanisms relating to trade, which include *a granel* 'in bulk', *mercader* 'merchant', *oferta* 'offer', *tarifa* (from Ar.) 'tariff'.

Many other borrowings reflect the practical skills of the Catalans: *avanzar* 'to advance', *avería* 'breakdown, damage', *caja* 'box', *cañivete* 'small knife', *cartel* 'poster', *cordel* 'cord', *cotejar* 'to compare', *crisol* 'crucible', *doblegar* (?) 'to fold, bend, twist', *escayola* 'plaster of paris, stucco', *esmalte* 'enamel', *faena* 'task', *farol* 'lantern, streetlamp', *forcejar* 'to struggle', *gafa(s)* 'hook; spectacles', *grúa* '(mechanical) crane', *maestre* 'master of order of chivalry', *metal* 'metal', *molde* 'mould, cast', *nivel* 'level', *paleta* 'trowel, shovel', *pantalla* 'lampshade', *sastre* 'tailor', *traste* 'fret (of guitar)', *trasto* 'piece of junk', *viaje* 'journey'. Some of the terminology of printing and writing is also of Catalan origin: *imprenta* 'printing', *papel* 'paper', *prensa* 'press', *tilde* 'tilde, accent'.

A number of words relating to the natural world are borrowings from Catalan, including *becada* 'woodcock', *bosque* 'wood, forest', *caracol* 'snail', *clavel* 'carnation', *dátil* 'date', *follaje* 'foliage', *palmera* 'palm tree'.

Some military terms, of more distant ultimate origin, probably passed to Castilian via Catalan; these include *capitán* 'captain', *coronel* (?) 'colonel', *cuartel* 'barracks'. The same is probably true of the following terms related to dress, etc.: *falda* (from Gmc.) 'skirt', *guante* (from Gmc.) 'glove', *palafrén* (from OFr.) 'palfrey', etc.

A number of verbs and abstract nouns of Catalan origin can be exemplified by *añorar* 'to miss', *congoja* 'anguish', *retar* 'to challenge', *trajinar* 'to transport, bustle', *ultraje* 'outrage'.

Finally, the following miscellaneous list of catalanisms reflect the somewhat broad range of sematic fields affected: *borracho* (?) 'drunk', *cohete* 'rocket', *esqueje* 'cutting (of plant)', *follón* 'arrogant, cowardly', *pila* 'pile', *plantel* 'seedbed', *pólvora* 'gunpowder', *quijote* 'cuisse (of armour)', *ristre* 'lance-socket (in armour)', *sardana* 'Catalan dance', *seo* 'cathedral', *sor* 'sister (in religious titles)', *retablo* 'altarpiece', *verdete* 'verdigris'.

The best source of information on the Catalan borrowings made by Castilian continues to be Corominas & Pascual 1980–, although, until the appearance of vol. 6 of this work, one is dependent upon the indices of the earlier edition (Corominas 1954–7). Also to be consulted is Colón 1967b.

4.12   Lusisms

Under this term we include words borrowed from either Portuguese or Galician, since it is usually impossible, on grounds of form, to distinguish between loans from these sources. Lusisms have passed into Spanish with some facility since the Middle Ages; the use, in Medieval Castile, of Galician-Portuguese as the language of the love-lyric is responsible for some of the earliest, such as *coita* 'sorrow', *coitado* 'sorrowful', *ledo* 'joyful', although the first two terms were replaced by *cuita*, ~ *ado* and the last later fell from use. Later medieval borrowings include *afeitar* 'to shave' (formerly also 'to apply makeup'), *afeite* 'makeup' (now antiquated), as well as other words referring to the emotions, such as *enfadarse* 'to become angry', *desenfadar* 'to quieten', *desenfado* 'carefree', *enfadoso* 'irksome'.

The largest group of Portuguese borrowings refers, unsurprisingly, to the world of the sea and ships, since Portuguese expertise in these fields anteceded that of Spain. Such loans include *angra* 'creek', *balde* 'pail, bucket', *buzo* 'diver', *callao* 'pebble beach' (restricted to seaman's language, except in the Canaries), *cantil* and *acantilado* 'cliff', *carabela* 'caravel', *chubasco* 'squall', *estela* 'wake', *garúa* 'drizzle' (chiefly used in American Spanish), *laja* 'flat stone' (restricted to Andalusia and America), *marejada* 'swell' (unless it is a catalanism), *monzón* 'monsoon', *pleamar* 'high tide', *tanque* 'water tank', *vigía* 'lookout', *virar* 'to tack'. Closely related are names of fish and other sea creatures: *almeja* 'clam', *cachalote* 'sperm whale', *chopa* 'black bream', *mejillón* 'mussel', *ostra* 'oyster', *perca* 'perch', *sollo* 'sturgeon'.

The establishment of Portugal's maritime empire allowed borrowing by Portuguese of words from many oriental languages. Some of this originally exotic vocabulary was then passed on to Spanish: *bambú* 'bamboo', *biombo* 'folding screen', *cacatúa* 'cockatoo', *carambola* 'cannon (in billiards)', *catre* '(camp) bed', *cha* 'tea' (ousted, after the seventeenth century, by *té*, which probably entered via French), *charol* 'varnish; patent leather', *(juegos) malabares* 'juggling', *pagoda* 'pagoda'.

Other words borrowed, or probably borrowed, from Portuguese or Galician include: *barullo* 'confusion', *basquiña* 'skirt', *bicho* 'creature', *brincar* 'to gambol', *caramelo* 'sweet', *corpiño* 'sleeveless bodice', *despejar* 'to clear', *laya* 'type, quality', *macho* 'mule', *mequetrefe* 'whippersnapper', *mermelada* 'jam', *sarao* 'soirée', *traje* 'suit; costume', *vaivén* 'swaying, bustle'.

For further discussion of borrowings from Portuguese, see Salvador 1967, and Corominas & Pascual 1980–.

4.13   Italianisms

The earliest borrowings made by Spanish from Italian are found towards the end of the Middle Ages, but it is in the sixteenth and seventeenth centuries that such loans reach their apogee, owing principally to the prestige of concepts emanating from Renaissance Italy and to the military involvement of Spain in the Italian Peninsula. Borrowing has continued, particularly in the field of music, down to the present, but became relatively infrequent after the eighteenth century. It should be noted that not all italianisms originate in Tuscan; some (particularly maritime terms) are borrowings from Genoese, Venetian, Milanese, etc., or from southern Italian or Sicilian varieties.

Words relating to the arts constitute one of the largest groups of italianisms in Spanish. In the vocabulary of literature and philosophy, we find *esdrújulo* 'proparoxytonic', *novela* 'novel', *soneta* 'sonnet', *terceto* 'tercet'; *folleto* 'pamphlet', *humanista* 'humanist', *parangón* 'comparison'. In the language of the theatre are to be found *bufón* 'buffoon', *comediante* 'actor', *payaso* 'clown', *saltimbanqui* 'acrobat', and in that of art, *acuarela* 'water colour', *arabesco* 'arabesque', *caricatura* 'caricature', *cartón* 'cartoon', *claroscuro* 'chiaroscuro', *destacar* 'to highlight', *diseño* 'design', *encarnado* 'red', *esbelto* 'slender', *esfumar* 'to tone down', *fresco* 'fresco', *grotesco* 'grotesque', *grupo* 'group', *miniatura* 'miniature', *modelo* 'model', *pintoresco* 'picturesque', *temple* 'tempera', *ultramarino* 'ultramarine'. The following architectural terms are also borrowed from Italian: *apoyar* 'to support', *balaustre* 'banister', *balcón* 'balcony', *casino* 'small house' (later 'casino'), *cúpula* 'cupola', *escayola* 'stucco', *fachada* 'façade', *fontana* 'fountain', *pedestal* 'pedestal' (via French), *pórtico* (?) 'portico', *terraza* 'terrace', *zócalo* 'plinth', while in sculpture we find *busto* 'bust', *medalla* 'medal, plaque', *relievo* 'relief', *terracota* 'terracotta'. As in the case of all European languages, borrowing by Spanish of Italian musical terms is extremely frequent; such loans include *alto* 'alto', *bajo* 'bass', *barítono* 'baritone', *contralto* 'contralto', *soprano* 'soprano', *tenor* 'tenor'; *mandolina* 'mandoline', *piano* 'piano', *viola* 'viola', *violín* 'violin', *violoncelo, -chelo* 'cello', *violón* 'double bass'; *aire* 'melody', *aria* 'aria', *batuta* 'baton', *cantata* 'cantata', *cavatina* 'cavatina', *compositor* 'composer', *concierto* 'concert, concerto', *dúo* 'duet', *fantasía* 'fantasia', *fuga* 'fugue', *fusa* 'demisemiquaver', *libreto* 'libretto', *madrigal* 'madrigal', *ópera* 'opera', *serenata* 'serenade', *solista* 'soloist', *solo* 'solo', *sonata* 'sonata', *sordina* 'mute', *tempo* 'tempo', *tocata* 'tocata'. Names of dances include *pavana* 'pavan', and *tarantela* 'tarantella'.

Italian military terms were borrowed in profusion by Spanish in the sixteenth and seventeenth centuries, although one or two of the following items are first attested in Spanish earlier or later than the Golden Age: *alerta* 'alert', *asalto* 'assault', *atacar* 'to attack', *batallón* 'battalion', *bombarda* 'bombard', whence *bombardear* 'to bomb', *canjear* 'to exchange (prisoners, etc.)', *cañón* 'cannon', *centinela* 'sentinel', *colina* 'hill', *coronel* 'colonel', *destacar* 'to detach (soldiers)', *duelo* 'duel', *embestir* 'to attack', *emboscada* 'ambush', *emboscar* 'to ambush', *escolta* 'escort', *escopeta* 'shotgun', *escuadrón* 'squadron', *generalísimo* 'supreme commander', *granada* 'grenade', *guardia* 'guard', *infante* 'infantryman', *marchar* (?) 'to march, go', *mosquete* 'musket', *mosquetero* 'musketeer', *penacho* 'plume', *saquear* 'to plunder', *zapar* 'to sap'. Words referring to defensive building are particularly well represented: *bastión* 'bastion', *ciudadela* 'citadel', *cuneta* 'cunette, ditch', *escarpa* 'escarpment', *muralla* 'defensive wall', *parapeto* 'parapet', *reducto* 'redoubt'.

Italian is one of the languages, together with Portuguese, Catalan and various Germanic languages, which have contributed substantially to the maritime vocabulary of Spanish. This semantic field is represented by the following loans, among others: *bogavante* 'stroke, first oarsman' (unless from Catalan), *brújula* 'compass', *corsario* 'corsair', *chusma* 'gang of galley slaves', later 'rabble', *dársena* 'dock', *escolla* 'reef', *fragata* 'frigate', *góndola* 'gondola', *mesana* 'mizzenmast', *piloto* 'pilot', *zarpar* 'to weigh anchor'.

Significant numbers of italianisms relate to commerce and industry, reflecting the Italian domination of these fields in the early modern period. Among others we find: *avanzar* 'to be in excess (over a calculated amount)' (later 'to advance'), *balance* 'balance (in accounts)', *bancarrota* 'bankruptcy', *banco* 'bank', *en bruto* 'gross', *cero* 'zero', *contrabando* 'contrabando', *crédito* 'credit', *débito* (?) 'debit, debt', *depósito* 'deposit', *factura* 'bill', *letra de cambio* 'bill of exchange', *mercancía* 'merchandise', *mercante* 'merchant', *millón* 'million', *monte de piedad* 'pawnshop', *montepío* 'pawnshop', *negociante* (?) 'businessman, -woman', *neto* 'net', *póliza* '(insurance) policy', *saldar* 'to liquidate', *saldo* 'bargain sale'. Particular commodities whose names are of Italian origin include *brocado* 'brocade', *cartulina* 'Bristol board', *granito* 'granite', *índigo* 'indigo', *porcelana* 'porcelain', *tafetán* 'taffeta' (or from Catalan).

A number of italianisms can be observed in the wider fields of social life, reflecting to some extent the imitation of Italian manners, principally in Spain's Golden Age. Words relating to general human characteristics and activities include *aguantar* 'to hold back, endure', *aspaviento* 'fuss', *bizarro* 'gallant, dashing', *bravata* 'piece of bravado', *brusco* (?) 'abrupt', *campeón* 'champion', *canalla* 'rabble; swine', *capricho* 'caprice', *cortejar* 'to woo', *cortejo* 'retinue', *cortesano* 'courtly', *chanza* 'joke', *charlar* 'to chat', *charlatán* 'garrulous', *chulo* 'swaggering, flashy', *desfachatado* 'insolent', *estafar* 'to swindle', *estrafalario* 'eccentric', *farsante* 'charlatan', *fogoso* 'spirited', *garbo* 'gracefulness', *mafia* 'Mafia', *rufián* 'pimp; villain', *supercheria* 'fraud'. In the field of games and similar activities, we find *cucaña* 'greasy pole', *empatar* 'to tie, draw', *regata* 'regatta', *trucos* 'billiards', *tute* 'tute (the card game)'. The fields of education and transport produce *gaceta* 'gazette', *pedante* 'pedant'; *carroza* '(horse-drawn) carriage', *esguazar* 'to ford', *ferroviario* 'railway (adj.); railwayman', *pista* 'track', *valija* 'suitcase'. In the field of religion we observe *camposanto* 'churchyard', *carnaval* 'Carnival', *plebe* (?) 'people', *sotana* 'cassock'.

In the fields relating to private life, we find terms relating to the house, such as *cantina* 'wine cellar, bar', *celosía* 'lattice window', *chaveta* 'securing peg', *pérgola* 'pergola', *toalla* (?) 'towel', some referring to dress and adornment, including *capucho* 'hooded cloak', *corbata* '(neck)tie', *filigrana* 'filigree', *perla* (?) 'pearl', *recamar* 'to embroider in relief' (taken by Italian from Arabic), *turbante* 'turban', some related to food, like *café* 'coffee', *caviar* 'caviar', *macarrones* 'macaroni', *menestra* 'mixed vegetables', *salchicha* 'sausage', and some which refer to the body and illness, such as *belleza* 'beauty', *caricia* 'caress', *chichón* (?) 'bump (on the head)', *malaria* 'malaria', *pelagra* 'pellagra'.

The physical world is apparently less well represented than others. We find some names relating to the natural world, *anchoa* 'anchovy' (probably via Catalan), *carroña* 'carrion', *pichón* 'young pigeon', *tarántula* 'tarantula', *pistacho* 'pistachio', *remolacha* 'beet', and some topographical terms, *cascada* 'waterfall', *golfo* 'gulf' (but, more probably, this is a catalanism; see 4.11), *gruta* 'cavern', *pantano* 'marsh; reservoir'.

In addition, a small number of rather general terms has been borrowed by Spanish from Italian: *bagatela* 'trifle', *estropear* 'to spoil', *fiasco* 'fiasco', *flamante* 'splendid', *fracasar* 'to fail', *manejar* 'to handle', *pillar* 'to grasp, steal', *premura* 'urgency'.

The main sources of further information on italianisms in Spanish are Terlingen 1943 and 1967, and Corominas & Pascual 1980–.

4.14   Word-formation

The vocabulary of Spanish can be said to consist of three components. In addition to words inherited from Latin (popular and semi-learned words, see 4.1), and to words borrowed from other languages (4.2–13), the Spanish lexicon includes items which have been created, through word-formation, by means of the language's internal resources. The term 'word-formation' includes reference to **prefixation** (4.14.1), **derivation** (4.14.2), and **composition** (4.14.3).

4.14.1   Prefixation

Latin prefixes were in close relationship with the prepositions of the language (see the discussion at 3.8.1), in that many particles which functioned as prepositions also functioned as prefixes, usually with similar sense. However, not all the particles that have survived as prepositions have also survived as prefixes.

Many prefixed Latin words ceased at an early stage to be analysed by speakers as consisting of {prefix + base morpheme} and developed thereafter as unitary words. This is exemplified by cases like PROFECTU > *provecho* 'advantage', where Latin /f/ has been given the treatment normally accorded to this phoneme in intervocalic position (i.e./-f-/ > OSp. /β/, MSp. /b/; see 3.5.3.2[2]). Similarly, DECOLLĀRE > *degollar* 'to cut the throat', where /k/ is given intervocalic treatment (> /g/). Where speakers continued to perceive the morphological complexity of a word, any consonant or consonant group which follows the prefix (and therefore stands at the beginning of the base morpheme) is treated in the same way as if it were in word-initial position. Thus, DĒFĒNSA 'forbidden (land)' must for some centuries have continued to be perceived as a complex word, since it develops to *dehesa* 'unenclosed pasture', showing the Latin /f/ is here given word-initial treatment (becoming /h/, later /∅/, as in FŪMU > *humo* 'smoke', etc.; see 2.5.6, 2.6.4). In a small but crucial number of cases, the complex structure of the prefixed Latin word has continued to be perceived as such throughout its history, as in APPREHENDERE 'to seize' (in relation with PREHENDERE 'id.') > *aprender* 'to learn' (still in relationship with *prender* 'to seize').

It is cases like APPREHENDERE > *aprender* which provided the model (in spoken Latin or at any later stage including the present) for the creation of new words by the addition of a prefix to a pre-existing verb, noun, adjective or adverb (examples of prefixed adverbs can be seen at 3.4). The prefixes which have a continuous history from Latin to Spanish (and which served and serve to create new words) are discussed below. No distinction is made, in the examples, between simple prefixation and **parasynthesis**, in which a prefix and a suffix are simultaneously added to a stem (as in *des-* + *alm-* + *ado*→*desalmado* 'heartless') and where the parasynthetic nature of the structure is recognizable by the absence from Spanish of words consisting of the same prefix and the same stem, or of the same stem and the same suffix (in this case, by the absence of such words as **desalma* or **almado*). It should also be noted that, unlike Classical Latin, spoken Latin and its successors (including Spanish) allow sequences of two or more prepositions.

AD-
The Latin meaning ('to, towards', etc.) has been almost entirely lost from this prefix, and its descendant *a-* is generally void of sense. It is used above all to create verbs from nouns or adjectives (e.g. *agrupar* 'to group', *amontonar* 'to pile up', *apaciguar* 'to pacify', *atormentar* 'to torment', *agravar* 'to aggravate', *amortecer* 'to deaden'), but may appear in other formations (e.g. *adiós* 'goodbye').

The form *ad-* appears in a number of prefixed forms borrowed from Latin: *adaptar* 'to adapt', *adherir* 'to adhere', *admirar* 'to admire, wonder at', etc.

DIS-
The notion of 'separation' inherent in the Latin prefix was later expanded to include 'away from' (absorbing DĒ-) and 'out of', so that it came into competition with EX-, and in particular with the compound prefix DĒ + EX-, which (at least before stems beginning with a consonant) shared the same phonetic outcome as DIS-, namely *des-*. The competition with EX-, whereby Spanish came to have two prefixes, *des-* and *es-*, of identical meaning and similar structure, explains the frequent alternation in Old Spanish and modern non-standard speech between these two prefixes (e.g. *destender* ~ *estender* 'to spread, extend'). However, the modern standard language has resolved these cases of alternation, usually on etymological grounds (so that *estender* is preferred, and is erroneously respelled *extender*, on the basis of EXTENDERE). Examples of *des-* include: *desconfiar* 'to distrust', *descoser* 'to unsew', *desdecir* 'to retract', *desechar* 'to discard', *deshacer* 'to undo', *deshonrar* 'to dishonour', *desmentir* 'to deny', *desviar* 'to deflect'.

Forms in *dis-*, *di-*, or *de-* betray their learned origins: *discernir* 'to discern', *disforme* 'deformed', *divertir* 'to amuse', *denegar* 'to refuse'.

IN-
This prefix retains the Latin sense 'in(to), on', and its form in Old Spanish is generally *en-*, even before /p/ and /b/ (reflecting the neutralization of /m/, /n/ [and /ɲ/] in syllable-final position), although modern spelling distinguishes *en-* from *em-*, in imitation of the Latin alternation between IN- and IM-. *En-* ~ *em-* is used to create verbs from nouns or adjectives: *embarrar* 'to cover with mud', *emborrachar* 'to make drunk', *empapelar* 'to paper', *empeñar* 'to pledge,

pawn', *encabezar* 'to lead', *enganchar* 'to hook'; *engordar* 'to fatten', *enloquecer* 'to go or drive mad', *enrasar* 'to make level'. Occasionally it is used to create new verbs from existing verbs: *embeber* 'to soak up', *encoger* 'to shrink', etc.

In a few instances, IN- was compounded with EX-, producing the sequences *ens-* or OSp. *enx-*, MSp. *enj-*: *ensalzar* (< *IN EX ALTIĀRE) 'to exalt', *ensanchar* 'to widen', *enjalbegar* (< *IN EX ALBICĀRE) 'to whitewash', *enjuagar* (< *IN EX AQUĀRE) 'to rinse', *enjugar* (< *IN EX SUCĀRE) 'to dry'.

The learned descendant of IN-, Spanish *in-*, has two values, the first of which is indistinguishable from that of popular *en-*: *inmiscuir* 'to mix', *innato* 'inborn', *inspirar* 'to inspire'. The second, negative, value of Latin IN- is also widely imitated in Spanish, not only under the form *in-* ~ *im-*, but under forms which imitate the Latin assimilation of N before L and R: *insensato* 'senseless', *impiedad* 'impiety', *impopular* 'unpopular', *ilegítimo* 'illegitimate', *ilimitado* 'unlimited', *irreal* 'unreal', *irrespetuoso* 'disrespectful'.

EX-

The popular descendant of EX- is OSp. *es-* (sometimes now respelled *ex-* but without phonological change). It has been seen (DĬS-, above) that *es-* has since Latin times been in competition with *des-* in the sense 'out of'. Forms with this prefix include *escapar* 'to escape', *escardar* 'to weed', *escoger* 'to choose', *extender* 'to spread'.

Learned use of this prefix, in the form *ex-*, extends from borrowings of forms which already displayed this prefix in Latin (in which case we also find examples of *e-*: *emanar* 'to emanate', *exhibir* 'to exhibit', *extirpar* 'to eradicate'), to the addition of the prefix to stems not found in Latin with EX- (*excéntrico* 'eccentric', *excarcelar* 'to release from prison'), and its semi-independent use before certain nouns (*ex primer ministro* 'ex-prime minister', *ex presidente* 'ex-president').

INTER-

The popular descendant of this prefix, *entre-*, appears in relatively few forms, but shows considerable development of sense from the Latin 'between' (as in *entrecomillar* 'to place in inverted commas') to 'partially' (*entreabrir* 'to half open', *entresacar* 'to thin [the hair, etc.]'), 'reciprocally' (*entreayudarse* 'to help one another', *entrecruzar* 'to intertwine'), or 'intermediate' (*entrecano* 'greying [hair])', *entrefino* 'of medium quality').

Words which display the learned form of this prefix, *inter-*, are most frequently borrowings or calques from other languages, typically French or English (e.g. *interferir* 'to interfere', *intermuscular* 'intermuscular'), although some are borrowings made directly from Latin by Spanish (e.g. *interrumpir* 'to interrupt').

TRANS-

The Latin sense 'across' rarely appears in the popular reflex of this prefix, *tras-* (e.g. *trasvolar* 'to fly across'). Instead we find other meanings such as 'behind' (*traslapar* 'to overlap', *trastienda* 'back room (behind a shop'), 'during' (*trasnochar* 'to stay up late'), or 'excessively' (*trastornar* 'to disrupt').

No doubt because of the frequent reduction (at least in conversational style) of syllable-final /ns/ to /s/ (see Navarro 1961: 112), the learned form of this prefix, *trans-*, is in many cases interchangeable with the popular form, both forms appearing with the same stem (e.g. *trasmitir* ~ *transmitir* 'to transmit').

SUB-   Although the popular reflex of the preposition sŭB has now all but disappeared, that of the prefix sŭB-, *so-*, is reasonably well represented in Spanish. Most frequently it retains the Latin sense 'under': *sobarba* 'double chin', *socavar* 'to undermine', *solapar* 'to overlap', *solomillo* 'sirloin', *someter* 'to subdue', *soterrar* 'to bury'. Occasionally, this prefix is used to attenuate the action indicated by the stem: *soasar* 'to roast lightly', *sofreír* 'to fry lightly'.

The learned form of the same prefix, *sub-*, may indicate location, as in *subsuelo* 'subsoil', *submarino* 'submarine', *subrayado* 'underlining', but more often has the metaphorical value of 'less than' the notion expressed by the stem, e.g. *subdesarrollado* 'underdeveloped', *subvalorar* 'to underrate'.

SUPER-   The relatively frequent popular descendant of this prefix, *sobre-*, appears with the senses 'above' (e.g. *sobrecama* 'bedspread', *sobrenadar* 'to float'), 'after' (e.g. *sobremesa* 'after-dinner chat', *sobrevivir* 'to survive'), and 'in excess' (e.g. *sobrecargar* 'to overload', *sobremanera* 'exceedingly', *sobresueldo* 'bonus').

Probably under the influence of English, the learned form of the prefix, *super-*, has enjoyed an enormous productivity in recent decades. It shows the same range of meanings as the popular form, but with the sense of 'excess' being by far the most frequent: *superestructura* 'superstructure', *supervivencia* 'survival', *supercompresión* 'super-charging', *superpoblación* 'overpopulation'.

RE-   In the case of this prefix, it is impossible to distinguish popular and learned reflexes, on the basis of form; both types of transmission of course produce *re-*. However, on the basis of meaning it may be possible to make some distinction, since it seems likely that the repetitive sense now sometimes associated with *re-* is a recent development, due to influence from Latin or from other modern languages which commonly display the repetitive meaning of this prefix (e.g. French or English). Examples of this development include *reanudar* 'to renew', *reaparecer* 'to reappear', *rehacer* 'to remake'. Traditional senses include reference to place (e.g. *recámara* 'dressing room' [i.e. 'a place beyond a bedroom'], *recocina* 'scullery', *rebotica* 'room behind a chemist's shop'), and occasionally to time (e.g. *redolor* 'discomfort remaining after an accident'), but most usually the prefix simply emphasizes the notion expressed by the stem: *rebién* 'very well indeed',

> *rebuscar* 'to search thoroughly', *recalentar* 'to overheat',
> *remoler* 'to grind up', *repudrir* 'to rot completely', *retemblar*
> 'to shake (violently)'.

Other prefixes derived from Latin are almost exclusively learned. PER- and PRŌ-, whose prepositional correlates merge as *por* (see 3.8.1), only in one instance behave in parallel fashion, in the development PERFĬDIA > *porfía* 'stubbornness'. *Per-* is found, with intensifying value, in the language of the rustic characters of Renaissance drama (probably reflecting the rural speech of the Salamanca area; see Penny 1990a), and with similar value in the rural speech of present-day Asturias, but is absent from standard Castilian except in learned formations like *perdurar* 'to last', *perjurar* 'to commit perjury', but also 'to curse repeatedly'. *Pro-* is always learned (e.g. *promedio* 'average', *prometer* 'to promise').

All of the following, ultimately of Latin origin, have entered Spanish through writing, their frequency increased today by the many anglicisms which display them: *pos(t)-* (<POST-), *ante-* (<ANTE-), *pre-* (<PRAE-), *com-~con-~co-* (<COM-, the correlate of the preposition CUM), *retro-* (<RETRŌ-), *contra-* (<CONTRĀ-), *extra-* (<EXTRĀ-), *intra-* (<INTRĀ-), *infra-* (<INFRĀ-), *supra-* (<SUPRĀ-), *circun-~circum-* (<CIRCUM-), *ultra-* (<ULTRĀ-); e.g. *posguerra* 'post-war period', *anteponer* 'to antepose', *preindustrial* 'preindustrial', *condueño* 'joint owner', *contraproducente* 'counterproductive', *retroceder* 'to move back', *extraterrestre* 'extraterrestrial', *intranuclear* 'intranuclear', *infraestructura* 'infrastructure', *supranacional* 'supranational', *circunlocución* 'circumlocution', *ultramarinos* 'groceries'. A particularly productive sub-set of learned prefixes comprises quantifying expressions, exemplified by the following: *bisabuelo* 'great-grandfather', *bipolaridad* 'bipolarity', *maxifalda* 'maxi-skirt', *minifundio* 'small farm', *multicolor* 'multicoloured', *pluriempleo* 'moonlighting', *semifinal* 'semifinal', *sesquióxido* 'sesquioxide', *vicetiple* 'chorus girl'.

The stock of Spanish prefixes has similarly been enriched by the introduction of a number of forms whose origin is ultimately Greek but whose current frequency is again probably due to the influence of English, where these prefixes are especially numerous in scientific and journalistic language (see Pratt 1980: 185–91). The prefixes concerned are exemplified by the following selection of words: *antioxidante* 'antirust', *autopromoción* 'self-promotion', *hipertensión* 'hypertension', *macroeconómico* 'macroeconomic', *microorganismo* 'micro-organism', *pericráneo* 'pericranium', *polivalencia* 'polyvalency', *protohistoria* 'protohistory' (see also 4.14.3).

4.14.2 Derivation

The addition of suffixes to pre-existing stems in Spanish serves two contrasting purposes: first, the creation of a word which refers to a different concept (albeit a related one) to that referred to by the original word, and second, the addition of a nuance which reveals the speaker's attitude to the concept concerned. In the latter case, no new concept is involved; the original word and the derived word refer to the same concept. To exemplify the two processes we may consider, first, the relationship between *vaca* 'cow' and *vacada* 'herd of cows'. It is evident that the derived form *vacada* indicates a concept which is different from (but related to) the concept indicated by the base-word. However, if one compares, secondly, the word *gordo* 'fat' with its derivative *gordito* 'nice and fat, chubby', it is clear that the concept referred to is essentially the same in each case, but that in the case of *gordito* the speaker's attitude to the concept is approving and affectionate.

However, these two derivational processes are not always as sharply distinguished as this discussion suggests; they overlap in two ways. On the one hand, the 'same' suffix may serve both derivational purposes. The ending -*ito* which conveys overtones of affection in *gordito* expresses no such nuance in *carrito*; in this case, the concept referred to ('trolley') is a different one from that indicated by *carro* (viz. 'cart', 'car', etc.). Similarly, the -*azo* which appears in *vinazo* 'coarse wine' (or, sometimes, 'magnificent wine'!) clearly carries emotive value but does not alter the basic reference (to 'wine'), while the 'same' element in *cabezazo* invokes reference to a different concept ('head-butt') from that of the base word *cabeza* ('head'). On the other hand, the emotive nuance added to a concept by the addition of a suffix may be closely related to an element of objective meaning. Thus, there is often a correlation between the affectionate response of the speaker and relative smallness of the referent (e.g. *gatito* 'kitten'), or between the repugnance expressed by the speaker and the relative bigness or coarseness of the referent (e.g. *novelón* 'long boring novel').

Despite the difficulties posed by the overlaps between these two derivational processes, it is useful to keep them separate in discussion. Further, the standpoint taken here is that where emotive nuances are associated with a given suffix, such nuances predominate over any element of objective meaning which may also be present. This view is in accordance with that expressed in a fundamental study of the suffixes concerned (Alonso 1935) and can further be justified by reference to Gooch 1970. In what follows, we shall distinguish the two types of derivation by using the label **lexical** for the types which produces new names for new concepts, and **affective** for the type which expresses the speaker's attitude towards the concept evoked.

4.14.2.1   Lexical derivation

Suffixes may be used to create new nouns, adjectives and verbs. Each of these categories will be considered in turn.

A derived noun may have as its base another noun, an adjective or a verb. Below are listed the main suffixes (i.e. those which remain productive or which at some stage have been so) which may be applied to each type of base, together with the source of each suffix and representative examples of each combination.

Base	Suffix MSp. (OSp.)	Source	Example
Noun	-ada	-ĀTA	*puñalada* 'stab'
	-ado	-ĀTU	*bocado* 'mouthful'
	-aje	Fr. -age (< -ATICU	*aprendizaje* 'apprenticeship'
	-al ~ -ar	-ĀLE	*trigal* 'cornfield' *olivar* 'olive grove'
	-azgo (-adgo)	-ATICU	*noviazgo* 'courtship'
	-azo	-ĀCEU	*vistazo* 'glance'
	-ero	-ĀRIU	*joyero* 'jeweller'
	-ía	-ĪA (<Gk. ια)	*abadía* 'abbey'
	-ismo	-ĪSMU (<-ισμός)	*espejismo* 'mirage'
	-ista	-ĪSTA (<-ιστης)	*modista* 'dressmaker'
	-o, -a	-U, -A	*manzano* 'appletree'
Adjective	-dad	-TĀTE	*tenacidad* 'tenacity'
	-dumbre	-TŪMINE	*reciedumbre* 'strength'
	-era	-ĀRIA	*cojera* 'lameness'
	-ez	-ITIE	*vejez* 'old age'
	-eza	-ITIA	*rareza* 'rarity'
	-ismo	-ĪSMU (<-ισμός)	*humanismo* 'humanism'
	-ista	-ĪSTA (<-ιστής)	*izquierdista* 'leftish'
	-or	-ŌRE	*grosor* 'thickness'
Verb	-ada, -ida	-ĀTA, -ĪTA	*huida* 'flight'
	-ado, -ido	-ĀTU, -ĪTU	*alumbrado* 'lighting'
	-aje	Fr. -age (< -ATICU	*tatuaje* 'tattoo'
	-ando	-ANDU	*graduando* 'graduand'
	-ante, -(i)ente	-ANTE, -(I)ENTE	*amante* 'lover'
	-anza ~ -ancia, -(i)encia	-ANTIA, -(I)ENTIA	*alabanza* 'praise' *ganancia* 'profit' *creencia* 'belief'
	-e, -o, -a		*derrumbe* 'demolition' *derribo* 'demolition' *marcha* 'progress'
	-ero (-uero) ~ -orio	-ŌRIU	*atracadero* 'quay' *lavatorio* 'washing'
	-mento ~ -miento	-MENTU	*pulimento* 'shine' *llamamiento* 'appeal'
	-ón, -ona	-ŌNE	*tumbona* 'deckchair'
	-or	-ŌRE	*pensador* 'thinker'
	-ura	-ŪRA	*armadura* 'armour'
	-zón, -ción	-TIŌNE	*hinchazón* 'swelling' *turbación* 'confusion'

It can be seen that in a number of cases, the form of the suffix has not been arrived at through regular phonological change. That is, a number of suffixes have passed into Spanish as a result of the borrowing of Latin words which contained the suffixes concerned, after which the suffix could become available for application to inherited stems. The learned suffixes concerned are: *-ia, -ismo, -ista, -ante, -(i)ente, -ancia, -(i)encia, -orio, -mento, -ción*. In a few cases, such learned forms compete with inherited forms of the same Latin suffix; this can be seen in the case of *-anza/-ancia, -ero/-orio, -mento/-miento -zón/-ción*. In some of these cases, the learned form (e.g. *-ancia, -ción*) is today more productive than the popular form; in the remaining cases (*-ero, -miento*) the reverse is true. Similarly, *-aje* results from the borrowing of French words from the Middle Ages onwards, and coexists with inherited *-adgo*, later *-azgo*, the latter now unproductive.

Certain of the suffixes used to derive nouns from verbs, namely *-ero, -or, -ura*, descend from Latin suffixes which were applied to participles. This structural feature continues to characterize Spanish, so that in the cases concerned we find participial *-ad-, -ed-,* or *-id-* between stem and suffix.

Derivation of nouns in *-o* from others in *-a*, and vice versa, is a relatively unproductive process, but accounts historically for such pairs in Spanish as *manzano* 'appletree'/*manzana* 'apple', *cesto* '(small) basket'/*cesta* '(large) basket', etc. On the other hand, deverbal nouns in *-e, -o, -a* are quite frequent and the process continues to be productive.

Derived adjectives may be based, similarly, on nouns, verbs, or on other adjectives:

Base	Suffix	Source	Example
Adjective	-ado	-ĀTU	*azulado* 'bluish'
	-enco	?	*azulenco* 'bluish'
	-iento	-ENTU	*avariento* 'miserly'
	-ino	-ĪNU	*blanquecino* 'whitish'
	-ista	-ĪSTA (<-ιστής)	*socialista* 'socialist'
	-izo	-ĪCEU	*rojizo* 'reddish'
	-oide	Gk. -οειδής	*negroide* 'negroid'
	-oso	-ŌSU	*verdoso* 'greenish'
	-usco	-ŪSCU	*pardusco* 'greyish'
	-uzco	-ŪSCU	*blancuzco* 'whitish'
Noun	-al ~ -ar	-ĀLE ~ -ĀRE	*invernal* 'wintry'
			seglar 'secular, lay'
	-ano	-ĀNU	*mediano* 'average'
	-ense	-ĒNSE	*ateniense* 'Athenian'
	-eño	-INEU	*panameño* 'Panamanian'
	-ero	-ĀRIU	*playero* 'beach'
	-és	-ĒNSE	*montés* 'wild'
	-esco	-ISCU	*gigantesco* 'gigantic'
	-ico	-ICU	*borbónico* 'Bourbon'

	-í	Ar. -î	*iraní* 'Iranian'
	-il	-ĪLE	*estudiantil* 'student'
	-ino	-ĪNU	*cristalino* 'crystalline'
	-ón	-ŌNE	*narizón* 'long-nosed'
	-oso	-ŌSU	*miedoso* 'fearful'
	-udo	-ŪTU	*orejudo* 'big-eared'
Verb	-able, -ible	-ABILE, -ĪBILE	*inoxidable* 'rustless'
			movible 'movable'
	-ado, -ido	-ĀTU, -ĪTU	*apagado* 'dull, weak'
			aburrido 'boring'
	-ante, -(i)ente	-ANTE, -(I)ENTE	*titubeante* 'shaky'
	-ero	-ĀRIU	*decidero* 'mentionable'
	-ivo	-ĪVU	*impulsivo* 'impulsive'
	-izo	-ĪCEU	*olvidadizo* 'forgetful'
	-ón	-ŌNE	*mirón* 'nosy'
	-or	-ŌRE	*embriagador* 'intoxicating'

It will be seen that adjectives derived from other adjectives for the most part denote colours related to those denoted by the base. Adjectives in *-ista* function also as nouns.

As in the case of derived nouns, we find cases of competition between popular and learned descendants of the same Latin suffix; thus popular *-és* coexists with learned *-ense*. Again as in the case of derived nouns, some deverbal adjectives have a participle as their base; this is generally so in the case of *-ero, -izo,* and *-or*.

Derived verbs are again based upon nouns, adjectives or verbs. The principal productive types of derivatives are listed below:

Base	Suffix	Source	Example
Verb	-ear	-IDIĀRE (< -ίξειν)	*toquetear* 'to finger'
	-ecer	-ĒSCERE	*embebecer* 'to delight'
Noun	-ar	-ĀRE	*salar* 'to salt'
	-ear	-IDIĀRE (< -ίζειν)	*cabecear* 'to nod'
	-ecer	-ĒSCERE	*anochecer* 'to grow dark'
	-ificar	-IFICĀRE	*glorificar* 'to glorify'
	-izar	-IZĀRE (< -ίζειν)	*tapizar* 'to carpet'
Adjective	-ar	-ĀRE	*igualar* 'to make equal'
	-ear	-IDIĀRE (< -ίζειν)	*blandear* 'to weaken'
	-ecer	-ĒSCERE	*blanquecer* 'to whiten'
	-ificar	-IFICĀRE	*amplificar* 'to amplify'
	-guar	-IFICĀRE	*santiguar* 'to bless'
	-izar	-IZĀRE	*fecundizar* 'to fertilize'

It can be seen that both the suffixes *-ear* and *-izar* descend ultimately from the same Greek causative suffix -ίζειν. The latter was adapted, as it passed into early spoken Latin by oral transmission, to -IDIĀRE, whose later development to Spanish *-ear* is regular (see 2.5.2.2[4]). The suffix *-ear* is applied straightforwardly to nouns and adjectives, but to verbs usually by means of an infix (e.g. *toqu + et + ear, freg + ot + ear, gim + ot + ear*) which generally has 'repetitive' value.

Gk -ίζειν was borrowed a second time by (later literary) Latin, in the form -IZĀRE, which was later taken through writing into medieval Spanish as -*izar*. Perhaps under the influence of other modern languages, where the corresponding suffix (-*ise*, -*ize*) is very productive, -*izar* has become one of the most frequent means of creating new verbs.

Latin -IFICĀRE also shows dual development. Via popular transmission, it shows the expected regular changes Ī > /e/, voicing of intervocalic -F- and -C- to [β] and [γ] respectively, and loss of pretonic I: *[-eβγár]. At this stage, /β/ was modified to a closing glide (as in the case of OSp. /βd/; 2.5.5 end), but then metathesized with the following consonant: *[-eβγár] > *[-euγár] > [-eγwár]. Pretonic /e/ was then raised to /i/ by assimilation to the following glide (cf. AEQUĀLE > OSp. *egual* > *igual* 'equal'): -*iguar*. When transmitted through writing, -IFICĀRE shows the usual minimal change to -*ificar*.

It will be noted that all the productive verbal suffixes belong to the -*ar* class, with the exception of -*ecer*, which usually appears in parasynthetic derivatives. In the Middle Ages, this type often competed with non-derived verbs in -*ir* (*escarnir ~ escarnecer, gradir ~ agradecer, guarnir ~ guarnecer, resplandir ~ resplandecer*, etc.), eventually ousting the simple verb in each case.

4.14.2.2   Affective derivation

In 4.14.2 we defined affective derivation as the process of adding suffixes which reveal the speaker's attitude towards the concept denoted by the base. The view was also expressed that the affective content of the suffixes concerned was more salient than any objective meaning (such as 'small-ness', 'largeness', 'coarseness', etc.) the suffixes might also convey. Each of the main affective suffixes of Spanish will be discussed here, with comments on emotive and objective content, whether the suffix lends itself to lexicalization (the denotation of a concept different from that of the base and with loss of affective value), and with consideration of its origin. The suffixes may be applied to nouns, adjectives and participles, or adverbs.

-*ito*   denotes approval/affection and is diminutive in value: *osito* 'teddy bear', *librito* 'nice (little) book', *crecidito* 'nice and tall (of child)', *bajito* 'small but nice'. Its Latin origins are hazy; it may have been extracted from certain personal names (JŪLITTA, BONITTA, SALVITTUS), but must have acquired frequent use in spoken Latin, since it is well represented in Romance (Fr. -*et*, -*ette*, It. -*etto*, -*etta*, Cat. -*et*, -*eta*, etc.). The form of the Latin suffix appears to have alternated between *-ĪTTU, whence Sp. -*ito*, and *-ĬTTU, from which the remaining Romance forms descend, including Fr., Occ., Cat. *-et*, borrowed by Castilian as *-ete* (see below). The suffix *-ito* is infrequently represented in thirteenth- and fourteenth-century texts (there is only one example in Berceo, who makes frequent use of other affective suffixes, and one in Juan Manuel) but gains in frequency in those fifteenth-century writers who most closely reflect the spoken language (the Archpriest of Talavera, Fernando de Rojas, etc.). Its frequency grows among similar writers of the Golden Age (especially Santa Teresa), whereafter it gradually displaces competitors (chiefly *-illo* and *-ico*) until it achieves its present dominance. Only in Andalusia does *-illo* retain its status as the preferred affectionate suffix.

-ico   is also affectionate and also has diminutive value: *besico* 'sweet little kiss', *malico* 'poorly', *un tantico* 'a wee bit'. Its origins are unknown, it has few Romance cognates, and its history until the Golden Age closely parallels that of *-ito*. But since that period, *-ico* has retreated from Castilian (being used now only in a limited range of forms) and remains frequent only in Navarre, Aragon, Murcia and Eastern Andalusia, and parts of Spanish America, where it is often the preferred affectionate form.

-in   plays a similar role to that of *-ito* and *-ico* (it is affectionate and diminutive): *pajarín* 'sweet little bird', *pequeñín* 'tiny, wee (fellow)'. However, it lends itself to numerous lexicalizations: *comodín* 'joker (in cards)', *futbolín* 'table football', etc. It may represent a development of the Latin suffix -ĪNUS, used to indicate the young of certain animals (e.g. PALUMBĪNUS [PULLUS] 'young dove') and throughout its history has been commonest in the western half of the Peninsula (Ptg. *-inho*, Gal. *-iño*, Ast. *-in*, León and Extremadura *-ino*). It has always had some frequency in Castilian, but cannot be freely applied to any base.

-illo   Although affectionate (and diminutive) for most of its history, this suffix now often has a slightly pejorative tone: *asuntillo* 'an unimportant piece of business', *empleíllo* 'rotten little job', *novelilla* 'piffling novel', *envidiosillo* 'pettily envious'. It also gives rise to frequent lexicalizations: *camilla* 'stretcher', *casilla* 'pigeonhole', *molinillo* 'coffee grinder', *pitillo* 'cigarette, fag'. It is the first of the suffixes considered here which has a clear Latin antecedent, -ĔLLUS, which was certainly diminutive and probably affectionate. Its descendant, *-iello*, was the commonest Old Spanish affectionate diminutive, and was gradually replaced by *-illo*, spreading from the Burgos area (see 2.4.2.5). In the Golden Age, *-illo* is still dominant (and still affectionate) but since that time has been challenged by *-ito* as the 'normal' Castilian diminutive form and has acquired its current slightly pejorative tone (except in Andalusia).

Lat. -ĔLLUS was applied directly to nouns and adjectives in -US and -A, but in the case of nouns and adjectives with other endings an infix -(Ĭ)C- was inserted. Since the /k/ of this infix was commonly intervocalic, it evolves to OSp. /dz/, MSp. /θ/:

*PAUPERCELLU (for PAUPERCULU) > OSp. *pobreziello* > MSp. *pob-recillo*. The extension of the use of this infix is dealt with at the end of this section.

-ejo   This suffix is generally pejorative in value and has diminutive sense when applied to nouns: *animalejo* 'wretched creature', *calleja* 'alley', *lugarejo* 'tin-pot village', *medianejo* 'poor to middling'. It gives rise to a certain number of lexicalizations: *candilejas* 'footlights'. The Latin antecedent of *-ejo*, -ŬLUS, was attached directly to nouns in -US and -A (e.g. FLAMMA→ FLAMMULA) but to other nouns by means of the infix -(Î)C- (PAUPER→PAUPERCULUS). In this respect, -ŬLUS was like -ĔLLUS (see *-illo* above) and the two suffixes were probably also similar in their affectionate/diminutive value. However, unlike -ĔLLUS, -ŬLUS was atonic (see 2.3.1), and in the case of nouns in -US and -A there was a strong tendency in spoken Latin to re-place atonic -ŬLUS with tonic -ĔLLUS: ROTA→ROTULA 'little wheel' > ROTELLA (> *rodilla* 'kneecap' > 'knee'). Where -ŬLUS continued to be productive (i.e. when combined with the infix -ÎC-: -ÎCŬLUS), it lent itself to frequent lexicalization, including cases where the suffixed form displaced the original base-form, which thus lost all affectionate/diminutive value: OVICULA (for OVIS) 'sheep', AURICULA (for AURIS) 'ear', APICULA (for APIS) 'bee' (whence *oveja, oreja, abeja*). The change in value, from affectio-nate to derogatory, is already apparent in Old Spanish, where *-ejo* has a value similar to that which it has in the modern language.

-uelo   is now most frequently pejorative in tone and may have diminutive value: *autorzuelo* 'insignificant writer', *ojuelos* 'mean little eyes', *gentezuela* 'petty riff-raff', *gordezuelo* 'nastily small and fat'. It easily lends itself to lexicalization: *habichuela* 'French bean', *hoyuelo* 'dimple'. Its Latin antecedent, -ŎLUS, was at first inherently atonic (see 2.3.1) and was applied to forms which displayed hiatus between the two final syllables: FILIUS→FILIOLUS, FLUVIUS→FLUVIOLUS. Under such phonological conditions, spoken Latin transferred the stress from the antepenultimate to the penultimate syllable (see 2.3.1, end), thus converting the suffix from atonic to tonic and ensuring its continued identity (FILIOLU > *hijuelo* 'offspring'). The suffix *-uelo* was very frequent in Old Spanish and apparently retained the affectionate value of its Latin ancestor. During the Golden Age, it continues to be well represented, but then declines in frequency and acquires its current predominantly pejorative tone. It has already been remarked that *-uelo* is often attached to its base by means of the infix *-(e)z*, borrowed from structures like OSp. *simpleziello*: *ladronzuelo* 'little thief'.

-ete   has above all a jocular tone (making it especially open to ironic use) and generally diminutive value: *comedieta* 'insubstantial little play', *curete* 'jolly old priest', *pillete* 'young rascal', *tacañete* 'pretty stingy'. It appears particularly frequently in lexicalized forms: *boquete* 'hole', *camioneta* 'van', *chincheta* 'drawing pin', *salmonete* 'red mullet'. This suffix has the same (obscure) origin as *-ito* but has reached Spanish as a result of borrowing of French/Occitan/Catalan words in *-et*. It may appear with the infix which originated in -ICELLUS (*trenecete* 'a joke of a train'), but may not be applied to bases with absolute freedom.

-uco   has pejorative tone and diminutive value, where it appears (albeit infrequently) in the standard language: *casuca* 'mean little house', *frailuco* 'petty little friar'. It gives rise to occasional lexicalized forms: *hayucos* 'beech mast'. By contrast, in the Cantabria region, this suffix is the commonest affectionate morpheme. Its origin is uncertain, but it may be a variant of *-ico*, on the pattern of other suffixes which share the same consonantal pillar combined with different vowels (e.g. *-azo, -izo, -uzo*).

-ucho   is (like *-uco*) pejorative in tone and often diminutive in value: *aldeúcha* 'miserable little village', *animalucho* 'wretched creature', *feúcho* 'rather ugly', *medicucho* 'tenth-rate doctor', *tabernucha* 'grotty little bar'. It provides only occasional lexicalizations: *aguilucho* 'eaglet'. Its origin is unclear, as is its history in Spanish.

-ón   As applied to words denoting or referring to people, this suffix is generally pejorative, and augmentative in the sense that it implies an 'increase' or 'excess' of some quality: *feón* 'very ugly', *maricón* 'pansy', *mujerona* 'hefty great woman', *sargentona* 'bossy woman', *valentón* 'boastful', *zampón* 'very greedy'. As applied to non-personal concepts, *-ón* still implies 'excess' and is pejorative in tone, except where 'excess' can be interpreted as desirable: *caserón* 'great big house', *gotón* 'big drop', *novelón* 'boringly long novel'. There are many cases of lexicalization of words containing *-ón: abejón* 'drone', *pimentón* 'paprika', *velón* 'oil lamp'; however, a number of lexicalized cases show that *-ón* may have diminutive value: *cordones* 'shoelaces', *ratón* 'mouse', *tapón* 'plug, stopper', *terrón* 'clod of earth; sugar lump'.

The notion of 'excess' was present in the Latin antecedent, -ŌNE, of this suffix (e.g. NĀSŌ, NĀSŌNIS 'big-nosed') and probably also the pejorative tone which springs from the notion of excess. However, we have already seen (4.14.2.1) that *-ón* extended its role to form lexical derivatives of various types. As an affective suffix, *-ón* may now be added with considerable (but not complete) freedom to a wide range of bases.

-azo   is similar to *-ón* in its derogatory tone and its 'augmentative' value: *acentazo* 'heavy, unpleasant accent', *broncazo* 'big row', *olaza* 'threatening wave'. Again like *-ón*, its pejorative note may be replaced by an approving tone where 'excess' is seen as desirable: *bodaza* 'slap-up wedding', *torazo* 'fine big bull'. There are significant numbers of lexicalizations: *barcaza* 'barge', *espinazo* 'backbone'.

As Malkiel (1959) shows, this suffix originates in Lat. -ĀTĬo and is to be regarded as historically separate from the homophonous -*azo* 'blow', which descends from -ĀCEU (see 4.14.2.1). As the examples given show, derogatory/augmentative *-azo* has a feminine counterpart *-aza*, whereas *-azo* 'blow' does not. However, both suffixes have been frequent throughout the history of Spanish and remain fairly highly productive.

-ote   is almost always pejorative in tone and 'augments' the concept expressed by the base to which it is attached: *frescote* 'cheeky devil', *machote* 'tough guy', *palabrota* 'swear-word', *seriote* 'glum'. It gives rise to frequent lexicalizations: *barrote* 'bar (of cage, etc.)', *camarote* 'cabin (in ship)', *capota* '(woman's) bonnet; hood (of car)'. The suffix *-ote* appears to have entered Spanish by borrowing from Gallo-Romance (or was extracted from individual borrowings of French/Occitan words ending in *-ot*). If it indeed has Gallo-Romance origins, we should note the change of sense from 'diminutive' in Gallo-Romance to 'pejorative/augmentative' in Spanish.

-aco   is pejorative in tone and appears to convey no connotation of size: *libraco* 'rotten old book', *pajarraco* 'ugly bird'. It is a relatively unproductive suffix whose obscure origins may lie, like those of *-uco*, in vocalic variation on the theme represented by *-ico*.

-acho   is similarly pejorative and only occasionally connotes 'increase' of the concept indicated by the base: *covacha* 'nasty cave', *poblacho* 'dump of a village', *populacho* 'common herd', *ricacho* 'filthy rich'. The suffix *-acho* may have the same origin as pejorative *-azo* but have entered Spanish via the Mozarabic dialect (where -ātīo > /-átʃo/). At all events, it is today relatively infrequent and unproductive.

-ajo   is strongly pejorative: *cintajo* 'tawdry ribbon', *latinajos* 'dog Latin', *pequeñajo* 'runtish', *trapajo* 'tatter'. It frequently gives rise to lexicalizations: *cascajos* 'rubble', *estropajo* 'scourer', *rodaja* '(round) slice'. It probably descends from -ACŬLUS, where -A- originally belonged to the base and -C- is the infix which in Latin linked certain bases to diminutive suffixes (see *-ejo*, and *-illo* above). Alternatively, *-ajo* may represent a variant of *-ejo* and/or *-ujo*.

-ujo   is always pejorative and occasionally diminutive: *blandujo* 'soggy', *ramujo, ramuja* 'dead wood', *tapujos* 'jiggery-pokery'. It is of limited productivity and its origins are similar to those of *-ajo*.

Spanish has a considerable number of other pejorative suffixes, but which are quite unproductive, in some cases appearing with no more than a single base. These include *-ángano* (*curángano* 'wretched priest'), *-ango* (*querindango* 'pathetic lover'), *-astre* (*pillastre* 'miserable young scoundrel'), *-astro* (*camastro* 'miserable bed'), *-engue* (*blandengue* 'contemptibly feeble [person]'), *-ingo* (*señoritingo* 'contemptible young gentleman'), *-orio* (*papelorios* 'rubbishy papers'), *-orrio* (*villorrio* 'tenth-rate village'), *-orro* (*chistorro* 'crude joke'), *-ute* (*franchute* 'Frog [= Frenchman]'), *-uza* (*gentuza* 'rabble, scum').

It should be noted that affective suffixes (and, to a much lesser extent, the suffixes responsible for lexical derivation [4.14.2.1]) may appear in sequences of two or more items joined to a single base. Such sequences usually consist of suffixes with the same or similar affective quality: *chiquitillo* 'little boy', *chiquitín* 'tiny', *riachuelo* 'insignificant stream', *valentonazo* 'utterly boastful man'. Where there is an apparent conflict of affective values, it is usually the case that the first suffix combines with the base to form a lexicalization and only the second retains affective value: *saloncito* 'attractive little room', *caperucita* 'charming little hood'.

The appearance (and origin) of the infix *-(e)c/z-* has been noted (see *-illo*, *-ejo*, above). Although it originated between -ĔLLUS and a base ending otherwise than in -US or -A, and continues in such forms (e.g. *florecilla*), this infix has extended its use in the course of time in two ways; firstly, there are cases where the infix has come to be used before other appreciative suffixes (*ladronzuelo*, *florecita*); and secondly, there are many cases in which the infix has come to be used with bases ending in /o/ or /a/: *manecita*, *huertecillo*, *pueblecito*, *viejecito*, etc. The latter forms are often ones in which the base displays a diphthong in either the final or the penultimate syllable, but are far from universal in the Spanish-speaking world; in general, American and Canarian Spanish prefers forms without infix (*manita*, *huertito*, *pueblito*, *viejito*).

For further discussion of the history of the 'diminutives' from the Middle Ages, see Náñez 1973. For additional detail on the current value of the suffixes considered here, see Alemany 1920, Alonso 1935, Alvar & Pottier 1983: 363–80, Gooch 1970, from the last of whom a number of glosses have been taken.

4.14.3 Composition

Creation of new vocabulary by compounding two or more lexemes is today a relatively frequent process in Spanish. Such composition reveals differing degrees of fusion between the contributing elements, ranging from simple juxtaposition (where the second element modifies the first, e.g. *tren correo* 'mailtrain', *ciudad dormitorio* 'dormitory town, bedroom community') through union without modification (e.g. *sordomudo* 'deaf and dumb', *abrelatas* 'tin opener', *tocadiscos* 'record-player'), union via modification to /i/ of the final vowel of the first element (e.g. *machihembra* 'tongue and groove', *rojiblanco* 'red and white'), to parasynthetic composition, in which two lexemes are compounded at the same time as a suffix is added (e.g. *estadounidense* 'American', *sietemesino* 'seven-month'). The classification adopted here is based upon the grammatical function of the words which enter into the compound and examples will be drawn from the various types of compounding just mentioned.

Noun + noun.   It is normal for the second noun to modify the first: *perro guardián* 'guard dog', *hombre rana* 'frogman', *buque-hospital* 'hospital ship', *aguamiel* 'mead', *telaraña* 'spider's web', *zarzamora* 'blackberry (bush)'. In *aguanieve* 'sleet', *machihembra* 'tongue and groove', *puerco espín* 'porcupine', the two elements are coordinated rather than showing subordination of one (the second) to the other. Parasynthetic composition can be seen in *salpimentar* 'to season'.

Noun + adjective.   This combination produces, on the one hand, co-ordinated nominal expressions (e.g. *aguardiente* 'eau-de-vie', *bancarrota* 'bankruptcy', *camposanto* 'cemetery', *guardia civil* 'civil guard', *Nochebuena* 'Christmas Eve') and, on the other, a wide range of adjectival expressions in which the second element is syntactically subordinated to the first (e.g. *barbirrojo* 'red-bearded', *cariancho* 'broad-faced', *cejijunto* 'bushy-browed', *corniabierto* 'wide-horned', *cuellilargo* 'long-necked', *maniabierto* 'open-handed', *ojinegro* 'black-eyed', *patizambo* 'knock-kneed', *peliagudo* 'thorny [problem]', *puntiagudo* 'pointed', *rabicorto* 'short-tailed'; *cabizbajo* 'crestfallen' no doubt represents a modification of earlier **cabezibajo*, which accords with this pattern).

Adjective + noun.   In this case, we find coordinated expressions which function as nouns: *bajamar* 'low tide', *cortocircuito* 'short circuit', *cortometraje* 'short film', *extremaunción* 'extreme unction', *mediodía* 'midday'.

Adjective + adjective.   The result of composition (inevitably of coordinating type) between two adjectives may give rise to a new adjective (*agridulce* 'bitter-sweet', *rojiblanco* 'red and white [striped]', *sordomudo* 'deaf and dumb', *verdinegro* 'dark green'), or to a noun (*altibajos* 'vicissitudes', *claroscuro* 'ciaroscuro').

Verb + noun.   This combination, in which the verb is imperative or present indicative and the noun functions as its direct object, has always constituted a frequent type of composition in Spanish: *abrelatas* 'tin opener', *aguafiestas* 'spoilsport', *cortaplumas* 'penknife', *cortafuego* 'fire-break', *espantapájaros* 'scarecrow', *guardacostas* 'coastguard', *guardarropa* 'wardrobe', *hincapié* 'firm footing', *pasatiempo* 'pastime', *picamaderos* 'woodpecker', *portaaviones* 'aircraft carrier', *portavoz* 'spokesperson', *rompecabezas* 'puzzle', *rompehielos* 'icebreaker', *sacacorchos* 'corkscrew', *saltamontes* 'grasshopper', *tragaperras* 'fruit machine'. Less frequently, the noun of the compound does not function as direct object of the verb, but has one of a variety of other roles: *cortafrío* 'cold chisel', *girasol* 'sunflower', *trotaconventos* 'go-between'.

Pronoun + verb.   This type is rare, but appears in the very common expression *quehacer* 'chore'.

Verb + verb. Such coordinated combinations, with or without the copula /i/, provide new nouns: *duermevela* 'the state of being half-asleep', *pasapasa* 'sleight of hand', *de quitaipón* 'detachable', *vaivén* 'swaying; bustle'.

Syntagmatic compounds. These compounds, all with nominal function, originate in a variety of sequences of words, as they occur in connected speech: *ciempiés* 'centipede', *correveidile ~ correvedile* 'gossip', *hazmerreír* 'laughingstock', *metomentodo* 'busybody', *padrenuestro* 'Lord's Prayer', *tentemozo* 'prop', *tentempié* 'snack'.

In addition to the types of composition discussed, we find a further type, which is of recent origin and now relatively frequent, and which represents a position intermediate between composition and prefixation. A 'prefixoid' (an element typically ending in /o/, but also in /i/ or /e/, and usually derived through writing from a Greek or Latin noun or adjective) is combined with a second element, which may be an inherited or borrowed word. It has been suggested (Pratt 1980: 186–9) that the profusion of such formations is one manifestation of the influence of English on the modern Spanish language. The 'prefixoids' involved include *aero-:* (*aerofotografía* 'aerial photography'), *ambi-:* (*ambigenérico* 'ambigeneric'), *archi-:* (*archiconocido* 'known by all'), *auto-:* (*autorretrato* 'self-portrait'), *bio-* (*biomecánica* 'biomechanics'), *electro-:* (*electrodomésticos* 'electrical household appliances'), *euro-:* (*eurocomunista* 'Euro-communist'), *ferro-:* (*ferroníquel* 'ferronickel'), *filo-:* (*filosoviético* 'admiring of the Soviet Union'), *hidro-:* (*hidroelectricidad* 'hydroelectricity'), *macro-:* (*macroempresa* 'big business'), *micro-:* (*microfilm* 'microfilm'), *mono-:* (*monocarril* 'monorail'), *moto-:* (*motosegadora* 'motor scythe'), *multi-:* (*multigrado* 'multigrade'), *núcleo-:* (*núcleo-electricidad* 'nuclear energy'), *poli-:* (*polideportivo* 'sports hall'), *proto-:* (*prototipo* 'prototype'), *radio-:* (*radiofaro* 'radio beacon'), *semi-:* (*semidesnudo* 'half-naked'), *tele-:* (*teledirigido* 'remote controlled', *telediario* 'TV news bulletin'), *termo-:* (*termonuclear* 'thermonuclear'), *tri-:* (*tricolor* 'three-coloured'), *zoo-:* (*zoogeografía* 'zoogeography').

5
Semantics

The development of the meaning of words is an important part of the history of a language, and it can be argued that of all the elements of language, meaning is least resistant to change. Yet the semantic history of Spanish words has received relatively little attention from scholars. An important source of information is Corominas & Pascual 1980–, but etymological dictionaries such as this do not give systematic and consistent detail on the developing meaning of the words of the language, let alone of the causes of change. In the absence of a full-scale historical dictionary of Spanish (the Spanish Academy's *Diccionario histórico de la lengua española* [Real Academia Española 1972–] has not yet reached the letter B–), any discussion of its semantic development is inevitably incomplete and is likely to be at least partially inaccurate.

Existing historical grammars of Spanish lack chapters dealing exclusively or predominantly with semantic development and what follows is an (admittedly provisional) attempt to fill this identifiable gap. It should also be made clear that there are no 'rules' of semantic development which might be comparable with statements of, say, phonological development; examples of semantic change remain just that: examples. The structure of the discussion follows Ullmann's (1962) account of meaning-change, distinguishing between its causes, its nature, and its consequences.

5.1 Causes of semantic change

Since the appearance of Ogden and Richards's now classic treatment of meaning (1923), it has been accepted that there is no direct relationship between the words (or symbols) of language and the things and events of the 'real world'. This relationship is indirect and mediated by the mental constructs (or concepts) by which we represent the world to ourselves. It is the interrelationship between symbol and concept (wherein lies the essence of 'meaning') that falls within the domain of linguistics and any change in this relationship constitutes an instance of semantic change. The relationship between symbol and concept is possibly more unstable than other aspects of language and its disruption may be caused by any of a number of factors, of which Ullmann (1962) distinguishes the following six.

5.1.1   Linguistic causes

Changes of meaning may be occasioned by the frequent collocation of two or more words. That is, if words frequently occur together in the same speech-context, (part of) the meaning of one may be transferred to the other, and eventually this transferred sense may come to belong to the 'receiving' word even in the absence of the 'donating' word. It is well known that many of the negative words of Romance were originally positive in sense but acquired their negative value by frequent collocation with the negative particle NON and its descendants. In the Latin of Spain and some other areas, the phrase HOMINE NATU, literally 'a man born', first acquired the sense 'anyone (at all)'; in combination with NŌN, it therefore meant 'no one (at all)', and this sense eventually predominated even in the absence of NON. Early Old Spanish shows examples of *omne nado* in the sense 'no one', but through ellipsis (see 5.2.4) *nado* alone is then found with this meaning. Subsequent modification of the form of *nado* (see 3.5.5) produces OSp. and MSp. *nadie*.

More widely in spoken Latin, a parallel phrase REM NĀTA (for the persistence of final -M here, see 2.5.4) meant at first 'anything (at all)'. At first only in conjunction with NŌN, but eventually even in the absence of NŌN, it meant 'nothing (at all)', and from this now negative phrase descend the various Old Spanish words with this meaning : ellipsis of REM produces OSp, and MSp. *nada*, but the alternative ellipsis of NĀTA produced *ren* in the Navarro-Aragonese region. In general, Lat. RĒS (Acc. REM) 'thing' was replaced in spoken Latin by CAUSA, and this replacement intermittently included the phrase REM NĀTA, producing *CAUSA NĀTA, whence OSp. *cosa (nada)*, with the same transfer of negative sense as in the case of (REM) NĀTA > *nada*. In recent Spanish, the phrase *en absoluto* has undergone similar negative development, so that its most frequent meaning is now 'not at all'.

5.1.2   Historical causes

Any change of a concept which is not accompanied by a corresponding change of symbol constitutes a semantic change. Since all concepts (whether they refer to things, institutions, abstract notions, etc.) are subject to at least gradual change, and since the symbols (or words) which reflect these concepts are slower to be replaced (or may not be replaced at all), it follows that any (non-linguistic) historical development is likely to provoke a semantic change. Many examples of this kind of shift are trivial or well known (thus, the symbol *coche* continued to be used [at least in Spain] even though the concept it represented evolved from 'horse-drawn vehicle' to '[motor-propelled] car'), but others may be less easy to reconstruct, often because of the remoteness in time of the change concerned. Examples of semantic change motivated by evolution of the concepts concerned (and ultimately by the evolution of their referents, the things and events of the 'real world' to which the concepts correspond) include the following:

> Latin created the form *CALCEA (derived from CALCEUS 'shoe') to indicate 'stockings', newly-adopted from the Germanic north. During the Middle Ages, the garment became longer and longer until it stretched from feet to waist; the descendant of Lat. *CALCEA (OSp. *calça*) now therefore meant approximately 'tights', and this sense can be seen in *CMC* 3085–6: *calças de paño en sus camas metió,/ sobr' ellos unos çapatos que a grant huebra son.* Later development of the garment, its sixteenth-century division into two parts, did necessitate certain changes of name: the lower portion, from thighs to feet (approximately 'hose') was specified as *medias calças*, later abbreviated to *medias*, a label which continues to be applied to 'stockings', although now only to a women's garment; meanwhile the upper part, from waist to thighs, continued to be labelled by means of the term which once indicated the undivided garment, although the term now meant 'breeches' and had a more specific equivalent (*calçones*). For these changes in the sense of *calzas*, see Jaberg 1926.
>
> In accordance with its etymon (Ar. *qâḍī*), Sp. *alcalde* when first borrowed meant 'judge (according to Islamic law)'. The functions of the post were subsequently broadened to include administrative activities, so that in Golden Age Spanish the term *alcalde* indicates an official who is both magistrate and mayor. Since that time, the judicial functions of the post have been lost and the term now means exclusively 'mayor'.
>
> *Alférez* (< Ar. *fâris* 'horseman') Spanish 'horseman' > 'best horseman (of a squadron)' > Golden Age Spanish 'standardbearer' > 'second lieutenant'.
>
> *Alguacil* (< Ar. *wasîr* 'chief minister') OSp. 'governor of a town in Islamic Spain' > OSp. 'magistrate' > GA 'constable' > MSp. 'minor court official; town-hall messenger'.
>
> *Barbero* (a late medieval derivative of *barba* 'beard'), like corresponding words elsewhere in Europe, indicates a 'barber/surgeon/dentist' until at least the eighteenth century, later becoming limited to the sense 'barber'.

5.1.3   Social causes

A change in a word's meaning may take place when the word ceases to be part of the vocabulary of all or most speakers of the language concerned and becomes restricted to the technical vocabulary of a particular social group (typically a trade, a profession or an interest-group). When this happens, there is normally an accompanying restriction of the word's meaning. Thus a form *ORDINIĀRE 'to organize' came to be restricted to farming language and its sense was restricted (via 'organizing the chores of the cowshed'?) to that of 'to milk'. Similarly, *afeitar* (a borrowing from

Latin AFFECTĀRE 'to devote oneself') was restricted first to the sense OSp. 'to adorn, beautify', then to the Golden Age 'to beautify with makeup; to shave', and later to the latter sense only. *Botar*, a medieval borrowing from Old French, at first has the general sense 'to throw', which the verb retains in some varieties of Spanish (including most American varieties); however, Peninsular Spanish has seen its restriction to the meaning 'to launch', no doubt as the word ceased to be part of the common vocabulary and became limited to that of boatbuilders. However, some other (metaphorical) senses of *botar* also survive, as well as intransitive 'to bounce'.

The reverse process, by which a word broadens its meaning as it passes from the language of a social sub-group into that of the whole community, is also widely attested. From the language of gaming, where Sp. *azar* (< Ar. *zahr* 'dice') meant at first an 'unfortunate throw of the dice', the word has passed into more general use, widening its sense to that of 'misfortune' or 'chance (lucky or unlucky)'. *Armario*, when first borrowed from Latin in the Middle Ages, maintained its connection with *arma* and meant 'armoury'; its sense was soon widened to its current value of 'cupboard'.

5.1.4 Psychological causes

Changes of meaning which spring from the mental state of particular speakers, who have creatively extended the sense of words by using them metaphorically, are manifold in language and this process will be considered in more detail in 5.2.1. However, there is a specific psychological cause of semantic change which is particularly powerful (and which has been studied in detail): **taboo**. 'Taboo' is a term which indicates a prohibition on the mention of a particular word, for a variety of reasons which vary from culture to culture but which show some inter-cultural constants (see, for example, Meillet 1921). Since the concept related to a tabooed word nevertheless has to be referred to in some fashion, a frequent solution is to resort to a **euphemism**, that is, to a word or expression which for some reason can replace the tabooed item. It follows that a word used euphemistically undergoes semantic change in the form of an addition to its earlier sense or senses, but it is also probably the case that once a word's 'euphemistic' sense comes to be widely used, this fact prevents (or at least militates against) the word's use in its earlier sense, since speakers are likely to be unwilling to risk their non-euphemistic intention being interpreted in a euphemistic way. In other words, an expression which has acquired a new, euphemistic, sense is likely to rapidly lose its earlier, non-euphemistic, sense or senses.

Examples of euphemism are frequently due to one or other of three types of taboo: fear taboo, delicacy taboo, or decency taboo.

5.1.4.1   Fear taboo

The fear which forbids use of certain words in a particular culture (and which brings about a change of sense in their euphemistic replacements) is often of a religious or superstitious kind. It is well known that the prohibition placed upon the Jews against the use of the name of God led to the use of euphemisms such as that translated into English as 'Lord', or into Spanish as 'Señor'. But it is not solely the names of supernatural beings which are subject to taboo; the names of perfectly 'worldly' concepts may be similarly tabooed if there is an association in speakers' minds between some 'worldly' referent and some feared supernatural referent. The classic case is that of the weasel, which in some cultures, including many Western European ones, is seen as endowed with certain supernatural forces, mostly evil. In most of the Romance-speaking world, the Latin name of the weasel, MUSTĒLA, has been replaced by euphemisms, which have consequently undergone dramatic meaning-change. Within the Peninsula (see Menéndez Pidal 1964a: 396–405), *mustela* remains in Catalan and in one area of Southern Galicia, together with (originally) affectionate derivatives of the same base in Northern León and Western Santander (*mostolilla*). Elsewhere, we find similarly propitiating terms: affectionate derivatives of DOMINA 'lady' in the West (Ptg. *doninha*, Gal. *don(oc)iña, donicela*, Leonese *donecilla*, etc.), *paniquesa* (no doubt referring to the animal's colouring) in the northeast (NE Castile, Navarre, Aragon), *comadreja* (an originally affectionate derivative of *comadre* 'neighbour') in most of Castile, Murcia and Andalusia (whence its introduction to Spanish America), together with many other forms in Asturias and Santander.

Taboos on animal names are not infrequent. Lat. VULPĒS 'fox' scarcely survives; in Spain it is replaced by a derivative VULPĒCULA, originally affectionate and no doubt propitiatory, but soon lexicalized and surviving as *gulpeja* until the fourteenth century. Its first euphemistic replacement (*raposa ~ rabosa*), referring to the animal's bushy tail, was itself largely displaced by *zorra*, probably a nominalization of a borrowing from Basque meaning 'lazy'. In Andalusia we find euphemistic use of personal names, such as *juanica, maría, maría garcía, mariquita*.

Other fear taboos include avoidance of the words meaning 'left', owing to the popular association between this concept and evil or the Devil. Of the Latin terms for 'left', LAEVUS, SCAEVUS, SINISTER, only the latter survives, partially, in Romance; in Old Spanish it appears as *siniestro* (with /ie/ under the influence of its antonym *diestro*). Thereafter, it is retained only in the sense 'sinister', reflecting the association just mentioned, and in the sense 'left' is replaced by another borrowing from Basque, namely *izquierdo*. It will be noted that foreign borrowings may serve the same purpose as euphemisms in providing replacements for tabooed words.

5.1.4.2 Delicacy taboo

The tendency to avoid words referring to concepts considered disagreeable may also lead to the use of euphemisms. The concepts concerned include those associated with disease, death, mental or physical infirmity, crime, etc. Examples of Spanish words which have acquired their current sense through the effects of delicacy taboo include the following:

> *Cretino* 'cretin' is a borrowing from French and originates in a dialectal form of Fr. *chrétien* 'Christian', used euphemistically.
>
> *Tullido* 'crippled' is the only surviving modern Spanish part of the Old Spanish verb *toller ~ tullir* 'to take away, deprive'.
>
> *Matar* 'to kill' may owe its origin to the euphemistic use of a verb whose original meaning was different. Late Lat. MATTUS 'stupid, stupefed' may have served as the base of a derived verb *MATTĀRE 'to stun, stupefy', which then underwent meaning-change through its euphemistic use.

Modern Spanish has a host of expressions which may be used euphemistically to express the notion 'to kill': *cargarse a uno, dar el pasaporte, dar el paseo, liquidar, eliminar*, some of which may be calques of similar English euphemisms. Similarly, we find many terms used as euphemisms for 'to steal, rob': *coger, pillar, apañar, aliviar, trabajar, raspar*. Expressions which in the same way may mean 'to die' include *reventar, estirar la pata*, etc. For these euphemisms, see Beinhauer 1968.

5.1.4.3 Decency taboo

The motive for semantic change in this case is the avoidance of mention of words related to sex, and to certain parts of the body and their functions. The following cases illustrate the semantic consequences of this kind of taboo:

> *Manceba* and *barragana* 'concubine' originally meant 'young woman', as can be seen by reference to their masc. counterparts *mancebo* 'youth' and OSp. *barragán* 'id.'
>
> *Fulana* 'lover, concubine, prostitute' (cf. *fulano* 'so-and-so').
>
> *Ramera* 'prostitute' probably earlier meant 'inn-keeper's wife; (female) innkeeper'.
>
> *Buscona* 'prostitute' and *buscón* 'thief' are probably euphemistic derivatives of *buscar* 'to seek' whose original sense was 'seeker'.
>
> *Amiga* and *querida* 'mistress'.
>
> *Parir* 'to give birth' is increasingly avoided, when reference is to humans, in favour of euphemistic *dar a luz, alumbrar*.
>
> *Embarazada* originally 'encumbered' or *en estado* (a reduction of *en estado interesante*) often replace *preñada* 'pregnant'.
>
> *Aseo* and *servicio(s)* have euphemistically extended their sense as replacements for *retrete* 'lavatory'.

Religious and sexual oaths may also be subject to decency taboo, with the effect that another word (usually one which shares a syllable or more of its form with the tabooed item) may change its sense to enable it to replace the original oath. Thus *¡caracoles!* (lit. 'snails') may replace *¡carajo!* (lit. 'penis').

Further exemplification of the effects of taboo can be seen in Kany 1960.

5.1.5   Foreign influences which cause semantic change

Coexistence between two languages (typically in the form of their use by substantial numbers of bilingual individuals or in the form of frequent translation between them) may lead to modification of the meanings of words in either or both of the languages concerned. Where two words (one belonging to each of the languages concerned) are approximate translation equivalents, any additional meaning belonging to one of the words may be transferred to the other. **Semantic loan** of this kind has no doubt taken place in some degree between Spanish and each of the languages with which it has been in contact over the centuries, but two particular instances of foreign influence on the meaning of Spanish words (that of Arabic and English) have received particular attention and will be considered here.

Although, in the early centuries (eighth–tenth) of the Reconquest, bilingualism between Arabic and Castilian must have been limited to small numbers of individuals, the following period (late eleventh–fourteenth centuries) saw the expansion of Castile into territories where substantial numbers of Arabic-speakers continued to use their traditional language at the same time as learning Castilian. In the same period, translation of Arabic works, at first into Latin via the vernacular and then definitively into Castilian, became extremely frequent. The conditions for semantic loan were therefore more than satisfied and a good number of cases have been identified. Not all are beyond dispute, but there is reasonable evidence that the following words, all of Latin origin, acquired their sense through influence from Arabic (see Lapesa 1980: 154–7).

> *Adelantado* 'placed in front' > 'military governor of an overseas territory', in imitation of Ar. *muqaddam* 'placed in front; chief'.
> OSp. *casa* 'house' > 'town' through the influence of Ar. *dār* 'house; town' (although the sense 'town' has now been lost from *casa*).
> OSp. *correr* 'run' > 'depredate'; cf. Ar. *gāwara* 'run; depredate' (again, the acquired sense was later lost).
> *Criar* 'to feed, rear, educate' > 'to grow (hair, fur, feathers)'; cf. Ar. *rabba* 'id.'
> *Hidalgo* 'noble' < OSp. *fijodalgo* 'noble' (literally 'son of wealth'), by imitation of Arabic expressions containing *ibn* 'son of' and having metaphorical value (e.g. *ibn ad-dunyā* 'son of wealth; rich man').
> *Infante* 'son of the king', until the thirteenth century also 'son of a nobleman'; cf. Ar. *walad* 'child; son of the king'. In this case, after the semantic extension, the original sense ('child') was entirely lost.

Plata 'silver' (< *PLATTA 'flat') may have acquired its sense by semantic loan from Ar. *luǧayn* or *waraqā*, both 'lamina (i.e. a thin plate); silver'. The later, American-Spanish, development of the sense of this word to 'money' is a more 'normal' case of semantic development, through association of ideas.

OSp. *poridat* 'secrecy, intimacy' (< PŪRITĀTE 'purity') perhaps acquired this sense by loan from derivatives of Ar. *ḥalasa* 'to be pure'.

Semantic influence of English on Spanish is widely attested (see Pratt 1980: 160–76), and often condemned by purists. It is particularly evident in the case of paronyms (pairs of words, one belonging to each of the two languages, which are obviously related in form but which have different meanings), the 'false friends' of the unwary translator. In this case, semantic loan can be said to turn 'false friends' into 'true friends' or at least 'truer friends'. The following instances of semantic loan due to paronymy (not all equally frequent, but most now well established) are among the many that have been identified. Where there is a traditional term, with which the new form has entered into competition, it is given in brackets:

> *administración [gobierno]* 'administration, government', *agenda [orden del día]* 'agenda', *apartamento [piso]* 'flat, apartment', *arruinar [dañar, estropear]* 'to ruin', *ataque* 'attack (e.g. heart)', *base* '(military) base', *cereales* 'cereals (as generic)', *círculo [sector, ambiente]* 'circle', *complejo* 'complex (in the psychological and industrial sense)', *congelar* 'to freeze' (e.g. prices or salaries), *crucial [crítico]* 'crucial', *duplicar [copiar]* 'to duplicate', *editor [redactor]* '(newspaper) editor', *estudio* '(film or TV) studio', *factoría [fábrica]* 'factory', *fatiga* '(metal) fatigue', *firma [empresa]* 'firm', *flota* 'fleet (of cars)', *honesto [honrado]* 'honest', *humor [gracia]* 'humour', *ignorar [pasar por alto]* 'to ignore', *incidente [suceso]* 'incident', *liberar [libertar]* 'to liberate', *literalmente [al pie de la letra]* 'literally', *nativo [natural]* 'native', *permisivo* 'permissive', *planta* '(industrial) plant', the noun *plástico* 'plastic', *proceso [procedimiento]* 'process', *satélite* 'satellite (with reference to space technology, politics, or town planning)', *simple [sencillo]* 'simple', *soda [seltz]* 'soda(water)', *tanque* '(military) tank', *torpedo* '(naval) torpedo', *verificar [comprobar]* 'to verify'.

However, semantic loan from English is also evident in cases where no paronymy is involved, e.g. *cadena* 'chain (of shops)', *canal* '(TV) channel', *cumbre* 'summit (meeting)', *escoba* 'sweeper (in football)', *estrella* '(film, etc.) star', *mariposa* 'butterfly (in swimming)', *muestra* '(statistical) sample', *ventilar* 'to ventilate (an issue)'.

Semantic loan from English may also take the form of **loan translation** (or **calque**), in which the separate words of an English expression are individually translated, giving rise to new compounds, some of which have already been considered in 4.14.3, since it is possible in some cases that an English model is not involved. Such loan translations include compounds consisting of two nouns (*buque escuela* 'training ship', *perro guardián* 'guard dog', *ciudad dormitorio* 'dormitory town, bedroom community', *encuentro [en la] cumbre* 'summit meeting', *hombre rana* 'frogman', *horas punta* 'rush hour', *madre patria* 'motherland', *cine club* 'cine club', *misión rescate* 'rescue mission', *año luz* 'light year', *hora cero* 'zero hour', *tiempo récord* 'record time', *tren miniatura* 'miniature train'), compounds comprising verb + noun (*calientaplatos* 'plate warmer', *cortacésped* 'lawnmower', *limpiaparabrisas* 'windscreen-wiper(s)', *portaaviones* 'aircraft carrier', *rompehielos* 'icebreaker'), noun + adjective (*caja fuerte* 'strongbox', *elefante blanco* 'white elephant', *guerra fría* 'cold war', *mesa redonda* 'round table', *perro caliente* 'hotdog'), or adjective + noun (*próximo oriente* 'Near East', *tercer mundo* 'Third World', *tercer programa* 'Third Programme'). Such loans may also include more complex structures, such as noun + *de* + noun: *beso de la vida* 'kiss of life', *cruce de cebra* 'zebra crossing', *fuera de juego* 'offside', *máquina de coser* 'sewing machine', *tubo de ensayo* 'test tube'.

5.1.6   The need to name a new concept

As new concepts become current in a linguistic community, there simultaneously arises an evident requirement for a means of expressing the new concept. The solution may be to borrow a word from another language (sections 4.2–13 are primarily concerned with this solution), to create a new term through word-formation (see 4.14.1, 4.14.2.1, 4.14.3), or to extend the sense of an existing word. In the case of Spanish (as with many languages), it is often difficult to distinguish between the latter process and semantic loan, that is, to know whether an extension of sense occurred spontaneously in Spanish or whether it is due to imitation of an extension of sense which took place in another language. The only firm guide here is the date of first attestation of the extended sense in the language concerned. Thus it is likely that *platillo volante* is a loan translation of Eng. *flying saucer*, rather than an independent creation within Spanish. By contrast, it is clear that the developments *león* 'lion' > 'puma', *piña* 'pine-cone' > 'pineapple', *tigre* 'tiger' > 'jaguar' are not due to foreign models.

5.2   Types of semantic change

Ullmann (1962, based on Roudet 1921) classifies semantic changes according to two criteria; on the one hand, a distinction is made between those changes which originate in an association of meanings and those which originate in an association between word-forms; on the other hand, a contrast is drawn between those changes which are motivated by similarity (either of meaning or form) and those which stem from contiguity (either of meaning or form), where 'contiguity' indicates 'juxtaposition' in a broad sense, as when the meanings concerned refer to things which appear together in the real world or when the words concerned are frequently collocated. This classification may be stated (now adding labels to each of the four types of semantic change involved) thus:

Change based on:	Association of meanings	Association of word-forms
similarity	metaphor	popular etymology
contiguity	metonymy	ellipsis

5.2.1   Metaphor

Many words have acquired their current sense (or one or more of their current senses) by having been used at one time or another as metaphors. The metaphor is fundamentally a comparison, in which one concept (the one which the speaker essentially has in mind) is compared with another (which the speaker sees as having some similarity with the first). If the name of the second concept, as a result of this metaphorical process, is used to replace the name of the first concept and the metaphor gains acceptance in the linguistic community concerned, it follows that a new sense has come to be associated with an existing word.

While the literal (or traditional) sense of a word continues to be present alongside the metaphorical sense, the metaphor concerned may be regarded as a 'living' metaphor, unless the two senses come to be regarded as unrelated, in which case one is simply faced with an instance of polysemy (more than one sense attached to a single word). By contrast, where the traditional sense is abandoned and only the metaphorical sense survives, the metaphor is best described as 'dead' and is only recognizable as a metaphor in the light of historical information not normally available to the speaker. Thus, it is likely that the sense 'mountain-range' which belongs to *sierra* is the result of metaphorical use of *sierra* 'saw' (< SERRA 'id.'). But whether native speakers regard *sierra* 'mountain range' as a (living) metaphor, rather than a case of polysemy, is open to dispute.

Many types of metaphor have been recognized, of which the most frequent will be exemplified here. 'Anthropomorphic' metaphors transfer names of parts of the body to inanimate objects: *boca* 'mouth (of river)', *entrañas* 'bowels (of the earth)', *manecillas* 'hands (of clock)', *ojo* 'eye (of needle)', *pata* 'leg (of table)', etc. The reverse process is also common: *caja (del pecho)* '(rib-)cage', *globo (del ojo)* 'eyeball', *nuez (de la garganta)* 'Adam's apple', etc. The same process can be seen in a number of dead metaphors: *pierna* 'leg' < PĔRNA 'ham', OSp. *tiesta* 'head' (like Fr. *tête*, etc.) < TESTA '(flower) pot', *yema* 'tip (of the finger)' < GEMMA 'shoot (of plant)'.

Animal metaphors, in which animal names are applied to plants or inanimate objects, can be seen in *diente de león* 'dandelion', *pata de gallo* 'goose foot'; *araña* 'chandelier', *gato* 'jack', *gatillo* 'trigger', *grúa* '(mechanical) crane' (< OSp. *grúa* 'crane [ornith.]', later changed to *grulla*).

The metaphorical use of originally concrete terms to convey non-concrete (e.g. abstract) notions can be exemplified by: *coz* 'kick' (< CALCE 'heel'), *depender* 'to depend' (also 'hang' < DĒPENDERE 'hang'), *fuente (de ingresos)* 'source (of income)', *pensar* 'think' (< PĒNSĀRE 'to weigh (up)'), *sembrar (odios)* 'to sow (discord)'.

'Synaesthetic' metaphors, which allow adjectives associated with one corporeal sense to be used in connection with another, are as frequent in Spanish as in other languages: *voz fría* 'cold voice', *voz dulce* 'sweet voice', *sonidos penetrantes* 'piercing sounds', *colores chillones* 'loud colours', *chillido agudo* 'shrill cry', etc.

5.2.2   Metonymy

Unlike metaphor, which forges links between previously unrelated concepts, metonymy exploits previously existing links between the names of things which are already linked in the 'real world'. It may be defined as the process of applying to a concept the name of an already related concept. The types of relationship involved (and therefore the types of metonymy) are several.

Spatial metonymy, where the name of an object is applied to another which is in physical contiguity with it, can be seen in: *acera* 'pavement, sidewalk' (< OSp. *façera* 'façade [of a row of buildings facing a street or square]'), *cadera* 'hip' < *'buttock' (< VL CATHEGRA [CL CATHEDRA] 'chair'), *asiento* 'backside' (< 'seat'), *boca* 'mouth' (< BUCCA 'cheek'), *mejilla* 'cheek' (< MAXILLA 'jaw'), *carrillo* '(lower) cheek' (earlier 'jaw'). For the facial terms mentioned, and others, see Wright 1985.

Temporal metonymy allows shifts of sense along the temporal axis: *ahora* 'now' may also mean 'soon, presently'; *verano* ('summer') until the Golden Age meant 'late spring' (by contrast with *estío* 'summer') but has become synonymous with *estío*, which is now restricted to literary register; *almuerzo* means 'breakfast' in Old and Golden Age Spanish (as it still does in American and regional Peninsular Spanish) but in urban Peninsular Spanish has come to mean 'lunch'; *cena* 'dinner' descends from CENA 'main meal (taken at about 3 pm)'.

Synecdoche, the application of the name of part of a larger concept to the whole of that concept, or vice versa, can be regarded as a kind of metonymy: *almiar* 'haystack' (<[PERTICA] MEDIĀLE 'central pole', around which haystacks in Spain are commonly built), *boda* 'wedding' (<*'marriage vows' < VŌTA 'vows'), *césped* 'lawn' (<CAESPITE '[piece of] turf'), *cimientos* 'foundations' (<CAEMENTŌS 'building stones'), *puerto* 'harbour' (<PORTU 'harbour entrance').

Other types of metonymy include the use of a name of a substance to indicate something made from that substance (*alambre* 'wire' <*'bronze wire' < AERAMEN 'bronze[work]'), the use of proper nouns to indicate an associated product (*jerez, montilla, champán, coñac*, etc.), and the use of abstract terms to indicate some associated concrete notion (*cuenta* 'account, bill', *cura* 'priest', *encuadernación* 'binding [of a book]', *guardia* 'policeman').

5.2.3 Popular etymology

This process, which essentially changes the form of 'unmotivated' (i.e. structurally isolated) words in order to make them conform to pre-existing families of words to which they do not historically belong, may also result in some change of meaning, usually quite subtle. A well-known case is that of *vagabundo* 'tramp', which through popular etymology often appears in colloquial speech as *vagamundo*, thereby specifying its sense as 'one who wanders the world'. Similarly, when OSp. *berrojo* 'bolt' (<*VERRUCULU) was modified to *cerrojo*, by attraction to *cerrar* 'to close', its meaning was no doubt also modified, associating it exclusively with the closing of doors, etc. Other examples include *tinieblas* 'darkness' (<OSp. *tiniebras*), where association with *niebla* 'fog' has not only changed the form of the word but has arguably added the notion of 'fogginess' to that of 'darkness' in *tinieblas*, and *pulgar* 'thumb' (<OSp. *polgar*), where it may be that, as the form of the word became more like that of *pulga* 'flea', speakers have come to associate the meaning 'flea' with *pulgar* (perhaps envisaging the thumb as a suitable weapon for killing fleas).

5.2.4 Ellipsis

We have seen (5.1.1) that when two words are frequently collocated, the meaning of one may be added to that of the other. A further change is the deletion (or ellipsis) of one of the words, so that the other bears the whole semantic burden of the originally compound expression. A frequently observed effect of such change is that in a noun + adjective phrase the noun is deleted and the adjective thereby takes on the function and meaning of a noun: *ábrego* 'south wind' (<[VENTU] AFRICU 'African wind'), *aguijada* 'goad' (<[PERTICA] *AQUILEĀTA [for ACŪLEĀTA] 'sharpened pole'), *albér-chigo* 'clingstone peach' (<[MALU] PERSICU 'Persian fruit'), *almiar* 'hay-stack' (<[PERTICA] MEDIĀLE 'central pole'; see 5.2.2), *armiño* 'stoat; ermine' (<[MŪRE] ARMENIU 'Armenian mouse'), *avellana* 'hazelnut' (<[NUCE] ABELLĀNA 'nut from Abella [in Campania]'), *breva* 'early fig' (<[FĪCU] BIFERA 'figtree bearing fruit twice per year'), *campana* 'bell' (<[VĀSA] CAMPĀNA 'vessels from Campania'), *ciruela* 'plum' (<[PRŪNA] CĒREOLA 'wax-coloured plums'), etc.

5.3 Consequences of semantic change

Irrespective of the cause of a semantic change or the general type to which it belongs, if one examines the meanings of words before and after a change, one can observe two broad semantic effects. On the one hand, there may be modification of the range and complexity of meaning of the word concerned, while on the other, it may undergo a change in any affective nuances which it possesses.

5.3.1 Change of semantic range

One consequence of meaning-change is a movement from greater gener-ality to greater specificity or the reverse. It should be noted that the first of these movements is accompanied by an increase in the 'amount' of meaning conveyed, while the change towards greater generality is accompanied by a decrease in the 'amount' of meaning. In this context, 'amount' refers to the number of separately identifiable components which make up the total meaning of the word. Thus, as Lat. SECĀRE 'to cut' becomes more specific in sense and is restricted to the meaning 'to reap' (Sp. *segar*), additional components of meaning ('with a scythe, machine, etc.', 'appropriate to grass, corn, etc.') can be recognized in the word. By contrast, as STĀRE 'to stand' becomes more general in sense (>Sp. *estar*), it loses such compo-nents of its meaning as 'in vertical position'. In the following examples of increase in specificity and complexity, it will be noted that where a Latin word has been transmitted to Spanish by more than one channel, the learned form concerned usually retains the unrestricted Latin meaning (see 2.2.4).

> *Adobar* 'prepare (meat for sausage); to tan (leather)' <OSp. *adobar* 'prepare, provide with'.
> *Anegar* 'to drown' <ĒNECĀRE 'to kill (especially by strangling or stifling)'.
> *Ánsar* 'wild goose' <OSp. *ánsar* 'goose' (cf. Juan Manuel *ánsares bravos*) <VL ĀNSAR (CL ĀNSER) 'goose'.
> OSp. *arienço* 'a medieval coin/weight' <ARGENTEU '(made) of silver'.
> *Boda* 'wedding' <*'marriage-vows' <VŌTA 'vows'.
> *Bruma* 'mist, haze' <OSp. *bruma* 'winter' <BRŪMA 'id.'.

Cebo 'fodder; bait (for fishing)' < CIBU 'food'.

Colgar 'to hang' < COLLOCARE 'to place' (cf. the unrestricted learned term *colocar* 'to place').

Comulgar 'to take communion' < COMMUNICĀRE 'to communicate' (cf. the unrestricted learned term *comunicar* 'to communicate').

Cuero 'leather' < CORIU 'skin (of people and animals)' (although some varieties of Spanish, especially American, retain the unrestricted sense).

Cuñado 'brother-in-law' < OSp. *cuñado* 'relation by marriage' < COGNĀTU 'blood-relation'.

Dehesa 'open pasture' < DĒFĒNSA 'forbidden (land)' (i.e. 'forbidden to huntsmen'?).

Guisar 'to cook' (or, with even further specialized sense, 'to casserole') < OSp. *guisar* 'to prepare, arrange' (derived from *guisa* 'manner').

Ponzoña 'poison' < POTIŌNE 'drink, potion'.

Rezar 'to pray' < OSp. *rezar* 'to recite, say aloud' < RECITĀRE 'id.' (cf. the unrestricted learned term *recitar* 'to recite').

Siesta 'siesta' < OSp. *siesta* 'mid-day heat' < SEXTA (HŌRA) 'sixth (hour)' (cf. the unrestricted sense of the learned numeral *sexta* 'sixth').

Tañer 'to play (an instrument)' < OSp. *tañer* 'to touch; to play (a musical instrument)' < TANGERE 'to touch'.

The reverse process, generalization of sense with loss of complexity, is probably rarer, but nevertheless provides frequent examples in the development of Spanish. Again, any learned correlates will normally retain the Latin sense, in this case a more specific sense.

Asir 'to grasp', as a derivative of *asa* 'handle', earlier meant 'to grasp by the handle'.

Barro 'mud' until the Golden Age meant only '(potter's) clay', a specific sense also still available in the word.

Compañero 'companion' < OSp. *compaño* 'id.' < Late Lat. COMPĀNIŌNE 'table companion' (lit. 'one who eats bread with another').

Cosa 'thing' < CAUSA 'cause; matter, question' (cf. learned *causa* 'cause').

Dinero 'money' < DĒNĀRIU '(a specific) coin'.

Grande 'large in size, morally great, etc.' < GRANDE 'large in size'.

Hallar 'to find' < AFFLĀRE 'to breathe out', perhaps via the meanings 'to follow the scent' and 'to find the prey', with reference originally to hunting-dogs.

Lograr 'to succeed' < OSp. *lograr* 'to enjoy the fruits of', perhaps via 'to enjoy, possess' and 'to acquire' (e.g. *lograr los deseos* 'to achieve one's desires', whence *lograr hacer*, etc.).

Palabra 'word' < PARABOLA 'comparison, allegory', probably via 'phrase, sentence'.

Parientes 'relatives' < OSp. *parientes* 'parents'.

A particular sub-group of cases of meaning-generalization is constituted by instances in which a proper noun has acquired the status of a common noun. Some examples are trivial and well-known (e.g. *un donjuan, un quijote*), but others require historical information for their elucidation. Thus, the nineteenth-century expression *quevedos* 'spectacles' owes its origin to portraits of Quevedo wearing spectacles, while *asesino* 'murderer' descends from Ar. *ḥaššāšī* lit. 'hashish-drinkers', the name of an eleventh-century Muslim sect with the reputation for butchering opponents.

5.3.2   Change of affectivity

The emotive overtones which accompany many words (revealing an attitude, on the part of the speaker, of hostility, contempt, approval, fondness, etc., towards the concept concerned) are as subject to change as any other semantic component, and in broad terms may show development of either pejorative or favourable sense.

Development of pejorative meaning may be the result of various processes, including use of the word as a euphemism (see 5.1.4), association of ideas, prejudice, etc. For example:

> *Algarabia* 'gibberish; uproar' < Ar. *'arabíya* 'the Arabic language'.
> *Cautivo* (a semi-learned descendant of CAPTĪVU 'captive') underwent a series of changes, in adjectival use, of increasingly pejorative tone: 'captive' > 'wretched' > 'wicked, evil' (its commonest Golden Age sense, perhaps reinforced by Italian *cattivo* 'bad'), although the meaning 'captive' has alone survived.
> *Necio* 'foolish' < NESCIU 'ignorant'.
> *Simple* 'simple, half-witted' (alongside other senses) < SIMPLU 'simple'.
> *Siniestro* 'sinister' < OSp. 'left' < SINISTRU 'id.' (see 5.1.4.1).
> *Villano* 'boorish' (derived from the descendant of VĪLLA 'farm') < 'rustic' < 'rural'.

The opposite process, development of favourable sense, is again motivated by a wide range of factors, and can take the form of movement from unfavourable to less unfavourable meaning (usually through hyperbole, as in the case of *terrible, horrible* or in that of *lamentar* 'to regret' < 'to lament, grieve') or movement from derogatory to favourable meaning, as in the following cases:

> *Caballo* 'horse' < CABALLU 'nag; workhorse'.
> *Calle* 'street' < CALLE '(cattle-)path'.
> *Casa* 'house' < CASA 'hut, cottage'.
> *Condestable* 'High Constable' < COMITE STABULĪ 'officer in charge of the stable'.
> *Corte* 'court'/*Cortes* 'Parliament' < COHORTE 'enclosure, farmyard', via 'division of a Roman military camp' > 'body of troops (belonging to that division)' > 'Imperial guard' > 'palace'. The originally rural sense survives in dialectal *corte* 'cowshed'.
> *Ministro* 'minister' < MINISTRU 'servant'.

A particular case of appreciative sense development can be seen in the so-called *voces mediae*, words whose tone is essentially neutral but which may take on favourable or unfavourable overtones in different contexts. Such words may eventually take on permanently pejorative or favourable sense. Many are concerned with the notion of luck:

> *Accidente* 'accident' is now unfavourable despite its neutral origins (a borrowing of ACCIDENS, -TIS 'occurring').
>
> *Fortuna* 'fortune' has acquired favourable overtones, as can be seen more clearly in its derivative *afortunado* 'fortunate'.
>
> *Sino* 'fate' is normally interpreted as having unfavourable associations.
>
> *Suerte* 'luck' implies 'good luck' (e.g. in wishing someone ¡*Mucha suerte!*), as can also be seen by the necessity to add an adjective (e.g. *mala suerte*) to indicate 'bad luck'.

References

ArL   Archivum Linguisticum
BHS   Bulletin of Hispanic Studies
BRAE   Boletín de la Real Academia Española
CLHM   Cahiers de Linguistique Hispanique Médiévale
CQ   Classical Quarterly
HR   Hispanic Review
JHP   Journal of Hispanic Philology
L   Language
MR   Medioevo Romanzo
NRFH   Nueva Revista de Filología Hispánica
PMLA   Publications of the Modern Language Association
RF   Romanische Forschungen
RLiR   Revue de Linguistique Romane
RPh   Romance Philology
VKR   Volkstum und Kultur der Romanen
ZRP   Zeitschrift für romanische Philologie

Abercrombie, David. 1967. *Elements of General Phonetics*. Edinburgh University Press.

Aebischer, Paul. 1971. 'Le pl. -ās de la 1ère decl. latine et ses résultats dans les langues romanes', *ZRP*, 87: 74–98.

Alarcos Lorach, Emilio. 1965. *Fonología española*, 4th edn. Madrid: Gredos.

Alemany Bolufer, José. 1920. *Tratado de la formación de palabras en la lengua castellana: la derivación y la composición: Estudio de los sufijos y prefijos empleados en una y otra*, Madrid: Suárez.

Allen, Jr., J. H. D. 1976. 'Apocope in Old Spanish' in *Estudios ofrecidos a Emilio Alarcos Llorach*, ed. M. V. Conde *et al.*, vol. I. Universidad de Oviedo: 15–30.

Alonso, Amado, 1935, 'Noción, emoción, acción y fantasía en los diminutivos', *VKR*, 8: 104–26; reprinted in his *Estudios lingüísticos: Temas españoles*, 2nd edn. Madrid: Gredos, 1961: 161–89.

    1943. *Castellano, español, idioma nacional: historia espiritual de tres nombres*, 2nd edn. Buenos Aires: Losada.

    1951. 'La "ll" y sus alteraciones en España y América' in *Estudios dedicados a Menéndez Pidal*, vol. II, Madrid: CSIC: 41–89; reprinted in his *Estudios lingüísticos: Temas hispanoamericanos*, 3rd edn. Madrid: Gredos, 1967: 159–212.

    1967. *De la pronunciación medieval a la moderna en español*, vol. I, 2nd edn. Madrid: Gredos.

1969. *De la pronunciación medieval a la moderna en español*, vol. II. Madrid: Gredos.

Alonso, Dámaso. 1962. *La fragmentación fonética peninsular*, published as *Enciclopedia lingüística hispánica*, vol. I (Supplement). Madrid: CSIC.

Alvar, Manuel. 1978. 'Para la historia de "castellano"' in *Homenaje a Julio Caro Baroja*, ed. A. Carreira *et al.*, Madrid: Centro de Investigaciones Sociológicas, 71–82.

Alvar, Manuel, *et al.* (eds.) 1960. *Enciclopedia lingüística hispánica*, vol. I, *Antecedentes. Onomástica*. Madrid: CSIC.

1967. *Enciclopedia lingüística hispánica*, vol. II, *Elementos constitutivos y fuentes*. Madrid: CSIC.

Alvar, Manuel, and Sebastián Mariner. 1967. 'Latinismos' in Alvar 1967: 3–49.

Alvar, Manuel, and Bernard Pottier. 1983. *Morfología histórica del español*. Madrid: Gredos.

Baldinger, Kurt. 1972. *La formación de los dominios lingüísticos en la Península ibérica*, 2nd edn. Madrid: Gredos.

Beinhauer, Werner. 1968. *El español coloquial*, 2nd edn. Madrid: Gredos (German original: *Spanische Umgangssprache*. Bonn: Dümmlers, 1958).

Blake, Robert J. 1988a. 'Aproximaciones nuevas al fenómeno [f] > [h] > [Ø]' in *Actas del I congreso internacional de historia de la lengua española*, eds. M. Ariza, A. Salvador, A. Viudas, vol. I. Madrid: Arco Libros, 1988: 71–82.

1988b. 'Ffaro, Faro or Haro?: F doubling as a source of linguistic information for the Early Middle Ages', *RPh*, 41 (1987–8), 267–89.

Blase, H. 1898. 'Zur Geschichte des Futurums und des Konjunctivs des Perfekts im Lateinischen', *Archiv für lateinische Lexicographie und Grammatik*, 2: 313–43; translated as 'De la historia del futuro y del perfecto de subjuntivo en latín', in *Introducción plural a la gramática histórica*, ed. Francisco Marcos Marín. Madrid: Cincel, 1982: 147–69.

Blaylock, Curtis. 1986. 'Notes on the chronology of a morpho-phonological change in Golden-Age Spanish: the loss of -d- in proparoxytonic forms of the second person plural verbs', *HR*, 54: 279–85.

Boyd-Bowman, Peter. 1956. 'The regional origins of the earliest Spanish colonists of America', *PMLA*, 71: 1152–72.

1964. *Índice geobiográfico de 40.000 pobladores españoles de América en el siglo XVI*, vol. I. Bogotá: Instituto Caro y Cuervo.

Buesa, Tomás. 1967. 'Elementos constitutivos: americanismos' in Alvar 1967: 325–48.

Bynon, Theodora. 1977. *Historical Linguistics* (Cambridge Textbooks in Linguistics). Cambridge University Press.

Canfield, D. Lincoln. 1981. *Spanish Pronunciation in the Americas*. University of Chicago Press.

Castro, Américo. 1936. *Glosarios latino-españoles de la Edad Media* (*RFE, anejo* 22). Madrid: Centro de Estudios Históricos.

Coleman, R. G. G. 1971. 'The origin and development of Latin HABEO + infinitive', *CQ*, n.s., 21: 215–32.

Colón Domenech, Germán. 1967a. 'Occitanismos', in Alvar 1967: 154–92.

1967b. 'Catalanismos', in Alvar 1967: 193–238.

Corominas, Joan. 1954–7. *Diccionario crítico etimológico de la lengua castellana*. Madrid: Gredos; Berne: Francke.

Corominas, Joan, and José A. Pascual. 1980–. *Diccionario crítico etimológico castellano e hispánico*, 5 vols (of 6). Madrid: Gredos.

Craddock, Jerry R. 1980. 'The contextual varieties of yod: an attempt at systematization' in *Festschrift for Jacob Ornstein: Studies in General Linguistics and Sociolinguistics*, ed. Edward L. Blansitt, Jr. and Richard V. Teschner. Rowley, MA: Newbury House: 61–8.

1985. 'The tens from 40 to 90 in Old Castilian: a new approach', *RPh*, 38: 425–35.

Dalbor, John B. 1980. *Spanish Pronunciation: Theory and Practice*, 2nd edn. New York: Holt, Rinehart and Winston.

Dardel, Robert de. 1964. 'Considérations sur la déclinaison romane à trois cas', *Cahiers Ferdinand de Saussure*, 21: 7–23.

De Gorog, Ralph. 1980. 'L'Origine des formes espagnoles *doy, estoy, soy, voy*', *CLHM*, 5: 157–62.

Dworkin, Steven N. 1988a. 'The interaction of phonological and morphological processes: the evolution of the Old Spanish second person plural verb endings', *RPh*, 42 (1988–9), 144–55.

1988b. 'The diffusion of a morphological change: the reduction of the Old Spanish verbal suffixes *-ades, -edes* and *-ides*', *MR*, 13 (1988), 223–36.

England, John. 1982. '*Ser* and *aver* with the past participles of intransitive verbs in the works of Don Juan Manuel', *Don Juan Manuel: VII centenario*. Universidad de Murcia & Academia Alfonso X el Sabio: 117–33.

1984. 'Observaciones sobre las nuevas formas femeninas en el castellano del siglo XIII' in *Estudios dedicados a James Leslie Brooks*, ed. J. M. Ruiz Veintemilla. Barcelona: Puvill, for University of Durham: 31–44.

1987. 'New feminine forms in Old Spanish: the fourteenth and fifteenth centuries', *BHS*, 64: 205–14.

Eseverri Hualde, Crisóstomo. 1945. *Diccionario etimológico de helenismos españoles* (Pampilonensia: Publicaciones del seminario diocesano de Pamplona, serie B, vol. I), Burgos: Aldecoa.

Fernández Galiano, M. 1967. 'Helenismos' in Alvar 1967: 51–77.

Galmés de Fuentes, Álvaro. 1955–6. 'Influencias sintácticas y estilísticas del árabe en la prosa medieval castellana', *BRAE*, 35: 213–75, 415–51; 36: 65–131, 255–307.

1967. 'Dialectalismos' in Alvar 1967: 307–24.

1983. *Dialectología mozárabe*. Madrid: Gredos.

Gamillscheg, Ernst. 1967. 'Germanismos' in Alvar 1967: 79–91.

González Palencia, Cándido. 1926–30. *Los mozárabes de Toledo en los siglos XII y XIII*, 4 vols. Madrid: Instituto de Valencia de Don Juan.

Gooch, Anthony. 1970. *Diminutive, Augmentative and Pejorative Suffixes in Modern Spanish: A Guide to their Use and Meaning*, 2nd edn. Oxford: Pergamon.

Harris, Martin B. 1971. 'The history of the conditional complex from Latin to Spanish: some structural considerations', *ArL*, n.s., 2: 25–33.

1978. *The Evolution of French Syntax: A Comparative Approach*. London: Longman.

1982. 'The "Past Simple" and the "Present Perfect" in Romance' in *Studies in the Romance Verb*, ed. N. Vincent and M. Harris. London: Croom Helm: 42–70.

1986. 'The historical development of conditional sentences in Romance', *RPh*, 39: 405–36.

Hartman, Steven Lee. 1974. 'An outline of Spanish historical phonology', *Papers in Linguistics*, 7: 123–91.

Henríquez Ureña, Pedro. 1932. *Sobre el problema del andalucismo dialectal de América* (Biblioteca de Dialectología Hispánica, 1). Buenos Aires: Instituto de Filología.

Herman, Joseph. 1967. *Le Latin vulgaire*. Paris: Presses Universitaires de la France.

Jaberg, Carl, 1926. 'Zur Sach- und Bezeichnungsgeschichte der Beinbekleidungen in der Zentralromania', *Wörter und Sachen*, 9 (2): 137–72.

Jungemann, Frederick H. 1955. *La teoría del sustrato y los dialectos hispano-romances y gascones*. Madrid: Gredos.

Kany, Charles E. 1960. *American-Spanish Euphemisms*. Berkeley: University of California Press.

Klein-Andreu, Flora. Forthcoming. 'Losing ground: a discourse-pragmatic solution to a problem in the history of Spanish' in *Categories of the Verb in Romance: Discourse Pragmatic Approaches*, ed. Suzanne Fleischmann and L. Waugh. London: Croom Helm.

Lapesa, Rafael. 1951. 'La apócope de la vocal en castellano antiguo: intento de explicación histórica' in *Estudios dedicados a Menéndez Pidal*, vol. II. Madrid: CSIC: 185–226.

1970. 'Las formas verbales de segunda persona y los orígenes del "voseo"' in *Actas del Tercer Congresso Internacional de Hispanistas*, ed. Carlos H. Magis. Mexico City: Colegio de México, for Asociación Internacional de Hispanistas: 519–31.

1975. 'De nuevo sobre la apócope vocálica en castellano medieval', *NRFH*, 24: 13–23.

1980. *Historia de la lengua española*, 8th edn. Madrid: Gredos.

1982. 'Contienda de normas lingüísticas en el castellano alfonsí' in *Actas del Coloquio hispano-alemán Ramón Menéndez Pidal*, ed. Wido Hempel and Dietrich Briesemeister. Tübingen: Niemeyer: 172–90.

Lausberg, Heinrich. 1965. *Lingüística románica*, vol. I, *Fonética*. Madrid: Gredos.

1966. *Lingüística románica*, vol. II, *Morfología*. Madrid: Gredos.

Lloyd, Paul M. 1987. *From Latin to Spanish*, vol. I, *Historical Phonology and Morphology of the Spanish Language* (Memoirs of the American Philosophical Society, 173). Philadelphia: The American Philosophical Society, 1987.

Lyons, John. 1968. *Introduction to Theoretical Linguistics*. Cambridge University Press.

Macpherson, I. R. 1975. *Spanish Phonology: Descriptive and Historical*. Manchester University Press; New York: Barnes and Noble.

Malinowski, Arlene. 1983. 'The pronouns of address in contemporary Judeo-Spanish', *RPh*, 37: 20–35.

Malkiel, Yakov. 1949. 'The contrast *Tomáis–Tomávades, Queréis–Queríades* in Classical Spanish', *HR*, 17: 159–65.

1957–8. 'Diachronic hypercharacterization in Romance', *ArL*, 9: 79–113 and 10: 1–36.

1959. 'The two sources of the Hispanic sufix *-azo, -aço*', *L*, 35: 193–258.

1963–4. 'The interlocking of narrow sound-change, level of transmission, areal configuration, sound symbolism: Diachronic studies in the Hispano-Latin consonant clusters CL-, FL-, PL-', *ArL*, 15: 144–73, 16: 1–33.

1971. 'Derivational transparency as an occasional co-determinant of sound change: A new causal ingredient in the distribution of -*ç*- and -*z*- in ancient Hispano-Romance (1)', *RPh*, 25: 1–52.

1974. 'New problems in Romance interfixation (1): The velar insert in the present tense (with an excursus on -*zer*/-*zir* verbs)', *RPh*, 27: 304–55.

1976. 'From falling to rising diphthongs: The case of Old Spanish *ió* < *éu (with excursuses on the weak preterite; on the possessives; and on *judío, sandío*, and *romero*)', *RPh*, 29: 435–500.

1982. 'Interplay of sounds and forms in the shaping of three Old Spanish consonant clusters', *HR*, 50: 247–66.

Mańczak, W. 1976. 'Espagnol classique *Tomáis, Queréis* mais *Tomávades, Queríades*', *Kwartalnik Neofilologiczny*, 23: 181–6.

Marcos Marín, Francisco. 1982. 'Observaciones sobre las construcciones condicionales en la historia de la lengua española', *NRFH*, 28: 86–105; repr. in *Introducción plural a la gramática histórica*, ed. Francisco Marcos Marín. Madrid: Cincel: 186–204.

Martinet, André. 1974. *Economía de los cambios fonéticos: Tratado de fonología diacrónica*. Madrid: Gredos.

Meillet, Antoine. 1921. 'Quelques hypothèses sur des interdictions de vocabulaire dans les langues indo-européennes', *Linguistique historique et linguistique générale*, vol. I, 281–91.

Mendeloff, H. 1960. *The Evolution of the Conditional Sentence Contrary to Fact in Old Spanish*. Washington: The Catholic University of America Press.

Menéndez Pidal, Ramón. 1958. *Manual de gramática histórica española*, 10th edn. Madrid: Espasa-Calpe.

1960. 'Dos problemas iniciales relativos a los romances hispánicos' in Alvar 1960, lix–cxxxviii.

1964a. *Orígenes del español: Estado lingüístico de la Península Ibérica hasta el siglo XI*, 5th edn. Madrid: Espasa-Calpe.

1964b, ed. *Cantar de mio Cid*, vol. I, *Gramática*, 4th edn. Madrid: Espasa-Calpe.

Montgomery, Thomas. 1976. 'Complementarity of stem-vowels in the Spanish second and third conjugations', *RPh*, 29: 281–96.

1978. 'Iconicity and lexical retention in Spanish: stative and dynamic verbs', *L*, 54: 907–16.

1979. 'Sound-symbolism and aspect in the Spanish second conjugation', *HR*, 47: 219–37.

1980. 'Vocales cerradas y acciones perfectivas', *BRAE*, 60: 299–314.

1985. 'Sources of vocalic correspondences of stems and endings in the Spanish verb', *Hispanic Linguistics*, 2: 99–114.

Müller, Bodo. 1963. 'Span. *soy, estoy, doy, voy* im Lichte der romanischen Endungsneubildung mit flexionsfremden Elementen', *RF*, 75: 240–63.

Náñez Fernández, Emilio. 1973. *El diminutivo: Historia y funciones en el español clásico y moderno*. Madrid: Gredos.

Navarro Tomás, Tomás. 1961. *Manual de pronunciación española*, 10th edn. Madrid: CSIC.

Nebrija, Antonio de. 1492. *Gramática de la lengua castellana*, ed. Antonio Quilis. Madrid: Editora Nacional, 1980.

Ogden, C. K. and I. A. Richards. 1923. *The Meaning of Meaning: A Study of the Influence of Language upon Thought and of the Science of Symbolism*, 1st edn. London: Kegan Paul [the edition used is the 10th (1949)].

Penny, Ralph J. 1972a. 'The reemergence of /f/ as a phoneme of Castilian', *ZRP*, 88: 463–82.

    1972b. 'Verb-class as a determiner of stem-vowel in the historical morphology of Spanish verbs', *RLiR*, 36: 343–59.

    1976. 'The convergence of B, V and -P- in the Peninsula: a reappraisal' in *Medieval Studies Presented to Rita Hamilton*, ed. A. D. Deyermond. London: Tamesis: 149–59.

    1980. 'Do Romance nouns descend from the Accusative? Preliminaries to a reassessment of the noun-morphology of Romance', *RPh*, 33: 501–9.

    1983a. 'The Peninsular expansion of Castilian', *BHS*, 60: 333–8.

    1983b. 'Secondary consonant groups in Castilian', *JHP*, 7: 135–40.

    1987. 'Derivation of abstracts in Alfonsine Spanish', *RPh*, 41: 1–23.

    1988. 'The Old Spanish graphs "i", "j", "g" and "y" and the development of Latin $G^{e,i}$- and J-', *BHS*, 65: 337–51.

    1990a. 'The stage jargon of Juan del Encina and the castilianization of the Leonese dialect area' in *Golden Age Literature: Studies in Honour of John Varey by his Colleagues and Pupils*, ed. Alan Deyermond and Charles Davis. London: Queen Mary and Westfield College: 155–66.

    1990b. 'Labiodental /f/, aspiration and /h/-dropping in Spanish: the evolving phonemic values of the graphs *f* and *h*' in *Cultures in Contact in Medieval Spain: Historical and literary essays presented to L. P. Harvey* (King's College London Medieval Studies, III), ed. David Hook and Barry Taylor, London: King's College.

Pensado Ruiz, Carmen. 1984. *Cronología relativa del castellano* (Acta Salmanticensia, Filosofía y Letras, 158). Universidad de Salamanca.

Pottier, Bernard. 1967. 'Galicismos' in Alvar 1967: 127–51.

Pountain, Christopher J. 1983. *Structures and Transformations: The Romance Verb*. London: Croom Helm; Totowa, NJ: Barnes and Noble.

    1985. 'Copulas, verbs of possession in Old Spanish: the evidence for structurally interdependent changes', *BHS*, 62: 337–55.

Pratt, Chris. 1980. *El anglicismo en el español peninsular contemporáneo*. Madrid: Gredos.

Quilis, Antonio. 1980. 'Le Sort de l'espagnol aux Philippines: un problème de langues en contact', *RLiR*, 44: 82–107.

Quilis, Antonio and Joseph A. Fernández. 1969. *Curso de fonética y fonología españolas*, 4th edn. Madrid: CSIC.

Real Academia. 1972–. Real Academia Española, *Diccionario histórico de la lengua española* [vol. I (A-alá), vol. II, fasc. 11–15 (álaba-alzo) so far published]. Madrid: RAE.

Ridruejo, Emilio. 1982. 'La forma verbal en -*ra* en español del siglo XIII (oraciones independientes)' in *Introducción plural a la gramática histórica*, ed. Francisco Marcos Marín. Madrid: Cincel, 170–85.

Robson, C. A. 1963. 'L'*Appendix Probi* et la philologie latine', *Le Moyen Âge*, livre jubilaire, 39–54.

Rohlfs, Gerhard. 1960. *La diferenciación léxica de las lenguas románicas* (Publicaciones de la *Revista de Filología Española*, 14). Madrid: CSIC.

Rojo, Guillermo and Emilio Montero Cartelle. 1983. *La evolución de los esquemas condicionales (potenciales e irreales desde el poema del Cid hasta 1400)* (*Verba*, anexo 22). Universidad de Santiago de Compostela.

Roudet, L. 1921. 'Sur la classification psychologique des changements sémantiques', *Journal de Psychologie*, 18: 676–92.

Sala, Marius. 1979. 'Sobre el vocabulario del judeo-español' in *Festschrift Kurt Baldinger zum 60. Geburtstag*, ed. M. Höfler, H. Vernay, L. Wolf, vol. II. Tübingen: Niemeyer: 910–16.

Salvador, Gregorio. 1967. 'Lusismos' in Alvar 1967: 239–61.

Samuels, M. L. 1972. *Linguistic Evolution* (Cambridge Studies in Linguistics, 5). Cambridge University Press.

Terlingen, Johannes H. 1943. *Los italianismos en español desde la formación del idioma hasta principios del siglo XVII*. Amsterdam: N. V. Noord-Hollandsche Uitgevers Maatschappij.

Terlingen, Juan. 1967. 'Italianismos' in Alvar 1967: 263–305.

Togeby, Knud. 1963. *Mode, aspect et temps en espagnol*, 2nd edn. Copenhagen: Munksgaard.

Trudgill, Peter. 1986. *Dialects in Contact* (Language in Society, 10). Oxford: Blackwell.

Ullmann, Stephen. 1962. *Semantics: An Introduction to the Science of Meaning*. Oxford: Blackwell.

Väänänen, Veikko. 1968. *Introducción al latín vulgar*. Madrid: Gredos.

Valesio, P. 1968. 'The Romance synthetic future pattern and its first attestations, I', *Lingua*, 20: 113–61.

Vincent, Nigel. 1982. 'The development of the auxiliaries HABERE and ESSE in Romance' in *Studies in the Romance Verb*, ed. Nigel Vincent and Martin Harris. London: Croom Helm.

Whinnom, Keith. 1954. 'Spanish in the Philippine Islands: a sociolinguistic survey', *Journal of Oriental Studies*, Hong Kong, 1: 129–94.

1956. *Spanish Contact Vernaculars in the Philippines*. Hong Kong: University Press; London: Oxford University Press.

Wilkinson, Hugh E. 1971. 'Vowel alternation in the Spanish -*IR* verbs', *Ronshu* (Aoyama Gakuin University, Tokyo), 12: 1–21.

1973–5. 'The strong perfects in the Romance Languages', *Ronshu* (Aoyama Gakuin University, Tokyo), 14 (1973): 157–94, 15 (1974): 23–44, 16 (1975): 15–31.

1976. 'Notes on the development of -KJ-, -TJ- in Spanish and Portuguese', *Ronshu* (Aoyama Gakuin University, Tokyo), 17: 19–36.

Wright, Leavitt Olds. 1932. *The -ra Verb-form in Spain: the Latin Pluperfect Indicative Form in its Successive Functions in Castilian* (University of California Publications in Modern Philology, vol. XV, no. 1). Berkeley: University of California Press.

Wright, Roger. 1976. 'Semicultismo', *ArL*, n.s., 7: 14–28.

1982. *Late Latin and Early Romance in Spain and Carolingian France* (ARCA Classical and Medieval Texts, Papers and Monographs). Liverpool: Francis Cairns.

1985. 'Indistinctive features (facial and semantic)', *RPh*, 38: 275–92.

Zamora Vicente, Alonso. 1967. *Dialectología española*, 2nd edn. Madrid: Gredos.

Index of Latin words

AB 103, 195
ABELLĀNA 266
-ĀBILE 245
ABSTINĒRE 92
ACCEPTĀRE 92
ACCEPTŌRE 75
ACCIDENS 269
ACCIPITER 75
*ACCU 129
-ĀCEU 55, 243, 249
ACŪLEĀTA 266
-ACULUS 250
ACŪTIARE 57
ACŪTU 47
AD 74, 102, 195, 196
AD- 238
ADDŪCERE 160, 190
ADDŪCŌ 153, 160
ADDUCTU 193
ADDŪXĪ 186
ADHŪC 118
*ADPĀCĀRE 11
AEQUĀLE 246
AERĀMEN 108, 265
AERĀMINA 108
*AERĀMINE 108
AFFECTĀRE 257
AFFECTIŌNE 92
AFFLĀRE 9, 267
AFRICU 73, 265
ALBA 30
-ĀLE 243, 244
ALEUM 52
ALIĀS 117
ALID 133
ALIĒNU 46
ALIQUIS 133
ALIQUIS ŪNUS 133
ALIQUOD 74, 76, 133
ALIU 41, 55
ALIUD 133
ALIUM 52

ALIUS 133
ALTER 133
ALTUS 114, 115
ALUMNUS 66
ALUNNUS 66
AMĀBAR 137
AMĀBOR 137
AMĀRELLU 10
AMĀRER 137
AMĀRU 10
AMĀTUS 137
AMBITĀVĪ 185
AMER 137
AMETHYSTUS 111
AMĪCĪ 57
AMITĒS 112
AMPLU 36, 63, 64
-ANDU 243
-ĀNE 11
ANGLUS 50
ANGULUS 50
ANIMA 78
ANNU 40, 62, 64
ANNUS 107
ANSA 66
ĀNSAR 266
ĀNSER 266
ANTE 117, 196, 197
-ANTE 243, 245
ANTE- 241
-ANTIA 243
-ANU 244
APERĪ 166
APERTU 193
APERUĪ 186
APICULA 42, 248
APIS 248
APPREHENDERE 237
APPREHENDĪ 187
APTĀRE 91
AQUA 71, 73
*AQUILEĀTA 266

ARĀNEA 41, 55
ARĀTRU 28
ARBOR 110
ARDEŌ 184
ARDUUS 116
-ĀRE 244, 245
ĀREA 40, 41
ARĒNA 8
ARGENTEU 266
ARGENTU 10
ARGILLA 60
-ĀRIA 243
-ĀRIU 243, 244, 245
ARMA 109, 110
ARMAE 109
ARMENIU 266
ARMUM 109
ARSĪ 184, 187
ASA 66
*ASCIĀTA 70
ASCIOLA 55
ASINU 76
-ĀTA 243
-ATICU 243
-ĀTIŌ 249, 250
ATQUE 129
ATRIBUĪ 185
-ĀTU 243, 244, 245
AUDĪBAM 168
AUDIĒBAM 167
AUDIŌ 150, 154, 165
AUDĪRE 28, 189
AUDĪRE HABEŌ 175
AUDĪRE HABET 176
AUDĪTU 192
AUDĪTUM 141
AUGURIU 42, 56
AUGUSTU 28, 59
AURICULA 248
AURIS 4, 45, 248
AUSCULTAT 42
AUT 199

AVICELLU 9
AVIS 64

BACULUS 4, 65
BALIAT 65
BAPLO 65
BĀSIU 41, 56
*BASSIĀRE 197
BASSUS 197
BELLU 9
BENE 44, 65, 85, 117
BIBĒBAM 168
BIBERE 65
BIFERA 76, 266
BINU 71
BIXIT 65
BLANDU 83
BONITĀTE 77
BONITTA 246
BONU 44
BONUS 117
BŌS 105
BOVE 113
BOVĒS 113
BOVIS 105
BRACCHIA 109
BRACCHIU 54, 63
BRACCHIUM 109
BRŪMA 266
BUCCA 65, 264

CABALLICĀRE 72
CABALLU 62, 64, 65, 73, 268
CABALLUS 2, 5
CADERE HABET 176
CADŌ 150, 151, 154
CAECU 8, 47
CAELU 45, 47, 57
CAEMENTŌS 265
CAEMENTU 48
CAESAR 5
CAESPITE 265
CALAMELLU 51
CALCE 50, 264
*CALCEA 54, 57, 63, 256
CALCEUS 256
CALCOSTEGIS 59
CALCOSTEIS 59
CALDA 50
CALIDA 50
CALLE 268
CAMPĀNA 266

CAMPSĀRE 8
CANNA 62
CANTĀ 147, 166
CANTĀBAM 74, 138, 141, 167
CANTABANT 138
CANTĀBĀTIS 140
CANTĀBIMUS 173
CANTĀBIT 173
CANTĀBŌ 141, 173
CANTAMUS 138
CANTANDŌ 191
CANTANS 191
CANTANT 49
CANTĀRAM 141, 146, 171
CANTĀRE 189
CANTĀRE HABĒBAM 178
CANTĀRE HABEŌ 174
CANTĀREM 141, 169
CANTĀRIM 146
CANTĀRŌ 146
CANTĀS 49
CANTĀSSEM 141, 170
CANTĀTE 139, 147
CANTĀTIS 138
CANTĀTU 192
CANTĀVERAM 141, 142, 146, 171
CANTĀVERĀTIS 140
CANTĀVERIM 141, 142, 146, 178
CANTĀVERĪS 178
CANTĀVERIT 178
CANTĀVERŌ 141, 142, 146, 178
CANTĀVĪ 41, 141, 142, 179
CANTĀVIMUS 173
CANTĀVISSEM 141, 142, 146, 169, 170
CANTĀVISTĪ 179
CANTĀVIT 173
CANTEM 141, 152
CANTĒS 138
CANTHARU 51
CANTŌ 49, 138, 141, 151
CAPANNA 28, 57
CAPIAM 56, 164
CAPIMUS 150
CAPIŌ 150, 151, 164
CAPISTRU 48
CAPIT 85
CAPITA 109
CAPITĀLE 78
CAPITULU 78

CAPRA 36, 73, 83
CAPTĀRE 11
CAPTIĀRE 55, 64
CAPTĪVU 268
CAPUT 109, 198
CARNIS 105
CARŌ 105
CARRICĀRE 72
CARRU 72
CĀRU 47
CĀRUS 137
CASA 67, 73, 268
CĀSEU 9, 45
CASTELLU 46, 221
CASTRU 221
CATĒNA 10, 68
CATĒNĀTU 11, 50, 78
CATHEDRA 264
CATHEGRA 264
CATTU 83
CAULE 47
CAUSA 28, 45, 73, 267
*CAUSA NĀTA 255
CAVA 8
CAVET 85
CECIDĪ 189
CENTĒNĪ 11
CENTĒNU 11
CENTUM 135
CERASIA 41
CERASIUS 110
*CERCIU 10
CĒREOLA 266
CERESIA 41
CERTUS 133
CERVĒSIA 41
CERVU 27
-CEU 245
CIBĀRIA 10
CIBĀTA 10
CIBU 10, 68, 267
CICERE 112
CICŌNIA 42
CILIA 42
CINCTU 193, 194
CĪNQUE 27
CINXĪ 187
CIRCĀ 57, 197, 198
CIRCIU 10
CIRCUM- 241
CISTA 27, 46, 64
CITO 49
CITRĀ 198
CĪVITĀTE 78

CLĀMĀRE 63, 64
CLAUSA 63
CLĀVE 63, 73
CLAVĪCULA 62
CLOACA 52
CLUACA 52
COĀGULU 41
COCHLEĀRE 48, 109
COCTU 193
CŌGITĀRE 48, 76
COGNĀTU 267
COGNŌSCŌ 155
COGNŌVĪ 186
*COGNŌVUĪ 186
COHORTE 268
CŌLĀRE 157
CŌLĀTIS 157
COLLACTEU 70
COLLIGIS 41
COLLOCĀRE 267
COLOBRA 46
COLOMNA 39
*COLOPU 83
COLUMELLU 11
COLUMNA 1, 39
COM- 241
COMITE 77, 268
COMMUNICĀRE 267
COMPĀNIŌNE 267
COMPLEŌ 149
CŌMPLĒRE 190
CŌMPUTĀRE 77
CON-BATTUŌ 149
CONCĒPĪ 189
CONCIPIŌ 149
CONDŪXĪ 186
CŌNFUNDERE 68
CONFUNDŌ 149
CONIUGES 53
CŌNSILIU 42
CONSŌLĀRĪ 157
CŌNSTĀRE 36
CONSUTŪRA 34
CONTRĀ 198
CONTRĀ- 241
COPERTU 193
COQUŌ 153
CORIU 42, 45, 267
CORNU 83, 107
CORNUA 107
CORŌNA 28, 57
CORPORA 107, 108
CORPUS 107, 108
CORRIGIA 34, 41, 55, 70

CORTICE 112
CORTICEA 48
COVA 29
COXĪ 186
COXU 41
CRĀS 8, 118
CRASSU 83
CRĒDE 166
CRĒDĒBAM 145
CRĒDERE 176, 181, 191
CRĒDIDĪ 181
CRĒDŌ 145
CREPĀRE 29
CRĒSCERE 70
CRĒTA 83
CRUCE 33
CRŪDU 69
CUBITU 47, 78
CUCUMERE 112
CUCURRĪ 189
CŪIU 70
CŪIUS, -A, -UM 8, 132
CULMEN 108
CULMINA 108
*CULMINE 108
CULTELLU 46, 61
CUM 74, 103, 120, 195
CUM- 241
CUMULU 78
CUNEA 40
CUNEU 42
CŪPA 47, 57, 68
CUPIDĪTIA 78
CUPPA 36, 40, 47, 68, 82, 83
CUPRU 113
CŪRĀRE 48
CURCULIŌNE 42
CURRERE 28
CURSU 193
CUSCULIU 42
CȲMA 197

DAMNU 71
DĀRE 185, 190
*DAXĀRE 10
DĒ 102, 103, 195
DĒ- 238
DE UNDE 49
DĒBEAM 152
DEBĒBAM 168
DĒBENDŌ 191
DĒBEŌ 147, 149, 150, 152, 156, 173

DĒBĒRE 10, 34, 149, 189
DĒBĒRE HABEŌ 175
DĒBĒS 150
DĒBET 86
DĒBITA 78
DĒBUĪ 186, 191
DECEM 134
DECIMU 76
DECOLLĀRE 237
DEDĪ 181, 185, 189
DĒFĒNSA 68, 237, 267
DEFĒNSU 193
DELĒVĪ 180
DEM 162
DĒMAGIS 8
DĒNĀRIU 267
DENTĒS 36
DEORSUM 118
DĒPENDERE 264
DESTRUXĪ 186
DĒVŌTĀ 118
DEXTRU 31
DIA 168
DĪC 74, 167
DĪCERE 159, 190, 193
*DĪCĪRE 159
DĪCIS 99, 100
DĪCIT 57
DĪCŌ 99, 149, 153
DICTU 193, 194
DIĒS 113
DIGITU 59, 67
DĪMIDIUM 102
*DIRECTIĀRE 55, 64
DIRECTU 41
DIS- 238, 239
DISPENDĪ 186
DĪXĪ 61, 62, 91, 185, 186
DŌ 162
DOLEAT 154
DOMINA 258
DOMINE 72
DOMĪNICU 76, 77
DOMINŌ 104
DOMINU 49
DOMINUM 104
DOMINUS 107, 112
DOMNE 72
DŌRIU 45
DORMĪERAM 171
DORMĪĪ 180
DORMIŌ 160
DORMĪRE 190
DORMĪRUNT 180

DORMĪSSEM 170
DORMĪVERAM 171
DORMĪVERŌ 178
DORMĪVĪ 180
DORMĪVISSEM 170
DORSUM 66
DOSSUM 66
DUĀS 134
DUCENTĪ 133
DUCENTŌS 135
DULCE 60
DUM 117, 118, 200
DUM INTERIM 200
DUO 133
DUO MĪLIA 134, 136
DUŌDECIM 51, 77, 134
DUŌS 134
DUPLU 73
DŪRACINU 76

Ē 196
ECCE 129
ECCU 129
ECCUM 118
EFFECTU 92
EGŌ 119
EIUS 126, 128
-ELLUS 247, 248, 251
ĒNECĀRE 266
-ĒNSE 69, 244
-ENTU 244
EŌ 164
EŌRUM 126, 128
EPISCOPU 77
EPITHEMA 78
EQUA 9, 44, 58, 64, 73
EQUUS 2
ERAM 143, 169
EREMU 76
ĒRĪCIU 54, 57, 64
ERIGŌ 154, 160
ERIS 162, 169
ES 161
-ĒSCERE 245
ESSE 5, 162, 167, 169, 191
*ESSERE 5, 191
EST 161, 169
ESTIS 161
ET 198, 199
EX 195, 196
EX- 238, 239
EXAGIU 55, 74
EXĀMEN 92
EXCELLENTE 92

EXCONSPUŌ 150
EXERCĒRE 92
EXPĒNSU 194
EXTENDERE 238
EXTRĀ 196
EXTRĀ- 241
EXTRĀNEU 41

FABULA 32
FABULĀRE 117
FABULĀRĪ 8, 32
FAC 167
*FACE 167
FACERE 57, 79, 189
FACERE HABET 177
FACEREM 170
FACIAT 151
FACIE 56, 195
FACILE 117
FACIMUS 148, 166
FACIŌ 150, 153
FACIT 57
FACITE 148
FACITIS 148, 166
FACTU 61, 64, 91, 193
FĀGEA 41, 55, 64, 110
FĀGUS 110
FALCE 50
*FĀRE 190
FARĪNA 79, 80
FASCE 50, 70
FASCĒS 58, 87
FECE 70
FĒCERAM 170, 183
FĒCERIM 183
FĒCERŌ 183
FĒCERUNT 183
FĒCĪ 40, 43, 183, 185, 187
FĒCIMUS 183
FĒCISSEM 170, 183
FĒCISTĪ 183
FĒCISTIS 183
FĒCIT 183, 187
FEL 74, 108
FĒMINA 78
FERIŌ 154
FERRĀRIU 56
FERRE 191
FERRU 80
FERVEŌ 149
FERVERE 9
FESTA 46
FĪCĀRIA 110
FĪCTU 61

FĪCU 46, 79, 266
FĪCUS 110
FIDE 75
FIDĒLE 49, 75
FĪLIOLU 34
FĪLIOLUS 248
FĪLIU 46, 64, 79
FILIUS 34, 248
FĪLU 79
FINDERE 157
FLACCIDU 41, 58, 63, 64, 76, 83
FLÁMMA 63, 64, 68, 248
FLAMMULA 248
FLOCCU 46, 62
FLŌRE 47
FLŌREŌ 149
FLORĒSCERE 155
FLUVIOLUS 248
FLUVIUS 248
FOCU 40
FOEDU 45, 46
FOETĒRE 157
FOLIA 40, 41, 55, 109
FOLLE 79
FONTE 79
FORĀS 117, 196
FORĪS 196
FŌRMA 11, 30, 79
FŌRMĀCEU 11
FŌRMŌSU 9, 47
FŌRMOSUS 39
FORMUNSUS 39
FORTE 79, 80
FORTIA 40
FORTIOR 115
FORTIS 114, 115
FORTISSIME 118
FORTISSIMUS 115
FORTITER 117
FORTIUS 118
FRANGŌ 154
FRĀTRE 11
FRAXINU 62
FRAXINUS 110
FRECARE 47
FRICARE 47, 157
FRĪCTU 61, 193
FRIDENANDU 77
FRĪGIDU 59, 80
FRONTE 46, 79
FRŪCTA 110
FRŪCTUS 110
FUGĪ 186

FUGIŌ 42, 149, 151, 154
FUĪ 188
FŪMU 47, 237
FURNU 79, 80

GALLICU 72
GALLĪNA 59
GALLU 62, 71
GAUDIU 59
GEIUNA 58
GELĀRE 58
GEMMA 58, 264
GENARIUS 58
GENERU 29, 59, 78
GENESTA 46, 48, 58
GENUCULU 42, 58
GERMĀNA 11
GERMĀNU 11, 58
GINGĪVA 60
GINGĪVĀS 58
GLATTĪRE 83
GLĪRE 83
GLĪRIS 105
GLĪS 105
GLOBELLU 83
GRADUS 113
GRANDE 267
GRANDIS 117
GRĀTIS 117
GREGE 41
GROSSU 83
GRŪIS 4, 105
GRUNNĪRE 62
GRŪS 4, 105
GURGULIŌNE 42
GUTTA 59, 68, 82
GYPSU 58, 59, 64, 74

HABEAM 56, 151, 154, 164
BABĒBAM 167, 169
HABEŌ 164, 173
HABEŌ CANTĀTU 179
HABEO CANTĀTUM 141
HABET 162
HABITU 193
HABUERIM 146, 179
HABUERŌ 146, 179
HABUĒRUNT 183
HABUĪ 45, 184, 185
HĀC 118
HEDERA 76
HERBA 44, 58, 74
HERĪ 43, 118
HIC 37, 38, 119, 129

HĪC 37, 38, 118, 119
HIERAX 53
HINC 198
HISPANIA 55
HODIĒ 41, 118
HOMINE 78
HOMINE NĀTU 133
HONŌRĀRE 77
HŌRĀ 118, 267
HORDEOLU 56
HOSPITĀLE 77
HUMERU 29, 78

-ĪA 243
IACEAT 151
IACEŌ 153
IACERE 57
IACET 58, 64
IACTĀRE 58
IACUĪ 185
IĀIŪNU 58
IAM 74
IAM MAGIS 118
IANUĀRIU 58
IANUARIUS 53, 58
ĪBAM 169
IBĪ 118
-ĪBILE 245
-ICELLUS 249
-ĪCEU 244
-ICU 244
-ICULUS 248
ĪDEM 129
-IDIĀRE 245
IEIŪNA 58
IENUĀRIUS 58
*IFFANTE 66
-IFICĀRE 78, 245
IINIPERU 58
-ĪLE 245
ĪLEX 110
ĪLICĪNA 110
ILICŌ 118
ILLA 118
ILLĀC 118
ILLAM 119
ILLĀS 119
ILLE 119, 129, 131
ILLĪ 119
ILLĪC 74, 118
ILLINC 197
ILLĪS 119
ILLŌRUM 126, 128
ILLŌS 119

ILLUD 119
ILLUM 119
IM- 238
IMPLEŌ 149
IMPLĒRE 63
IMPULSAT 42
IN 74, 117, 196
*IN EX ALBICĀRE 239
*IN EX ALTIĀRE 239
*IN EX AQUĀRE 239
*IN EX SUCĀRE 239
IN- 238
*INADDŌ 149
INCITAMENTO 56
INDE 118
-INEU 244
INFĀNTE 66, 112
INFLĀRE 63
INFRĀ- 241
INGENERĀRE 29, 51, 78
*ĪNGUINE 78
INSTANTE 92
ĪNSULA 76
INTCITAMENTO 56
INTEGRU 41
INTEGRUM 34, 36
INTELLECTUM 142
INTELLĒXĪ 142
INTER 196
INTER- 239
INTERIM 117, 188
INTRĀ- 241
INTRŌ 196
-ĪNU 244, 245, 247
INVIARE 30
IOCU 57
IOVIS 49
IPSA 91
IPSE 66, 129, 131
IPSŌS 69
ĪRE 9
IS 119, 129
-ISCU 244
-ĪSMU 243
ISSE 66
-ĪSTA 243, 244
ISTE 119, 129
*ĪSULA 76
-ITER 117
-ITIA 243
-ITIE 243
*-ITTU 246
-ĪTU 245
ĪTUM 143

IUDICĀRE 78
IŪDICĒS 59
IUGU 74
IŪNCTU 198
IUNCU 60
IUNGERE 198
IŪSTU 59
IUSTUS 53
ĪVERAM 143
ĪVERIM 143
ĪVERŌ 143
ĪVĪ 143, 188
ĪVISSEM 143
-ĪVU 245
-IZĀRE 245

JOHANNE 72
JŪLITTA 246

LABIU 41
LAC 41, 108
LACRYMA 36
LACTE 41, 108
LAEVUS 258
LAICU 41
LAMBERE 68
LANCEA 52
LANCIA 52
LATERA 107, 108
LATERĀLE 76
LATUS 107, 108, 198
LAVAT 86
LAXĀRE 10
LAXIUS 117, 198
LĒCTIŌNE 92
LECTORĪLE 62
LECTU 41
LĒGĀLE 71
LĒGE 113
LĒGĒS 113
LĒGĪ 189
LEGŪMEN 108
LEGŪMINA 108
*LEGŪMINE 71, 108
LENDINE 78
LENS 78
LENTĀ 118
LENTEU 40
LENTICULA 61
LEŌ 105
*LEŌNIS 105
LEVĀRE 157
LEVIS 37
LĒVIS 37

LEVŌ 158
LIBER 37
LĪBER 37
LĪBERĀRE 76
LIGĀRE 59, 67
LIGNA 42, 61, 62, 109
LĪMITĀRE 50
LIMPIDU 41
LINGUA 217
LITTERA 76
LOCĀLE 57
LOCŌ 118
LONGE 117, 198
LŪCEŌ 149
LŪCĒS 70
LUCTA 42
LŪCTU 92
LUMBU 28
LUMBUS 66
LŪMEN 108
LŪMINA 108
*LŪMINE 108
*LUMMUS 66

MACULA 63
MAGIS 9, 116, 117
MAGISTER 112
MAGISTRU 59
MĀIŌRE 55, 116
MĀIŌRĒS 74
MĀIU 55, 64
MALE 75, 117
MALU 71
MALUM 37
MĀLUM 37
*MANCLA 63
MĀNE 118
*MĀNEĀNA 118
MANICA 51
MANSĪ 185
MANSIŌNE 56
MANU 47
MANŪS 49, 113
MARE 49, 75, 108
MARMORE 102
MARTIU 54, 57, 63
MASTICĀRE 77
MATAXA 41, 61
MĀTERIA 40, 41, 45, 113
MĀTERIĒS 113
*MATTĀRE 259
MATTIANA 54, 63
MATTUS 259
MAURICELLU 76

MAURU 47
MAXILLA 64, 264
MAXIME 116
MĀXIMUS 116
MĒ 119
MEA 127
MĒCUM 120
MEDIĀLE 265, 266
MEDIĒTĀTE 136
*MEDIPSIMUS 129
MEIERE 148
MEL 74, 108
MELIŌRE 55, 116
MENS 105, 117
MĒNSA 9, 66, 74, 101, 102, 104, 112
MĒNSĀ 102, 104
MĒNSAE 102
MĒNSAM 102, 104
MĒNSĀRUM 102
MĒNSĀS 102
MĒNSE 49, 69
MĒNSĒS 69
MĒNSĪS 102
MENTE 118, 200
MENTIS 105, 117
-MENTU 243
MENUS 39
MERCĒDE 49, 69
MERĒSCŌ 155
MERULA 46
MESA 66
MESE 69
MESSE 69
MĒTIŌ 159
METIPSIMUS 129
MĒTĪRĪ 190
METU 47
MEUS 125
MIHĪ 43, 119
MĪLIA 134, 136
MĪLLE 72, 134, 135
MINĀCIA 70
MINIMĀRE 78
MINIMUS 116
MINISTRU 268
MINŌRE 116
MINUERE 148
MINUS 39, 74, 118, 199
*MISCULĀRE 89
MĪSĪ 186
MISSU 193, 194
MITTERE 193
MODIU 221

MOLĪNU   34
MOLLIĀRE   55
MOLLIŌ   160
MOLUĪ   186
MOMORDĪ   189
MONEŌ   149
MONĒRE   193
MONITU   193
MŌNSTRĀRE   157
MONTE   104
MONTĒS   74, 104
MONTIS   104
MŌRA   109
MORIOR   149
MORTUU   51, 193
MORTUUS EST   142
MOVĒ   166
MOVEŌ   156
MŌVĪ   189
MULIERE   34, 36, 48, 51,
      55, 74
MULTU   42, 49, 61, 62, 64
MULTUM   116, 117
MŪRE   266
MUSTĒLA   258

NĀSCOR   155
NĀSŌ   249
NĀTA   255
NĀTU   194
NĀVIGĀRE   71
NEBULA   76
NEC   74, 199
NEC ŪNUS   133
NEGĀRE   59
NEGŌ   156
NĒMŌ   133
NERVIU   41
NESCIU   268
NICEAM   56
NIGRA   73
NIHIL   133
NISEAM   56
NISI   199
NŌBĪSCUM   120
NOCTE   41, 61
NŌDU   10, 69
NŌMEN   108
NŌMINA   108
NŌMINĀRE   48
*NŌMINE   108
NŌN   118, 255
NŌNĀGINTĀ   8, 135
NŌNGENTĪ   133

NŌNGENTŌS   136
NŌS   119, 125
NŌSCUM   120
NOSTER   125
NOSTRĪS   102
NOVĀCULA   41, 61, 74
NOVE   47
NOVEM   134
NOVENDECIM   135
NOVIU   41, 56
NOVU   47, 65, 68, 74
NŪBĒS   67
NŪBIS   113
NUCĀLIS   110
NUCĀRIA   110
NUCE   266
*NŪDU   10
NŪDU   69
NŪLLUS   133
NUMQUAM   117
NURA   111
NURUS   31, 111
NUX   110

OB   196
OCTINGENTŌS   136
OCTO   41, 134
OCTŌBER   10
OCTŌDECIM   135
OCTŌGINTĀ   135
*OCTŪBER   10
OCULU   41, 61, 64
*OFFERĪRE   191
OFFERRE   191
-OLUS   248
OMNIS   133
-ŌNE   243, 245
OPERA   107, 108, 109, 110
OPERAE   109
OPTIMUS   116
OPUS   107, 108, 109
*ORDINIĀRE   256
-ŌRE   243, 245
ORICLA   4, 45
-ŌRIU   243
OS   37, 109
ŌS   37
OSSA   109
OSSU   44, 69
OSSUM   44, 109
OSTREA   41
-ŌSU   244, 245
OVA   109
OVICULA   248

OVIS   248

PĀCĀRE   11
PĀCE   49, 56, 70
PACEM   153
PACĒS   153
PACŌ   153
PALEA   41
PALUMBA   28
PALUMBĪNUS   247
PĀNĀRIA   48
PĀNE   49, 75
PANNU   71
PANTICE   77, 112
PARABOLA   267
PARĒTE   51
PARIĒTE   49, 51, 69
PARIŌ   149
PĀSCERE   58
PASSAR   9
PASSARE   112
PASSER   9, 112
PASSU   87
PATER   47
PATRE   73
PATRĒS   49
PAUCĪ   102
PAUCU   45
PAUPER   115, 248
PAUPERA   115
*PAUPERCELLU   248
PAUPERCULU   248
PAUPERE   76
PAUSĀRE   48
PECTINĀRE   62
PECTORA   107, 108
PECTUS   107, 108
PEDE   75
PĒIŌRE   55, 70, 116
PELLE   72
PĒNSĀRE   157, 264
PER   196, 197
PER HOC   199
PER-   241
PERDERE   181
PERDIDĪ   181
PERFIDIA   241
PERNA   264
PERSICA   66
PERSICU   221
PERTICA   265, 266
PESSICA   66
PESSIMUS   116
PETŌ   150

PETRA   36, 40, 44, 47, 82
*PETTIA   70
PIGNORA   41, 62, 107, 108, 109
PIGNUS   107, 108
PIGRITIA   73
PILU   46
PĪNUS   110
PIRA   71, 109
PISCE   50, 70
PISCĒS   58, 64
PLACEAT   73, 151
PLACITU   77
PLACUĪ   185
PLACUIT   73
PLĀGA   63, 71
PLAGIA   70
PLANGŌ   154
PLANU   63
PLATEA   62
*PLATTA   261
*PLATTU   63
PLEBES   65
PLĒNA   40, 46
PLEVIS   65
PLICĀBAM   153
PLICĀRE   10, 48, 63, 100, 153
PLICEM   100, 153
PLICĒS   100
PLICET   100
PLICŌ   153
*PLŌPPU   63
PLŌRĀRE   64
PLŪS   9, 116
PLUTEU   63
PLUVIA   42, 56
PODIU   41, 55, 74
POELLA   52
POENA   45, 46
POMPELŌNE   76
PŌNAM   151
PŌNERE   151
PŌNŌ   151, 154
PŌPULU   63
POPULU   76
POPULUS   37
PŌPULUS   37, 110
PORCU   60
PORCUS   36
PORTĀTICU   78
PORTU   265
POSITU   193
POSSE   191

POSSEM   170
POSSUM   166
POST   117, 162, 197, 200
*POST COCCEU   70
POST TRANS   197
POST-   241
POSTQUAM   200
*POSTU   193
PŌSUĪ   185
POTE(S)T   74
POTEAM   166
*POTEŌ   166
*POTĒRE   191
POTĒS   166
POTIŌNE   267
POTUĪ   166, 185, 191
POTUISSEM   170
PRACTICA   92
PRAE-   241
PRAECŌNE   48
PRAECOQUU   221
PRAEDĀ   102
PRAEMIU   41, 56
PRAESĒPE   29
PRĀTA   107
PRĀTU   47
PRĀTUM   107
PRECARE   57
PREHENDERE   237
PREHENDĪ   187
PRĒNSU   194
PRETIARE   57
PRĪMĀRIUS   136
PRĪMUS   136
PRŌ   196, 197
PRŌ-   241
PRŌFECTU   68, 237
PROMPTU   92
PROPE   198
PROPTER   196
PRŪNA   266
PUELLA   52
PUGNU   42, 61, 64, 91
PŪLICE   112
PULLUS   247
PULVERE   112
*PULVUS   112
PUNCTU   187
PUPPE   112
PŪRITĀTE   261
PUTEOLU   34
PUTEU   54, 64
PUTREŌ   149
PUTRĒRE   161

QUADRĀGINTĀ   8, 34, 73, 135
QUADRINGENTŌS   135
QUADRU   73
QUAE   132
QUAERERE   84
QUAERIT   45
QUAESĪVĪ   187
QUĀLE   84
QUĀLIS   132, 133
QUAM   199
QUANDŌ   118, 199
QUĀRTUS   136
*QUASSICĀRE   84, 87
QUATTUOR   74, 84, 134
*QUATTUOR CENTŌS   135
QUATTUŌRDECIM   77, 84, 135
QUEM   74, 132
QUĒTU   51
QUĪ   132
QUIA   199
QUID   132, 199
QUĪDAM   133
QUIĒTU   51
QUĪLIBET   133
QUĪNDECIM   57, 84, 135
QUĪNGENTŌS   60, 84, 136
QUĪNQUĀGINTĀ   135
QUĪNQUE   27, 134
QUĪNTUS   136
QUISQUE   133
QUOD   199
QUŌMŌ   84, 118, 200
QUŌMODŌ   84, 118, 200

*RABIA   41, 113
RABIĒS   113
RACĒMU   57
RADIĀRE   55, 64
RADIU   41, 70
RĀDŌ   151
*RĀMA   110
RĀMUS   110
RAPHANU   51
RAPÔN   148
RAUBÔN   148
RE-   240
RECIPERE   160, 190
RECIPIŌ   149
RECITĀRE   267
RECUPERĀRE   51
REDDERE   181
REDDIDĪ   181

REDDŌ 150
REGĀLE 59, 67
RĒGE 113
RĒGĒS 113
RĒGĪNA 70
REGULA 32, 33, 61, 74
RĒGULĀRIS 32
REM NĀTA 133, 255
REMANEAT 151
REMANSĪ 186
RĒMU 68
RENIŌNE 48
REPAENITEŌ 149
RĒS 113
RESECĀRE 76
RESPONDĪ 185
RESTE 112
RĒTE 108
RETINA 51, 78
RĒTIS 108
RETRŌ 197, 198
RETRŌ- 241
RĒX 113
*RĪCUS 217
RĪDEŌ 149, 150, 159
RIGĀRE 157
RINGERE 60
RINGĪ 60
RĪPA 197
RĪPĀRIA 48
RĪSĪ 186
RŌBORA 108
*RŌBORE 28, 108
RŌBUR 108
RŌDAT 151
ROGĀRE 9
RŌMĀNICĒ 117
ROSA 69, 112
ROTA 47
*ROTULĀRE 61
ROTUNDU 28
RUBEU 42, 56
RUGĪTU 59
*RUPTIĀRE 70
RUPTU 68, 193

SAECULU 46
SAGITTA 34, 59
SALE MURIA 42
SALIAM 152
SALIŌ 150, 152, 154
SALĪS 150
SALĪVIT 74
SALVITTUS 246

SĀNĀRE 9
SANCTIFICĀRE 78
SANGUINE 51, 78
SAPIAM 41, 73, 151, 164
SAPIAT 45
SAPIŌ 164
SAPIT 86
SAPPHĪRUS 111
SAPUĪ 45, 73, 185
SCAEVUS 258
SCAMNU 91
SCHOLA 36
SCRĪBERE 159, 190
SCRĪPSĪ 185, 186
SCRĪPTU 193
SĒ 119
SECĀRE 67, 266
SĒCUM 120
SECUNDUM 198
SECUNDUS 136
SĒCŪRU 48, 71
SED 199
SEDĒ 167
SEDEAM 55, 70, 151, 162, 191
SEDEAT 41
SEDĒBAM 169
SĒDECIM 135
SEDĒRE 68, 162, 167, 176, 191
SEDĒTE 167
SĒDĪ 185
SEGŪSIU 45
SELLA 46
SĒMINĀMUS 157
SĒMINĀRE 157
SĒMITA 75, 76, 77
SEMPER 74
SENATUS 47
SENIŌRE 48, 55, 112
SENTIAM 173
SENTIŌ 110, 159
SENTĪRE 75, 100, 190
SENTĪS 100
SENTIT 100
SĒPIA 41
SEPTEM 134
SEPTEMBER 92
SEPTEMBRIS 66
SEPTENDECIM 135
SEPTIMĀNA 50, 77
SEPTINGENTŌS 136
SEPTUĀGINTĀ 135
SEQUERE 57, 71

SEQUĪ 57, 71
SEQUOR 150
SERENA 47
SERRA 47, 263
SERVIŌ 159
SESCENTŌS 136
SETTEMBRES 66
SEX 62, 134
SEXĀGINTĀ 135
SEXTA 46, 267
SĪ 199, 201
SIBĪ 43, 65, 119
SĪC 118
SICCU 67, 71
SIGNA 42
SIGNAS 46
SIGNIFICĀRE 92
SIGNU 92
SIMPLU 268
SINATUS 47
SINE 75, 195
SINISTER 209, 258
SINISTRU 31, 268
SIRENA 47
SĪVI 65
SMARAGDUS 111
SOCRA 111
SOCRU 73
SOCRUS 31, 111
SOLEŌ 154
SOLIDU 76
SŌLITĀRIU 76
SOLLEMNE 92
SOLŪTU 193
SOMNIU 42
SPARGŌ 60, 154
SPARSĪ 187
SPECLUM 50, 60
SPECULU 41
SPECULUM 50, 60
SPERĀRE 36
STABLUM 50
STABULĪ 268
STABULUM 50
STAGNU 61
STĀRE 36, 185, 266
STEM 162
STETĪ 185, 189
STŌ 162
STRICTU 41, 61, 62, 194
SUA 127
SUB 197
SUB- 240
SUBEŌ 160

SUBĪRE   190
SUBRĪSĪ   186
SUCCUTIŌ   149
SUFERRE   191
*SUFFERĪRE   191
SUFFERŌ   150
SULCU   60
SULFUR   108
*SULFURE   108
SUM   74, 143, 161
SUMUS   161
SUNT   161
SUPER   197
SUPER-   240
SUPERBIA   41
SUPRĀ-   241
SURSUM   118
SUSPECTA   48
SUSTUS   53
*SUTIS   162
SUUS   125

TĀLEOLA   34
TAM   74
TAM MAGNU   41
TANGERE   267
TANGŌ   60, 154
TARDE   117
-TĀTE   243
TAURU   28, 45
TAXŌ   217
TAXU   61
TAXUS   110
TĒ   119
TĒCTU   41
TĒCUM   120
*TEGLA   60
TEGULA   42, 60, 61, 64
TEMPLUM   102
TEMPORA   107, 108
TEMPORĀNU   50, 76
TEMPUS   107, 108
TENĒ   166
TENEBRAE   34
TENEŌ   151, 154
TENSA   66
TEPIDU   41
TEPIDUS   36
TERRA   82
TERSIO   54
TERTIĀRIUS   136
TERTIO   54
TERTIUS   136
TESA   66

TESTA   264
TETIGĪ   187
TIBĪ   43, 119
TIMĒBAM   167
TIMĒBŌ   173
TIMUĪ   186
TINCTU   194
TINXĪ   187
-TIŌNE   243
-TIS   138
TOLLŌ   154
TŌNSŌRIĀS   88
TOPAZIUS   111
*TORCERE   60
TORMA   39
TORQUERE   60
TORRĒRE   148
TŌTU   47
TŌTUS   133
TRACTU   194
TRAHŌ   150, 151, 154
TRANS   197, 198
TRANS-   239
TRAXĪ   185, 186
TRECENTŌS   135
TREDECIM   134
TREMULĀRE   78
TRĒS   133, 134
TRIENTA   59
TRIFOLIU   113
TRĪGINTA   59, 135
TRISTIS   4, 115
TRĪSTITIA   70
TRISTUS   4, 115
*TROPĀRE   9
TRUCTA   42
TŪ   119, 123
TUA   127
-TŪMINE   243
TUNC   117
TURBIDU   42
TURMA   39
TURRE   72
TURRĒS   71
TURTURE   112
TUSSĪRE   149
TUUS   125

ŪBER   108
ŪBERA   108
*ŪBERE   108
UBĪ   118
ULMUS   110
ULTRĀ   197, 198

ULTRĀ-   241
-ULU   248
-ULUS   248
UMERU   9
ŪNA   130, 134
UNDE   118
ŪNDECIM   134
UNDECIM   77, 134
ŪNU   134
ŪNUS   130, 133
-ŪRA   243
URSU   69
URSUS   44
-ŪSCU   244
-ŪTU   245

VACCA   65
VACLUS   4, 65
VĀDAM   151, 154, 165
VĀDĀMUS   148
VĀDĀTIS   148
VADE   167
VĀDIMUS   148
VĀDITIS   148
VĀDŌ   165
VADU   69
VALDE   116
VALEAT   65
VALEŌ   154
VALLĒS   62
VAPULO   65
VĀS   109
VĀSA   109, 266
VĀSUM   109
VECES   39
VECLU   41
VECLUS   50, 61
VENDAM   173
VĒNDĒBAM   167
*VENDEDISSEM   170
VĒNDERE   10, 148, 181,
      189
VĒNDIDĪ   180, 181, 185
VĒNDITE   148
VENDŌ   147, 150, 156
VENERIS   78
VENĪ   40, 43, 166
VĒNĪ   43, 49, 142, 185, 187
VENIENDŌ   191
VENIŌ   151, 154, 173
VENĪRE HABĒBAT   145
VENĪRE HABET   145
VENĪS   85
VENIT   37, 138

VĒNIT 37, 187
VENTU 265
VENTUS EST 142
VERĒCUNDIA 42, 56
VĒRITĀTE 76
VERMICULU 61
*VERRUCULU 265
VERSUS 195
VERVĀCTU 65
VESPA 46
VESPERA 46
VESTER 125
VETULU 41, 61
VETULUS 34, 50, 61
VIBA 65
VICES 39
VĪCĪ 189
VĪCĪNU 57, 64, 159
VICLUS 61
VICTU 193
VIDEAM 163
VIDEAT 41
VIDEŌ 55, 150, 163

VIDĒRE 176, 191
VĪDĪ 185, 188
VĪGINTĪ 135
VĪLLA 268
VĪMEN 108
VĪMINA 108
*VĪMINE 108
VINCENTIUS 54
VINCENTZUS 54
*VINCICULU 60
VINDĒMIA 40, 41, 56
VINDICĀRE 75, 77
VĪNEA 52, 55, 64
VINIA 52
VĪNU 49
VĪNUM 107
VIRDIA 56
VIRDIS 5, 50
VIRIDIS 5, 34, 50
VĪSIŌ 210
VĪSU 193
VĪTA 29, 46, 64, 65
VITREU 41

VITULUS 61
VĪVA 65
VIVĒBAM 168
VĪVERE 65, 159
VĪVU 65
VĪXĪ 187
VĪXIT 65
VŌBĪSCUM 120
VOLŌ 173
VOLŪTU 193
VOLVERE 65
VŌS 119, 123, 125
VŌSCUM 120
VOSTER 125
VŌTA 109, 265, 266
VULPĒCULA 258
VULPĒS 258
VULTURE 42, 62

ZANUARIO 53
ZERAX 53

Index of Spanish words cited

Words are modern Spanish unless followed by an abbreviation: OSp. = Old Spanish, JS = Judaeo-Spanish, Phil = Philippines Spanish, Gal = Galician, Ptg = Portuguese.

a 74, 102, 103, 195, 196
a través 197
ábaco 214
abadengo 12
abadía 243
abajo 118
abarca 210
abedul 209
abeja 42, 248
abejón 249
abierto 193
abismo 212
abolengo 12
abonar 227
ábrego 73, 265
abrelatas 251, 252
absoluto (en~) 255
abstener 92
aburrido 245
acá 118
acaba 85
acacia 214
açada OSp. 70
academia 213
açaguán OSp. 222
acantilado 233
accidente 269
aceite 219, 223
aceituna 219
acelga 219, 221
acentazo 249
aceptar 92
acequia 219
acera 264
acetar 92
aceutar 92
achicoria 214
-aço OSp. 54
açor OSp. 75

acordeón 228
acrílico 231
actoritat 211
actuario 231
acuarela 234
açuela OSp. 55
adaptar 238
adarga 218
adarme OSp. 219, 221
adelantado 260
además 8, 197
adereçar OSp. 55, 64
aderredor OSp. 198
adestrar OSp. 157
adherir 238
adiestrar 157
adiós 238
administración 261
admirar 238
-ado 192
adobar 216, 266
adobe 219
adral 76
adta OSp. 195
aduana 219, 222
aducho OSp. 193
aducir 160
adugo OSp. 153
adurá OSp. 176
aduxe OSp. 186
aduzco 160
aduzir OSp. 153, 190
adversario 211
aerofotografía 253
aeropuerto 231
aerosol 231
afanar 216
afecto 92
afeitar 233, 256

afeite 233
aferrar 232
afeto 92
afeuto 92
afición 92
afortunado 269
agenda 261
agoiro OSp. 42
agora OSp. 118
agosto 28, 59
agradecer 149, 246
agravar 238
agridulce 252
agrupar 238
agua 71, 73
aguafiestas 252
aguamiel 252
aguanieve 252
aguantar 236
aguardiente 252
agudo 47
aguijada 265
aguilucho 249
agüero 42, 56
ahí 118
ahora 118, 264
ahorrar 219
ai JS 23
aire 213, 235
ajedrez 220, 221
ajenjo 212
ajeno 46
ají 228
ajo 41, 55
ajuar 222
al OSp. 133
al- 218
alabanza 243
alabastro 213

alacena 219
alacrán 220, 221, 222
alambique 220, 221, 222
alambre 108, 265
álamo 209
alarde 218, 221, 222
alarife OSp. 219, 220,
     221, 222
alazán 221
alba 30, 85, 211
albacea 222
albahaca 220
albañal 219
albañil 219, 222
albaricoque 219, 221
albéitar 219, 220, 223
alberca 219
albérchigo 221, 266
albardero 219
albergue 216
albóndiga 220
albornoz 220
alcachofa 219, 221
alcaide 218, 223
alcalde 219, 256
alcanfor 220, 221
alcantarilla 219
alçar OSp. 86, 88
alcaraván 220, 222
alcatraz 220
alcázar 218, 221, 222
alcoba 219
alcohol 220
alcurnia 220
aldaba 219
aldea 219, 223
alderredor OSp. 198
aldeúcha 249
alemana 115
alerce 220
alerta 235
alfabeto 213
alfageme OSp. 220
alfalfa 219, 221
alfamar OSp. 221
alfanje 218
alfarero 219
alfayate OSp. 220
alfeña OSp. 221
alfeñique 220, 221
alférez 218, 256
alfil 220
alfiler 219
alfombra 219

alfónsigo 219
alforja 221
alforjas 218
algarabía 221, 268
algarroba 219, 221
álgebra 220
algo 74, 76, 133
algodón 219, 222, 223
alguacil 222
alguazil OSp. 256
alguien 133
algún(o), -a 133
alhaja 220
alhamar 221
alhelí 220, 223
alheña 220, 221, 223
alhucema 220
aliar 225
alicates 219, 222
aliso 210
aliviar 259
aljibe 219
allá 118, 195, 198, 197
allén OSp. 197, 198
allende 197
allí 23, 74, 118
alma 78
almacén 219
almáciga 220
almadía 219
almanaque 220, 221
almazara 219
almeja 233
almenas 218
almez 220, 223
almiar 265, 266
almíbar 220, 221
alminar 220
almirante 218
almirez 219
almocadén 222
almocafre 219
almogávar 222
almohada 219
almohaza 219
almoneda 219
almoraduj 220
almotacén OSp. 222
almud 221
almuédano 220
almuerzo 264
alondra 209
aloquín 222
alquiler 219, 222

alquimia 220, 221
alquitrán 220
alrededor 195, 198
altibajos 252
alto 114, 235
altramuz 220
alubia 219
alud 210
alumbrado 243
alumbrar 259
alva OSp. 30, 85, 211
amanezient OSp. 192
amante 243
amarillo 10, 23
amario JS 23
amarrar 226
amatista 111
ambición 211
ambigenérico 253
ameba 231
amenaza 70
ametista OSp. 111
ametisto OSp. 111
amiga 259
amontonar 238
amor 111
amortecer 238
amplificar 245
ampolla 212
amputación 211
analgesia 231
ananá(s) 229
anarquía 214
anatomía 213
ancho 63, 64
anchoa 236
ancla 212
andamio 219
andas 112
andes OSp. 112
andide OSp. 189
andove OSp. 185
andude 186
anegar 266
anemia 214
anestesia 214
anfibio 214
angra 233
anguila 232
ánima 211
animalejo 248
animalucho 249
anís 232
anochecer 245

anorak 230, 231
ánsar 266
ante 197
anteponer 241
antes 117
antes que 200
antídoto 214
antigo OSp. 114
antigua 114
antiguo 114
antioxidante 241
antiquísimo 117
antología 214
antorcha 225
ántrax 214
añadir 149
añil 220, 221
año 40, 62, 64, 104
año luz 262
añorar 233
apaciguar 238
apagado 245
apagar 11
apañar 259
apartamento 261
apellido 211
aplausos 211
apoplejía 213
apórtar 157
apoyar 234
aprender 237
aprendizaje 243
aprise OSp. 187
aquel 129
aquelarre 209
aquello 130
aquén de OSp. 198
aquesse 130
aqueste 130
aquí 118
árabe 222
arabesco 234
arado 28
araña 41, 55, 264
árbol 111, 112
arcabuz 226
arcaico 214
archiconocido 253
arcilla 60
ardí 184
ardido 216
ardite 226
arena 8
arenga 215

arenque 216, 225
argolla 223
argumento 211
aria 235
arienço OSp. 10, 266
aristocracia 214
aritmética 213
arma 109, 110
armadura 243
armario 257
armiño 266
armonía 213
arpa 216, 217
arpende 209
arpía 214
arqueología 214
arquitecto 220
arrabal 219
arrayán 220
arrepentirse 149
arriba 85, 118, 195, 197
arroba 219
arrojar 61
arroyo 210
arroz 219, 221
arruinar 261
arte 112
arteria 213
ártico 213
arzilla OSp. 60
asalto 235
asamblea 226
ascensión 211
ascua 210
aseo 259
asesino 220, 268
asfixia 214
asgo 154
así 118
asiento 264
asir 267
asno 76, 89, 94
aso OSp. 154
aspaviento 236
astener 92
asteroide 214
astrólogo 213
astronomía 213
astrónomo 213
asuntillo 247
ata OSp. 195
atacar 235
atalaya 218
ataque 261

atar 91
ataracear 148
ataúd 220
ataviar 215
ateniense 244
ateo 214
aterrizaje 227
atesar OSp. 157
atiesar 157
átomo 213
atormentar 238
atracadero 243
atreví 185
atril 62
atrove OSp. 185
auctoridat 211
aún 118
aunque 200
auto-stop 230
autógrafo 214
autonomía 214
autopromoción 241
autopsia 214
autoridad 211
autorretrato 253
autorzuelo 248·
avalancha 227
avanzar 232, 235
avariento 244
ave(s) (vb) OSp. 164
avellana 266
aver OSp. 163, 177
avería 232
avestruz 226
aviación 227
aviespa OSp. 46
avión 227
avispa 46
-avo 137
avrá OSp. 175
ayer 43, 118
ayuno 58
ayuso OSp. 118
azabache 222
azafata 220
azafrán 219
azahar 220
azar 257
azogue 220
azor 75
azote 223
azotea 219
azúcar 219
azucena 220

azuda 219
azufre 108
azul 220, 221
azulado 244
azulejo 219
azulenco 244
azumbre 219, 222

babor 226
babucha 227
bacalao 226
bachiller 225
badén 222
bagatela 236
bailar 225
bajamar 252
bajito 246
bajo 195, 197, 235
bala 216
balada 226
balance 231, 235
balaustre 234
balcón 234
balde 233
ballena 213
balsa 210
baluarte 226
bambú 233
ban OSp. 85
bancarrota 235, 252
banco 215, 235
banda 215, 216
bando 65, 85, 216
banquete 226
bantam 231
baño 212
baquelita 231
barba 265
barbecho 65
barbero 220, 256
barbirrojo 252
barcaza 249
barítono 235
barón 216
barraca 232
barragán OSp. 259
barragana OSp. 259
barrica 226
barricada 226
barrio 219
barro 210, 267
barrote 250
barullo 234
barvecho OSp. 65

base 214, 261
basquiña 234
bastión 235
batallón 226, 235
batata 229
batea 229
batería 226
batuta 235
baúl 226
bautismo 212
bautizar 212
baxar OSp. 31
baxo OSp. 85, 197
baya 225
bayoneta 226
bebé 228
beber 65
bebrá OSp. 76
becada 232
becerro 210
begonia 228
beige 227
béisbol 231
bejuco 229
belleza 236
bellota 220
bendición 211
berça OSp. 56
berenjena 219
bermejo 61
berro 209
berrojo OSp. 265
besamel(a) 227
besico 247
beso 41, 56
beso de la vida 262
bestséller 231
betún 232
bever OSp. 65
bevi OSp. 187
bevir OSp. 65, 159
bevrá OSp. 175
biblia 212
bibliografía 214
biblioteca 213
bicho 234
bicicleta 227
bidé 227
bidma OSp. 78
biela 227
bien 44, 65, 117
bienes 85
bikini 231
billar 227

billete 226
biografía 214
biombo 233
biomecánica 253
bipolaridad 241
bisabuelo 241
bisonte 214
bistades OSp. 85
bisturí 227
bisutería 227
bivi OSp. 187
bivir OSp. 65
bivo OSp. 65, 85
bivrá OSp. 175
bizarro 236
bizma 78
blanco 216
blancuzco 244
blandear 245
blandengue 250
blandir 216, 225
blando 83
blandujo 250
blanquecer 245
blanquecino 244
blasfemar 212
bloque 227
blusa 227
bob 231
bobina 227
bobsleigh 231
boca 65, 263, 264
bocado 243
boda 109, 113, 265, 266
bodaza 249
bodega 212
boga 227
bogavante 235
bohío 229
boina 209
bolo 94
bolos 94
bolsa 227
bolver OSp. 65
bombarda 235
bombardear 235
bondad 77
boom 231
boquete 248
borbónico 244
borde 226
borracho 233
bosque 232
bota 209

botar 216, 257
botella 227
botón 226
boutique 228, 231
boxeo 231
boz OSp. 65, 85
braço OSp. 54, 63
braga 209
bramar 215
brasa 215
bravata 236
braza 109, 228
brazo 109
brecha 226
bretona 115
breva 76, 266
brezo 209
brigada 227
brigadier 227
brincar 234
brío 209
brocado 236
broker 231
broncazo 249
brote 215
bruces (de~) 209
brújula 235
bruma 266
bruñir 216
brusco 236
bruto (en~) 235
bucle 227
buen 114
buenísimo 117
bueno 44, 71, 98
buey 85, 113
búfalo 213
bufón 234
buganvilla 228
buitre 42, 62
bujía 227
bulevar 228
bullir 161
bunker 231
buque 216, 232
buque-hospital 252
buque escuela 262
burdel 226
burgesas OSp. 115
burgués 115
buró 227
burocracia 227
buscón 259
buscona 259

busto 234
butaca 229
butifarra 232
buzo 233

ca OSp. 199
cab(e) OSp. 198
cabalgar 72
caballo 2, 62, 65, 268
cabaña 28, 57, 209
cabdal OSp. 78, 91
cabe 85
cabecear 245
caber 85
cabestro 48
cabeza 242
cabezazo 242
cabildo 78
cabizbajo 252
cable 226
cabo 109, 113
cabo (prep) OSp. 198
cabra 73, 83
cabrá 177
caça OSp. 86, 88
cacahuete 229
cacao 229
caçar OSp. 55, 64
cacatúa 233
cacerola 227
cachalote 233
cachorro 209
cacique 229
cada 133, 212
caddie 231
cadena 68, 261
cadera 264
cadete 227
cadrá OSp. 176
cadré OSp. 175
café 236
çafir OSp. 111
cagarruta 224
çahanoria OSp. 222
cahiz 219
caigo 151, 154
caja 90, 232, 263
caja fuerte 262
cal OSp. 72
cal 212
calafatear 232
calamar 232
calça OSp. 54, 63
calças OSp. 256

calibre 226
calientaplatos 262
caliente 158
calor 112
calzas 256
callao 233
calle 268
calleja 248
callente 158
calles 72
cama 210
cámara 212, 231
camarote 250
camastro 250
cameraman 231
camilla 247
camino 209
camión 227
camioneta 248
camisa 209
campana 266
campeón 236
campiña 224
camping 230
camposanto 236, 252
camuflaje 228
canal 261
canalla 236
cancha 229
candado 10, 50, 78
cándido 211
candilejas 248
canesú 227
cangilón 224
caníbal 229
canjear 235
canoa 229
canónigo 213
cansar 8
canso (part) 194
canta 95
cantaba 74
cantan 49
cántaro 51
cantas 49, 95
cantata 235
cantava OSp. 74
canté 41
cantil 233
cantina 236
canto 49, 98
caña 62, 212
cáñamo 212
cañivete 216, 232

cañón   235
caoba   229
caos   213
capacho   224
capacidad   211
capellán   225
caperucita   251
capitán   232
capitel   225
capota   250
capricho   236
capucho   236
capuz   224
caqui   230
cara   195
carabela   233
carabina   226
caracol   232
caracoles   260
carajo   260
carambola   233
caramelo   234
caramillo   51, 213
cardíaco   213
cargar   72
cargarse   259
cariancho   252
caricatura   234
caricia   236
caridad   211
caridat   211
caries   211
carmesí   223
carmín   226
carnaval   236
carné   228
caro   47
carpintero   209
carra   195
carria   195
carrillo   264
carrito   242
carro   72, 209, 242
carroña   236
carroza   236
carta   213
cartaginés   115
cartel   231, 232
catón   234
cartucho   226
cartulina   236
casa   22, 67, 73, 86, 88,
     90, 260, 268
casa OSp.   89

cascabel   225
cascada   236
cascajos   250
cascar   84, 87
caserón   249
casilla   247
casino   234
cassette   231
casta   216
castellano   25
castidad   211
castidat   211
castiello OSp.   46
castillo   46, 221
catálogo   214
catar   11
catarro   213
catástrofe   214
cátedra   213
catedral   213
catide OSp.   189
católico   213
catorce   84, 135
catorze OSp.   84
catre   233
caucho   229
caudal   78, 91
causa   267
cautivo   268
cavalgar OSp.   72
cavallo OSp.   62, 64, 65,
     73
cavar   85
cavatina   235
caviar   236
caxa OSp.   86, 88, 90
cayo OSp.   151, 154, 229
caza   90
cebada   10
cebo   267
cebolla   23
ceca   222
cedo OSp.   49
ceja   42
cejijunto   252
celidonia   214
celo   213
celosía   236
cementerio   213
cena   264
cencerro   209
cénit   220
centeno   11
centinela   111, 235

cerca   57, 195, 198
cereales   261
ceresa OSp.   41
cereza   41, 212
cerezo   110
cero   220, 235
cerrojo   265
certas OSp.   117
cerúleo   211
cervesa OSp.   41
cerveza   41, 209
césped   265
cesta   46, 64, 212, 244
cesto   244
cevo OSp.   68
cibdad OSp.   78
cibera   10
cibernética   231
ciclamato   231
ciclo   214
ciego   8, 47
cielo   45, 47, 57
ciempiés   253
cien(to)   135
ciertas OSp.   117
cierto   133
cierzo   10
cifra   220, 222
cigoña OSp.   42
cigüeña   42
cilindro   213
cima   212
cimiento   48
cimientos   265
cinemascope   231
cinco   22, 134
cincuenta   135
cine club   262
cingo OSp.   155
cintajo   250
cinto OSp.   193
cinxe OSp.   187
ciño   155
círculo   261
circunlocución   241
ciruela   266
cisma   213
ciudad   78
ciudad dormitorio   251,
     262
ciudadela   235
cizaña   212
claraboya   226
clarete   226

claridad 211
claridat 211
claroscuro 234, 252
clavel 232
clavija 62
clérigo 213
clima 111, 213
clínico 214
clip 231
clisé 228
cobaya, -o 229
cobdicia OSp. 78
cobdo OSp. 78
cobre 113
coca 229
coçe OSp. 50
cocer 90
cocodrilo 213
coche 255
cocho OSp. 193
codeso 212
codicia 78
codo 47, 78
cofonder OSp. 68, 149
coger 259
coges 41
cogombro OSp. 112
cohete 233
cohombro 112
cohonder OSp. 68
coiro OSp. 42
coita 233
coitado 233
cojera 243
cojo 41
col 47
colar 157
coldcream 231
cólera 211, 213
colesterol 231
colgar 267
cólico 213
colina 235
collaço OSp. 70
colmillo 11
colmo 78
colocar 267
color 112
coma 213, 231
comadreja 258
comandar 227
combater OSp. 149
combatir 149
combrá OSp. 176

comedia 213
comediante 234
comedieta 248
comején 229
comendaçión 211
cometa 214
comidrá OSp. 175
comigo OSp. 121
comité 227
como 84, 118, 200
como quier(a) que
    OSp. 201
comodín 247
compañero 267
compaño OSp. 267
complejo 261
complir OSp. 190
complot 227
compositor 235
comulgar 267
comunicar 267
con 74, 195
con(n)usco OSp. 121
cóncavo 211
concebir 149
concepto 211
concha 212
concibrá OSp. 175
concierto 235
conde 50, 77
condestable 268
condición 211
cóndor 229
condueño 241
condugo OSp. 155
conduje 187
conduxe OSp. 186
conduzco 155
confortar 157, 211
confundir 68, 149, 161
congelar 261
congoja 233
conmigo 121
conmiseración 211
cono 213
conocer 155
conosco OSp. 155
conozco 155
conquerir OSp. 194
conquistar 194
conquisto OSp. 194
consejo 42
conserje 226
consigo 121

consigrá OSp. 175
consintrá OSp. 175
consolar 157
consomé 227
consuelo (vb) 157
contáiner 231
contar 77
contigo 121
continuo 34
continúo 34
continuó 34
contra 198
contrabando 235
contralto 235
contraproducente 241
contrición 211
control 227
conuve OSp. 186
convite 232
convoy 226
convusco OSp. 121
coñac 227, 265
copa 40, 47, 68, 82
cope OSp. 185
copyright 231
coqueta 227
corbata 236
corbeta 227
corcel 225
corcho 112, 113, 224
cordel 226, 232
cordobesa 115
cordones 249
córner 231
corneta 111
corniabierto 252
coro 213
corona 28, 57
coronel 226, 232, 235
corpiño 234
correa 34, 41, 55, 70
correo 226, 251
correr 28, 260
correvedile 253
correveidile 253
corsario 235
corsé 227
cortacésped 262
cortafrío 252
cortafuego 252
cortaplumas 252
corte 268
cortejar 236
cortejo 236

cortés 69, 115
cortesa 115
cortesano 236
corteses 69
corteza 48
cortocircuito 252
cortometraje 252
cosa 28, 45, 73, 267
cosa (nada) OSp. 255
coscojo 42
coser 90
cosmético 231
cosmos 214
costura 34
cotejar 232
cotidiano 211
cotizar 227
covacha 250
coxe OSp. 186
coyote 229
coz 50, 264
cozer OSp. 153
cracking 231
cráneo 214
cras OSp. 8, 118
cráter 214
crawl 231
creçer OSp. 70
credidito 246
creçrá OSp. 175
credito 235
creencia 243
creer 167, 191
crei 185
crema 226
cremallera 227
crepúsculo 211
crerá OSp. 176
cretino 259
creyendo 192
criar 260
criatura 211
crisantemo 214
crisis 214
crisol 232
cristalino 245
criterio 214
crítico 214
crol 231
crónica 213
croquet 231
croqueta 227
cross country 231
crove OSp. 185

cruasán 228
cruce de cebra 262
crucial 261
crucificado 211
crudelísimo 117
crudo 69
crúo OSp. 69
cruz 33, 50
cuadro 73
cuádruplo 136
cuajo 41
cual 84, 132, 133
cualquier 132
cualquiera 133
cuando 118, 199
cuandoquiera 133
cuarenta 8, 34, 73, 135
cuarentena 136
cuartel 232
cuarto 136
cuatro 74, 84, 134
cuatrocientos 135
cuba 47, 57, 68
cubierto 193
cubo 213
cucaña 236
cuchar 109
cuchara 48, 212
cuchiello OSp. 46, 61
cuchillo 46, 61
cuego OSp. 153, 155
cuellilargo 252
cuelo 157
cuemo OSp. 118, 200
cuend OSp. 50
cuenta 265
cuento 136
cuentra OSp. 198
cuerda 212
cuerno 83, 107
cuero 42, 45, 267
cuerpo 108
cueva 8, 29
cuévano 212
cuezo 155
cuidar 48, 76
cuita, -ado 233
culebra 46
culuebra OSp. 46
cumbre 108, 261
cumplir 149
cundir 216
cuneta 235
cuña 40, 42

cuñado 267
cuño 42
cupón 227
cúpula 234
cura 111, 265
curángano 250
curar 48
curare 229
curete 248
cuyo, -a 8, 70, 128, 132

cha 234
chacal 227
chalé 227
chamorro 210
champán 228, 265
champiñón 228
champú 231
chanza 236
chaparro 209
chaqueta 227
charco 210
charlar 236
charlatán 236
charol 234
chárter 231
chato 63
chaveta 236
cheviot 231
chícharo 112, 224
chichón 236
chicle 229
chile 229
chimenea 225
chimpancé 228
chinche 224
chincheta 248
chiquitillo 251
chiquitín 251
chirimía 226
chirivía 219, 224
chistorro 250
chocolate 229
chopa 233
chopo 63, 110
choza 63
chozo 63
chubasco 233
chulo 236
chusma 235
chutar 231

dado 220
dama 226

damajuana 227
damisela 226
dáncing 230
daño 71
danzar 225
dardo 216, 225
dársena 235
dátil 232
dé 163
de 103
deán 225
debajo 118
debate 227
debda OSp. 78
debe 86
deber 10, 34
débito 235
debrá OSp. 177
debut 228
debutar 228
decena 136
decidero 245
decir OSp. 86
decir 149
decoro 211
dedo 59, 67
defender 211
defesa OSp. 68
defeso OSp. 193
deflación 231
degollar 237
dehesa 68, 237, 267
dejar 10
delantal 232
delante 197
delantre 197
deleite 225
delfín 214
demandide OSp. 189
demás 8
demientre OSp. 117, 200
democracia 214
denante OSp. 197
denegar 238
dentro 196
depender 264
depósito 235
depués OSp. 197
derecho 41
derribo 243
derrumbe 243
des OSp. 195, 196
desalmado 238
desante OSp. 197

desastre 226
descapotable 227
desconfiar 238
descoser 238
desde 94, 195, 196, 197
desdecir 238
desdén 225
desdeñar 94
desechar 238
desenfadar 233
desenfado 223
desertar 227
desfachatado 236
deshacer 238
deshonrar 238
deshuesar 157
desiderio OSp. 210
desmayar 216, 225
desmentir 238
desnudo 69
desossar OSp. 157
despachar 226
despejar 234
despise OSp. 186
déspota 214
después 117, 195, 197
destacar 234, 235
destender OSp. 238
destruxe OSp. 186
destruyes 165
desviar 238
detalle 227
detergente 231
detrás 195, 198
deuda 78
devaluación 231
deve OSp. 86
dezir OSp. 22, 86, 87, 88, 153
dezmar OSp. 157
di (imper) 74, 167
di (pret) 189
día 110, 168
diablo 213
diácono 213
dialecto 214
diamante 213
diámetro 214
diarrea 213
dices 100
dicho 193
diecisiete 135
diente de león 264
diestro 31, 157, 258

diez 134
diezmar 157
diezmo 76, 89, 94, 136, 157
digo 100, 153, 154
dije 61, 91, 187
diluvio 211
dínamo 111
dinastía 214
dinero 267
dintel 226
diptongo 213
dirá 176, 177
directo (en~) 230
disc-jockey 231
discernir 238
disentería 214
diseño 234
disforme 238
disgusto 94
divertir 238
dixe OSp. 61, 62, 91, 186
dixera OSp. 87
dixiendo OSp. 192
dixo OSp. 22, 86, 88
dize OSp. 57
dizir OSp. 159, 190
do OSp. 118, 162
doblaje 228
doble 73, 136
doblegar 232
doblo 73
doce 51, 77, 134
docena 136
dócil 211
doldrá OSp. 176
dolfín OSp. 214
domientre OSp. 117, 200
domingo 76, 77
don 49, 72
don(oc)iña Gal 258
doncel 225
doncella 225
donde 49, 118
donecilla 258
donicela Gal 258
doninha Ptg 258
donjuan 267
doping 231
dormir 160
dos 134
doscientos 135
dosis 214
doy 162

dozavo   137
doze OSp.   77
dozientos OSp.   135
dragón   213
drama   214
dribbling   231
dubda OSp.   91
ducha   227
duda   91
duela   154
duelga OSp.   154
duelo   235
dueño   113
duermevela   253
duermo   160
Duero   45
dues OSp.   49, 134
dulce   60
dumping   231
dúo   235
duplicar   261
duplo   136
duque   225
durante   196
durazno   76

e   198
ea JS   23
ecelente   92
ecepción   211
echar   58
eclipse   213
ecología   231
economía   214
editor   261
efecto   92
efeto   92
ejecución   211
ejercer   92
el   23, 129, 131
él   119, 129
ela OSp.   131
elar OSp.   58
elas OSp.   131
electrodomésticos   253
elefante   213
elefante blanco   262
elepé   231
eliminar   259
elipse   214
ell OSp.   131
ella   23, 119
ellas   119
ello   119

ellos   119
elos OSp.   131
emanar   239
embajada   226
embarazada   259
embarrar   238
embebecer   245
embeber   239
embestir   235
embiar OSp.   30
emborrachar   238
emboscada   235
emboscar   235
embriagador   245
embrión   214
empapelar   238
empatar   236
empeñar   238
empeño   108
emplear   225
empleíllo   247
empós OSp.   197
empués OSp.   197
empuja   42
emular   211
en   74, 196
enaguas   229
enante OSp.   197
encabezar   239
encarnado   234
encia   60
encías   58
enciclopedia   214
encima   118, 197
encina   110
encoger   239
encontra OSp.   198
encuadernación   265
encuentro cumbre   262
end(e) OSp.   118
enderredor OSp.   198
endosar   227
enebro   58
enero   58
enfadarse   233
enfadoso   233
enfrente   197
enganchar   239
engendrar   29, 51, 78
engorar   209
engordar   239
engranaje   227
engrossar OSp.   157
engruesar   157

enjalbegar   239
enjambre   108
enjuagar   239
enjugar   239
enloquecer   239
enojar   225
e(n)mendar   211
enojo OSp.   42
enrasar   239
ensalzar   239
ensanchar   239
ensayo   55, 74
ensordecer   149
entero   34, 41
entonces   50, 117, 118
entrañas   263
entre   196
entreabrir   239
entreayudarse   239
entrecano   239
entrecomillar   239
entrecruzar   239
entrefino   239
entregar   157
entremés   232
entrenar   228
entresacar   239
entride OSp.   189
enviar   30
envidiosillo   247
enzia OSp.   60
enzias OSp.   58
eñader Osp.   149
epidemia   214
epigrama   214
epilepsia   213
epitafio   211
epíteto   214
equipar   227
era   40, 41, 169
eres   162
erguir   154, 160
erigir   211
erisipela   214
erizo   54, 64
ermano OSp.   58
ermita   213
ervage OSp.   58
erzer OSp.   154
-és   69
es   162
esa   91
esbelto   234
escalfar   232

escalope   228
escanciar   216
escaño   91
escapar   239
escardar   239
escarnecer   216, 246
escarnir OSp.   216, 246
escarola   232
escarpa   235
escayola   232, 234
escena   214
escoba   261
escoger   239
escollo   235
escolta   235
escontra OSp.   198
escopeta   235
escopir OSp.   161
escrevir OSp.   190
escribir   159
escrise OSp.   186
escrito   193
escrivir OSp.   190
escuadrón   235
escucha   42
escuela   22, 36, 213
escullirse   215
escupir   150
escurrir   161
esdrújulo   234
ese   129
esfera   213
esfinge   214
esfumar   234
esgrimir   216, 225
esguazar   236
esient OSp.   192
eskola JS   22
eslip   231
esmalte   216, 232
esmeragde OSp.   111
esmeralda   111, 213
esmoquin   36
esnob   36
eso   119, 130
espada   212
espantapájaros   252
España   25, 55
español   25, 225
española   115
españon OSp.   25, 115, 225
espargo OSp.   60, 154, 155
espárrago   212
esparto   212

esparzir OSp.   154
esparzo   60, 155
espejismo   243
espejo   41
espera OSp.   213
esperar   36
espeso OSp.   86, 193
espesso OSp.   86
espeto   216, 217
espía   215, 217
espiar   215
espinazo   249
espiquer   231
espise OSp.   186
esplendor   211
esponja   212
espuela   215
espuerta   212
esqueje   233
esqueleto   214
esquí   228
esquife   232
esquila   216, 226
esquilar   216
esquina   216
esquizofrenia   231
essa OSp.   91
essos OSp.   69
estaca   215
estadounidense   251
estafar   236
estandarte   216, 225
estaño   61
estar   36, 266
este   129
este   94
esté   163
estela   233
estender OSp.   238
esternón   227
estide OSp.   189
estío   264
estirar la pata   259
esto   119, 130
estó OSp.   162
estómago   213
estonz OSp.   50, 117, 118
estopa   212
estopaçio OSp.   111
estopaza OSp.   111
estopazo OSp.   111
estoria OSp.   213
estove OSp.   185
estoy   162

estrafalario   236
estrecho   41, 61, 62
estrella   261
estrés   231
estribo   216
estribor   226
estropajo   250
estropear   236
estuche   225
estuco   234
estude OSp.   186
estudiantil   245
estudio   261
etcho JS   22
éter   214
etimología   226
etiqueta   226
eurocomunista   253
evidencia   211
ex primer ministro   239
ex presidente   239
examen   92
excarcelar   239
excavación   211
excelente   92
excéntrico   239
excepción   211
excreción   211
exercer   92
exerçiçio OSp.   87
exhalación   211
exhibir   239
explotar   227
extender   238, 239
exterior   116
extirpar   239
extraño   41
extremaunción   252
eya JS   23

fablar OSp.   30
fábrica   211
fábula   32, 33
façe OSp.   50
facer OSp.   79, 81
façera OSp.   264
faces OSp.   58, 87
fachada   234
factoría   261
factoring   231
factura   235
fading   231
faena   232
fago OSp.   153

faisán 226
falda 216, 232
falleztra OSp. 176
falso 79
fama 79
fambri JS 22
fanega 219
fantasía 235
far OSp. 189
fará OSp. 177
farándula 226
faraute OSp. 216
farina OSp. 79, 81, 90
farmacia 214
farol 232
farsante 236
fase 214
fasta OSp. 195
fatiga 261
favorito 227
faya OSp. 55, 64
fayar JS 23
faz OSp. 50, 70, 87, 195
faza OSp. 195
faze OSp. 57
fazer JS 22
fazer OSp. 57, 153, 189
fazerá OSp. 177
fazia OSp. 195
fe 75, 113
feçes OSp. 70
fecundizar 245
fech OSp. 148, 167
feches OSp. 148, 166
fecho OSp. 61, 64
femos OSp. 148, 166
fénix 214
feo 45, 46
feón 249
fer OSp. 189
ferá OSp. 177
ferir OSp. 154
Fernández 12
Fernando 12, 77
ferrá OSp. 175
férrea 211
ferrero OSp. 56
ferroníquel 253
ferroviario 236
feúcho 249
fez OSp. 70
fezes OSp. 70
fezo OSp. 187
fiasco 236

ficha 227
fideos 220, 224
fiel OSp. 74
fiel 49, 75
fieltro 216
fier(g)o OSp. 154
fierro OSp. 90
fiesta 46
figo OSp. 79, 81
figura 79
fijo OSp. 64, 79, 81, 86
fijodalgo OSp. 260
fijus JS 22
filigrana 236
film 228
film(e) 231
filmar 228
filo OSp. 79, 81
filología 214
filosofía 213
filosoviético 253
financiero 227
finanazas 227
finojo OSp. 42
firma 261
firme 115
fito OSp. 61
fixo OSp. 86
fiz(e) OSp. 184, 187
fizo OSp. 187
flamante 236
flamígero 211
flan 228
flas(h) 231
flauta 226
flecha 216, 225
fleco 46, 62
flema 213
flete 216
flor 47
florecer 149
florecilla 251
florecita 251
florir OSp. 149
flota 261
flueco OSp. 46, 62
fobia 231
foca 214
foçe OSp. 50
fogón 232
fogoso 236
foja OSp. 55
follaje 232
folleto 234

follón 233
fonda 220
fondo OSp. 30
fonética 214
fontana 234
footing 230
forcejar 232
forjar 226
forma 79, 81, 91
forma OSp. 79, 81, 91
forno OSp. 79, 81, 90
fortísimo 117
fortuna 269
fósforo 214
foto 111
foz OSp. 50
frac 227
fracasar 236
fragata 235
fraile 225
frailuco 249
frambuesa 227
francesa 115
franchute 250
frango OSp. 154
franzir OSp. 154
frañer OSp. 154
frasco 216
frase 214
fregar 157
frego 157
fregotear 246
freisno OSp. 62
frenesí 226
frente 46, 79, 195, 197
fresa 226
fresco 215, 234
frescote 250
fresno 62, 110, 134
friego 157
frío 59, 81, 91
frito 61, 193, 194
fruente OSp. 46, 79, 81
fruncir 216
fruta 110
fruto 110
fudré OSp. 175
fudredes OSp. 176
fue 188
fuego 40
fuel-oil 231
fuelle 79, 81
fuente 30, 79, 81, 264
fuera (adv) 195, 196

fuera de juego 262
fueras OSp. 117
fuerte 30, 79, 80, 81, 90, 114
fuertísimo 117
fuerza 40
fuga 235
fui 185, 186, 188
fulana 259
fulano 220, 259
fulgente 211
funesto 211
furmiga JS 22
fusa 235
fusil 227
fútbol 231
futbolín 247
fuxe OSp. 186
fuye(s) OSp. 165
fuyo OSp. 151, 154
fuyrá OSp. 176

gabán 222
gaceta 236
gafa(s) 232
gaína JS 23
gala 226
galán 226
galante 227
galera 232
galgo 72
galimatías 227
galón 226
galopar 225
galpón 229
galleta 227
gallina 23, 59
gallo 62, 71
gana 216
ganancia 243
ganar 216
gancho 209
gandul 220
gangrena 213
ganso 216
garaje 227
garantía 227
garbo 236
García 209
garra 220
garrapata 210
garúa 233
gasoil 231
gatillo 264

gatito 242
gato 83, 264
gavilán 216
gazapo 210
gazpacho 224
géiser 230
gelo OSp. 122
generalísimo 235
génesis 112
gentezuela 248
gentuza 250
geografía 214
geometría 213
gerifalte 216
gigante 213
gigantesco 244
Gimeno 209
gimotear 246
girasol 252
globo 263
glorificar 245
gobernalle 232
gol 231
golf 231
golfo 232, 236
golpe 83, 212
góndola 235
gongo 230
gordezuelo 248
gordito 242
gordo 242
gorgojo 42
gota 59, 68, 82
gotón 249
gozo 59
gradir OSp. 149, 246
graduando 243
gramática 213
gran 114
granada 235
granate 225
grande 114, 267
granel (*a~*) 232
granito 236
graso 83
grave 85
greda 83, 212
greña 209
grey 41
grifo 213
gripe 228
gris 226
groggy 231
grogui 231

grosella 227
grosor 243
grotesco 234
grúa 232, 264
grueso 83, 157
grulla 264
gruñir 62
grupo 234
gruta 236
guacamayo 229
guadaña 215, 217
guadañar 215
Guadiana 222
guagua 18
guajolote 229
guanaco 229
guano 229
guante 216, 232
guarda 111, 215
guardacostas 252
guardar 215, 217
guardarropa 252
guardia 12, 111, 235, 265
guardia civil 252
guardián 12
guarecer 215
guarir OSp. 215
guarnecer 149, 215, 246
guarnir OSp. 149, 215, 246
guasa 229
guateque 229
guayaba 229
guerra 215, 217
guerra fría 262
guiar 215
guinda 216
guisa 118, 215, 217
guisante 224
guisar 267
gulpeja OSp. 258
gusano 210

ha 162
habemos 164
haber 163
habichuela 224, 248
habla 33
hablar 8, 32, 81
habrá 177
hace 57
hacer 22, 57, 79, 81
haçer OSp. 87
haces (noun) 58

hacia 195, 196
haga 151
hago 150, 154
haiga 154
hallar 9, 23, 267
hamaca 229
hambre 22
handicap 231
hará 177
harina 79, 81
hasta 195, 220
hata OSp. 195
hato 215
hay 162
haya (noun) 41, 55, 110
haya (verb) 56, 151, 154, 164
haz 50, 113, 167
hazaña 220
hazer OSp. 87
hazmerreír 253
hazte 94
he 163
hecho 22, 61, 91, 193
heder 157
helar 58
hélice 214
hembra 78
hemorragia 214
hemos 164
henchir 63, 149
hender 157
heraldo 226
hereje 225
herencia 211
herir 154
hermana 11
hermano 11
hermoso 9, 47
herrero 56
herver 149
hervir 9, 149
hetcho JS 22
heterodoxo 214
hice 40, 43, 184
hidalgo 260
hidroelectricidad 253
hiedo 157
hiedra · 76
hiel 74, 108
hiena 214
hiendo 157
hierba 44
hiero 154

hierro 81
higo 46, 79, 81, 110,
higuera 110
hijo 34, 46, 79, 81, 88
hijuelo 34, 248
hilo 79, 81
himno 213
hincapié 252
hinchar 63
hinchazón 243
hiniesta 46, 48
hinojo 42, 58
hipertensión 241
hipopótamo 214
hipótesis 214
historia 213
hit 231
hito 61
hockey 231
hoja 40, 41, 109, 113
holding 231
holgazana 115
hombre 78
hombre rana 252, 262
hombres 94
hombro 9, 29, 78
homenaje 225
homónimo 214
honesto 261
honor 111
honrar 77, 78
hora 213
hora cero 262
horas punta 262
horchata 232
horizonte 214
horma 79, 81, 91
hormazo 11
hormiga 22
horno 79, 81
horrible 268
horrísono 211
hostal 77, 225
hotel 227
hoy 41, 118
hoyuelo 248
hoz 50
hube 46
hucha 216, 226
huebos OSp. 107, 109
huérfano 212
huertecillo 251
huertito 251
hueso 44, 109, 157

huesso OSp. 69
hueva 109
huevo 109
huida 243
huigo 154
huir 149
hule 229
hulla 227
humanismo 243
humanista 234
húmedo 211
húmido 211
humo 47, 237
humor 261
huracán 229
huye(s) 165
huyo 42, 151

i 198
iba 169
idea 214
ides OSp. 9, 165
idioma 214
ido 9
-ido 192
iglesia 213
ignorar 261
igualar 245
iguana 229
ilegítimo 239
ilimitado 239
imos OSp. 9, 165
impiedad 239
impopular 239
imprenta 232
impreso 194
impulsivo 245
incidente 261
ínclita 211
incurrir 161
índigo 236
infanta 112
infante 112, 235, 260
inferior 115, 116
inflación 231
infraestructura 241
ingente 211
ingle 78
inmiscuir 239
inmóvil 211
innato 239
inojo OSp. 58
inoxidable 245
insensato 239

inspirar 239
instante 92, 211
interesante 227
interesante (en
    estado~) 259
interferir 239
interior 115, 116
intermuscular 239
interrumpir 239
interviewar 231
interviú 231
interviuvar 231
intranuclear 241
intriga 227
invernal 244
Íñigo 209
ir 9
iraní 225
irgo 160
irreal 239
irrespetuoso 239
is (dial.) 165
-ísimo 117
isla 76
istante 92
iva OSp. 169
izar 226
izquierdista 243
izquierdo 209, 209, 258

jabalí 220, 223
jabón 215
jade 227
jaguar 229
jamás 118
jamón 225
jarabe 220
jardín 216, 226
jarra 219
jaspe 213
jaula 225
Javier 209
jazmín 221
jefe 226
jengibre 225
jeque 221
jerez 265
jerigonza 226
jersey 231
jibia 41, 224
jícara 229
jinete 218
jockey 231
jofaina 219, 223

jogar OSp.   48, 190
jóquey 231
jornada 226
jornal 226
joroba 220
joya 225
joyero 243
Juan 72
juanica 258
judgar OSp.   78
judía 224
judo 230, 231
juego 57
jueves 49
juezes OSp.   59
jugar 48, 87, 190
jumper 231
junco 60
júnior 231
junto 198
jurel 232
justo 59
juzgar 78

kárate 230, 231
karting 231
kayak 230, 231
kilt 231
kimono 230, 231
kindergarten 230
knock-out 231

la 119, 131
labio 41
labor 112
lacio 41, 58, 63, 64, 76, 83
lado 108, 195
ladral OSp. 76
ladrona 115
ladronzuelo 248, 251
lágrima 212
laico 214
laja 233
lama 209
lamer 68
lámpara 212
laringe 214
las 119
lastimar 213
latinajos 250
latir 83
laurel 225
lava 86
lavatorio 243

laya 209, 234
le 119
leal 71
leasing 231
lección 92
lech OSp.   50
leche 41, 50, 108
lecho 41
ledo 233
leer 167
légamo 209
legaña 209
lego 41, 213, 214
legua 209
legumbre 71, 108
lejos 117, 198
lema 214
lenteja 61
leña 42, 61, 62, 109
león 104, 113, 229, 262
leonés 115
leonesa 115
lepra 213
les 119
letra 76
letra de cambio 227, 235
letril OSp. 62
levar OSp. 157
levita 227
lexar OSp. 10
lexos OSp. 198
ley 113
leyendo 192
liar 67
liberar 261
libraco 250
librar 76
libreto 235
librito 246
lición 92
liendo OSp. 192
liendre 78
lienzo 40
ligar 59
ligero 226
limón 219
limosna 213
limpiaparabrisas 262
limpio 41
linage OSp. 87
linaje 225
linax OSp. 87
lince 214
lindar 50

linde 112
lingote 227
linterna 212
liquidar 259
lirón 83
lisonja 226
literalmente 261
lo 119
loadora 115
lob 231
loción 231
logar OSp. 48, 57
lógica 213
lograr 267
lomo 28
loro 229
los 119
losa 209
lote 227
LP 231
lucha 42
lucir 149
luctuoso 92
luego 118
lueñe OSp. 117, 198
lugar 48, 57
lugarejo 248
lugo OSp. 155
lumbre 108
luto 92
luviello OSp. 83
luz (dar a~) 259
luzco 155
luzes OSp. 70

llacio OSp. 41, 58, 63, 83
llaga 63, 71
llama 63, 64, 68, 229
llamamiento 243
llamar 63, 64
llano 63
llave 63, 73
llegar 10, 48, 63
llegue 100
llena 40
lleno 46
llevar 158
llorar 64
llosa 63
lluvia 42, 56

maçana OSp. 54, 63
macarrones 236
machihembra 251, 252

macho 224, 234
machote 250
macroeconómico 241
macroempresa 253
madeja 41, 61
madera 40, 41, 45, 113
madexa OSp. 41, 61
madre patria 262
madrigal 235
madroño 210
maes OSp. 199
maestre 225, 232
maestro 59
mafia 236
magnético 214
maguer(a) OSp. 200, 212
maguey 229
maíz 229
mal 75, 114, 117
malabares (juegos~) 234
malaria 236
maleta 226
malico 247
malla 93, 225
mallo 93
malo 71
manager 231
mançana OSp. 54, 63
manceba OSp. 259
mancebo 259
mancha 63
mandioca 229
mandolina 235
manecillas 263
manecita 251
manejar 236
manera 201
manga 51
maní 229
maniabierto 252
manifestar 211
manita 251
manjar 225, 232
mano 47, 110, 113
manos 49
manteca 210
manzana 244
manzano 243, 244
mañana 118
maquila 219
maquillaje 227
maquillarse 227
máquina 214
máquina de coser 262

mar 49, 75, 108
maravedí 219
março OSp. 54, 63
marcha 243
marchar 226, 235
marejada 233
marfil 220
maría 258
maría garcía 258
maricón 249
mariposa 261
mariquita 258
marisma 224
marketing 231
marmita 226
mármol 212
marrón 227
marta 216
mártir 213
más 9, 116, 117
mas 199
mascar 77
mass-media 231
mastranzo 224
matar 259
matasen 87
matassen OSp. 87
matava OSp. 85
match 231
mate 229
matemáticas 214
maxifalda 241
maya 93
mayo 55, 64, 93
mayor 55, 115, 116
mayores 74
mazapán 220
me 119
me(e)smo OSp. 130
mear 148
mecha 225
medalla 234
medianejo 248
mediano 244
medias 256
medicucho 249
mediodía 252
medir 159
meismo OSp. 130
mejilla 264
mejillón 233
mejor 55, 86, 88, 90, 115, 116
melena 220

melodía 213
menestra 236
mengano 220
menguar 148
menor 115, 116
menora 115
menos 74, 118, 199
mensaje 226
menta 214
-mente 118
mente 211
mequetrefe 234
mercader 232
mercancía 235
mercante 235
merced 49, 69, 124
mercet OSp. 69
merecer 155
merengue 227
meresco OSp. 155
merezco 155
mermar 78
mermelada 234
mes 49, 69
mesa 9, 73, 113
mesa redonda 262
mesana 235
mesclar OSp. 89
meses 69
mesmo 130
mesón 56, 225
metáfora 214
metal 232
meteoro 214
metomentodo 253
metro 213
mexilla OSp. 64
mezclar 89
mezquino 220, 223
mezquita 220
mi(s) 49, 126
mí 43, 119
mía(s) 126
mico 229
microfilm 253
microorganismo 241
midir OSp. 159, 190
mido 159
mie OSp. 49
mie(s) OSp. 126
miedo 47
miedoso 245
miel 74, 108
-miente OSp. 118

mientra(s) 117, 200
-mientre OSp. 118
mientre OSp. 197, 200
mierla OSp. 46
mies 69
miesses OSp. 69
mil 72, 136
mill OSp. 72, 136
millón 136, 235
mimbre 108
miniatura 234
minifalda 231
minifundio 241
ministro 268
mío(s) 126
miope 214
mirla 46
mirón 245
mirto 214
mise OSp. 186
mísero 211
misión rescate 262
mismo 130
mis(s)o OSp. 194
misterio 213
místico 214
mitad 136
moʃka JS 22
moçarabe OSp. 222
moda 226
modelo 111, 234
modista 227, 243
modo 201
mojar 55
molde 232
moldrá OSp. 176
moler 156
molinillo 247
molino 34
mollir OSp. 161
monaguillo 213
monarca 214
monasterio 213
monitor 231
monocarril 253
mont OSp. 50
monte 50
monte de piedad 235
montepío 235
montes 74
montés 69, 115, 244
montesa 115
montilla 265
monzón 233

mora 109
morcillo 76
morena 212
morir 149
moro 47
morrá OSp. 175
morsa 228
morziello OSp. 76
mosca 22
mosquete 235
mosquetero 235
mostolilla 258
mostrar 157
moto 111
motosegadora 253
movible 245
mozárabe 222
muchacho 224
mucho 42, 61, 62, 64, 117
muelo 156
muelle 232
muerto 51, 193
muestra 261
muestro 157
mugier OSp. 55, 74, 86, 88
mujer 34, 48, 51, 55
mujerona 249
mújol 232
muleto 224
multicolor 241
multigrado 253
múltiple 136
mullir 160
mullo 160
muñir 149
muralla 235
museo 214
música 213
muy 49, 62, 116
muyt OSp. 62

nacer 155
nada 133, 255
nadi OSp. 133
nadie 133, 255
nadir 220
nado OSp. 133, 194, 255
nailon 231
naipe 232
nao 232
naranja 219, 221
narciso 214
narizón 245

narria 209
nasco OSp. 155
nasque OSp. 187
nativo 261
náusea 214
nava 210
navaja 41, 61, 74
navegar 71
nazco 155
necio 268
negar 59, 156
negociante 235
negra 73
negroide 244
nervio 41
neto 235
neumonia 214
ni 74, 199
niames 229
niebla 76
nief OSp. 50
niego 156
nieve 50
nin OSp. 199
ningún(o), -a 133
nivel 232
no 74, 118, 199
nocaut 231
nocturno 211
noch OSp. 50
noche 41, 50, 61
Nochebuena 252
nogal 110
noguera 110
nombrar 48
nombre 108
non OSp. 74, 118, 199
nonaenta OSp. 135
nopal 229
noria 219
nos 119
nosotros 119
novela 234
novelilla 247
novelón 242, 249
noveno 136
noventa 8, 135
noviazgo 243
novio 41, 56
nozir OSp. 161
nube 104, 113
nubes 67
nubífero 211
nuca 220

núcleoelectricidad 253
nudo 10, 69
nuef OSp. 50, 134
nuera 31, 111
nuestro 126
nueve 47, 50, 134
nuevo 47, 65, 68, 74
nuez 110, 263
nul, nulla OSp. 133
nunca 117, 118
nutria 224
nuves OSp. 67
nylon 231

ñandú 229

o 199
o OSp. 118
obispo 77
objeto 211
obra 109, 110
obús 227
océano 214
ocelote 229
ocre 226
octavo 136
octubre 10
ocheno OSp. 136
ochenta 135
ocho 41, 134
odrá OSp. 176
odré OSp. 175
oferta 232
off (en~) 231
offset 231
offside 231
ofrecer 191
ofrir OSp. 191
oigo 150, 154
oír 28, 161, 165
ojalá 200, 220
ojinegro 252
ojo 22, 41, 61, 64, 263
ojuelos 248
ola 220, 221, 223
olas 94
olaza 249
olivar 243
olivo 212
olmo 110
olvidadizo 245
ombro OSp. 78
omne OSp. 78
omne nado OSp. 255

once 77, 134
ond(e) OSp. 118
onrrar OSp. 77
onze OSp. 77
ópera 235
opio 214
orçuelo OSp. 56
orden 112
ordeñar 256
oreja 248
orejudo 245
órgano 213
orgullo 216
origen 111, 112
ortografía 213
os 119
osito 246
oso 44
osso OSp. 69
ostentar 211
ostra 41, 212, 233
ostria OSp. 41
otri OSp. 133
otrie OSp. 133
otrien OSp. 133
otro 133
ove OSp. 45, 185
oveja 248
overol 231
ovillo 83
oxalá OSp. 200
oye(s) 165
oyo OSp. 150, 154, 165

pabellón 226
pacer 58
paçes OSp. 70
padre 47, 73
padrenuestro 253
padres 49
paella 232
pago (part) 194
pagoda 234
paja 41
pajarín 247
pájaro 9, 112, 113
pajarraco 250
paje 226
pala 95
palabra 29, 213, 267
palabrota 250
palafrén 225, 232
palas 95
paleta 232

palmera 232
paloma 28
palombika JS 22
palta 229
pampa 229
Pamplona 76
pan 49, 75
panameño 244
pança OSp. 77
panera 48
paniquesa 258
pantalón 227
pantalla 232
pantano 236
panty 231
panza 77, 112
paño 71
papa 213, 229
papagayo 225
papel 232
papelorios 250
paquete 226
par OSp. 196
par 231
para 195, 196
para que 200
parabla OSp. 29
paradoja 214
paraíso 213
paralelo 214
páramo 210
parangón 234
parapeto 235
pardusco 244
pareçrá OSp. 175
pared 49, 51, 69
paréntesis 214
paret OSp. 69
parientes 267
parir 149, 259
parking 230
parlamento 227
parlar 226
parodia 214
parque 226
parrá OSp. 175
parra 215
parroquia 213
part OSp. 50
parte 50, 137
partrá OSp. 175
pasapasa 253
pasaporte (dar el~) 259
pasatiempo 252

Pascua 213
paseo (dar el~) 259
paso 113
passo OSp. 22, 86, 87, 89
pata 263
pata de gallo 264
paté 228
patio 226, 232
patizambo 252
patriarca 213
patrimonio 211
patriota 227
pavana 235
payaso 234
paz 49, 50, 70
pazes OSp. 70
peaje 226
peçe OSp. 50
peces 58
peçes OSp. 64
pecho 108
pedante 236
pedestal 234
pedir 150
peinar 62
pelagra 236
peliagudo 252
peligro 29
pelo 46
pelotón 228
peluca 226
pena 45, 46, 212
penacho 235
penalty 231
pendra OSp. 62
pensador 243
pensar 157, 264
peño 108
peonía 214
peor 55, 70, 115, 116
pequeñajo 250
pequeñín 247
pera 71, 109
perca 233
perdello(=perderlo) 190
perdiz 212
perdrá OSp. 175
perdurar 241
pereza 73
perfil 226
pergamino 213
pérgola 236
pericráneo 241
periferia 214

periglo OSp. 29
periodo 214
perjurar 241
perla 236
permisivo 261
pero 199
perro guardián 252, 262
perro caliente 262
personal 227
pesar 157, 201
pescueço OSp. 70
pesebre 29
peso 157
pestaña 210
petaca 229
petate 229
petunia 229
peyndra OSp. 62
pez 50, 70
piano 235
picamaderos 252
picaporte 232
pick-up 231
pichón 236
pidrá OSp. 175
pie 75
pieça OSp. 70
piedra 40, 44, 47, 82, 212
piel 72
pieles 72
pielles OSp. 72
pienso 157
pierna 264
pijama 230, 231
pila 233
Pilipinas 24
pilotaje 226
piloto 235
pillar 236, 259
pillastre 250
pillete 248
pimentón 249
ping-pong 231
pingüino 227
pino 110
pintoresco 234
pinzas 226
piña 229, 262
pique (echar a~) 226
piquete 226
piragua 229
pirámide 112
pista 236
pistacho 236

pitillo 247
pizarra 209
plaça OSp. 62
placa 226
placer 73
planeta 111, 213
plango OSp. 154, 155
planta 261
plantel 233
plañir OSp. 154
plaño 155
plástico 261
plata 261
plática 92
platillo volante 262
playa 70
playback 231
playero 244
plaza 62, 212
plazco 155
plazdo OSp. 77
plazo 77
pleamar 233
plebe 236
plega OSp. 73, 151
plego OSp. 155
pleita 224
plogo OSp. 73
plogue OSp. 185
plugo 73
pluriempleo 241
poblacho 250
pobre 76, 115
pobrecillo 248
pobreziello OSp. 248
poco 45
poder 191
podiendo OSp. 192
podrá 175
podrir 161
poeta 213
polaina 225
polgar OSp. 48, 265
polideportivo 253
polivalencia 241
póliza 235
polo 214
polución 231
polvo 112
pólvora 233
pollo 93
pon 167, 167
pon(r)rá OSp. 176
pondrá 176, 177

pongo 151, 154
pony 231
ponzoña 267
pop 231
popa 112
populacho 250
por 103, 195, 196, 197
por a OSp. 196
porcelana 236
porfía 241
poridat OSp. 261
porná OSp. 176
porque 200
porrá OSp. 176
portaaviones 252, 262
portadgo OSp. 78
portavoz 252
portazgo 78
pórtico 234
posar 48
posguerra 241
postal 227
póster 231
poyo 41, 55, 74, 93
pozo 54, 64, 86, 88
pozuelo 34
práctica 92
prado 47, 107
pregón 48
preindustrial 241
premio 41, 56
premura 236
prenda 41, 62, 108, 109
prender 237
prensa 232
preñada 259
preso OSp. 194
prestar 157
preste 225
pretender 157
preto JS 22
prieto 22
primas OSp. 117
primer(o) 49, 114, 136
primo 136
princep OSp. 50
príncipe 50
prisco 221
prise OSp. 187
prisma 214
problema 214
proceso 261
prodigio 211
profeta 111, 213

programa 214
prólogo 213
promedio 241
prometer 241
pronóstico 213
pronto 92
protohistoria 241
prototipo 253
provecho 68, 237
provisto 194
próximo oriente 262
proyección 211
psiquiatría 214
pude 185
pudiendo 192
pudrir 149, 161
pueblecito 251
pueblito 251
pueblo 76
puede 74
pueder JS 22
puedet OSp. 74
puedo 166
puerco 60
puerco espín 252
puerto 265
pues 117, 162, 197, 200
puesto 193
puesto que 200
pulga 112, 113
pulgar 48, 265
pulimento 243
pullover 231
pulpo 212
puma 229, 262
puna 229
puntiagudo 252
puñalada 243
puño 42, 61, 64, 91
púrpura 212
purpúreo 211
puse 185
pusiendo OSp. 192

quadro OSp. 73
qual OSp. 84, 132
quando OSp. 199
quántum 231
quaraenta OSp. 73, 135
quark 231
quarto OSp. 136
quatorze OSp. 84
quatro OSp. 74, 84, 134
que 132, 199

quedo   51
quehacer   252
quepa   56, 164
quepo   151, 164
querer   8, 84
querida   259
querindango   250
quero JS   22
querrá   175, 177
queso   9, 45
quevedos   268
qui   OSp.   132
quien   74, 132
quien (pl)   132
quienquiera   132, 133
quiero   22, 45
quijote   223, 268
quilate   219
quilla   226
quimera   214
quimono   231, 230
quince   57, 84, 135
quinientos   60, 84, 136
quinqué   227
quintal   219
quinto   136
quiñentos OSp.   136
quiosco   228
quirófano   214
quise   187
quiste   214
quitaipón (de~)   253
Quixote   88

rábano   51, 212
rabé   222
rabel   222
rabia   41, 113
rabicorto   252
rabosa   258
rádar   231
radiofaro   253
raglán   231
rama   110
ramera   259
ramo   110
ramuja   250
ramujo   250
rancho   226
rango   227
rapar   148, 215, 217
rape   232
raposa   258
raquitismo   214

rareza   243
rasgar   76
raspar   259
ratón   249
raya   70
rayar   55, 64
rayo   41
rayo (vb)   151
razimo OSp.   57
real   59, 67
realengo   12
reanudar   240
reaparecer   240
rebién   240
rebotica   240
rebuscar   241
recalentar   241
recamar   148, 220, 236
racámara   240
recebir OSp.   160
recibir   149, 160
recibo   85
recibrá OSp.   175
reciedumbre   243
recitar   267
recobrar   51
recocina   240
recodir OSp.   161
récord   231
recordman   230
recudrá OSp.   175
red   108
redolor   240
redondo   28
redor OSp.   198
reducto   235
refrán   226
regaliz   212
regar   157
regata   236
regla   33
regular   32
rehacer   240
rehén   218, 222
reina   70, 135
reír   149, 159
reja   32, 33, 61, 74
relievo   234
reloj   232
relox OSp.   87
remandrá OSp.   176
remanga OSp.   151
remanir OSp.   151
remase OSp.   186

remo   68
remolacha   236
remoler   241
ren OSp.   133
render OSp.   150
rendir   150
reñir   60
repintrá OSp.   175
repiso OSp.   194
reportaje   227
repudrir   241
repuso   186
resgar   76
resorte   227
resplandecer   246
resplandir OSp.   246
respuse OSp.   186
restaurant(e)   228
resuelto   193
retablo   233
retar   233
retemblar   241
retreta   227
retrete   232, 259
retroceder   241
retrovisor   230
reventar   259
rey   113
rezar   87, 267
riachuelo   251
ribera   48
ricacho   250
rico   215, 217
riego   157
rienda   51, 78
riestra OSp.   112
rima   225
rímel   231
ring   231
rinoceronte   214
riñón   48
río (vb)   150, 159
rise OSp.   186
ristra   112
ristre   233
ritmo   213
robar   148, 215
roble   28, 108
robot   231
roçar OSp.   70
rodaballo   224
rodaja   250
rodaje   227
rodilla   248

Rodrigo 12
Rodríguez 12
rogar 9
roido OSp. 48, 59
rojiblanco 251, 252
rojizo 244
rol 231
romance 25
romançe OSp. 117
rompecabezas 252
rompehielos 252, 262
ropa 215, 217
rosa 69, 104, 113
roto 68, 193, 194
round 231
royo 151
rubio 42, 56
rueca 215
rueda 47
rufián 236
rugby 231
ruido 48, 59
ruiseñor 225
Ruiz 12
ruleta 228
rústico 211
rutina 227
ruvio OSp. 56
Ruy 12

sábana 212
sabana 229
sabe 85, 86
saber 164
sabidora 115
sabrá 177
sacacorchos 252
sacar 215
saco 212
sacudir 149
saeta 34, 59
sal 112
sal (vb) 167
sal(r)rá OSp. 176
sala 216
salar 245
salchicha 236
saldar 235
saldo 235
saldrá 176, 177
salgo 154
saliod OSp. 74
saliot OSp. 74
salir OSp. 177

salmo 213
salmonete 249
salmoyra OSp. 42
salmuera 42
salo OSp. 154
saloncito 251
salpimentar 252
saltamontes 252
saltimbanqui 234
salvaje 226
san 49
sanar 9
Sancho 209
sangre 51, 78
santiguar 245
santo 49
sapo 210
saquear 235
sarao 234
sardana 233
sargentona 249
sarna 210
sarro 210
sastre 220, 232
satélite 261
satén 227
sátiro 214
saya 209
scriptgirl 231
sé 164, 167
se 119
se (conj) OSp. 199
se(d)ze OSp. 135
sea 41, 55, 70, 151, 162
seco 67, 71
sed (vb) 167
sedía OSp. 169
seer OSp. 68, 162, 167,
191
segar 67, 266
seglar 244
seguir 57, 71, 150
según 49, 118, 198
segund OSp. 198
segundo 49, 136
seguro 48, 71
seis 62, 134
self(-service) 231
semana 50, 77
sembrar 157, 264
sembro OSp. 157
semidesnudo 253
semifinal 241
semilla 224

sémola 232
sen OSp. 195
senda 75, 76, 77
sentidor 115
sentir 75, 159
seña 42
señas 46
señor 48, 55, 112
señora 112, 113
señoría 124
señoritingo 250
seo 233
sepa 41, 45, 73, 151, 164
septiembre 92
séptimo 136
ser 5, 162, 191
será 176
sera 215
serenata 235
seriote 250
serna 209
servicio(s) 259
servilleta 226
servir 159
sesenta 135
sesquióxido 241
sesseno OSp. 136
set 231
seteno OSp. 136
setenta 135
setiembre 92
setmana OSp. 77
sevoya JS 23
sexta 267
sexto 136
seyendo OSp. 192
shetland 231
shorts 231
show 231
sí 43, 118, 119
si 199
sieglo OSp. 46
siella OSp. 46
siempre 74
siendo 192
siente 100
sientes 100
siento 100, 159
sierra 47, 263
siesta 46, 136, 267
siete 134
sietemesino 251
siglo 46
significar 92

signo 92
sigrá OSp. 177
silueta 227
silla 46
símbolo 214
simetría 214
simple 136, 261, 268
simpleziello OSp. 248
sin 75, 118, 195
síndrome 231
sines OSp. 195
sinfonía 214
siniestro 31, 268
siniestro OSp. 258
sinificar 92
sino 92, 199, 269
sinon OSp. 199
sinónimo 214
sinsonte 229
sintaxis 213
sintir OSp. 159, 190
síntoma 214
sirena 214
sirvo 159
sismo 214
sistema 214
sitio 215
sketch 231
slam 231
slip 231
smash 231
smoking 230
so (vb) OSp. 162
so (prep) OSp. 74, 197
so(s) OSp. 126
soasar 240
sobarba 240
soberbia 41
sobir OSp. 161, 190
sobre 197
sobrecama 240
sobrecargar 240
sobremanera 240
sobremesa 240
sobrenadar 240
sobresueldo 240
sobrevivir 240
socaire 232
socarrar 209
socavar 240
socialista 244
soda 261
sodes OSp. 162
sofá 227

sofreir 240
sofrir OSp. 191
solapar 240
solemne 92
solene 92
solista 235
solo 235
solomillo 240
soltar 194
soltero 76
solver 194
sollo 233
someter 240
somier 227
somos 162
son 162
sonata 235
soneto 234
sonrise OSp. 186
sope OSp. 45, 73, 185
sopiendo OSp. 192
soprano 235
sor 233
sorber 157
sordina 235
sordomudo 251, 252
soroche 229
sospecha 48
sota 232
sotana 236
soterrar 240
sove OSp. 185, 186
soy 74, 162
sparring 231
speaker 231
spot 231
spray 231
sprint 231
stock 231
stress 231
su(s) 126
suave 85
subdesarrollado 240
subir 160
submarino 240
subo 160
subrá OSp. 175
subrayado 240
subsuelo 240
subvalorar 240
sue(s) OSp. 126
suegra 31, 111
suegro 73
sueldo 76

suelgo OSp. 154
suelo (vb) 154
suelto 193, 194
sueño 42
suerte 269
suéter 231
suflé 228
sufrir 150, 191
sumiller 226
supe 46, 73
superchería 236
supercompresión 240
superestructura 240
superior 116
superiora 115
superpoblación 240
superstición 211
supervivencia 240
supranacional 241
suprí Phil 24
surco 60
surgir 232
suso OSp. 118
suspense 231
suyo(s), -a(s) 128
sweater 231

tabaco 220
tabernucha 249
taburete 226
tacañete 248
táctica 214
tacha 226
tachuela 226
tafetán 236
tajador 115
tajuela 34
talento 212
tallo 212
tamaño 41
tambor 218
tan 74
tándem 231
tango OSp. 60, 155, 154
tanque 233, 261
tantico 247
tanxe OSp. 187
tañer 154, 267
taño 60, 155
tapa 215
tapioca 229
tapir 229
tapizar 245
tapón 249

tapujos 250
taquígrafo 214
taracear 148
tarantela 235
tarántula 236
tarde 117
tarea 220, 221
tarifa 219, 232
tatuaje 243
taxugo OSp. 216
taza 219
te 119, 125
té 230, 234
teatro 213
techo 41
teja 42, 61, 64
tejo 61, 110
tejón 215, 217
telaraña 252
telediario 253
teledirigido 253
temblar 78
templar 157
temple 234
tempo 235
temprano 50, 76
ten 166
tenacidad 243
ténder 231
tendrá 177
tener 164
tengo 151, 154
tenis 231
tenor 235
tentemozo 253
tentempié 253
teología 87, 213
teoría 214
terapéutica 214
tercer(o) 49, 114, 136
tercer mundo 262
tercer programa 262
terceto 234
tercio 137
termonuclear 253
terracota 234
terraza 234
terrible 268
terrón 249
tesis 214
tesoro 213
testuz 224
texo OSp. 61
texugo OSp. 216

ti 43, 119
tibio 41
tiburón 229
tiempo 108, 113
tiempo récord 262
tienes 74
tierra 82
tieso 157
tiesta OSp. 264
tigre 214, 229, 262
tijeras 88
tilde 232
timonel 232
tinieblas 34, 265
tiniebras OSp. 265
tinto 194
tinxe OSp. 187
tío, -a 212
tisera(s) OSp. 88
tísico 213
tisú 227
titubeante 245
tiza 229
to(s) OSp. 126
toalla 236
tocadiscos 251
tocata 235
tocayo 229
todo 47, 133
toldo 216
toldrá OSp. 176
toller OSp. 259
tomar acta 227
tomate 229
tomo 214
topacio 111, 213
topografía 214
toquetear 245, 246
Tor 72
torazo 249
torcer 60
toro 28, 45
torpedo 261
torre 72, 212
torres 71, 72
tórtola 112
tos 94
toser 149
tostar 148
tove OSp. 185
toviendo OSp. 192
trabajar 259
tragaperras 252
tragedia 213

traidora 115
traigo 151, 154
trailer 231
traje 187, 234
trajinar 233
transistor 231
transmitir 240
trapajo 250
tráquea 214
tras 198
traslapar 239
trasmitir 240
trasnochar 240
trasqui OSp. 187
traste 232
trastienda 240
trasto 232
trastornar 240
trasvolar 239
traxe OSp. 186
tray OSp. 167
trayo OSp. 151, 154
trébol 113
trece 134
trecho OSp. 194
tred OSp. 167
tregua 215
treinta 135
trémulo 211
tren 251
tren miniatura 262
trenecete 249
tres 134
trescientos 135
tricolor 253
trigal 243
trinchar 226
trinchera 226
triple 136
triscar 216, 217
triste 115
tristeza 70
trolebús 231
tropa 226
trópico 214
trotaconventos 252
trotar 225
troxe OSp. 185, 186
trucha 42
trucos 236
truje 186
truxe 186
tú 23, 119, 123–5
tu(s) 125, 126

tubo de ensayo 262
tucán 229
*tude OSp. 186
tudiere OSp. 186
tue(s) OSp. 126
tuelgo OSp. 154
tuelto OSp. 194
tullido 259
tullir OSp. 259
tumbona 243
tuna 229
turbación 243
turbante 236
turbio 42
turismo 228, 231
turista 228
turrar 148
tute 236
tuviese 87
tuviesse OSp. 87
tuyo(s), -a(s) 125, 128
tweed 231

u 199
ubre 108
-udo OSp. 193
-uir 151
ulterior 116
ultraje 233
ultramarino 234
ultramarinos 241
un(a) 130, 134
un(o) 134
undulación 211
urdir 161
urraca 209
usted 124
ustedes 18, 124
útiles 227

vaca 65, 242
vacada 242
vades OSp. 148
vado 69
vagabundo 265
vagamundo 265
vaiga 154
vais 165
vaivén 234, 253
val 112, 167
val(r)rá OSp. 176
valdrá 176, 177
valentón 249
valentonazo 251

valgo 154
valija 236
valle 72, 112
valles 62, 72
valo OSp. 154
vamos 148, 165
van 85
vando OSp. 65, 85
vaniloco 211
varón 216
vasallo 209
vaso 109
vaya 151, 154
ve (imp, ver) 167
vea 41, 163
vedar 157
vedri JS 22
vee(s) OSp. 163
veer OSp. 191
vega 210
veinte 135
vejez 243
velón 249
ven 40, 43, 85, 166
vencejo 60
vender 10, 31
vendimia 40, 41, 56
vendrá 176, 177
vengades OSp. 159
vengamos 159
vengar 75, 77
vengo 151, 154
veno OSp. 187
ventilar 261
veo 55, 150, 163
ver 191
verá 176
veraño 264
verdad 76
verde 5, 34
verdete 233
verdinegro 252
verdoso 244
vergel 225
vergoña OSp. 42
vergüença OSp. 56
vergüeña OSp. 42, 56
verificar 261
verná OSp. 176
verrá OSp. 176
vestidas 85
veyendo OSp. 192
vezino OSp. 57, 64
vi 188

viaje 232
vianda 225
vicetiple 241
vicuña 229
vida 29, 46, 65
vide OSp. 188
video 231
videocassette 231
vido OSp. 188
vidrio 41
viejecito 251
viejito 251
viejo 34, 41, 61
viendo 192
viene 94
vienes 85, 94
viento 85
viernes 78
viéspera OSp. 46
vigía 233
vihuela 225
villano 268
villorrio 250
vinagre 232
vinagreta 232
vinazo 242
vine 43, 49, 187
vino 49, 107, 113, 187
viña 55, 64
viola 235
violín 235
violón 235
violoncelo, -chelo 235
virar 233
visión 210
víspera 46
visque OSp. 187
vistazo 243
visto 193
vistrá OSp. 175
vitrina 227
viva 85
vivir 65, 159
vivo 86
vo OSp. 162
voacé 124
volibol 231
volleyball 231
volver 65
vos 23, 123–5
vos OSp. 119
vosotros 119, 124
voy 85, 162
voz 65, 85, 86

vucé 124
vuced 124
vuelto 193
vuesarced 124
vuestra merced 124
vuestro 126
vusted 124

wélter 231

xeque OSp. 221
xugar OSp. 87

y OSp. 118, 162
y (conj) 198
ya 74, 118
ya que 200
yace 58
yacer 57
yaga OSp. 151
yago OSp. 153, 155
yaz 167
yazca 151

yazco 155
yazdrá OSp. 176
yaze OSp. 55, 64
yazer OSp. 57, 153
yazrá OSp. 175
yedra OSp. 76
yegua 9, 44, 58, 64, 73
yelmo 215, 217
yema 58, 264
yera 76
yerba 44
yergo 154, 155, 160
yermo 76, 212
yerno 29, 78
yerva OSp. 58, 74
yeso 58, 212
yesso OSp. 58, 59, 64, 74
yo 119
yogue OSp. 185
yuca 229
yuezes OSp. 59
yugo 74
yuso OSp. 118

yusto OSp. 59

zafiro 111
zaga 218, 222, 223
zagal 220
zaguán 219, 222
zampón 249
zampoña 213
zanahoria 219, 222
zapar 235
zaragüelles 222
zarigüeya 229
zarpar 235
zarza 210
zarzamora 109, 252
zócalo 234
zona 214
zoogeografía 253
zopilote 229
zorra 258
zurdo 209

Subject index

Capital letters indicate sounds of Latin.
Hyphens indicate position in the word: e.g. H-=initial /h/ in Latin; /-t-/=intervocalic /t/;
/-s/=final /s/.
Spellings are indicated by italics.

Ablative 101
accent: nature 34; pitch vs stress 95;
    position in Latin 33; shift 34,
    147, 167 178; shift in verbs 139;
    types 35
Accusative 101
address 123
adjective 114
adverbial 's' 117
affective derivation 246
affectivity 268
agent 103, 195
Alfonso X the Learned 15
allophone 27
Almohads 14
Almoravids 14
alternation 114; in verbal stem
    (consonantal) 153; in verbal stem
    (vocalic) 156
America 82, 88–90, 93–4, 120–1, 124,
    128, 133, 139, 144, 147, 188;
    discovery and conquest 18
American Spanish 93
Amerindian languages 19, 228
amerindianisms 228–29
analogy 31, 99, 100, 105, 109, 147, 160,
    184
analytic 99
Andalusia 14, 20, 26, 82, 89, 94, 121,
    124, 223, 258
Andes 93
anglicisms 230–31
animate 106
anterior 141
antihiatic consonant 165
aperture 39
apodosis 201

Appendix Probi 4, 50, 52, 59, 61, 65,
    66, 105, 115, 121
Arabic 14, 16, 89, 195, 200, 217; Arabic
    article al- 218; as source of
    semantic loan 260; as transmitter
    of loans from other languages 221
arabisms 148, 217; lost from
    Spanish 220; phonological
    adaptation 221–23; syntax and
    phraseology 13
Aragon 14, 120, 258
Aragonese 15, 192
Araucanian 228
Arawak 228
archaism: Latin of Spain 7
Argentina 18, 19, 125
article: lacking in Latin 130; OSp.
    extension of use 131
aspect 140; vs tense 140
assimilation 60, 77, 176, 185;
    anticipatory, progressive,
    mutual 27
asterisked forms 5
Asturias 82, 258
atonic (vowel, syllable) 38;
    (vowels) 47
augmentative 249
Augustine, St 174, 204
Auto de los reyes magos 15, 138

b and *v* in OSp. 65
/b/ > [u̯] syllable-final 96; /b/+[j] 56;
    /b/ = *b* (OSp.) 30; /b/ and /β/
    merge in OSp. 84, 96
/β/ = *v* (OSp.) 29, 30; sources 73
-B- 65, 68; -B- = -V- in spoken
    Latin 65; -B- and -V- merge 96

Balearics 15, 131
Basque 6, 14, 17, 79, 87, 208, 258;
    loans from Basque 208
Basque country 82
bilingualism 208
-BL- 83
Bolivia 124
-BST- 92
Buenos Aires 19
Burgos 7, 13, 14, 16, 25, 82
Byzantium 11

-C- 71, 83; -C 74; C+[j] 96; C and G
    palatalized 96; -C-+glide 73;
    CC+[j] 96; -CC- 71
Cádiz 14, 21, 90
Caesar 102
calque 261
Canaries 17, 90, 124, 133
Cantabria 13, 14, 79, 82
cardinal 133
Carib 228, 229
case 101, 119
case-endings 101, 114
Castile 25, 93
Castilian 13, 25
Catalan 1, 15, 17, 215, 216, 223, 231,
    258
catalanisms 231
Catholic Monarchs 14
çeçeo 89
ceceo 90
Celtic 6, 208; influence on consonant
    system 66
Central America 19, 125
Chile 125
chronology of phonological change 95
Cicero 174, 203
-CL- 61, 83, 96; palatalization 63
clitic 119
collective 109
Colombia 125
Columbus 18, 228
comparative 116
comparison 103; of adjectives 115; of
    adverbs 118
complementary distribution 27, 91
composition 237; adjective+adjective
    252; adjective+noun 252;
    noun+adjective 252;
    noun+noun 252; pronoun+verb
    252; verb+noun 252; verb+verb
    253
conditional 145, 146, 177, 205

conditional perfect 143, 145, 146
conditional sentences 201–7
conditions: impossible 201, 203;
    improbable 201, 203; open 201,
    202
conjunction 198
conservatism: Hispanic Latin 8
consonant system: OSp. 84; Latin 52
coordination 198
Córdoba 14, 90
Cortés 18
Costa Brava 131
count-noun 122
-CR- 73, 83
creoles 24
-CT- 61, 92, 96; -CT 62
Cuba 18

-D- 68; -D 74; -D- made final 75
/d/+[j] 55; lost in verbal endings 138
Dative 101
decency taboo 259
declension 113
deferential 123
definite article 131; with
    possessive 127
degrees of aperture 39
delicacy taboo 259
demonstrative 128
derivation 237, 241; adjectives 244;
    nouns 243; verbs 245
desinential [j] 156
diminutive 246
diphthongization 43, 96; in verb 156
diphthongs; Latin 37, 44; reduced in
    Latin 96; in spoken Latin 45
Disputa del alma y el cuerpo 210
dissimilation 28, 78, 159, 168
Don Quixote 88
doublets 33
-DR- 73
/dz/ in OSp.: sources 64

E and I merge in [j] 96
/e/ lost in final position 49, 96; in
    imperative 167; in imperfect
    subjunctive 170; in verbs 152
/ɛ/ > /e/ in Latin 96
economy of effort 86
Ecuador 125
ellipsis 265
enclitic 122
English 253; as source of semantic
    loan 261

epenthesis 28, 78, 176
-ĒRE and -ÉRE verbs merge 147
euphemism 257, 259
Extremadura 82, 93

f 81
F-> [h] 96
F- 68, 79; -FF- 68
/f/: emergence in Spanish 90
fear taboo 258
final (vowel, syllable) 38; (vowels) 49
FL- 63, 83, 96
foreign semantic influence 260
form-classes 147
forms of address 123
FR- 73
Franks 11
Fray Juan de Córdoba 87
French 1, 91, 105, 216, 224, 230;
    borrowed suffix 244
frequency 101
Fuero de Madrid 15
FUI as preterite of *ser* and *ir* 188
future 146, 173; contraction of
    stem 175; of *hacer* 177
future perfect subjunctive 144, 146, 179
future subjunctive 144, 146, 178, 202;
    decline 179; use in OSp. 179

/g/ + [j] 55; palatalized 58; grouped
    with preceding consonant 59;
    spreads in verbal stems 154
-G- 71
Galicia 11, 15, 17, 258
Galician 23
gallicisms 224-28
Gascon 79, 210
gem-names 111
geminate 52
gender 106
generalization (semantic) 267
Genitive 101
Germanic 148; influence on vowel-
    system 43; loans 215-17; their
    phonological adaptation 216-17
germanisms in spoken Latin 215
gerund 191
-GL- 83, 96
glide (palatal) 39-43
glide-formation 51
-GN- 61, 92, 96; -GN 62
-GR- 73; GR- 83
Granada 14, 21, 90

Greek 6, 130, 200, 211; Greek prefixes
    borrowed 241; Greek suffixes
    borrowed 245

h 81
/h/ in OSp. 79; /h/ = *f* (OSp.) 30; lost
    in Latin 53; lost in Spanish 96
H- 95
Hebrew 16
hellenisms 211-14; in Church
    Latin 212; in popular Latin 212
hiatus 35, 96, 168; lost in Latin 51
Hispano-Romance 13
homonymy 93
Huelva 90
hypercharacterization 112, 115
hypercorrection 207
hypothetical forms 5

/i/: consonantized in Latin 53
Iberian 6
/ie/ reduced to /i/ in OSp. 45
imparisyllabic 105
imperative 139, 147, 166
imperfect indicative 146, 167
imperfect subjunctive 169
imperfective 140
inanimate 106
inceptive verbs 155
incidence 31
indefinite article 130
indefinite pronoun 133
indicative 146
indirect statement 145
infinitive 189; reduction from four to
    three types 189
infix -(e)c/z- 251
infix -v(I)- lost 170
inherited vocabulary 208
initial (vowel, syllable) 38; (vowels) 47
innovation in Hispanic Latin 10
interrogative 132
intertonic (vowel, syllable) 38;
    (vowels) 50; loss of intertonics 96
Isidore, St, bishop of Seville 4
Islamic invasion 13
isolative change 29
Italian 1, 234
italianisms 234-36
Italic languages 9

[j]: combined with preceding
    consonant 53; in verbal
    endings 150, 156

/ĵ/: sources 64, 74; in spoken Latin 70; /ĵĵ/ in spoken Latin 70
Jews 21
jocular 248
Judaeo-Spanish 21, 93
Judezmo 21

/k/: + [j] in Latin 54; palatalized 56; grouped with preceding consonant 59; /kk/ + [j] 54; /kk/ palatalized 57
kinship-terms 111
/kt/ + [j] 54

-L- 71; -L 74; L- 83; -L- made final 75; -LL- 71; -LL- made syllable-final 72; palatalized 62
/l/ + [j] 55
/λ/ of spoken Latin gives OSp. /ʒ/ 96; sources 64
La Española 18
Ladino 21
laísmo 121–2
Latin suffixes borrowed 244
Latin: vulgar 2, 3; classical 2; vulgar contemporary with classical 3; pre-classical 7; sources of information about spoken Latin 4; spoken Latin 2
latinisms 210–11
latinization of Spain 6
le used as plural 122
learned suffixes 244, 245
learned words 32, 210
leísmo 121–2
lenition 57, 65, 96
León 14, 258
Leonese 15, 82, 192, 194
lexical derivation 242
lexicalization 246
Lima 18
loan translation 261
loísmo 20, 24, 122
-LT- 61; -LT 62
lusisms 233

M-, 68; -M 74, 95; -MM- 68
/m/ + [j] 56
macron 37
Madrid 16, 19, 82, 87, 93
Málaga 90
Mapuche 228
mass-noun 109, 122
Maya 288

-MB- 66, 96
merger 30; /ʃ/ and /h/ 90; /λ/ and /ĵ/ 93; in case-endings 103; of noun classes 113; of sibilants 89
metaphony 39, 48, 60, 187
metaphor 263
metathesis 29, 78, 96, 176, 185
metonymy 264
Mexico 18, 93, 124
-MN- 66, 92, 96
mood 146
morpheme 98
morpho-syntax 99
morphological change 99
morphology 98
Mozarabic 14, 89, 217
mozarabisms 223
-MPT- 92
multiple 136
Murcia 14, 93, 223, 258

-N- 71, 83; -N 74; -NN- 71; -NN- made syllable-final 72; -NN- palatalized 62
/n/ + [j] 55
/ɲ/: sources 64
Nahuatl 228, 229
Navarre 258
neuter 106, 119, 129
neutralization 27, 52, 77, 85; of voice 87; of locus 89
new concept 262
New York 24
-NF- 66
Nominative 101
non-deferential 123
non-finite 189
noun 101; noun classes 112
-NS- 96
-NST- 92
number 101; in verb 137
numeral 133

/o/: gives /u/ in Latin 96; lost in final position 49
/ɔ/: gives /o/ in Latin 96
oaths 259
Oblique 104
Occitan 215, 216, 224
occitanisms 224–28
ordinal 136
Oscan 9
Ottoman Empire 21
Oviedo 25

P- 68; +[j] 96; +glide 72; -PP- 68
/p/ +[j] 56
palatalization 54, 56, 60
palatals: creation of palatal order 53
Palencia 25
paradigm 98
Paraguay 125
parasynthesis 238
paronyms 261
paroxytonic 138
participle 192; short participle 194;
   strong participle 193; weak
   participle 192
partitive 136
passive 137
past subjunctive 143
pejorative 247, 250, 268
perfect 179; of intransitives 142; of
   transitives 141
perfective 140, 170
person (verb) 137
personal *a* 102
personal pronoun 119
Peru 18, 124
Philippines 24
phoneme 27
phonologization 90
phonotactics 77
pidgins 24
pitch-accent 35
Pizarro 18
PL- 63, 83, 96; -PL- 73
Plautus 102
pluperfect 141; 144; indicative 143,
   146, 204; subjunctive 204
Poema de mio Cid 15
polarization of gender and noun-
   ending 110
Pompeii 39
popular etymology 31, 265
popular words 32, 208
Portuguese 1, 21, 210, 215, 223, 233
possessive 125
-PR- 73
pre-Roman loans 208–10
prefixes 237; borrowed from
   Latin 241
prefixoid 253
preposition 102, 194; derived from
   noun 195; related to adverb 195
present indicative 146, 150
present participle 191
present subjunctive 146, 150
preterite 144, 146, 179; in -I 185, 187;

in SI 186; in -UI 184, 185; second-
   plural ending 183; strong preterite
   183; weak preterite 180
pretonic (vowel, syllable) 38
progressive aspect 144
pronoun 119
proparoxytonic 138
proper nouns 267
protasis 201
Provençal 91, 105
-PS- 66
-PT- 66, 92, 96
/pt/ +[j] 54

QU- 57, 83; -QU- 71
Quechua 228, 229

R- 83; -R- 71; -R- made final 75;
   -R 74; R+[j] 56, 96; -RR- 71;
   -RR- made syllable-final 72
-*ra* verb-form: as conditional 172; as
   imperfect subjunctive 172; as
   pluperfect 171
Reconquest 15, 82
reduplicative preterite 185, 189
register 2
relative 132
Romance 3; Romance languages 1;
   Romance consonant groups 75
romanization of Spain 5
-RS- 66, 96
Rumanian 1

s-+consonant 83; -s- 69; -s-+[j] 56,
   96; -s-+glide 73; -s 74; -ss- 69
/s/ and /θ/: syllable-final weakening 19,
   93
/-s/: transfer of grammatical function to
   preceding vowel
/ʃ/ in OSp.: sources 64
Salamanca 82
San Millán glosses 210
Santa Teresa 87
Santander 13, 82, 258
Saragossa 14
Sardinia 131, 132
secondary consonant groups 75, 96
semantic change: causes 256;
   consequences 266; types 262
semantic loan 260
semantic range 266
semantic specificity 266
semi-learned words 32, 208
seseo 20, 24, 90

Seville 14, 16, 17, 20, 21, 89, 90; Seville norm 19
sibilants 22; in OSp. 86; in Andalusia/America 89; deaffrication 96; locus-change 97; voiced merge with voiceless 97
sigmatic 186
/sk/ + [j] 54; /sk/ palatalized 57
sources of vocabulary 208
spelling 15; of OSp. *b, v* 85; of sibilants 87
split 30, 57, 59, 79
standard 3, 15, 82, 87
stative verbs 161
stem 153; stem-regularization 157
stem-vowel: preterite 187
stem-vowel variation 169, 171, 176, 178, 181, 190, 192, 193
stress-accent 35
subjunctive 144, 146, 147
subordination 199
substratum 79
suffix 243; suffixes conjoined 251
superlative 116
suprasegmental 33
Swabians 11
syllable 35; syllable-boundaries 35
syntagmatic compounds 253
syntax 98
synthetic 99

-T- 68; T + [j] 54, 96; -T 74; -TT- 68; TT + [j] 54, 96
/tʃ/: sources 64
taboo 257
Taíno 228
Tartessian 6
tense 145
-TL- 61
Toledo 12, 14, 16, 26, 82, 87, 223
Toledo/Madrid norm 19
tonic (vowel, syllable) 38; (vowels) 46
-TR- 73
tree-names 110

/ts/ in OSp.: sources 63; /ts/ in spoken Latin 70
/tts/ in spoken Latin 70
Tupí-Guaraní 228, 229
tuteo 19, 124

/ue/ reduced to /e/ in OSp. 45
Umbrian 9
Uruguay 125

v- 65
Valencia 15
variation: in Latin 2; diachronic 2; diatopic 2, 12; sociological 2
velars: syllable-final in Latin 60; syllable-initial in Latin 56
verb-classes 147
verb-ending variation 183
Virgil 102
Visigothic 215
Visigoths 11, 215
vocabulary 208
Vocative 101
voces mediae 269
voice 137
voiced fricatives: creation 53
voseo 20, 125
vowel-changes in spoken Latin 95
vowel-length 37; its loss 37
vowel-system of Latin 36

/w/ = v in Latin 29
word-formation 237
word-order 102; pronoun position 123

-x- 61, 92, 96; -x 62
-xC- 92

yeísmo 20, 23, 24, 93

/z/ in OSp.: sources 73
/ʒ/ in OSp.: sources 64, 74
zezeo 89